TEACHING
and LEARNING
ACROSS
CULTURES

TEACHING
and LEARNING
ACROSS
CULTURES

A Guide to Theory and Practice

CRAIG OTT

B
Baker Academic
a division of Baker Publishing Group
Grand Rapids, Michigan

Published by Baker Academic
a division of Baker Publishing Group
PO Box 6287, Grand Rapids, MI 49516-6287
www.bakeracademic.com

Printed in the United States of America

Library of Congress Cataloging-in-Publication Data
Names: Ott, Craig, 1952– author.
Title: Teaching and learning across cultures : a guide to theory and practice / Craig Ott.
Description: Grand Rapids, Michigan : Baker Academic, a division of Baker Publishing Group,
    [2021] | Includes bibliographical references and index.
Identifiers: LCCN 2020053956 | ISBN 9781540963109 (paperback) | ISBN 9781540964335
    (casebound)
Subjects: LCSH: Multicultural education—Religious aspects—Christianity. | Teaching—Religious
    aspects—Christianity.
Classification: LCC LC1099 .O83 2021 | DDC 370.117—dc23
LC record available at https://lccn.loc.gov/2020053956

21 22 23 24 25 26 27   7 6 5 4 3 2 1

In keeping with biblical principles of creation stewardship, Baker Publishing Group advocates the responsible use of our natural resources. As a member of the Green Press Initiative, our company uses recycled paper when possible. The text paper of this book is composed in part of post-consumer waste.

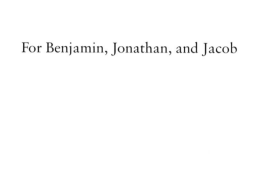

For Benjamin, Jonathan, and Jacob

Contents

List of Sidebars   xi

Preface   xiii

1. Understanding the Challenge   1

Who Is the Cross-Cultural Teacher?
The Challenges of Teaching across Cultures
What Does It Mean to Teach and Learn?
Culture and the Content of Teaching
Meeting the Challenge
About This Book

2. Culture and the Teaching Context   27

What Is Culture?
The Universal, Cultural, and Individual
Culture Change and the Cross-Cultural Teacher
The Dangers of Stereotyping and Ethnocentrism
Developing Intercultural Competency

3. Learning Styles, Teaching Styles, and Culture   47

Learning Styles: A Constructed and Contested Concept
Culture's Influence on Learner Preferences and Expectations
Teaching Styles in International Comparison
Implications for Teaching across Cultures

4. The Cognitive Dimension—*Part 1: Concrete and Abstract Thinking*   65

What Is a Cognitive Style?
Concrete and Abstract Orientations
Language, Literacy, and Cognition
Concrete Thinking and Critical Analysis
Approaches to Reasoning

5. The Cognitive Dimension—*Part 2: Teaching Concrete Thinkers* 89

Oral and Concrete Features of Biblical Literature
Teaching with Stories
Use of Metaphor and Object Lessons
The Wisdom of Proverbs
Case-Based Instruction
Other Methods and Media
Advantages of Decontextualized, Abstract Teaching

6. The Cognitive Dimension—*Part 3: Holistic and Analytic Cognitive Styles* 111

Holistic and Analytic Cognitive Styles
Field Dependence and Field Independence
Culture and Field Articulation
Cognitive Development and Culture
Implications for Instruction
Implications for Theological Education

7. The Worldview Dimension—*Part 1: The Influence of Worldview on Learning* 137

The Nature of a Worldview
Epistemology: How We Know What We Know
Causal Attribution: Why Things Happen
Understanding Time

8. The Worldview Dimension—*Part 2: Teaching for Worldview Change* 159

Worldview Change and Worldview Changers
Cognitive Approaches
Spiritual Approaches
Communal Approaches
Conclusion

9. The Social Dimension—*Part 1: The Influence of Social Hierarchy* 177

The Importance of Social Relations for Effective Teaching
The Nature of Status, Hierarchy, and Authority
The Role of Status
Authority and Student-Teacher Interactions
Patron-Client Relationships
From Authority-Based to Critical-Reflective Learning

10. **The Social Dimension—*Part 2: The Influence of Individualism and Collectivism*   201**

Characteristics of Individualism and Collectivism
Limitations of the Individualism/Collectivism Construct
The Role of Shame and Honor
Learner Motivation
Social Interactions in Instructional Contexts
Writing Style
Academic Integrity: Plagiarism and Cheating
Conclusion

11. **The Media Dimension—*Part 1: Instructional Methods*   229**

Observation and Traditional Learning
Teaching and Learning in a Foreign Language
Reading and Writing Assignments
Lecturing
Use of Visual Media
Song, Drama, and Other Arts

12. **The Media Dimension—*Part 2: Online Learning and Culture*   257**

The Hopes and Realities of International Online Education
Advantages of Online Learning in Cross-Cultural Perspective
Limitations of Online Learning in Cross-Cultural Perspective
Addressing the Cultural Challenges of Online Learning
Conclusion

13. **The Environmental Dimension   279**

The Physical Environment
The Societal Environment
The Institutional Environment

Works Cited   299

Index   329

Sidebars

1.1 Introducing Change   9

1.2 Resources for Developing a Christian Philosophy of Education in Cultural Perspective   15

1.3 A Hard-Learned Lesson   18

1.4 Resources on Biblical Contextualization   21

2.1 Experience in India   39

2.2 Resources for Developing Intercultural Competence   44

4.1 Concrete Thinkers' Understanding of Fictional Texts   76

5.1 Dimming the Stars?   94

5.2 Training Caregivers through Drama   95

5.3 Resources for Bible Storying and Oral Learners   96

5.4 Chronological Bible Storying and Leadership Development   97

5.5 Carrying the Hound to the Hunt   102

5.6 A Learning Activity Using Proverbs   104

5.7 Use of Proverbs in Evangelism   105

5.8 CHIMES for Oral Learners   108

6.1 Holistic Learners and Language Learning   112

6.2 Discerning the Relevant from the Irrelevant   114

6.3 Teaching Field-Dependent Learners   129

6.4 Providing Structure for Holistic Learners   130

6.5 Perceptions of Western Theology in the Majority World   132

7.1 Teacher Knows Best? 147

7.2 A Holistic Melanesian Worldview 151

8.1 Enlightened or Clueless? 163

8.2 The Power of a Story to Change Society 166

8.3 A Kenyan Burial Ceremony 175

9.1 A Question for Miss Yoshikawa 180

9.2 Exercise: Qualities That Determine a Person's Status in a Society 182

9.3 The Thai Experience 183

9.4 Introducing Problem-Based Learning in More Teacher-Centered Learning Contexts 197

9.5 Learning to Contradict the Teacher 198

10.1 Hypercompetitive Collectivists? Not an Oxymoron! 206

10.2 Exercise: From Direct to Indirect Communication 210

10.3 A Reprimand and a Thirsty Horse 211

10.4 A Visit to the Ice Cream Parlor 216

10.5 Blank Stares 218

10.6 What Is *Real* Cheating? 224

10.7 Homework Cartels 225

10.8 Tips for Teaching Collectivistic Learners 226

11.1 Maximizing Effectiveness When Teaching through a Translator 233

11.2 Understanding and Misunderstanding the *Jesus Film* 245

11.3 Getting from Here to There 247

11.4 Story in Song 250

11.5 Grain Banks, Loan Repayment, and Drama 252

11.6 The Power of Song and Drama in Public Health Education 255

12.1 Challenges of International Internet Access 264

13.1 Teaching and Learning in Under-Resourced Schools 283

13.2 Resources on Leadership and Culture 297

Preface

Anyone who has taught students of another culture, or anticipates doing so, knows the challenges they face. But they may be less aware that people from different cultures may approach teaching and learning in fundamentally different ways, which adds an unexpected layer of challenge to the task. Even seasoned teachers often find themselves bewildered by the enigmatic behavior of learners from an unfamiliar culture. This book examines those culturally related differences in teaching and learning, and offers guidance. Whether one is a formal teacher or professor, a community worker or trainer, a pastor or disciple-maker, this book seeks to provide readers with practical insight to understand and navigate those challenges. On the basis of the best cross-cultural research and illustrated with real-life experiences, it will explore ways to appreciate and engage learners from different cultures. It will not suggest cookie-cutter solutions or simplistic how-to guidelines but will point the way to deeper understanding, improved teaching effectiveness, and transformative relationships in the midst of complex intercultural encounters.

This work proceeds from a Christian conviction that the ultimate goal of all teaching is human flourishing, which has its ultimate root in biblical values and the restoration of the divine image through the redemptive power of the gospel. Although written largely from the perspective of a North American teaching abroad, I hope this volume will provide insight for readers whatever their background and whomever their students may be. Numerous excellent resources address more generally the topic of teaching and learning. Though often written from a Western perspective, they contain many valuable insights for teaching in any context. However, to keep this work focused on the cultural dynamics at play in teaching and learning, I have not drawn heavily upon that literature, and simply refer readers to it.

Writing about cultural differences is a tricky business. One is ever caught in the tension between identifying cultural commonalities that people share, and acknowledging individual differences. On the one hand, whenever an example from a particular country or culture is mentioned, unhelpful stereotypes can be created in the minds of readers. Differences may be wrongly understood as binary categories, pigeonholes into which people can be neatly placed that leave little space for diversity and change. On the other hand, excessive attention to nuance can lack clarity. Continual qualifying statements weary the reader and dull the impact. I have attempted to strike the right balance, but have at points no doubt erred to one or the other extreme. If a study cited or example given causes offense to anyone, know that it was not my intent. On the contrary: may these pages kindle an appreciation for human diversity, a curiosity to understand learners, and most importantly, the ability to see others not primarily as students, or as citizens of a nation, or as members of an ethnic group. But rather, may we see them first and foremost as persons created in the image of God with amazing potential. My hope is not only that this book will aid teachers in helping others realize that potential but also that teachers themselves reach their potential in that process.

This book is the fruit of forty years of living, learning, and teaching cross-culturally. Born an American, I lived for over twenty years teaching and ministering in Germany and central Europe, and since then I have worked on short assignments in over forty countries. There are many people to thank. During my doctoral studies, professors such as Jim Plueddemann, Lois McKinney, and my dissertation mentor Ted Ward introduced me to the fascinating inquiry into culture's influence on teaching and learning. For the last twenty-four years I have taught annually a graduate-level course, Teaching and Learning across Cultures, in both Germany and the US. Most of these students bring rich experience from around the globe. They have afforded me with literally hundreds of case studies on the challenges of cross-cultural teaching. I'm indebted to those students for many insights, interviews, and examples described in this book. I'm also fortunate to have qualified and devoted friends who improved this book. Jim Plueddemann, Jim Moore, Donald Guthrie, Te-Li Lau, Richard Trca, Bradley Wordell, and Keith Anderson reviewed the manuscript, in part or whole, and made helpful suggestions. I thank Trinity Evangelical Divinity School and the Evangelical Free Church of America for granting me two sabbaticals, which were largely devoted to researching and writing this volume. The editors and staff at Baker Academic have once again proven patient and professional at getting my work into the hands of readers. A special shout-out of appreciation goes to Jim Kinney, Eric Salo, and Brandy Scritchfield at Baker. Not least of all, I thank my loving wife, Alice, who has accompanied and encouraged me in the birthing process of this work.

Understanding the Challenge

CHAPTER OVERVIEW

- Who Is the Cross-Cultural Teacher?
- The Challenges of Teaching across Cultures
- What Does It Mean to Teach and Learn?
- Culture and the Content of Teaching
- Meeting the Challenge
- About This Book

The Rodgers and Hammerstein musical *The King and I* tells the nineteenth-century story of British school-teacher Anna Leonowens, who becomes governess to the children of King Mongkut of Siam. One of the musical's best-known songs is "Getting to Know You," which describes not only how she has become a student of her students, but how—as the lyrics go—she is "getting to feel free and easy, . . . getting to know what to say," and ultimately feeling "bright and breezy." Though highly romanticized, this captures in many ways the ideal attitude of every cross-cultural teacher: willingness to be a learner, striving to like and understand the students, and working toward a relationship that is honest, open, and relaxed. The teacher with the right attitude will truly be personally enriched by the experience.

But such an attitude and commitment are only the starting points for cross-cultural effectiveness as a teacher. Other challenges will abound that can sour that "bright and breezy" spirit. Here's a sampling:

- "My students just want me to tell them all the answers. They don't think for themselves."
- "I arrived and there was no PowerPoint projector. But it wouldn't have mattered since there were constant power outages."
- "Students complained bitterly when I assigned them even the simplest homework."
- "As a woman teacher, the boys showed me no respect and ignored my instructions."

- "They are great at memorizing large amounts of material, but don't seem to have critical reasoning skills."
- "I tried to develop personal friendships with some of my students. They nod and smile, but remain cool and distant."
- "Plagiarism is rampant, and I don't know what to do about it."
- "My contract stated that I would teach three hours per day, but when I arrived, my schedule included five hours per day."
- "I thought I could teach by using the lecture notes I had from seminary, but quickly had to scrap that idea, because students found my material too abstract and irrelevant."
- "When students write papers, they just seem to ramble and not come to the point. There is no clear thesis, no logical argument, and no compelling conclusion."

Jude Carroll describes these most common sources of misunderstanding and frustration for cross-cultural teachers in higher education: "(1) relations between teachers and students; (2) teaching methods (how they work and how they support learning); (3) assessment; (4) academic writing; and (5) academic/critical reading" (2015, 32). The list could go on.

Much of this book is devoted to addressing these and other issues, especially as they relate to student preferences and expectations. This chapter will define what is meant by *cross-cultural teaching*. Then, after describing some of the most common challenges and frustrations cross-cultural teachers encounter, we consider what is necessary to face the challenge and become more effective. Because there are differing understandings of what it even means to teach and learn, we will examine these basic concepts. Even the content of our teaching, especially theological teaching, must take culture into consideration; therefore, we briefly consider the importance of contextualization. Finally, an overview of the structure of this book will be provided.

Who Is the Cross-Cultural Teacher?

Teaching is one of the wonderful ways in which people invest in the lives of others. This may occur in a school, vocational training, adult continuing education, an English as a second language (ESL) class, individual mentoring, or a spiritual formation relationship. Today, more than ever, teachers, trainers, pastors, and people who have never formally taught before are traveling abroad to teach people of another culture. The low cost of airfare, the ease of international communication via the internet, and globalization in general have opened up to thousands of people opportunities for international teaching. International migration has also brought literally millions of people from the most diverse cultures into our schools and churches at home. Thus, the challenges of cross-cultural teaching are present nearly everywhere.

Today there are worldwide an estimated 420,000 Christian missionaries, of whom a high percentage are involved in some form of teaching, be it in formal schools and seminaries, or in the context of church and development work (Zurlo, Johnson, and Crossing 2020). Each year from America alone approximately 1.6 million people serve on international short-term mission assignments lasting from a few days to a few years (Wuthnow 2009, 170–71), and over 20 percent of these are explicitly in teaching roles of some kind (Priest 2010, 99). By one estimate there are some 250,000 native English speakers teaching ESL in some 40,000 schools and language institutes.[1] Annually the Fulbright Scholar Program sponsors some 1,200 US scholars and 900 visiting scholars who lecture internationally.[2] The list could go on documenting the growing number of persons involved in some form of teaching across cultures, all facing to a greater or lesser extent the kinds of challenges described above in bridging the cultural gap between teacher and learner.

Today, schoolteachers, professors, community workers, and pastors are increasingly involved in teaching ethnically or culturally diverse learners like never before. With increasing immigration and cultural diversity, schools have wrestled with the challenges of teaching in a classroom of learners from a variety of ethnic backgrounds, varying levels of English skills, and little or no familiarity with the expectations of school or university study in the US. There is a large literature devoted to teaching in the multicultural classroom. A teacher from an affluent suburb who teaches ethnic minority students in the inner city will encounter many of the cross-cultural challenges described in this volume.

Although teachers everywhere can benefit from insights discussed here, primarily in view is the teacher who has traveled to another country or location to teach students of a single culture significantly different from her own: for example, an American[3] science teacher teaching Chinese students in Beijing, a

1. John Bentley, "How Large Is the Job Market for English Teachers Abroad?," International TEFL Academy, last updated February 24, 2020, www.internationalteflacademy.com/blog/how-large-is-the-job-market-for-english-teachers-abroad.

2. United States Department of State, Bureau of Educational and Cultural Affairs, "Frequently Asked Questions," accessed November 5, 2020, https://eca.state.gov/fulbright/frequently-asked-questions.

3. Although the Americas include Central, South, and North America, for simplicity, this text uses the terms "America" and "American" to refer to the United States and its population.

German teaching English as a foreign language in Indonesia, or a Korean missionary teaching at a theological seminary in Chile. Our term *cross-cultural teacher* is not to be confused with a *cross-cultural trainer*, whose task is to help people (usually of his own culture) develop intercultural competency in preparation for an international assignment.

Most examples in this volume will be taken from formal teaching in schools. In non-formal teaching, such as seminars or workshops, similar cultural dynamics and challenges are at play, though the teacher may have a different role or status. The cross-cultural teacher may also be an after-school tutor, a church Sunday school teacher, a community health worker, a trainer for a corporation, an athletic coach, or in any other number of contexts in which teaching, in the broadest sense, is the task. The teaching assignment may be relatively long-term—as for a professor, development worker, or missionary teacher whose assignment lasts months or years—or for a relatively short period of time, such as for a visiting lecturer or short-term missionary whose teaching assignment lasts only a week or two.

The Challenges of Teaching across Cultures

Teachers tend to teach others in the same manner by which they were taught, and if they do change their teaching methods, it will be in ways that feel most natural to them. Teaching methods, expectations about relationships between teachers and learners, the institutional parameters of teaching, and even the physical conditions of teaching are all influenced by culture. Thus, teaching that comes naturally and is effective in one's home culture can become like the proverbial square peg trying to fit in a round hole when it is attempted in another culture. Or to switch metaphors, sometimes the cultural gap can be measured in millimeters and be easily bridged, but in other cases the gap resembles the Grand Canyon. Bridging the chasm seems daunting if not impossible!

The opening paragraphs of this chapter listed typical frustrations that teachers regularly experience due to culture conflict. Later chapters of this book will explore in detail the various dimensions of how culture influences teaching and learning, and the reasons behind those conflicts. Strategies will be proposed for reducing frustration and increasing teaching effectiveness. But first we will describe briefly just some of the challenges that a cross-cultural teacher commonly encounters, as a heads-up regarding some of the largest stumbling stones. These illustrate why effective teaching across cultures doesn't come naturally, and why the cross-cultural teacher needs not only pedagogical preparation but also personal preparation to meet the challenge.

Conflicting Expectations

At the root of much frustration experienced by cross-cultural teachers and learners are conflicting expectations. Culture defines appropriate ways for people to interact, how learning institutions function, and what it even means to learn. Culture therefore shapes the expectations that both teacher and learner bring to the teaching-learning experience. When a teacher and learners come from different cultures, divergent expectations and ensuing frustration or conflict are preprogrammed. The disconnect can relate to course content, teaching methods, roles, scheduling—nearly every aspect of teaching. For example, the teacher may plan for students to engage in lengthy class discussions, but learners desire formal lectures. Over twenty years ago, a comparative study of teaching in various countries concluded, "To put it simply, we were amazed at how much teaching varies across cultures and how little it varied within cultures" (Stigler and Hiebert 1999, 11). Despite globalization, the challenges persist today. This means that teaching expectations that are considered normal in one culture may well be in conflict with the expectations of other cultures. "Teaching is a cultural activity. We learn how to teach indirectly through years of participation in classroom life, and we are largely unaware of some of the most widespread attributes of teaching in our own culture" (11). When such firm but subconscious expectations are in conflict with the firm and subconscious expectations of a cross-cultural teacher, conflict and frustration are preprogrammed.

Often poor advance communication is also a source of conflicting expectations. Especially for short-term assignments, cross-cultural teachers depend on receiving accurate information about their students, teaching responsibilities, and classroom conditions. However, that information may be inadequate and come late or not at all. The teacher may arrive only to find that the number of teaching hours has changed, textbooks aren't available, power outages make use of electronic media impossible, class size is not as expected, or students do not possess the academic background or skills to perform as planned. One teacher arrived at a college in Nepal having prepared to teach an intensive one-week English course. Upon arrival he was informed that he would be teaching a theology course instead!

Steven T. Simpson describes how Western ESL teachers have misinterpreted China's invitation to come teach English as a desire for them to contribute pedagogical expertise and methodology. The Chinese, however, were more interested in these teachers' linguistic and cultural expertise to enrich their English ability. "When these two expectations are in conflict, the potential results are frustration and accusations of wrongful treatment, ignorance, and laziness of both sides, by both sides" (2008, 382). The effective cross-cultural teacher must learn to adjust expectations and negotiate such conflicts.

False Perception of Teaching Effectiveness and Learner Response

Even when teachers feel that they have been effective, their perceptions often don't reflect reality. One experienced English teacher from Canada described his first day of teaching in China this way:

> My students smiled and laughed continually. What a relief! They must have understood and thoroughly enjoyed the story, I thought. . . . My illusion that the students had at least a rudimentary grasp of the story was shattered that evening as I read their journals. Student after student, with the best spelling and grammar they could manage, thanked me for being their teacher, declared how much they appreciated my easygoing manner, and then, as politely as possible, proceeded to inform me that they understood nothing of the entire first day. (Squire 2007, 531)

Enthusiastic praise from learners or organizers may politely mask underlying problems. David Livermore (2004) compared, for example, the experience of

TABLE 1.1

Perceptions of American Pastors Teaching Abroad

American Pastors' Perceptions of Their Teaching	National Partners' Perceptions of the American Pastors' Teaching
"They're so hungry for the training we offer." "They listened so intently. They just hung on every word."	"You conclude that you're communicating effectively because we're paying attention when we're actually just intrigued by watching your foreign behavior."
	"It was a nice day but I don't think what they taught would ever work here. But if it makes them feel like they can help us in ways beyond supporting our ministry financially, we're willing to listen to their ideas."
"Teach biblical principles. Those are always the same."	"You describe a different Jesus than the one we know."
"Just teach the principles" without illustrations since they know that cultures differ.	Without illustrations, the national pastors complained they were given purely abstract information with no help in implementation.
"We have so much. They have so little."	"You call us backward. . . . You underestimate the effectiveness of our local church leaders."

Source: Summarized from Livermore 2004.

Americans teaching internationally with the experience of their students and discovered major disconnects, as illustrated in table 1.1.

Initial student enthusiasm about expatriate teachers can also be short-lived. Curiosity about meeting a foreigner or fascination with new teaching methods can fade quickly. A study of Chinese student satisfaction with expatriate English professors illustrates the point. First-year students were generally enthusiastic about their expatriate teachers. But by the fourth year their enthusiasm had melted away, and responses became generally negative (M. Li 2002; see table 1.2).

Teaching international students in one's own country can be just as challenging as teaching abroad. For example, in a study of 129 ethnic minority students in Montreal, the researcher found that "a majority felt that the teaching style of their teachers was not a match with their individual learning styles and a majority saw this as a reflection of cultural values" (Kandarakis 1996). This was believed to have compromised minority student performance.

Encountering Stereotypes and Prejudice

The potential for stereotyping exists across the board: the cross-cultural teacher faces the temptation to stereotype her students (discussed in the next

TABLE 1.2

Chinese Student Satisfaction with Expatriate English Professors

Chinese student views	Year 1	Year 4
	Percent who agree	
I prefer Chinese teachers' teaching.	31%	79%
Expatriate teachers' teaching is disappointing.	2%	56%
I can learn more in Chinese teachers' classes than in expatriate teachers' classes.	48%	92%
Expatriate teachers' teaching cannot match my expectations.	14%	74%
Expatriate teachers' techniques do not match my needs.	13%	71%
Chinese teachers adopt better teaching techniques than expatriate teachers.	3.2%	44.3%
Chinese teaching methods suit me better than the methods introduced by expatriate teachers.	26.9%	62.9%
Expatriate teachers do not know what our learning needs and expectations are.	32.7%	79%
Few expatriate teachers have lived up to our expectations.	38.4%	82.2%

Source: M. Li 2002, 14. Used by permission.

chapter), and her students are likely to stereotype *her* according to unflattering national caricatures or on the basis of various prejudices. This has a dampening effect on teacher credibility and teacher-learner relationships, and can distort seemingly objective teaching content. Americans may be stereotyped as arrogant, materialistic, immoral, and obese (to mention just a few). For example, a study of five thousand college students in eleven nations indicated perceptions of Americans as competent, but cold and arrogant. They regarded Americans with a mix of admiration and contempt. Furthermore, the United States was perceived as seeking dominance over other nations (Glick et al. 2006). Female teachers may encounter the stereotype that American women are sexually promiscuous, and they may experience sexual harassment (Rawlins 2012).

Self-perception often diverges dramatically from the stereotypical perceptions of others. This is illustrated in a study of national stereotypes involving twelve thousand Europeans in ten nations. The quality that Germans most often used to describe themselves was dutiful/diligent; 23 percent of Germans mentioned it. But only 4.3 percent of non-German Europeans attributed that quality to Germans. A quality non-Germans mentioned twice as frequently to describe Germans was militaristic/warlike, at 8.8 percent, but very few Germans—a miniscule 0.2 percent—used it to describe themselves.[4] This illustrates not only how self-perceptions can diverge from the perceptions of others but also the stubborn persistence of negative national stereotypes.

In addition to racial, national, and ethnic stereotypes, the cross-cultural teacher may encounter gender and age prejudices. One study involving one hundred university students in Tehran found a bias against female teachers and a preference for male teachers (Nemati and Kaivanpanah 2013). In many male-dominant cultures, men or even boys may feel that they have nothing to learn from women. An unmarried woman may be viewed as a social misfit, or perhaps of questionable character: "What's wrong with her that she is not married?" In other cultures age is an important factor for teacher credibility. If a cultural belief is that knowledge and wisdom come only with age, older persons feel they have nothing to learn from younger persons. One veteran missionary in an East Asian country reported how she received little respect as a teacher until her hair began to turn grey, at which point student response to her changed noticeably. The cross-cultural teacher can be blindsided by any number of unanticipated prejudices or stereotypes that undermine her credibility and effectiveness.

Stereotypes and prejudice will also be encountered by the increasing number of teachers and missionaries from Asia, Africa, and Latin America who travel abroad. In ethnically diverse countries such as Nigeria or India, a teacher

4. Study conducted by GfK Marktforschung in 2006, cited at http://www.bpb.de/lernen/grafstat/projekt-integration/134668/m-03-06-was-ist-typisch-deutsch.

may encounter prejudices from students of another ethnic group without even leaving their own country. This can block student receptivity and hinder the ability to teach and develop trusting relationships. On the other hand, cross-cultural teachers are in a unique position to help learners overcome such stereotypical thinking and attitudes. This will, however, demand considerable awareness, patience, humility, and skill on the part of the teacher.

Resistance to Change

North Americans especially value creativity and welcome innovation. When entering a teaching situation where common teaching methods or curriculum appear outdated or inappropriate, the expatriate teacher may attempt to introduce new methods and ideas. This can prove frustrating when working in a culture that values tradition. In some cultures, an attempt to change the status quo is interpreted as a criticism of leadership whereby leaders stand to lose face. When new ideas are introduced they may be received with polite, affirming nods in formal meetings, only to be ignored when it comes to implementation. Sidebar 1.1 illustrates one expatriate teacher's experience in this regard.

SIDEBAR 1.1

Introducing Change

A teacher in North Africa describes her experience in attempting to apply principles learned in a course on teaching across cultures:

As in the past two years, the board members of our training program expressed again the wish to see the instruction better adapted to the students and make it more practical. The general observation was that instruction was not making a practical difference and was to some extent over the heads of the students. So far we hadn't succeeded in implementing change so that the students would benefit more.

This summer I was able to apply what I had learned in the course on teaching across cultures. At first I encountered little understanding for my proposals and it took a considerable amount of convincing. I was rather surprised that even experienced teachers had little appreciation for the different learning preferences of the students. We finally agreed to reduce the theory by a third so as to employ more time with group projects and practical exercises. These were topics that were not very relevant for the students since they would only be important in the distant future.

There will be an orientation offered for the teachers whereby they will receive a template for their lesson plans as well as specific ideas how they can make their instruction more practical. Now we are simply hoping that at least a few of the teachers will welcome the new ideas and seriously consider implementing them.

Of course, it should be kept in mind that newcomers are rarely in a position to accurately assess a situation and identify what change is really necessary. One can easily overlook the fact that methods effective in one context are not necessarily effective in another, and there may be very good reasons why seemingly inappropriate methods are employed. The ability to accurately assess a situation comes only with extended experience and insight into the culture and history of the people or institution. Expatriates must earn the right to be heard by demonstrating humility, being a team player, and demonstrating effectiveness in practice. Even when one has made an accurate assessment of needed change, the process of implementing that change can be complex and bewildering. Different cultures have different approaches to decision-making that must be learned and respected.

Language Barriers

Cross-cultural teaching often entails overcoming a linguistic barrier. The teacher may be teaching in a language that is not her mother tongue, the students may be learning in a language that is not their mother tongue, or teaching may occur through an interpreter. If the teacher is teaching in a language that is not her mother tongue, preparation will likely take longer. Finding the appropriate vocabulary, following discussions, and locating textbooks and resources can all be formidable challenges. Unless the teacher's language proficiency is exceptionally strong, her teaching of complex material may lack depth and precision.

If the students are learning in a language that is not their native tongue, their language skills and vocabulary may not be adequate for the subject matter. The teacher may need to speak slowly and spend time explaining technical vocabulary or idioms. Students may find reading assignments tedious and time-consuming. Students' verbal skills may be so poor that the teacher has difficulty understanding class discussions or presentations. Students may be reluctant to participate in class discussions because they lack confidence in their language ability. Unless the cross-cultural teacher is a language instructor, she will probably not have the time or expertise to help students improve their language proficiency. This presents a particular challenge in higher education because proficiency in the language of instruction is so important to classroom interaction, written assignments, and understanding academic texts.

Teaching through an interpreter presents its own set of challenges, such as having materials translated in advance, the competency of the translator, and time lost through sequential translation. Chapter 11 will include an extensive discussion of teaching and learning in a foreign language.

Physical and Emotional Stress

The international sojourner often teaches under physical conditions that add an extra layer of stress and difficulty to the teaching task. Crossing international time zones can create jet lag and sleep problems. Extreme climates, such as tropical heat and humidity, can drain energy. Strange foods can cause digestive problems. Noise, air pollution, uncomfortable beds, traffic, security concerns, and a host of other conditions can make the assignment taxing.

The long-term sojourner will face the additional challenges of culture shock and learning to live in a strange culture. Continually having to interpret others' behavior and discern appropriate conduct, all while struggling to understand why everything is so different, can create enormous emotional stress at the personal level as well as in family and other relationships. If the teacher is working in an isolated location where there is little contact with other expatriates, he may feel that he has no one with whom he can talk, share frustrations, or seek counsel. But the sojourner who perseveres will have the advantage of developing deeper relationships with people of the host culture and may gain a deeper appreciation for that culture. How to develop intercultural competency will be addressed in chapter 2.

What Does It Mean to Teach and Learn?

One of the most fundamental challenges that a cross-cultural teacher may face relates to the most basic questions she may not think to ask. Our culturally colored glasses influence the very definitions of what we mean when we speak of teaching and learning. Consider how you answer the following questions:

- Has one really learned if one can only recall information? Or must one be able to use or apply that information?
- Is learning primarily about information *at all*, or is learning more about skill or wisdom?
- Is learning more an active process of the learner discovering knowledge, or more a passive experience of the learner receiving authoritative knowledge?
- What role do intuition, the transcendent, or meditation play in learning, if any?
- How do passing examinations and other requirements of formal education relate to being a productive and successful human being?

Answers to these questions do more than just reveal how a teacher (or learner) understands the goal of education: they will determine the teaching methods that teacher will adopt to achieve that goal. Some of these questions that relate to worldview will be discussed in chapters 7 and 8.

Western versus Non-Western Understandings

Whenever we attempt to speak of differences between social groupings of people, language becomes difficult. Should we speak of race, or ethnicity, or age, or education, or nationality? Each term has its own advantages and disadvantages, and deciding upon the appropriate terminology is the subject of much debate in academic circles. Words matter: they can shed light or foster harmful stereotypes and prejudices. There is no consensus about the best way to discuss human difference. In this volume a variety of terms and categories will be used, and a prominent one is the distinction between Western and non-Western cultures. This is admittedly imprecise and problematic. Globalization and human migration have made the term *Western* somewhat misleading. So let me clarify how I will use the term. By *Western* I do not refer primarily to geography (e.g., Europe, North America, Australia, etc.) nor only to people of European descent with light skin color. Rather, I use the term to describe cultural ideals rooted in European social and intellectual traditions. This would include, among other features, the legacy of the Enlightenment and—important to our subject—educational institutions and traditions. The Enlightenment describes the philosophical and cultural movement originating in the seventeenth and eighteenth centuries that defined knowledge in terms of that which is rational or demonstrable by empirical, scientific method. The autonomy of the individual in self-determination and the discernment of truth was elevated over tradition, religion, and other authorities.[5] These ideas have since evolved, and one can no longer speak of a cohesive Western worldview, but these elements are nevertheless present.

As a result of colonialism and globalization, features of Western culture have been exported, adopted, and adapted in many parts of the world, especially in higher education. Thus, we must be cautious about dichotomizing too much between Western and non-Western understandings. Influence has moved in the reverse direction, from non-Western contexts to the West. Nevertheless, Sharan B. Merriam's observation is no doubt correct: "Embedded in [the Western paradigm of learning] are the cultural values of privileging the *individual* learner over the collective, and promoting *autonomy* and *independence* of thought and action over community and interdependence" (2007, 1). In the 1970s, self-directed learning became almost educational

---

5. Although many aspects of these Enlightenment convictions have been questioned in academia, for example by postmodernism, at the popular level they are still for the most part tacitly assumed in Western culture.

orthodoxy (e.g., C. Rogers 1969; Knowles 1970). Self-realization also took priority over community responsibility. Although such views have since moderated, in the West it is still generally believed that the best way for students to learn is for them to discover for themselves, to ask questions, to experiment, to explore, and to process information; this is called a *constructivist view* of knowledge and learning. In most Western education, a high value is placed on learners developing critical and analytical skills, being willing to challenge ideas, and arriving at their own conclusions. Creative thinking is rewarded, innovation is seen as the way to progress, and tradition is regarded as quaint but unreliable. The scientific method is the path to discovery of new knowledge. Abstract conceptualization is understood as the way to solve complex problems. Even postmodern jabs have not fully dethroned the Enlightenment ideal: public truth is verifiable, objective, scientific, and rational; personal truth is private, subjective, and not verifiable. In the United States the relationship of religion and education is ambivalent at best, hostile at worst. Even private religious schools and colleges often struggle with the integration of faith and learning.

To state, perhaps, the obvious, many societies simply disagree. Knowledge in some cultures is vouchsafed in time-tested tradition or in the wisdom of elders. It would be arrogant for a young person to question authority, much less to become the creator of new knowledge. Religion may play an integral role in knowing, and is indeed hardly separable from life in general. Information, truth, and wisdom are to be received as communicated by an authoritative teacher, not discovered by the student. Authors such as Sanjay Seth in *Subject Lessons: The Western Education of Colonial India* (2007) challenge Western epistemology and reject Western axiomatic and universal modes of learning. Colonial powers sought to replace indigenous epistemologies and pedagogies with Western approaches, which have been widely adopted and adapted. But Seth suggests they are inadequate in non-Western contexts. Christina Paschyn warns that academics working in institutions outside the US and Europe "must be careful not to impose the same cultural ignorance, misconceptions, and false sense of superiority when teaching students of non-Western backgrounds" (2014, 224). Such critiques are highly controversial but point to fundamental tensions in pedagogy and epistemology.

In Islamic societies life is ideally to be guided by the Qur'an as the authoritative revelation of God's will. The very word *Islam* means "submission"—particularly submission to the will of Allah. This sets the tone for life and learning: the teacher is to be revered as one following in the footsteps of the prophet Muhammad. The famous Islamic philosopher Al-Ghazzali named imitation, logical reasoning, contemplation, and/or intuition as methods of learning (Kamis and Muhammad 2007, 30–31).

Perhaps the most extreme contrast to the Western educational tradition is found in traditional oral societies with little formal schooling and low literacy rates. There, learning is largely a matter of observation and imitation of daily tasks or occupational skills—how to hunt, cook, build a house, tend cattle, and so on—with little verbal explanation. Asking questions is neither welcomed nor necessary. In an oral culture, information, values, and traditions are communicated through storytelling, proverbs, drama, rituals, initiation rites, and the like. Botswanan Gabo Ntseane claims that "in the African context characterized by an oral instead of book-reading culture you don't pass useful information through books because learning simply will not happen" (2007, 114). Written communication allows information to be abstracted and disseminated; it is open to critical analysis; and it is separated from the author and context of its origin. Oral communication, on the other hand, is highly personal, communal, and contextual, and it is linked to the authority of the storyteller. The introduction of literacy into oral societies has many profound implications (Ong 1982, 77–113). Western-style schooling that encourages learners, especially children and youth, to ask questions is liable to be viewed as a threat to established authority and tradition, not to mention an embarrassment if elders cannot answer the questions. Even when oral societies become highly educated, features of orality persist.

Much, of course, depends on the desired learning objectives. Educational traditions and philosophies internationally also have much in common, particularly where forms of Western higher education have been adopted. Every educational tradition has its limitations, whether it is the need for oral cultures to become literate and think more abstractly in order to participate in the modern world, or Western pedagogy's failure to emphasize wisdom and communal responsibility or to give place to religion. This brief discussion serves simply to highlight that one challenge a cross-cultural teacher faces may be rooted in different answers to the most fundamental questions a teacher can ask: What constitutes knowledge? What does it mean to teach and learn? We will return to these questions in chapter 7.

The first few things the long-term cross-cultural teacher will want to do are to explore local understandings of teaching and learning, identify areas of potential conflict, and in conversation with local partners discuss strategies for cooperation that honors the values and convictions of all involved. Cross-cultural teachers should consciously examine their own philosophy of education while being slow to criticize others. (See sidebar 1.2 for helpful resources.)

We shall return in later chapters to many of these concepts and explore in more detail their cultural roots and how they play out in concrete teaching situations.

SIDEBAR 1.2

Resources for Developing a Christian Philosophy of Education in Cultural Perspective

Abdi, Ali A., and Dip Kapoor, eds. *Global Perspectives on Adult Education.* New York: Palgrave Macmillan, 2008.

Anthony, Michael, and Warren S. Benson. *Exploring the History and Philosophy of Christian Education: Principles for the Twenty-First Century.* Grand Rapids: Kregel, 2003.

Knight, George R. *Philosophy and Education: An Introduction in Christian Perspective.*

4th ed. Berrien Springs, MI: Andrews University Press, 2006.

Merriam, Sharan B., and Associates, eds. *Non-Western Perspectives on Learning and Knowing.* Melbourne, FL: Krieger, 2007.

Spears, Paul D., and Stephen R. Loomis. *Education for Human Flourishing: A Christian Perspective.* Downers Grove, IL: InterVarsity, 2009.

Formal, Informal, and Non-formal Learning

When speaking of what it means to learn, the distinction between formal, informal, and non-formal approaches to learning is important to keep in mind. Each approach has its own objectives, context, and methods. Though this typology was first developed in the 1970s, all three have been around much longer, are present in most societies, and share many commonalities across cultures.

Formal learning occurs in an institutional context such as a school or university, and usually has the goal of developing productive members of society, often with a professional qualification. Especially for children, socialization and impartation of national values are major objectives. Formal learning includes standardized curricula, learning assessed by exams or student assignments, and public recognition of successful completion by the granting of a certificate or diploma. Teachers must meet defined formal qualifications. Often the institutions themselves must meet the standards of accreditation agencies or school boards, and fulfill government regulations.

Informal learning occurs in the context of the home or community in the course of child rearing and daily social intercourse. There are no classrooms, defined curricula, exams, or formal structures. The objectives include enculturation, socialization, acquisition of life skills, character development, and often personal guidance or development. Most of what we know comes by informal means: how to talk, how to tie our shoes, table manners, cultural norms, and so on. As we have seen above, in traditional, nonindustrial societies vocational skills are often imparted informally. Play is an expression of informal learning. Personal mentoring or counseling might also be considered as types of informal learning.

Non-formal learning occurs in the context of semi-structured, more flexible settings such as workshops, professional or adult continuing education programs, religious institutions (e.g., church, synagogue, or mosque), community development projects, and the like. There are rarely any exams or formal assessment of learning. The objectives are narrowly defined and may address immediate needs (e.g., alleviation of poverty, learning a foreign language), professional advancement, personal interest, spiritual formation, or entertainment. Personal betterment or social change is often in view. Non-formal programs typically arise from grassroots needs and interests, as opposed to formal learning, which tends to be "top-down" and serve larger societal, institutional, or political concerns.

These categories are not hard and fast, though each comes with its own set of objectives, expectations, and rules (whether implicit or explicit). Again, the cross-cultural teacher must familiarize herself with these various forms as they are found in the host culture, and more particularly how they apply to the specific context of her teaching.

Institutional Standards and Procedures

Most teaching occurs in some institutional context, be it the family, a church, a school, a workshop, or a business. Each such institution forms a subculture with its own social norms, rules, standards, and expectations. In some ways the subculture conforms to the standards of the larger culture, and in some ways not. (As we shall see in the next chapter, this is one of the problematic aspects of relying upon studies that attempt to describe a national culture.) Hence, the cross-cultural teacher encounters the challenge not only of teaching students of another culture but also of working in a strange institutional environment. One might assume that as the level of formal education moves upward from elementary to secondary to tertiary, the cultural differences will gradually disappear. Internationally, there is some convergence in forms, structure, and content of higher education (Brock and Alexiadou 2013, 46–53); however, many significant differences remain. Learning assessment (e.g., testing, grading), expectations for student workloads, accrediting standards, teachers' or professors' interaction with students, and innumerable other differences will be encountered. A professor may also be frustrated by students who come to class unprepared, who lack motivation, or who are regularly absent from lectures.

Cross-cultural teachers encounter institutional procedures and standards that are not only unfamiliar but may seem unethical. This can especially be the case in terms of an institution's unwritten internal culture. Should students be admitted to a study program solely on the basis of academic qualifications, or do family relations, social standing, financial ability, or other factors enter into consideration? How does one deal with students found cheating or plagiarizing? Can diplomas or degrees be granted to students who have clearly not performed up to minimal passing standards? Such questions and many more can create no end of consternation for cross-cultural teachers who have strong convictions about such matters and are unable to see the issue from the perspective of the host.

Culture and the Content of Teaching

One final challenge must be addressed, and that is the matter of content. We tend to think that culturally adapting our teaching has primarily to do with teaching methods, or perhaps roles of teacher and student, but not the content. However, the cultural perspective of the teacher profoundly influences how subject matter is structured, taught, analyzed, and evaluated. For example, teaching history is more than mere dates and facts. (Yes, in 1492 Columbus sailed the ocean blue—but is Columbus a hero or a villain?) Even within Western academia, debates simmer about standards for writing history and how various biases and perspectives deeply influence the telling of the story (e.g., Cheney 1994; 2015; Nash, Crabtree, and Dunn 2000). The same might be said of a host of other disciplines. The challenge is only exacerbated when moving across cultures and encountering cultural stereotypes and popular postcolonial rhetoric. Differing standards for argumentation, valid evidence, plausibility, and credibility add to the confusion.

Teaching theology presents its own unique twist. Many cross-cultural teachers are long- or short-term missionaries teaching in schools, seminaries, or church education programs. Because the content of their teaching is related to the Bible and theology, they desire to be faithful to their message. They may equate their teaching outlines, doctrinal formulations, and eschatological charts with orthodoxy, and any tinkering with them may seem tantamount to heresy. Christians rightly believe that God's truth is equally true in any culture. So far so good. However, a naive and overly rigid approach can lead to theological myopia at best, or biblical irrelevance at worst, by failing to address culturally specific challenges and provide biblically and culturally compelling answers. Ultimately this fails to help Christians live as faithful followers of Christ in the face of challenges in their given context. While creeds or catechisms may indeed be equally *true* everywhere, they may not be equally *relevant* everywhere, and they are certainly not exhaustive—they don't say all that can or needs to be said.

Much of Western theology has developed in terms of abstract and analytical categories employing a strict linear logic (a matter we will return to in chap. 5). Non-Western Christians sometimes find this approach too rigid and artificial. In the words of Peter S. C. Chang (1984), Western theology is like "steak, potatoes, and peas" (neatly separate on the plate), while Asian theology is more like "chop suey" (mixed together). Both can be equally nutritious but not equally tasty to the consumer. Should theology be explicated in distinct analytic categories, or more holistically? However, "steak, potatoes, and peas" have dominated international theological menu. Chang argues that nonlinear theological discourse may be more accurately understood by nonlinear thinkers. (See also sidebar 6.4 on p. 130.) The story in sidebar 1.3 illustrates what can happen when a teacher naively attempts to import his favorite course material and underestimates the size of the cultural gap that is to be bridged.

We are speaking here of the need for *contextualization*. While some readers may associate this term with "compromise," in reality appropriate

---

SIDEBAR 1.3

A Hard-Learned Lesson

After returning to the US from teaching a course at a seminary in Southeast Asia, I was approached by a bright American student about to graduate with an advanced theological degree. He was headed to teach for several years at the very school where I had just been and was eager to hear about the students and the local situation. After a few minutes of conversation, he went on to describe with unbridled enthusiasm the textbooks he was intending to use there to teach systematic theology. I knew these texts to be of a particularly opaque philosophical nature, difficult for most American students to understand and utterly irrelevant, if not incomprehensible, to the students he would soon be teaching. When I inquired if he had taken any courses on contextual theology or inter-cultural communication, he confidently replied that such preparation was superfluous since his wife was a native of that very country to which he was headed. At the suggestion that he might consider leaving those texts at home and developing a more relevant approach for his future students, perhaps adopting locally written textbooks, his countenance fell and our conversation soon ended. Needless to say, it came as little surprise to later discover that his teaching assignment at that school was prematurely terminated and he, with his wife, was soon back in the US. This was a painful lesson on not underestimating the challenge of cross-cultural ministry, the dangers of overconfidence, and the need for contextualization of instruction.

contextualization leads to greater biblical faithfulness. Darrell Whiteman (1997) describes these three purposes of contextualization:

1. "To communicate the Gospel in word and deed and to establish the church in ways that make sense to people within their local cultural context, presenting Christianity in such a way that it meets people's deepest needs and penetrates their worldview, thus allowing them to follow Christ and remain within their own culture." (2)
2. "To offend—but only for the right reasons, not the wrong ones." (3)
3. "To develop contextualized expressions of the Gospel so that the Gospel itself will be understood in ways the universal church has neither experienced nor understood before, thus expanding our understanding of the kingdom of God." (4)

It would, of course, be foolishness to omit from theological teaching the accumulated theological insights and wisdom that the church has acquired over the centuries. But all too often, the content of theological teaching in non-Western contexts is adopted from Western curricula, textbooks, or classes with only minimal adaptations. While that may be a reasonable starting point, alone it is usually inadequate to address the most pressing questions that students face in their daily lives. Different challenges arise in different cultural settings, and the cross-cultural teacher must help students address those challenges on the basis of biblical teaching and wisdom. The teacher may not have encountered many of those questions in classes or textbooks at home, and thus those questions may not show up in the teacher's course outline or imported curriculum. Here are a few actual examples:

- Can a Christian parent curse a rebellious and disrespectful child? (asked in Taiwan)
- Are all dreams a message from God? If not, how do we know the difference? If some dreams are from God, how do we interpret them? (asked in Kenya)
- How do I honor my parents and ancestors without participating in ceremonies that seem to worship them? What is the difference between worshiping and honoring? (asked in Japan)
- If a Christian woman is kidnapped and then forcibly wed to a Muslim man, should that woman be considered married in the eyes of God? (asked in Kazakhstan)
- Of the two major Bible translations into Mongolian, one uses the name *Burhan*, which can have Buddhist connotations; the other uses

the name *Yertzuntsuiin Ezen*, which has more folk religious connotations. Which is best? (asked in Mongolia)

The Bible speaks much about blessings and curses, dreams from God, honoring parents, avoiding idolatry, the character of marriage, and the nature of God. Yet one would search Western theology books in vain for answers to these culturally specific questions.

An unprepared cross-cultural teacher can be quickly overwhelmed by such questions and feel inadequate to address them. And that may be good! The cultural outsider is rarely in a position to discern the nuances of language, the meanings behind certain symbols or practices, and the social implications of changing traditions. For this reason it is important not only to adapt teaching content to address such issues but also to actively involve local leaders and learners in discovering solutions.

Even though contemporary cultures differ greatly from the world of the Bible, we can find biblical principles that help address such issues. Paul G. Hiebert's (1987) "critical contextualization" model is perhaps the most helpful and widely used methodology for carefully assessing and biblically contextualizing traditional practices. Contextualization is a complex undertaking that demands both theological expertise and cultural insight. Globalization has further complicated the task (Ott 2015). Sidebar 1.4 provides a list of some of the most helpful literature on the topic of contextualization with which every cross-cultural theological teacher should become familiar.

Meeting the Challenge

This rather daunting list of challenges is not intended to scare readers away from a cross-cultural teaching assignment. The challenges are not insurmountable, but they must be faced with open eyes. Advance preparation can go a long way to sensitize teachers to the issues and equip them with strategies to deal with those issues proactively and constructively. That is the primary purpose of this book. In the course of these pages we'll discuss many more challenges that stretch the patience of teachers and learners. Whether these are related to pedagogical preferences and expectations, language, understandings of learning, or teaching content, cross-cultural teachers may react in a variety of ways. Jude Carroll (2015, 19–21) describes four possible responses: *denial, deficit, expecting students to adjust,* and *shared responsibility for adjustment and adaptation.* Let's look at these more closely.

Denial occurs when teachers simply recognize no real differences between cultures regarding the way a subject is to be taught. "Mathematics is mathematics wherever you teach it." "God's truth is the same everywhere." This overlooks the reality that even when the subject content is the same across cultures, many other factors—such as the way the content is communicated, the social relations between teacher and students, and work expectations— are different, and complicate the total instructional experience negatively, impacting learning.

The *deficit* response places the burden of learning solely upon the students. "They have poor work habits." "Their previous education didn't prepare them well enough." Difficulties in student learning are not the teacher's fault. Carroll comments, "Those who follow a 'students as problems' approach seem

---

SIDEBAR 1.4

Resources on Biblical Contextualization

Dowsett, Rose, ed. *Global Mission: Reflections and Case Studies in Contextualization for the Whole Church*. Pasadena, CA: William Carey, 2011.

Numerous case studies illustrate how Christians have responded to various specific contextual challenges from around the world.

Flemming, Dean. *Contextualization in the New Testament*. Downers Grove, IL: InterVarsity, 2005.

Shows how the entire New Testament engages culture and derives biblical principles for contextualization.

Hiebert, Paul G. "Critical Contextualization." In *Anthropological Reflections on Missiological Issues*, 75–92. Grand Rapids: Baker, 1994.

Presents a four-step process for biblically evaluating cultural practices and formulating contextualized responses.

Moreau, A. Scott. *Contextualization in World Missions*. Grand Rapids: Kregel, 2012.

Provides a comprehensive overview of models and methods of contextualization.

Moreau, A. Scott. *Contextualizing the Faith: A Holistic Approach*. Grand Rapids: Baker Academic, 2018.

Examines contextualization in terms of its social, mythic, ethical, artistic, ritual, experiential, and doctrinal dimensions.

Ott, Craig. "Globalization and Contextualization: Reframing the Task of Contextualization in the Twenty-First Century." *Missiology* 43, no. 1 (January 2015): 43–58.

Considers the additional challenges that globalization presents.

Tennent, Timothy C. *Theology in the Context of World Christianity*. Grand Rapids: Zondervan, 2007.

Examines traditional theological domains such as bibliology, soteriology, ecclesiology, and so on but engages non-Western conversation partners and employs non-Western categories.

Whiteman, Darrell L. "Contextualization: The Theory, the Gap, the Challenge." *International Bulletin of Missionary Research* 21, no. 1 (January 1997): 2–7.

A concise, classic statement on the nature and task of contextualization.

to assume that they themselves are good teachers—that it is just that they are faced with the wrong students" (2015, 19). A teacher's stereotypes or prejudices about students can further aggravate the situation. However, especially a teacher who has sojourned to teach in the context of another culture will have to take a more pragmatic approach and deal with the realities of the situation. Sidebar 1.3 describes a good example of what can happen to the teacher unwilling to adapt.

Expecting students to adjust typically assumes several things: (1) that adjustment of the student to the teacher is the right and necessary strategy, (2) that students are able to make the adjustment, and (3) that the teacher bears little if any responsibility to help the student change. While it will be necessary for an international student to adjust to the expectations of the host institution, it is less clear to what extent students should have to adapt to a cross-cultural teacher who has entered their native culture and institutional context. The general expectation in that case is that the teacher must adapt, not the learners. However, as we shall later see, there are situations where exposing students to unfamiliar pedagogies will enhance their learning and development. To whatever extent students are expected to adapt, it is normally a slow process that will be greatly aided by a patient teacher willing to coach students along the way.

To these negative responses might be added the temptation to attribute the difficulties or ineffectiveness of one's teaching to a problem with the local culture. "It is the culture's fault that the students don't, won't, or can't learn." While this may be a contributing factor, the real problem may be the incompetency of the teacher, which is entirely unrelated to culture. Regardless of where or in what culture a person teaches, there are no substitutes for good communication ability, a caring disposition, and basic pedagogical skills. To these, intercultural competency must be added when teaching across cultures. But without them, the best intercultural preparation will not make for good teaching.

This brings us to Carroll's ideal response: *shared responsibility for adjustment and adaptation.* Much of the rest of this book will address ways in which this can happen.

Pamela Gale George's research on American professors who have taught in cross-cultural contexts describes effective teachers as those who experienced and learned

- *to observe the cultures of their classrooms* and academic workplaces;
- *to modify the teaching methods*, hewed in American university tradition, to fit the new instructional demands;
- *to structure thoughtful learning environments* to maximize student comprehension and participation; and
- *to practice flexibility and patience* with their students and colleagues (George 1995, xi).

All of these lessons emphasize the importance of the cross-cultural teacher being aware of the need to adapt—not assuming that learners would or should adjust to her. Culture matters, and if cultural differences are not managed well, learning will be hindered and relationships strained. This demands patience and flexibility on the part of both teacher and learner.

About This Book

This book will simply dip its toe in the vast ocean of literature and research on the subject. Whole shelves in libraries are filled with books on any given topic that is discussed here in only a few pages or paragraphs. The book can only scratch the surface of the countless rich insights that practitioners have gained on the ground by teaching across cultures. I offer here a modest, but comprehensive, survey of the challenges and approaches to teaching across cultures.

Overview of the Content

Chapters 2 and 3 deal with two fundamental issues that must be clarified prior to discussion of more specific dimensions of teaching across cultures. Chapter 2, "Culture and the Teaching Context," will look at the nature of culture and culture change, the dangers of stereotyping, and steps toward developing intercultural competency. Chapter 3, "Learning Styles, Teaching Styles, and Culture," takes up the popular but complex topic of learning styles, how they relate to culture, and the extent to which adaptation to learning style is advisable.

The remaining chapters describe five dimensions of how culture influences teaching and learning, and discuss implications for effective cross-cultural teaching.

- *The Cognitive Dimension*, the way that learners process information (chaps. 4–6).
- *The Worldview Dimension*, questions regarding the nature of learning, causality, epistemology, tradition, and worldview change (chaps. 7–8).
- *The Social Dimension* of teacher roles and relationships in terms of social status, authority, collectivism and individualism, shame and guilt, and other aspects of social interactions in teaching-learning relationships (chaps. 9–10).
- *The Media Dimension*, how various instructional modes and media are received or understood in different cultures, including online learning across cultures (chaps. 11–12).

- *The Environmental Dimension*, the physical, institutional, and socio-political context of teaching in another culture (chap. 13).

Five dimensions of culture's influence on teaching and learning

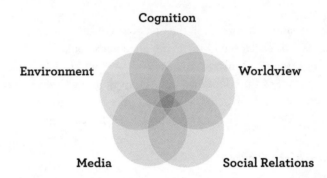

Cognition

Environment   Worldview

Media   Social Relations

These dimensions actually overlap and influence one another. They are considered here independently only for the sake of clarity. Each chapter includes sidebars with practical examples further illustrating the concepts. I hope that readers will not only find this discussion insightful and practical, but that they will also reflect personally on their own experiences as learners and teachers in light of their own culture and the culture of others.

To Keep in Mind while Reading This Book

There are two things that readers must keep in mind when reading this book if they are to benefit from it and not be misled by it instead! First, throughout this book there are examples and case studies from specific countries or ethnic groups. Readers may be tempted to say to themselves, "So *that's* how people learn in Kenya" (as an example). Resist this temptation! This by no means is an attempt to describe how all people in Kenya (or anywhere else) learn. Indeed, the example may even be an exception to the way most people learn in Kenya. (We will discuss the danger of stereotyping in chapter 2.) Recognizing the risk of such misunderstanding, I was tempted not to mention any country or ethnic group when giving examples, but that would have made for a very bland and abstract text. Specificity helps readers better visualize the dynamics that are at play, and better understand the broader principle or concept. In other words, readers need to focus on the principles, the dynamics, and how the example illustrates a concept, not on the specific country or people in the example. That said, all the specific examples, case studies, and illustrative quotations in this volume are from real-life experiences and are not made up. Those for which no source is cited are drawn from my own personal experience or from case studies written by my students.[6]

Second, some research cited in these pages was published fifteen or twenty years ago, or is even older. In the disciplines of social science, such dated research can be misleading because cultures and societies change so rapidly. I have chosen to cite some older studies not because they accurately describe the current situation in a given country or context but because they illustrate the fundamental nature of cultural differences that, although they may or may not still exist there, do exist elsewhere. For example, a study conducted fifteen years ago that compared German and Chinese college students may no longer reflect the nature of German and Chinese students today—but it may serve to illustrate cultural differences in other places. Even older studies can provide empirical evidence for the categories or concepts being presented and make clear that they are not hypothetical or merely anecdotal. Therefore, again, the reader should not focus on the specifics—in this example, German versus Chinese students—but rather on the dynamics, categories, and concepts being discussed and how they might be at play in other cultural contexts.

This means that readers should not look for formulas or checklists for teaching learners in a specific country or culture. Rather, seek to glean principles and tools that can be used and adapted for a variety of cultures. But learners in each local setting must be understood on their own terms and in their unique context, both as individuals and as members of a larger culture. This requires the cross-cultural teacher to enter each situation as a learner—a student of their students—not jumping too quickly to conclusions, but with patience and humility *getting to know them*. The cultural differences described in these pages are not boxes into which learners can be neatly categorized. Rather, I hope that the five dimensions of culture's influence on teaching and learning will provide teachers with tools to better understand their learners, appreciate them, and become more effective teachers helping learners reach their full potential.

6. Since 1997 I have regularly taught master's or doctoral-level courses on teaching and learning across cultures at the European School of Culture and Theology (Akademie für Weltmission) in Korntal, Germany, and at Trinity International University in Deerfield, Illinois, USA. The majority of my students have lived and taught cross-culturally for many years, and they themselves come from diverse cultural backgrounds. Their rich experience and insight provided many of the examples in this book. In some cases, examples are unattributed for reasons of security or confidentiality.

Culture and the Teaching Context

Culture is like the water we swim in or the air we breathe. We take it for granted; we barely know it exists. Much like the fish that doesn't realize that it is wet until it jumps out of the aquarium, we only become aware of our own culture when we enter the world of others and are exposed to other cultures. We naturally assume that our world is "normal" and others are exotic or distorted. In our day and age of cultural pluralism and globalization, we are constantly confronted with other cultures, languages, ethnicities, and ways of life, and we have increasingly become aware of human diversity in all its beauty and with all its challenges. The cross-cultural teacher enters into another aquarium, as it were, and must learn to swim in it. Or, to switch metaphors, cultures are much like games, each with its own rules and objectives. As we move into another culture, we must learn to play a new game, but without the advantage of a rule book or strategy manual. One should not underestimate the subtleties of cultural differences, even if on the surface two cultures appear very similar. To the casual observer, baseball and cricket may appear to be similar games, but the underlying rules are *very* different! In this chapter we will briefly explore the nature of culture, culture change, some pitfalls to avoid, and how to make healthy adjustments when living in another culture.

CHAPTER OVERVIEW

- What Is Culture?
- The Universal, Cultural, and Individual
- Culture Change and the Cross-Cultural Teacher
- The Dangers of Stereotyping and Ethnocentrism
- Developing Intercultural Competency

What Is Culture?

In English the word *culture* is sometimes popularly associated with an educated and usually affluent class of society who appreciate art, classical music, and literature. As in the musical *My Fair Lady*, some people (like Professor Henry Higgins) are cultured and others (like Eliza Doolittle) are not. However, this text will use the term in the social-scientific sense to describe the collective, learned characteristics of an identifiable group of people that make them distinct from other groups. As one wag put it, the simplest definition of culture is "the way we do things around here." But, of course, culture is more complex than that. There are nearly as many definitions of culture as there are anthropologists. Culture runs much deeper than observable behaviors, traditions, and customs and includes underlying values and convictions about the nature of reality. Michael Rynkiewich captures that complexity when he gives this definition:

> Culture is a more or less integrated system of knowledge, values, and feelings that people use to define their reality (worldview), interpret their experiences, and generate appropriate strategies for living; a system that people learn from other people around them and share with other people in a social setting; a system that people use to adapt to their spiritual, social, and physical environments; and a system that people use to innovate in order to change themselves as their environments change. (2011, 19)

A culture is composed of explicit or implicit norms for appropriate social behavior, how labor is organized and tasks delegated, how goods are distributed, how individuals and groups reach decisions, how power is exercised, what values have priority, how families are created and structured, and what beliefs give meaning to their collective existence. The term *worldview* is often used to describe the underlying convictions and conceptualization of reality that inform much of culture: how one understands time, causality, epistemology, and cosmology. Perhaps the most fundamental feature of culture is a common language that provides the basic tool of communication and coordination of social life. Other forms of symbolic communication such as art, music, rituals, clothing, and status symbols are important features of a culture. Anthropologist Clifford Geertz sees such symbolic systems as *the* central feature of culture; he defines *culture* as a "historically transmitted pattern of meanings embodied in symbols, a system of inherited conceptions expressed in symbolic forms by means of which men communicate, perpetuate, and develop their knowledge about and their attitudes toward life" (1973, 89). Myths, legends, stories, and religious systems embody and reinforce core cultural values and meanings. In all these regards, culture is learned, not biological or instinctive.

We must remember that a culture does not exist independently from a group of people. A culture is not an entity in itself. It is usually best not to speak of national cultures, such as *French culture*. We can speak of common traits, values, or beliefs that most French citizens share, but a nation is composed of people with a wide variety of individual personalities and preferences. France, like most nations, includes groups of people who do not share the cultural traits of the dominant French society. Furthermore, the cultural values, beliefs, practices, and institutions of France, like those of any other country or people, are ever changing. They are fluid, not fixed. While people everywhere have traditions that they cherish and that give them a sense of identity, it is all too easy to idealize or romanticize the concept of culture as if it were some kind of primordial essence that defines a people's existence. The idea of cultural identity becomes even more complex when one considers that in the modern world, many people identify with more than one culture or subculture. This is especially the case with immigrants and international sojourners. Most people experience a process of cultural hybridization, which will be discussed below.

Let's return for a moment to the illustration comparing culture to the rules of a game, such as basketball. There are variations in the rules of basketball: for example, college rules are different from professional NBA rules. But everyone would agree that both sports are still basketball. So too, within a larger cultural context there is diversity, although it could be said that all are members of the same broad culture. Also, the rules of a sport may change over time; basketball did not always have a shot clock or allow dunking. Cultures also change and adapt. Finally, a person may play more than one sport and choose which to play depending on personal preference, the people she is with, and the available court or field. So too, an individual may identify with more than one culture—discerning, adopting, adapting, or rejecting the norms and behaviors of the social group in which she finds herself.

Therefore, when we describe a culture, we are really describing *people* and how they relate to one another, structure their lives together, and give meaning to their collective existence. This understanding acknowledges that there is change and diversity in how a culture is experienced or expressed. To speak of a people's culture is an imperfect but convenient way to summarize the general characteristics and experiences shared by most people in a given social group. This is the sense in which the term *culture* is used in this volume.

The Universal, Cultural, and Individual

One way of understanding human differences and commonalities is to differentiate between what is universal, cultural, and individual (see fig. 2.1).

It has been said that individual people are more alike than cultures are. Individuals have much in common simply because, as humans, we all share common biological, social, psychological, and spiritual needs. We all need food and shelter, love our children, desire security and companionship, experience

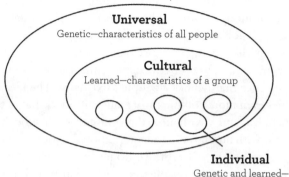

FIGURE 2.1

The universal, cultural, and individual

Based on ideas from Geert Hofstede, Gert Jan Hofstede, and Michael Minkov, *Cultures and Organizations: Software of the Mind*, 3rd rev. ed. (New York: McGraw-Hill, 2010), 6.

joy and sorrow, pass through life transitions (birth, childhood, puberty, adulthood, death), and have some sense of the transcendent. All mentally healthy people have the rational capacity to reflect upon themselves and the world. These characteristics are universal, and thus we can quickly relate to individuals from the most diverse backgrounds. From a biblical perspective, all humans—irrespective of background, nationality, ethnicity, age, or gender— are bearers of the divine image (Gen. 1:26–27; 9:6), which gives every person infinite value and potential. Although marred by the fall, that image is being renewed in Christ (Col. 3:10). Teachers must acknowledge their common humanity with learners, which overshadows their differences.

Culture describes specific shared strategies for how a group of people meet these basic needs, organize their collective lives, and interpret the world. Genesis 10 describes the Table of Nations and growing diversity of humanity, including different clans, livelihoods, and languages. With the confusion of human language at the Tower of Babel, human diversity was amplified (Gen. 11:9). Anthropologist Lothar Käser defines culture as a strategy that gives shape and coherence to human existence (2014, 37). If we compare universal human genetic characteristics to the hardware of a computer, culture would be its operating system and software (Hofstede, Hofstede, and Minkov 2010, 4–7). The characteristics of a culture are learned: language, appropriate behavior, social norms, beliefs and values, power structures, and so on. *Enculturation* is that process of learning or acquiring a culture. Every society has various ways of enculturating its children, including, but not limited to, child-rearing, schooling, rituals, storytelling, rewarding appropriate behavior, and correcting or punishing deviant behavior. Because culture is learned, a cultural outsider will not automatically understand the norms, symbolic systems, and living strategies of another culture. The newcomer will need to make extra effort to learn about the culture since so much of a culture is implicit and, at first, bewildering to an outsider. Cultural insiders may have few means of enculturating newcomers and will have varying degrees of patience with the ability of the newcomer to adapt.

Finally, every human being is not only a member of the human race, and is not only enculturated in a specific culture (or cultures), but is also an individual person. Each person has unique characteristics of their own such as personality, temperament, interests, aesthetic taste, talents and abilities, and physical appearance. Even identical twins are not exactly alike. Such characteristics of individuals are a mix of genetic features (e.g., appearance, natural abilities, and temperament) and learned experiences (e.g., enculturation, upbringing, education, and social standing). Some very restrictive cultures do not allow much freedom and individuality. For example, occupation, marriage partner, and social standing may not be matters of personal choice or merit. There may be many collective obligations. The struggle for survival may occupy most of one's existence. Other cultures, particularly more affluent societies, tend to allow much more freedom for individuality and personal choice. But individuals everywhere, even within cultures that demand a high degree of conformity, differ.

These distinctions between the universal, cultural, and individual are of importance to the cross-cultural teacher. The answer to many questions will depend on how we understand these categories. To what extent does effective cross-cultural teaching depend on adapting teaching to an individual student's learning styles or preferences, or in accommodating cultural expectations of teachers, or on simply understanding universal human characteristics of how all people learn? Are instructional methods that are effective in one culture readily transferrable to another culture because all people are basically the same, or are different methods necessary in another culture because culture so deeply shapes how people learn? A common mistake of newcomers to a culture is to mistake qualities of individual persons for characteristics of the general culture. Differences between a teacher and a student may be merely an indication of individual personality differences, not evidence of underlying cultural differences.

Culture Change and the Cross-Cultural Teacher

The cross-cultural teacher is inevitably an agent of culture change and globalization. No teacher is culturally neutral. Even when teaching a subject that seems culturally neutral, such as mathematics, the teacher brings himself into the classroom. No matter how well a teacher adopts the host culture, intentionally or unintentionally she brings learners into contact with new ideas, values, behaviors, and technologies. Is this a good thing? Many people think of a culture as a fixed, well-defined set of characteristics of a group of people that is essential to their identity. To introduce culture change is seen as compromising that identity, and thus "traditional culture" is to be preserved at all cost. European colonial powers denigrated local cultures as "primitive" and often sought to replace them with Western culture and "civilization." As the colonial empires were dismantled in the second half of the twentieth century, many formerly colonialized peoples attempted to preserve or redis-cover their traditional cultures to undo the evil of cultural imperialism. The sense of having been robbed of that identity can be painful. Culture is an important feature of a person's identity and the collective identity of groups. Accordingly, people celebrate their cultural heritage through art, music, lan-guage, and traditions, and often resist culturally homogenizing pressures of globalization and pop culture. For this reason, the cross-cultural teacher may be rightly sensitive about introducing culture change through his teaching.

However, it is easy to overly romanticize, idealize, and absolutize culture. *Cultural essentialism* is the view that all people belonging to a cultural group share largely fixed and inherent characteristics. For example, an essentialist would claim not merely that French people generally share certain characteris-tics but that those characteristics are *inherent* to a person being truly French. The concept of *Frenchness* is essentialized. Essentialists tend to categorize people according to those qualities. Thus, cultural essentialism easily leads to stereotyping and prejudice. Such understandings that emphasize fixed cultural boundaries and identities can also lead to social fragmentation and conflict between peoples, and they can overlook human commonalities. A pure "traditional culture" is a somewhat mythic ideal. Essentialist concepts of ethnicity, religion, tradition, and culture have been challenged (e.g., Barth 1998; Masuzawa 2005; Hobsbawm and Ranger 1983; Rynkiewich 2011). The boundaries between cultures and ethnic groups are not hard and impermeable but fuzzy and porous. The reality is that cultures are not static, but rather all cultures experience change—some for good, others for ill. People everywhere desire the benefits of education, medicine, and technology, which constitute culture change (Legrain 2006, 39). Furthermore, few would argue against the necessity of culture change where racism, caste discrimination, slavery, human trafficking, denigration of women, and other evils prevail.

In contrast to cultural essentialism is *cultural homogenization*—the view that through globalization all cultures are becoming more or less the same—in the words of Gwynne Dyer, putting "everybody's culture into an industrial strength blender" (cited in Stahl 2007, 335). A cross-cultural teacher who holds this view might think that because of this, there is no need to adapt or contextualize teaching to a specific culture. But this point of view is too simplistic. People around the world may eat pizza, wear jeans, and use cell phones: technology and global economic systems do shape cultural conformity in certain domains. But at a deeper, more fundamental level, people are not all becoming the same. Core cultural values, social norms, religious convictions, and patterns of social intercourse tend to stubbornly resist change. Radical nationalist and religious movements are often a reaction to the seemingly irresistible forces of globalization that some perceive as robbing people of their autonomy and culture.

The concept of *cultural hybridization* has become the more widely accepted theory of culture change as an alternative to essentialization and homogenization theories. This view argues that globalization brings culture change by fusing the local with the global. The local retains a certain priority; people do not entirely surrender their cultural identities in the face of global influences. But they do adapt and adopt some of them, assimilating elements from other cultures and rejecting others (e.g., Nederveen Pieterse 1995; 2020). All cultures change, and they always have. Globalization has only accelerated the rate of change, not by homogenizing but by hybridizing cultures.

Education is one of the most powerful agents of culture change, and the cross-cultural teacher brings an added dimension to such change by exposing learners to new ideas and his own cultural "otherness." If we consider culture change something normal, then "traditional culture" need not be pitted against global influences, or local against universal (Robertson 1995, 33). On the one hand, the cross-cultural teacher must respect and appreciate the host culture and resist imposing her foreign culture upon the students. On the other hand, a cross-cultural teacher can be a positive influence in helping her students understand and appreciate her culture, and others. In some cases she will play the unique role of a "bicultural bridge" (Hiebert 1994, 147–58), helping people navigate culture change and process the influences of globalization. This may occur explicitly through formal instruction but will also occur implicitly through the attitudes and values that the teacher informally models.

In this discussion one must keep in mind that culture, values, and beliefs are intertwined. To the extent that the teacher advocates concepts of human dignity, equality, justice, and a biblical worldview, these will have cultural consequences. In some cases, core features of a culture may be challenged. Christians believe that all humans are fallen and thus every culture is a mix of good and evil, and that therefore culture change is not only inevitable but often necessary. The real issues are what *kind* of culture change is occurring and how to process the influences of globalization so as to advance human betterment and curb human exploitation. When directly or indirectly addressing such matters, the teacher must be careful not to project the impression of superiority or condescension. The teacher will need great wisdom to discern the appropriate manner with which to engage the culture at this level. Such matters can only be taken up on the basis of a fair understanding of the culture and in a spirit of mutual learning and humility.

The Dangers of Stereotyping and Ethnocentrism

When relating to people of another culture, there are two particular pitfalls that can hinder effective teaching and undercut meaningful relationships: stereotyping and ethnocentrism. *Stereotyping* pigeonholes people, assuming that all people of a certain group are the same. *Ethnocentrism* assumes that one's own culture is superior to that of others, and proceeds to judge others accordingly. Western conceptions of non-Western pedagogies have historically been notoriously ethnocentric, and cross-cultural teachers will do well to familiarize themselves with those critiques before making value judgments or introducing change in other cultures (Paschyn 2014).

Stereotyping

Whenever learning about people of another culture or traveling to another country, one naturally has mental images of what the people are like. These impressions come from many sources: popular media, Hollywood depictions, anecdotal stories, news reports, and personal encounters with the people. Stereotyping is when we allow such general impressions or descriptions to cause us to suppose that all people of that group have the same basic characteristics. Even when one has studied the people's culture and history more carefully, the temptation is to form stereotypical images of the people—generalizations that rarely reflect the more complex reality and diversity of individuals within the culture. The fact is that given any set of characteristics, individual people of a culture will manifest those characteristics at diverse levels.

When thinking of various characteristics that might generally describe a culture, such as collectivism or individualism, it is best not to think in terms of categories, as if a culture (and people belonging to that culture) were *either* collectivistic *or* individualistic. Rather, we should think in terms of a continuum from one end of a spectrum to the other. All cultures and individuals will likely evidence some aspects of each end of the spectrum.

For example, consider this spectrum: *extravagant—generous—frugal—stingy.* In any given culture there will be persons who have each of these

FIGURE 2.2

Cultures may manifest general tendencies, but individuals vary within a culture

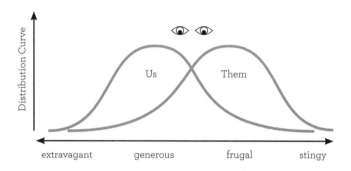

Source: Helmut Rez, Monika Kraemer, and Reiko Kobayashi-Weinszieher, "Warum Karl und Kiezon sich nerven: Eine Reise zum systematischen Verständnis interkultureller Missverständnisse," in *Interkulturelle Kommunikation: Methoden, Modelle, Beispiele,* ed. Dagmar Kumbier and Friedemann Schulz von Thun (Hamburg, Germany: Ro, Ro, Ro, 2011), 34. Used by permission.

characteristics to some extent, which will be evidenced differently in different situations. But it may still be true that the majority of persons in one culture tend to be more generous, while the majority of persons in another culture tend to be more frugal. This is illustrated in the bell curve distribution graph in figure 2.2.

When reading the literature that compares characteristics of different cultures or countries, we often find that only the average value for a culture is reported, which can give the wrong impression—for example, the impression that nearly all people of one culture are generous while those of another are all frugal. Stereotypes further distort the image of "culturally other" persons by portraying them in unrealistic, extreme terms. This is especially so when we compare our own culture with the culture of others, as illustrated in figure 2.3.

We view our own culture as diverse but tend to view other cultures as more extreme and less diverse. Rez, Kraemer, and Kobayashi-Weinszieher (2011, 34) call this the "Obelix distortion," recalling the tendency for the comic book figure named Obelix, a Gaul, to frequently declare, "These Romans are crazy!"

Even when certain behaviors are, in fact, commonly observed, the reasons behind those behaviors may not be culturally determined or rightly interpreted. For example, Western teachers often consider Asian students to be relatively passive and reticent to speak up in classroom discussions. However, research has demonstrated that this is both an overgeneralization and a misreading of the behavior. Most Asian students do desire to participate, and quietness is often due more to specific circumstances of the situation. They

FIGURE 2.3

Stereotyping a culture by seeing all its members as having the same extreme characteristics

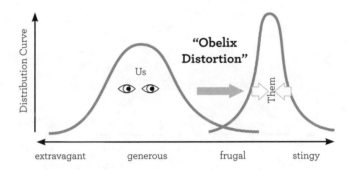

Source: Helmut Rez, Monika Kraemer, and Reiko Kobayashi-Weinszieher, "Warum Karl und Kiezon sich nerven: Eine Reise zum systematischen Verständnis interkultureller Missverständnisse," in *Interkulturelle Kommunikation: Methoden, Modelle, Beispiele*, ed. Dagmar Kumbier and Friedemann Schulz von Thun (Hamburg, Germany: Ro, Ro, Ro, 2011), 34. Used by permission.

are not culturally "pre-set" (Cheng 2000). Cortazzi suggests that they "are not passive but reflective. . . . Chinese students value thoughtful questions which they ask after sound reflection. . . . Less thoughtful questions may be laughed at by other students'" (cited in Kennedy 2002, 434).

Using Research on National Characteristics

Research investigating and comparing characteristics of people in different nations abounds. Much of it will be cited in this book. But how are we to avoid stereotyping when we read studies that describe characteristics of people from a given land? For example, Geert Hofstede's widely cited research describes Americans as highly individualistic with a factor value of 91, whereas Chinese have a value of only 20 and are thus considered more collectivistic.[1] But we know that not all Americans are equally individualistic, and not all Chinese are equally collectivistic. Such variability is not reflected in these absolute numbers. So, such information can reinforce the temptation to stereotype others—in this instance, to assume that *all* Chinese are highly collectivistic, irrespective of the circumstances, geographic location, or individual differences among Chinese persons.

Several dangers exist when considering comparative studies of this type, especially those that utilize bipolar measures (for example, measuring

1. Hofstede Insights, "Compare Countries," accessed November 5, 2020, https://www.hofstede -insights.com/product/compare-countries.

collectivism versus individualism). The first danger is either-or thinking, or one might call it black-and-white thinking, which can lead to pigeonholing and stereotyping: a person or a people is *either* this way *or* that way. The second danger is reductionism: the tendency to use one bipolar measure to attempt to explain the whole complexity of cultural difference or personality traits. A third problem is that much of the research has been done from an etic (cultural outsider's) perspective and fails to take into account emic (cultural insiders') perspectives (McSweeney 2002; Fougère and Moulettes 2007; Kim 2007; Signorini, Wiesemes, and Murphy 2009). However, one should not entirely dismiss such data but rather interpret it critically (Venkateswaran and Ojha 2019).

To best assess and appropriately utilize such national profiles and comparative studies, several things must be kept in mind. First, one must carefully examine how the data was collected, how the various factors are defined and measured, and whether the research was conducted in accordance with commonly accepted standards for credible social science research. One should consider the particular subjects of any given study: Are they urban or rural, well educated or poorly educated, old or young? Many if not most international comparative studies have students or managers as the subjects. Cultures can change rapidly; thus, research must be evaluated on the basis of how likely it is that conditions have changed since the study was conducted.

A second thing to keep in mind is that some studies look at how people of a culture currently experience certain factors ("as is"), while others look at what people *desire* for their culture ("should be"). This is not always immediately apparent when reading the data. The GLOBE Project, which involved "more than 200 researchers from 62 countries studying more than 17,000 mid-level managers,"[2] examined both current and desired states. Figure 2.4 illustrates how the two perspectives can vary greatly.

Third, one should not rely too heavily on a single study, a single methodology, or a single conceptualization of cultural differences. There are many ways to study cultural differences and characteristics. Sometimes different studies arrive at seemingly contradictory findings, as illustrated in figure 2.4 (which compares data from Hofstede with that of GLOBE[3]; see Venaik and Brewer 2008; 2010). This needn't cause us to be skeptical of all such research, but rather should force us to dig deeper into the methodology and exercise discernment.

Fourth, one should recognize such data such for what they are: generalizations about tendencies among particular groups of people. Generalizations

2. See https://globeproject.com/studies and House et al. 2004. GLOBE stands for Global Leadership and Organizational Behavior Effectiveness.
3. GLOBE values were converted to percentage by setting the maximum value 5.61 = 100%.

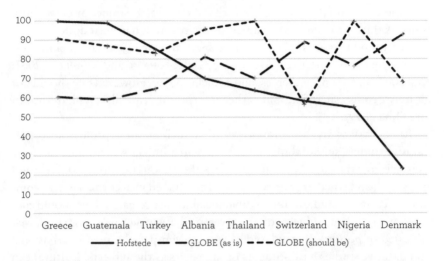

FIGURE 2.4

Comparison of Hofstede and GLOBE values for uncertainty avoidance

Uncertainty avoidance describes "the extent to which a society, organization, or group relies (and should rely) on social norms, rules, and procedures to alleviate unpredictability of future events. The greater the desire to avoid uncertainty, the more people seek orderliness, consistency, structure, formal procedures, and laws to cover situations in their daily lives." See "An Overview of the 2004 Study," GLOBE, https://globeproject.com/study_2004_2007.

can alert one to potential areas of frustration or conflict when entering another culture, which can be helpful. But one must still relate to each person as an individual who may or may not reflect broad country profiles. Furthermore, subgroups within a larger culture may not conform to national profiles. For example, one large comparative study of students in Singapore, Thailand, Austria, and Germany revealed that one cannot put much faith in generalizations about "Asian" or "European" learners: Only seven of twenty-three aspects of learning differed significantly between Asian and European students. Yet there were clear differences even within those groups: Asians compared to other Asians, and Europeans compared to other Europeans. "A number of clear Intra-Asian and Intra-European differences were identified" (Apfelthaler et al. 2007, 23).

The first time I taught a graduate-level course in the Philippines, I prepared by reading various studies about Filipino culture and learning preferences. I arrived expecting, among other things, that students would be largely passive in the classroom and deferential to my views as the professor. My experience proved the very opposite. These students engaged readily in class discussions and were not shy about challenging my views. When I asked another experienced professor about this disconnect, he explained that if I had been teaching younger students at a lower level, my expectations would have been largely fulfilled. However, nearly all these students were older, experienced pastors who had already become acquainted with more participative classroom teaching methods. The lesson learned was not that preparation is unimportant, but rather that stereotypes—even those based on academic studies—can be misleading (see also sidebar 2.1).

Familiarity with national profiles may alert us to potential differences. But each teaching situation must be understood on its own merits, and the teacher must remain flexible. Signorini and colleagues warn against using homogenous country profiles, and recommend focusing on micro-cultures that reflect more specific subcultures or institutions.

> We argue that culture cannot be reduced to immutable concepts such as nationality or other regional geopolitical constructs. Instead, we advocate the opposite

---

SIDEBAR 2.1

Experience in India

Many Western teachers are under the impression that all Indian students are passive learners who transcribe lectures, expect answers to exam questions to be dictated verbatim by the professor, and are reluctant to express their own opinions. Although that may be the case in many situations, the stereotype can be misleading. Jude Carroll observed a diversity of pedagogical approaches and learning experiences in Indian higher education:

> I visited one programme with a zero lecture policy, where students only learned and were assessed through projects, by giving presentations and through going on placements. No spoon-feeding here. In one postgraduate school [masters level in India], I sat in lectures where students used

response software to interact with the lecturer, and students looked to be on the edge of their seats as they followed him through the complex, theoretical material in English in order to answer questions on the lecture itself, none of which were right/wrong questions. Once, when asked to lecture myself, I was hard pressed to get through the material because students wished to challenge, question and extend what I was hoping to cover, jumping in to make their views known. The conclusion? That Indian students (and surely all national groups) will have had a range of experiences and that differences are more about assessment regimes, about expectations and the way in which teaching sessions are structured than they are about nationality or "heritage" (whatever that might be). (Carroll 2015, 120–21)

approach by starting with examining micro-cultures, for example, one particular learning setting in [higher education] in combination with an individual's
relevant experiences. This would allow us to develop "small" models, which
can gradually be expanded into larger models of "culture" and intercultural
learning. We suggest that culture is to be considered as fundamentally flexible
and dynamic. (Signorini, Wiesemes, and Murphy 2009, 262)

A final concern when utilizing cross-cultural studies is that much, if not
most, of the research is conducted from a decidedly Western perspective by
Westerners, who may impose biased categories (Fougère and Moulettes 2007;
Kim 2007). Studies in psychology and the behavioral sciences typically make
universal claims about human nature and derive categories of analysis by
conducting research on what Henrich, Heine, and Norenzayan call WEIRD
people—Western, Educated, Industrialized, Rich, and Democratic—who
they consider "particularly unusual compared with the rest of the species"
(2010). In other words, categories of human behavior derived from studying
Westerners are not necessarily valid when studying people in other cultures.

Throughout this book, numerous examples will be described in which
a specific ethnic group or nationality is mentioned by name. As noted in
chapter 1, these examples only serve to illustrate the point at hand and are
not intended to describe what is typical of an entire ethnic or national group.
Hence, readers should give attention more to the principles illustrated, and
less to the specific nationalities or locations.

Ethnocentrism

As was mentioned earlier, ethnocentrism is the tendency to see one's own
culture or ethnicity as superior or right and to see others as inferior or wrong.
People nearly everywhere naturally believe that their way of life is the best
way of life, and there is certainly nothing wrong with being proud of one's
culture or heritage. Some authors thus view ethnocentrism as a positive force
to resist cultural imperialism (see examples in Schleicher and Kozma 1992).
However, most observers view ethnocentrism as the dark side of cultural pride
because it judges others on the basis of how they measure up to one's own
cultural norms and values. It fosters human divisions, as opposed to human
unity and commonality.[4]

4. Tamás Kozma (1992) concludes, based on both the political and psychological ramifica-
tions of ethnocentrism, that "although it has a function, ethnocentrism is a negative social
epidemic, which may threaten both the individual and the society in the long run" (283), and
that although it may solidify personal and group identity, ultimately "it is dysfunctional in
promoting the survival of the social group" (284). He argues: "An education that concentrates
on the common future of mankind can be an alternative to ethnocentrism and other kinds of
social separation" (286).

The temptations of stereotyping and ethnocentrism are natural, and they are difficult to resist, but they bring on many negative effects, especially for the cross-cultural teacher. No one likes to be pigeonholed. Stereotyping fails to see individuals for who they are but rather sees and judges them as caricatures. This is both unfair and inaccurate. Ethnocentrism not only can blind one to the beauty of other cultures but can also lead to condescending attitudes that block meaningful relationships with others and the ability to learn from them. Learners will quickly pick up on a teacher's negative attitudes and close themselves off from closer relationships and new ideas the teacher brings. Ethnocentrism also blocks the teacher's ability to appreciate positive aspects of the culture. In the worst case, it can foster racism and prejudice. In later chapters we will see how stereotypes and ethnocentrism can play out in teaching situations.

Developing Intercultural Competency

The cross-cultural teacher must not only be ready to adapt teaching style and pedagogy to the learners of the host culture but will need to develop more general skills of intercultural competency. Any international sojourner who for the first time enters a new culture experiences what Joseph Shaules (2015) calls an "Oz moment." In the Hollywood film *The Wizard of* Oz, a tornado transports Dorothy from dreary Kansas to the colorful land of Oz, and she declares to her dog, "Toto, I've the feeling that we're not in Kansas anymore." When entering a strange culture, one may experience a host of responses, from fascination to fear. But to survive and thrive in Oz, one must go beyond marveling and musing to develop intercultural competency.

Navigating life in our native home culture comes naturally, intuitively, and for the most part unconsciously. Appropriate responses to countless daily situations come like a reflex. We take our culture for granted as the fish takes water for granted and knows instinctively how to swim. But in many ways, learning to navigate life in another culture means resisting our intuitions and retraining our natural reflexes of how we respond to everyday situations. Indeed, we may feel like the fish that doesn't know how to walk on dry ground! In the words of Shaules, "it's the intuitive mind—the autopilot of everyday life—that bears the brunt of intercultural adjustment" (2015, 69). Or, to return to the computer analogy, it involves adopting a new software for our minds. Because we enter the culture as adults, and not as children born and raised in the culture, that challenging process is disorientating and has a steep learning curve.

Intercultural competency has been defined as "a set of abilities, knowledge, attitudes and skills, that allow one to appropriately and effectively manage relations with persons of different linguistic and cultural backgrounds" (Portera

2014, 159). It is key to effective teaching and to a sense of personal well-being while living with and relating to persons of another culture. This is especially the case when the teacher lives in a foreign cultural context for a long time.

> In its simplest expression, intercultural competence development is about the capacity of individuals to respectfully engage and communicate with another so that they have the benefit of another person's cultural perspectives. Such capacity results in the ability to communicate and form relationships more effectively with persons who are different from us, and to see, interpret, understand, appreciate, and utilize what we have learned in new ways. (AHSE 2012, 43)

Resources are available for developing intercultural competency for teachers and international education administrators (e.g., Cushner and Mahon 2009; Paige and Goode 2009). Long-term international sojourners face adjustments beyond the classroom, such as dealing with culture shock, learning a foreign language, managing daily life, and navigating personal relationships that often operate according to different norms and expectations. Living in a foreign country, exploring a new culture, and making new international friends are among the joys of being a cross-cultural sojourner. But after the honeymoon is over, culture shock can create frustration and conflict, kill motivation, and even lead to depression. Adventure morphs into adversity. The new and exotic becomes the familiar and "stupid." If a cross-cultural teacher does not come to feel at home in the host culture, does not develop satisfying relationships with the hosts, or does not develop an appreciation for the culture, he can become discouraged, ineffective, and resentful.

Steven T. Simpson describes three phases of acculturation that Western teachers of English as a foreign language (EFL) experience in China: "baggage brought," "hand dealt," and "fertile soil."

> First, "Baggage Brought" refers to the prior "experience and expectations" of the Westerner; second, "Hand Dealt" refers to the awakening stage in which EFL teachers start to understand "the reality and constraints of the local context" in China; and third, "Fertile Soil" refers to the "emerging, personal, and professional issues" in which the Western teacher begins to negotiate decisions in a more culturally sensitive and professionally productive way. (Simpson 2008, 385, citing Wong 2000)

Developing intercultural competency and moving through these phases of acculturation requires adjustment in a variety of areas. Agostino Portera (2014, 160) discusses three areas—knowledge, attitudes, and skills—that are necessary for developing intercultural competency.

- *Knowledge* includes factors such as cultural awareness, self-awareness, and aspects of intercultural communication.
- *Attitude* includes flexibility, ability to listen, interpersonal intelligence, patience, acceptance, managing uncertainty, and the like.
- *Skills* include language and communication skills, observational and analytical ability, and interpersonal skills such as relationship building and conflict management.

We examine now more closely cultural self-awareness, knowledge, attitude, and experience as key dimensions of developing intercultural competency.

Self-Awareness

Experts agree that the first step in developing intercultural competency is to become more aware of one's own cultural identity, experience, values, prejudices, and attitudes. What is the "baggage" that we bring with us to a new cultural context? "Cultural self-awareness is a person's conscious ability to critically view and understand the objective and subjective cultures to which the individual belongs" (Madden 2015, 177).

One can improve intercultural competence by exploring one's own cultural identity, monitoring one's own attitudes, and identifying the related emotions (Weigl 2009). We can discover as much about ourselves as we do of others when we enter a new culture. Such self-understanding can help us maintain a sense of identity in the midst of cultural disorientation. It also helps us better identify why we are responding as we do to change and unfamiliarity, and how to process that experience in constructive ways. Journaling, sharing experiences with other sojourners, and soliciting honest feedback from persons from the host culture are ways to gain greater self-awareness and process the cross-cultural experience.

Some of these dynamics will be explored later as they relate more specifically to teaching. Sidebar 2.2 lists some of the excellent resources on that subject for further study.

Knowledge

General knowledge of a people—their history, traditions, customs, values, religion, and so on—not only illuminates the context of the teaching-learning experience but is also important to one's personal navigation of daily life in the new culture. Especially important are understandings of communication norms, social skills, and appropriate conflict resolution strategies. Gestures we use subconsciously, such as the degree of eye contact or bodily distance between conversation partners that we find natural, may be uncomfortable

SIDEBAR 2.2

Resources for Developing Intercultural Competence

Brislin, Richard. *Working with Cultural Differences: Dealing Effectively with Diversity in the Workplace*. Westport, CT: Prager, 2008.

Deardorf, Darla K., ed. *The SAGE Handbook of Intercultural Competence*. Thousand Oaks, CA: SAGE, 2009.

Elmer, Duane. *Cross-Cultural Servanthood: Serving the World in Christlike Humility*. Downers Grove, IL: InterVarsity, 2006.

Kohls, Robert L. *Survival Kit for Overseas Living*. 4th ed. Boston: Nicholas Brealy, 2001.

Moreau, A. Scott, Evvy Hay Campbell, and Susan Greener. *Effective Intercultural Communication: A Christian Perspective*. Grand Rapids: Baker Academic, 2014.

or offensive to others. Sometimes neither party can readily identify what it is that makes the relationship feel uncomfortable. Such basic rules of respectful communication need to be learned. The host may be patient with the sojourner's lack of social skill for a time, but the longer the sojourner lives in the country, the less patience and understanding he will receive from the hosts. Even more befuddling than basic communication challenges are the cultural differences in values, perceptions of time and causality, role expectations, status differentiation, and a long list of other factors that are not easily observed or identified. The more intentional one is about identifying and understanding such differences, the more likely one will be able to adapt behavior, minimize conflict, reduce personal frustration, and have a satisfying sojourn experience.

International sojourners today are often concerned about personal security, be it due to fear of crime, prejudice, health hazards, or other dangers. In many locations, gaining local knowledge of how to maintain personal security will be a high priority. Such knowledge improves one's safety and sense of well-being; it also can reduce or eliminate anxiety and suspicion, allowing the sojourner to relax and enjoy the positive aspects of the culture.

However, knowledge alone will not be adequate to insure the development of intercultural competency. David Livermore, director of the Cultural Intelligence Center, goes so far as to claim that "a mounting body of research suggests it would actually be better to not teach cultural differences at all if that's the only thing you're going to do. Dozens of studies find that cultural knowledge leads to stereotyping and perpetuating bias rather than building cultural intelligence" (2018). He argues that curiosity, humility, intersectionality,[5] and

5. *Intersectionality* here describes the awareness that a person's identity is a composite of overlapping and interrelated forms such as race, ethnicity, social class, and gender.

skills are critical to developing intercultural competency and avoiding stereo-typing. In other words, approaching people of another culture as a humble and inquisitive learner is more important than acquiring general knowledge that might create prejudice and block learning.

Attitude

Having the attitude of a humble learner is also essential to effective cross-cultural learning and living. In fact, studies have demonstrated that humility is a predictor of intercultural competence (Paine, Jankowski, and Sandage 2016). Respect (valuing other cultures and individuals), openness (withholding judgment), and curiosity and discovery (tolerating ambiguity) have also been identified as essential attitudes that characterize intercultural competency (AHSE 2012, 29–34). One must be open to new ideas and lifestyles that are not necessarily bad, just different. Resisting ethnocentrism does not entail surrendering my own culture or values, but does mean that I must be slow to judge and quick to learn. I attempt to appreciate cultural differences through the eyes of the culturally other. Questions that should be often asked and that are nearly always welcomed include:

- "I am new to your country and want to know more about you. Can you help me understand why . . . ?"
- "As a newcomer to your land, I realize that I may be ignorant of the appropriate behavior when. . . . Can you tell me what the appropriate response might be?"
- "I'm still learning how to respect and adopt local ways of getting things done. Can you give me advice on the best way to . . . ?"

The answers may not always make sense, and you may not always follow your hosts' guidance, but they can provide insight and help avoid unnecessary frustration or conflict.

Experience

There is no substitute for direct experience. To learn to swim, one must enter the water, and to learn to live and effectively interact in a new culture, one must venture out of the comfort of the familiar. Participating in social events and building new friendships with local people are indispensable. If culture defines the rules of society's game, to develop intercultural compe-tence, one must not only learn the rules but actually *play* the game. Only then does one acquire a real feel for the game and learn winning strategies (Carroll 2015, 28). In totally foreign circumstances, it can be crippling to know one may be misunderstood and may behave inappropriately. The temptation can be great to socialize exclusively with other expatriates. However, such fears and behavior only rob the sojourner of the very kind of practical learning experiences that are essential to developing relational skills and unveiling new insights into the host culture. Receiving and extending hospitality, spending time in public social spaces (such as markets, restaurants, parks, museums, or festivals), and seeking out other shared experiences with local people will not only provide opportunity to develop communication skills; they can also lead to deeper, more satisfying relationships.

Learning Styles, Teaching Styles, and Culture

CHAPTER OVERVIEW

- Learning Styles: A Constructed and Contested Concept
- Culture's Influence on Learner Preferences and Expectations
- Teaching Styles in International Comparison
- Implications for Teaching across Cultures

Before beginning our discussion of the five dimensions of culture's influence on learning, we must address the topic of learning styles more generally. Not only are individuals different in personality, ability, and taste, but it is claimed that individuals also learn differently. Thus it seems a matter of common sense that adapting teaching to a student's individual learning style will improve learning. Popular books and websites abound that describe how your child's success depends on identifying her learning style and appropriately accommodating it. Questionnaires and resources are marketed to determine that style. Teenagers famously claim that their learning style requires that, in order to learn effectively, they must listen to music while they study (their favorite music, of course, loudly)! Such simplistic approaches are rarely helpful. But what are we to make of the many theories, claims, and resources related to learning style? Furthermore, questions arise: To what extent does culture influence the predominant learning styles or preferences of whole ethnic groups? Is the concept of learning style useful to a cross-cultural teacher seeking to understand and adapt to cultural preferences in learning? How might culture influence learners' expectations? This chapter explores those issues, and then lays out the implications for cross-cultural teachers.

Learning Styles: A Constructed and Contested Concept

The term *learning style* is used in many different ways by educators and researchers, but it generally refers to natural or preferred conditions under which an individual person best learns. Sternberg and Grigorenko explain that core to the definition of an individual style is "its reference to habitual patterns or preferred ways of doing something (e.g., thinking, learning, teaching) that are consistent over long periods of time and across many areas of activity" (2001, 2). Two dimensions of learning often included in learning style theories are cognition and social relations. These dimensions will be discussed separately at length in later chapters.

Constructing Learning Style Theories

Most learning style theories focus primarily on individual learner preferences, personality, and inherent traits or abilities. They are often implicitly based on psychological essentialism—namely, that learning styles can be identified in distinct categories or types, are innate and fixed, and are predictive of learner performance. Thus, it is claimed that a key to effective teaching is adapting one's teaching style to the learning style of the student. Not only educators but parents and non-educators, too, are encouraged to utilize learning style theory to maximize learner potential and treat all people with fairness. It is often argued that minority communities are disadvantaged because schools fail to take into consideration the particular learning styles of such students. At least in Western cultures, most people have an intuitive sense that they learn better through some methods than through others. Accordingly, the idea of individual learning styles seems plausible, and it has been the subject of considerable theorizing and research.

The list of factors that theorists consider to constitute a learning style is varied and long. One might examine physical conditions (e.g., light, sound, temperature), social relationships, media (e.g., visual, auditory, kinesthetic), or motivational factors. Some theories focus more on personality or affective characteristics of a learner; others examine strategies for completing learning tasks and cognitive processes. Any combination of these factors might be considered a "learning style," so it is little wonder that there are numerous competing theories and conceptualizations. Serious research on learning styles began in the 1950s, took off in the 1970s, exploded in the 1980s, and its expansion has continued to the present (Nielsen 2012). The literature on learning style has become voluminous, producing over five thousand articles in academic journals alone.[1] A Google search of "learning style" yields over two and a half million web sources, indicating the enormous popular appeal of the concept.

1. Results from a search for academic articles under "learning styles" in EBSCO Academic Search Complete.

Contesting Learning Style Theories

Despite all the research and literature on learning styles, no scholarly consensus has yet emerged about how best to define, categorize, determine, or apply understandings of learning styles. This contributes to conceptual confusion, contradictory research findings, and conflicting recommendations. This alone should serve as a warning against simplistic approaches to understanding learning styles and their usefulness as a quick solution for navigating cross-cultural teaching.

An extensive review of learning style literature conducted by Coffield et al. (2004b, 135–36) found the following difficulties in the field, to name only a few:

- theoretical incoherence, conceptual confusion, and lack of consistent terminology
- a proliferation of some thirty learning style dichotomies and seventy-one learning style models
- "small-scale, non-cumulative, uncritical and inward-looking" research with little dialogue among leading proponents
- a "bedlam" of contradictory research findings
- theory that can lead to labeling and stereotyping, with a variety of negative consequences for teachers and students
- disagreement about research findings' implications for pedagogy
- overstated claims (particularly by the commercial learning styles industry)

Many other fundamental questions remain unanswered. For example, are styles more learned or more part of a person's fundamental makeup? Are they stable or malleable? What do they reflect more: ability or style? Is matching teaching style to learning style a real help or a hindrance? Not a few researchers question the validity of the concept of learning styles altogether, and some even call it a harmful myth (e.g., Riener and Willingham 2010; Scott 2010; Nancekivell, Shah, and Gelman 2020). Some studies have challenged the claim that adapting teaching style to learning style results in better learning outcomes (e.g., Massa and Mayer 2006). Of course, the validity of these critiques depends largely upon how learning styles are defined.

Attempts to measure learning styles, sort learners into neat categories, and offer formulaic pedagogies may belie a Western penchant for quick fixes to complex human phenomena. Possible cultural biases in such models make them particularly questionable for international usage. As one study concludes, "there are growing concerns that the application of learning styles concepts from Western cultures and research may not be valid in non-Western education contexts, due to fundamental differences in learning processes or misinterpretation of international students' learning behaviour" (Eaves 2011, 677). The validity of learning style tests across cultures has been researched and, indeed, found wanting (e.g., Yousef 2019).

Attempts to Determine Learning Style

Whereas there is little question that learners self-report differences in how they prefer to learn, the validity of learning style typologies and of instruments designed to determine learning style *has* been questioned. There is evidence that self-report learning style questionnaires are poor predictors of study techniques, recall processes, and student performance (Price and Richardson 2003; Kappe et al. 2009). In short, students don't necessarily know how they learn best. Coffield et al. (2004a) examined thirteen major learning style models and measuring instruments and found most of them psychometrically weak and vulnerable to problems of self-reporting. Other studies have come to similar conclusions regarding the weakness of most learning-style instruments (e.g., James and Blank 1993; Ferrell 1983; An and Carr 2017). Consider, for example, one of the most widely discussed and employed constructs for learning styles: David A. Kolb's (1984) experiential learning theory. His "learning style inventory" (LSI), a written self-test consisting of just twelve sets of four words to choose from, has been used extensively in numerous professional contexts as wide-ranging as education, management, medicine, counseling, and engineering. However, the LSI has been repeatedly scrutinized, and a long list of studies, including international studies, have found it to be based on weak theoretical foundations and to render poor psychometric performance (e.g., Atkinson 1991; De Ciantis and Kirton 1996; Garner 2000; Brew 2002; Henson and Hwang 2002; Metallidou and Platsidou 2008; Kappe et al. 2009).

Whether the problems lie in conceptualization or only in the measurement instruments, most of the commonly used learning style questionnaires do not consistently measure what they claim they do. Thus, the actual value of learning style questionnaires—and of learning style theory in general—may be less in determining well-defined student learning styles and more in serving as a discussion launcher about individual differences and raising self-awareness. Even if valid learning style questionnaires were available, they would be of little value for most cross-cultural teachers since they would be unavailable in the learners' language.

Matching Learning and Teaching Styles

Behind much learning style research is the underlying assumption that adapting teaching methods to an individual student's learning style will improve student learning. This would be especially important if learning styles were relatively fixed, stable attributes. But questions abound regarding the practical usefulness of that information and whether these seemingly obvious assumptions are valid. Two questions arise regarding strategies to match teaching and learning styles. First, is there empirical, experimental evidence demonstrating that pedagogical interventions based upon information gained from learning style inventories improves student learning? Second, even if such effectiveness can be demonstrated, how realistic is it for a teacher to adapt teaching style in a single classroom of students with presumably differing styles? Here again the evidence is ambiguous. One major review of the literature found, on the one hand, "ample evidence that children and adults will, if asked, express preferences about how they prefer information to be presented to them. There is also plentiful evidence arguing that people differ in the degree to which they have some fairly specific aptitudes for different kinds of thinking and for processing different types of information" (Pashler et al. 2008, 105). However, on the other hand, the same study found virtually no evidence that adapting teaching methods to student learning styles improved student learning. In fact, the authors continue, "Although the literature on learning styles is enormous, very few studies have even used an experimental methodology capable of testing the validity of learning styles applied to education. Moreover, of those that did use an appropriate method, several found results that flatly contradict the popular meshing hypothesis" (105).

Another comprehensive study and synthesis of over eight hundred meta-analyses relating to student achievement concluded, "Emphasising learning styles, coaching for tests, mentoring and individualised instruction are noted for their lack of impact" (Hattie 2009, 199). An and Carr go a step further in their review of the literature: "Learning styles theories clearly do a poor job of explaining the causes of individual differences in student learning. More important, the recommendation to 'teach to learning styles' does not result in improved learning. In many cases teaching to a learning style will result in stymied development and poor achievement because the approach to teaching does not address weaknesses" (2017, 412).

Often, research that seems to support the effectiveness of matching teaching and learning styles is based upon laboratory experiments in which extreme or unnatural conditions are set up that have little in common with ordinary classroom contexts. Consider also that for some learning objectives, a preferred learning style or mode may simply may not be the most effective method of learning. Can a person really learn to swim by reading a book if reading is their preferred learning style? The same logic may apply to many other learning domains. Obviously, many learning objectives will require teaching methods that may not match a preferred learning style or expectation.

Furthermore, unless one is teaching one-on-one, it is practically impossible to adapt teaching to accommodate all the diverse styles of students in larger class. As Coffield et al. comment, "The benefits of individualised teaching are often greatly exaggerated, although many teachers will admit that it is extremely difficult to ensure that learners are benefiting from specially tailored approaches when there is a large class to manage" (2004b, 51).

One can, however, choose to employ a wider range of teaching methods so as to offer something for every learner. Evidence shows that exposing students to learning style theory and encouraging them to experiment with mixed learning methods can increase motivation and lead to changes in their learning style scores (Bhagat, Vyas, and Singh 2015). But that would probably be good pedagogy in most cases anyway, with or without learning style knowledge. As we shall see below, there can be advantages to exposing students to alternative learning strategies and methods beyond their preferred style or expectations if those strategies and methods are introduced thoughtfully. Thus, one of the benefits of discussing learning style may be less in determining individual learner styles and individualizing teaching, and more in exposing teachers to a general awareness of learner diversity and encouraging them to employ a wider range of teaching methods, whoever their students are (Orsak 1990).

Is a Style Innate or Learned, Static or Malleable?

Many learning style theories assume that individual learning styles are innate and static features of an individual's personality and/or psyche. In this view, it follows that to be effective, instructional strategies must accommodate the learner's style and that not making such an effort would unfairly disadvantage the learner. But is this assumption justified? Is a person really biologically or psychologically locked into one way of learning and unable to adapt and learn in other ways? Bhagat, Vyas, and Singh (2015) found that over just three months of exposure to mixed learning methods, student learning styles changed, which points to the malleability of learning styles or preferences. Static learning style constructs may in fact be a reflection of Western values and anthropology. As Catherine Scott observes, "Learning styles as an idea chimes well with the individualist value system of our culture and fits its dominant, entity, model of human attributes but there is no credible evidence that it is a valid basis for pedagogical decision-making" (2010, 14).

In Western cultures, student performance is often attributed to innate student ability: "He's just not good at math," or "She is a natural at spelling." Other cultures take the opposite view, attributing student performance to hard work (e.g., Stevenson and Stigler 1992; Sato, Namiki, and Hatano 2004; Miyamato 1985). The truth no doubt lies somewhere in between. A similar logic is often at work regarding learning style: it can offer an excuse for poor student performance when a student and teacher are allegedly mismatched. The wiser strategy may be to not only help teachers expand their teaching styles but also to help students expand their learning styles and acquire new learning strategies and abilities.

Identifying and accommodating the dominant learning style of ethnic minorities has been proposed as a way to reduce minority discrimination in multiethnic classrooms. Indeed, ethnic minorities may enter a classroom that confronts them with an unfamiliar social environment and related learning challenges. Teachers will need to take such differences into account, for which a large literature on teaching in multiethnic classrooms will provide guidance. Learning style theory has been proposed as one way to address the challenge of ethnic diversity. But Gutiérrez and Rogoff (2003) argue that theories describing learning styles as static, categorical human attributes could have the opposite effect of providing yet another handle for stereotyping and prejudice. The challenge for ethnic minority students who struggle may be more one of unfamiliarity with skills needed for classroom learning, which could be acquired. Teacher awareness of such limitations can alert them to take appropriate measures to acquaint such students with the requisite skills and help them adapt. This may require adjusting classroom activities and culture, at least initially. But attributing poor performance to innate abilities or failure to match learning and teaching style is more likely to exacerbate the problem than to solve it.

The Way Forward

This critique of much of learning style theory is not intended to suggest that all learning style research is bad research, nor that the concept should be entirely abandoned. Future research, and more collaboration among researchers, might lead to greater consensus and to more valid, reliable findings. But the field is clearly not there yet, and this suggests that educators should exercise caution and restraint in utilizing current theories and tools, especially the use of questionnaires. Many researchers, such as those in the European Learning Styles Information Network, are attempting to bring more coherence to the field and seek stronger evidence for the validity of the construct (e.g., Zhang, Sternberg, and Rayner 2012). As we shall see in the following chapters, research on some dimensions of learning style, such as cognition, reasoning, and social dynamics, is better established and can provide reliable insight into how people think and learn.

Although the jury is still out regarding many aspects of individual learning styles, there is no question that culturally conditioned differences in learning preferences, expectations, and educational traditions have significant impact on the learning experience. Thus, in the following discussion we will speak of learning style more in the sense of learning preferences and expectations, and less in terms of fixed, innate types. As we have seen, strict, static, essentialized typologies regarding learner characteristics are problematic. But so long as we think more in terms of preferences, expectations, and malleable qualities, we are freer to explore issues around teacher-student style mismatches, and to consider ways to expand students' learning strategies and abilities. Because these differences do exist, teachers need to take them into account in their instructional strategies, especially as they relate to culturally conditioned, collective preferences and expectations, the topic to which we now turn.

Culture's Influence on Learner Preferences and Expectations

When we add the dimension of culture to our discussion of learner preferences and expectations, a different dynamic comes into focus: ways in which the cultural context has shaped the collective preferences and expectations of whole groups of learners. While individual differences remain—that is, diversity within a culture—collective preferences and expectations are shaped by generally accepted cultural norms regarding teacher-student relations, appropriate teaching and learning methods, and other educational factors. These collective preferences and expectations might be considered culture-specific learning styles. Teachers, too, are influenced by their cultural context regarding what makes for good teaching. Therefore, while allowing for individual differences, we can meaningfully speak of culturally preferred teaching styles.

Numerous international comparative studies of learning styles and preferences consistently reveal significant national differences. Even though most learning style measurement tools are of questionable value, this consistent finding indicates that learners from different cultures have, on average, different learning preferences and experiences (as self-reported). These culturally conditioned preferences and expectations have been formed through enculturation in general and by past learning experiences in particular. Lev Vygotsky (1978) emphasized how learning is socially mediated. Empirical research has corroborated the importance of the cultural framework of learning. For example, even the language spoken at home influences learner preferences (Maldonado Torres 2016). A study by Cornel Pewewardy (2002) reviewed the voluminous literature regarding learning styles of American Indian/Alaska Native students. He found an emphasis on social harmony, holistic perspectives, creativity, and nonverbal communication, and demonstrated how these preferences were linked to students' language, culture, and heritage. Such findings come as no surprise. Writers like Pewewardy argue that schools must adapt to these preferences and styles of particular ethnic groups. The questions are, of course, how much to adapt, and how such adaptation will facilitate student attainment of the desired learning outcomes. This is the challenge the cross-cultural teacher faces. Our discussion of the five dimensions of culture's influence upon learning will point practical ways forward.

Generally speaking, people are most comfortable with familiar methods and relations. Teacher methods or behaviors that depart from these expectations will—at least initially—create some dissonance and potentially impair learning effectiveness. The wise cross-cultural teacher will become well acquainted with such collective preferences and expectations, then judiciously determine whether and how to adapt teaching. This does not preclude the possibility of introducing unfamiliar learning experiences, but does mean that any such introduction should be done with intentionality, understanding, and awareness of possible unintended consequences. In fact, as we will see in later chapters, some studies indicate that mismatch of teaching and learning styles can lead to cognitive growth.

Carefully conducted empirical research and international comparative studies examining such collective learner styles according to nationality are of a different character than monocultural studies that are narrow in scope and individualistically conceived. As we explore the various dimensions of how culture influences learning, we will draw upon the best research related to cultural differences and their possible implications for teaching and learning. Many well-established human differences, such as cognitive styles and individualism/collectivism, do not describe a learning style per se. But such factors do influence the learning environment and process.

Broadly conceived international studies and national profiles, however, are of limited usefulness in determining the best instructional strategies. They can alert a teacher to potential challenges. But they are not context-specific: they may not differentiate between urban and rural contexts, formal and nonformal settings, whether learners are children or adults, and other nuanced factors that are hidden in a general national profile. Furthermore, although culture has a significant influence, it is not strictly determinative of learning preferences. For example, one study found that

> Contrary to the expectation that Asian learners have a propensity for rote learning, the Sri Lankan students reported the lowest score for memorising strategy and relatively high scores for concretising and analysing strategies. This could be indicative of the not so strong influence of culture on the use of learning strategies and thus powerful learning environments have a great potential in bringing about a change towards the greater use of more constructive learning strategies. (Marambe, Vermunt, and Boshuizen 2012, 314)

Due to the weaknesses of most questionnaires and measurement tools designed to determine learning style, Mina Eaves concludes that "there is a strong argument for non-psychometric studies of learning behaviour to be included in the study of culture-specific learning styles in the light of the limitations of the psychometric approach" (2011, 684). Such an approach would include more observation and qualitative research methods. The average cross-cultural teacher is unlikely to have the time or expertise to conduct careful research about her students' learning preferences and expectations. But she can seek to better understand them with relatively simple approaches that include some or all of the following:

- classroom observation of teachers who are described as the most effective teachers in that cultural setting
- observation of student response to different instructional methods and classroom management
- interviews with students, asking questions such as: "Describe to me the best teacher you have ever had. What was she like?" "What teaching methods were used?" "What would you think about a teacher who did . . . ?"
- interviews with native and expatriate teachers with wide experience in the culture, to learn from their experience
- experimentation with various methods and monitoring of learner response
- focus group in which students discuss their learning experiences

Of course, such inquiry demands considerable patience and commitment from the teacher. Findings are likely to be in shades of grey, not black and white. Observations must be carefully conducted since it is easy to misread students; for example, students who experience coursework as heavy, especially if in a second language, will tend to use reproductive learning methods. Eaves warns, "Therefore, generalising from the behaviour of international students or students learning in a second language to cultural patterns of learning styles may not be valid due to a possibly confounding factor of a perceived intensive workload affecting learning strategies" (2011, 683).

Teaching Styles in International Comparison

Just as learners have differing preferences or styles in how they learn, teachers have different preferences or styles in how they teach. Studies demonstrate that culture influences not only learner preferences and expectations but also instructional preferences and expectations. A few examples will illustrate the point. Cothran et al. (2005) studied the beliefs about teaching styles of 1,436 physical education teachers in seven countries. They found that teachers' use of styles was related to their beliefs about the styles. All countries were significantly different from each other in experience with teaching styles and in their beliefs about teaching styles. "For example, Korea and Portugal use reproductive methods most frequently. . . . England, Australia, and Canada used production styles more than Korea and Portugal" (198). In general, though, teachers in every country studied had a more positive view of reproductive learning methods (whereby the teacher takes more initiative in the learning process) than production learning methods (whereby the learner takes more initiative).

Other international comparisons of teacher styles consistently demonstrate clear national differences. Consider, for example, Stigler et al.'s (1999) study of mathematics teachers in Germany, Japan, and the United States. German and American teachers tend to begin with teacher-led instruction and follow it with an application phase of teaching, but Japanese teachers tend to reverse the order: "Problem solving comes first, followed by a time in which students reflect on the problem, share the solution methods they have generated, and jointly work to develop explicit understandings of the underlying mathematical concepts" (vi). Another study examined secondary teachers' attitudes about critical thinking; it found that American teachers positively endorsed critical thinking approaches, whereas Chinese teachers evidenced some resistance to them (McBride et al. 2002). Eaves surveys numerous qualitative studies comparing international learning styles "that suggest Western academic culture is associated with interactive, constructivist and student-centred values compared to a more teacher-centred type of academic culture found in many [Chinese and Confucian Heritage] cultures, influencing teaching and learning styles" (Eaves 2011, 684). The International Association for the Evaluation of Educational Achievement (IEA) has conducted numerous international comparative studies (www.iea.nl).

Culturally conditioned learner expectations clearly influence how students perceive and respond to teacher behaviors. For example, many Western educators claim that student autonomy facilitates learning. Chinese schoolteachers tend to be more authoritarian and have larger classes than American teachers, yet Chinese students perform well in international comparisons. Exploration of this paradox found that "the same controlling behaviors of teachers had different affective meanings for different cultural groups" (Zhou, Lam, and Chan 2002, 1162). "Students from the United States felt more controlled by their teachers and, in turn, reported that they were less motivated in their teachers' class. In contrast, students from China felt less controlled by their teachers and, in turn, reported that they were more motivated in their teachers' class" (1169). These studies indicate that not only do teachers of different cultures differ in their instructional strategies; students are conditioned to respond accordingly to those strategies. A cross-cultural teacher may therefore find students responding to his teaching in unexpected ways.

Implications for Teaching across Cultures

A teacher's awareness of differing preferences and expectations can alert her in advance to possible confusion or stress that may arise when she employs pedagogical methods that are unfamiliar or uncomfortable to her students. This does not mean that unfamiliar methods should not be employed, but they may need to be introduced gradually and with explanation of their pedagogical value. For example, in most Western schooling and higher education the expectation is that students will work individually on assignments and receive an individual grade for their performance. Requiring students to work in groups on assignments or projects for which all participants will receive the same common grade often meets with resistance. Explaining the value of group work, cooperation, and synergy as an important life skill can help overcome student resistance.

Teacher awareness of the diversity of learner preferences can provide impetus for the teacher to expand his repertoire of instructional methods. The reality is, teachers tend to teach in the manner in which they themselves prefer to learn. They often fall into a rut, always using the same instructional methods. But whatever the learning preferences and expectations of the students might be, employing a variety of methods is likely to make instruction more interesting and more memorable for everyone.

Discussing with learners their preferences and expectations can heighten their self-awareness and appreciation of diversity. The idea is not to create the expectation that the teacher will necessarily cater to their individual preferences, much less give them an excuse for failure if their expectations aren't met. On the contrary, such discussion can help students not only understand the value of exploring alternative approaches to learning but also expand their own learning strategies.

Aspects of Adaptation

There are at least four ways that teaching can be adapted to better match learner preferences: didactic adaptation, social adaptation, structural adaptation, and content adaptation.

- *Didactic adaptation*—the teacher's choice of instructional methods that fit the expectations and preferences of the learners. This is the aspect that is most often in view in the literature on matching teaching and learning styles.

- *Social adaptation*—promotion of social relations between teacher and learners, and among learners, that will respect cultural norms and facilitate learning. This may include a teacher adopting the role or status that his students regard as culturally appropriate, along with its implications for classroom behavior and the teacher's relationships with students.
- *Structural adaptation*—adaptation of the environmental conditions of the classroom or learning institution to be more conducive to learner participation and attentiveness. This may include a wide range of variables, such as seating arrangements, classroom temperature, and scheduling of class times and breaks. It may also include methods of assessment, such as examinations and grading.
- *Content adaptation*—crafting instructional content and learning objectives to be relevant and motivational to learners. As discussed in the previous chapter, the content that is taught may need to be contextualized for greater impact and relevance.

Match Teaching Styles with Learner Styles?

Although we have noted the practical difficulty of matching teaching and learning styles in classrooms where students represent a wide range of styles, the cross-cultural teaching situation presents a different setting. If the learners are from a relatively homogenous ethnic or cultural group, one can expect that there will be commonly shared, culturally conditioned learning preferences and expectations. There are several possible strategies for engaging cultural differences between the cross-cultural teacher and his students. In some situations, however, the cross-cultural teacher will not be entirely free to choose the level of adaptation. For example, standards for testing, accreditation, and other institutional norms may place constraints on the teacher's ability to be creative.

Throughout this book we will continually return to the question of the extent to which teaching should or should not be adapted to the preferences or styles of the learners. How we answer the question will depend on a variety of factors. For example, which of the five dimensions of culture's influence upon learning are we talking about? Each dimension will need to be considered on its own terms. Also, are we speaking of a short-term or long-term cross-cultural teacher? If the teaching assignment lasts only a few weeks, significant mismatch of preferences and expectations could potentially inhibit learning. On the other hand, if one teaches over the course of months or years there is time for both student and teacher to assimilate to one another, and new teaching methods can be introduced gradually. Finally, there is the question of what is to be gained or lost by mismatching teaching style with student learning style.

The following options exist regarding adaptation of teaching style to learner preferences and expectations: no adaptation (mismatch), full adaptation (match), partial adaptation (compromise), and adaptation with gradual introduction of alternate approaches (match to mismatch).

NO ADAPTATION

In *no adaptation* the teacher expects students to adapt to the teacher, and not vice versa. Some cross-cultural teachers may naively adopt this strategy by default. Others may adopt this strategy out of conviction that even if methods are unfamiliar, they are inherently essential to attaining the desired learning outcomes. Sometimes this will be the case; for example, when teaching practical skills such as riding a bicycle there is no substitute for experimentation and learning-by-doing. But most learning objectives can be attained by a variety of methods. Although at first learners may find the novelty of a foreign teacher with strange methods intriguing, over time the novelty can grow old and students may become frustrated, as evidenced in the study by Mingsheng Li (2002) cited in chapter 1. A teacher's stubborn insistence upon certain methods along with unwillingness to be flexible can lead to student resistance, and possibly conflict. Except for short-term teaching assignments with very limited learning objectives, this approach is, for obvious reasons, not generally recommended.

FULL ADAPTATION

With *full adaptation* the teacher decides to conform instruction as fully as possible to cultural or learner preferences and expectations. Such a stance is admirable in that it seeks to respect cultural traditions and avoid creating discomfort or confusion for students. All too often, cross-cultural teachers assume that their methods are better and prematurely disregard local methods. But although those local methods may seem backward, they may have a track record of effectiveness. For example, Western teachers typically undervalue rote learning and memorization as superficial, although in certain forms it can promote learning and understanding at a deep level (Kember 2000; Kennedy 2002). Research by Marton, Dall'Alba, and Tse (1996) found that memorization may precede or follow understanding. Mechanical memorization is different from memorization with understanding. Repetition while memorizing can contribute to understanding. In the words of one Chinese student, "Each time I would repeat I would have some new idea of understanding, that is to say I can understand better" (81). However, changing one's instructional style to conform to cultural preferences will limit instructional options and may make it difficult to attain some learning objectives. Teachers who fully accommodate local expectations are willing to pay that price because they see the negative consequences of mismatch outweighing the negatives of matching.

Making an effort to accommodate local learning preferences and traditions is particularly important in formal learning settings such as schools, universities, and seminaries. However, considerably more flexibility is possible in nonformal teaching contexts such as workshops, church-based training programs, and spiritual formation groups. It is unnecessary to limit instructional options as a matter of principle. Each situation, audience, and learning objective should be considered on its own merits. In many non-formal settings, creative or unfamiliar methods will be welcomed. However, it is usually a good idea to run ideas by a local leader to ensure that there is no unnecessary offense or confusion created, and to anticipate possible challenges.

Fully adapting to local expectations and preferences also may limit the potential for students' cognitive growth and expansion of their learning strategies. Unfamiliar teaching methods may promote these. For example, if students generally prefer the teacher to dictate lecture notes, answer all questions, and test for content mastery, it is unlikely that students will learn critical thinking skills. Eaves summarizes several studies indicating the value of introducing students to alternative teaching styles:

> Wong (2004) found that Asian international students in Australia expressed a preference for student-centred teaching and learning styles even though this approach differed from their previous experience in their home country. On another positive note, Bell (2007, 62) found that Thai postgraduate students in Australia reported developing self-efficacy in their studies mainly due to "a safe, non threatening study environment." Wallace and Hellmundt (2003) found that the learning behaviour of international students such as critical thinking was enhanced through the promotion of a student-centred and interpersonally interactive learning environment, which was also found to be beneficial for local students' learning processes. (Eaves 2011, 685)

Although mismatch of teaching and learning styles creates some discomfort, Bruce Joyce observes:

> Curiously, the more a given model of teaching was mismatched with the natural learning style of the student, the more it presented a challenge to the student to take an affirmative stance so as to pass through the period of discomfort and develop skills that permit a productive relationship with the learning environment. . . .

. . . Hence the challenge is not to select the most comfortable models, but to develop the skills to relate to a wider variety of models, many of which appear, at least superficially, to be mismatched with their learning styles. (Joyce 1984, 29)

PARTIAL ADAPTATION

Partial adaptation is a meeting halfway. The teacher decides that for some objectives, teaching will match learner preferences and expectation, but for other objectives there will be mismatch. As noted above, this is more advantageous than the first two options. If, for example, the teacher believes that a certain method is essential to achieving a given outcome, irrespective of the learner's culture, then learners would just need to "get over it" and accept the unfamiliar or less preferred method. As previously noted, evidence suggests that exposure to new learning strategies and instructional methods can contribute to cognitive growth. But if such methods are introduced too abruptly, learners may be left behind and become frustrated or confused. Thus, a fourth approach is recommended.

ADAPTATION WITH GRADUAL INTRODUCTION OF ALTERNATE APPROACHES

To quote Joyce again, "Nearly all learners have the potential to relate to a wide variety of learning environments, provided they are not made *too* uncomfortable and that they are provided with assistance to relate productively to any given environment" (1984, 30). The need for assistance in adapting to unfamiliar learning strategies and methods may be all the greater in a cross-cultural setting. In many cultures innovation is unwelcome and viewed with suspicion. Thus, teachers not only need to be careful about how they introduce new methods; they also should provide a clear rationale for *why* such methods are being employed. In institutional learning contexts, permission from administrative leaders and stakeholders may be necessary, so as to avoid the impression of disrespect for institutional or cultural traditions—and to avoid "surprises" should students file complaints.

Biblical Precedent for Mismatch?

Jesus's approach to teaching and spiritually forming his disciples is instructive. In many ways he taught similarly to the rabbis of his time. For example, in first-century Judaism, learning in a classroom was not the norm; it took place more in life situations. A disciple often accompanied his rabbi on travels, and during student days he would frequently spend the Sabbath with his master (Strack and Billerbeck 1965–69, 1:528; Aberbach 1967, 20). He could observe the master's lifestyle, thinking, and interactions with those who came and asked questions (Neudecker 1999, 255–56). "The disciples accompanied their sage as he went to teach, when he sat in the law court, when he was engaged in the performance of meritorious deeds" (Safrai et al. 1974–76, 946). We observe similar features in Jesus's relationship with his disciples.

However, Jesus also differed from the rabbis in significant ways. For example, disciples served their rabbis in menial tasks, which became a mark of scholastic distinction. "Discipleship was frequently called 'service to the sages' (Av 6:6)" (Neudecker 1999, 225). The student who failed to serve was considered an *Am ha-Aretz*, a "cunning rogue" (Aberbach 1967, 3). The teacher was even bound to receive the service of his students. A disciple was not allowed to stand next to or directly behind his rabbi during prayer; this being seen as disturbing, and as motivated by the desire to be seen close to the rabbi (15). Jesus, by contrast, "did not come to be served, but to serve" (Mark 10:45). Rabbis called their disciples "sons" (Wenthe 2006, 158), but Jesus called his disciples "friends" and "my mother and my brothers" (John 15:13–14; Matt. 12:49). Most astonishingly, he washed the disciples' feet (John 13:1–17), a gesture so shocking that Peter initially protested. Foot washing was considered a task too base for even a disciple, was rather reserved for slaves (b. Ketubbot 96; Neudecker 1999, 255), and was unthinkable for a rabbi (Mekhilta d'Rabbi Yishmael 21.2.).[2] So intimate was Jesus's relationship with his disciples that he allowed John to lay his head upon his breast (John 13:23, 25).

The verbal instruction of the rabbis was characterized by repetition and memorization, with question and answer (Riesner 1984, 190–98; Neudecker 1999, 252, 254). Though Jesus's teaching was memorable, memorization was not his method (Riesner 1984, 365–71). At times he taught with longer discourses, such as the Sermon on the Mount. But he also asked the disciples questions, forcing them to reflect and process his teaching. His parables typically included some twist that challenged conventional thinking, and "disequilibrated" his listeners (Foster and Moran 1985, 100). They had to reconsider previous ways of thinking, value systems, and understandings. He, however, did not destroy old moral and theological frameworks without providing new ones presented in positive teaching. His teaching was often illustrated with object lessons. Almost any object could become an instrument of visual and conceptual illustration in his hands: seeds, birds, fields, a fig tree, a coin, fish. He utilized verbal, visual, and emotive impact to make his teaching memorable rather than relying on rote repetition or writing (Habermas 2008, 87–150).

In summary, Jesus's teaching included both familiar and unfamiliar methods. His break with the traditions and expectations of a rabbi was intentional

2. https://www.sefaria.org/Mekhilta_d'Rabbi_Yishmael.21.2?lang=bi.

and not for the sake of novelty. He was even willing to shock, if necessary, to make his point. The deciding factor was not conformity but impact. His teaching objectives were fundamentally different from those of the rabbis; thus, different teaching methods were necessary. Cross-cultural teachers today must also make pedagogical decisions based less upon tradition or learner expectations than on the basis of suitability to their teaching objectives. Whatever the subject matter, Christian teachers will also want to demonstrate an exemplary lifestyle of service and concern for the well-being of the learner. Jesus lived and taught in ways that served his objective: to not only impart knowledge but also to transform lives. Teachers today will do well to follow his example.

The Cognitive Dimension

Part 1: Concrete and Abstract Thinking

Perhaps the most fundamental aspect of how people learn relates to how they think: how they perceive, process, and structure information; how they conceptualize and categorize their world; and how they craft arguments. This is the cognitive dimension of learning, the first of the five dimensions of culture's influence on teaching and learning.

CHAPTER OVERVIEW

- What Is a Cognitive Style?
- Concrete and Abstract Orientations
- Language, Literacy, and Cognition
- Concrete Thinking and Critical Analysis
- Approaches to Reasoning

These cognitive processes clearly differ among individuals, and different cultures have different predominant cognitive styles. "In short, culture affects not only what people think but also how they think" (Medin, Unsworth, and Hirschfeld, 2007, 616). Summarizing numerous empirical studies, Richard Nisbett writes in *The Geography of Thought*: "The research shows that there are indeed dramatic differences in the nature of Asian and European thought processes" (2003, xviii). Because cognitive style describes mental processes, it influences how people learn.

In this chapter we will examine theories of cognitive style relating to concrete versus abstract styles, and styles relating to reasoning processes. The next chapter will discuss the practical implications of this for cross-cultural teaching. (Readers who are less interested in the complexities of underlying theories may skip forward to chapter 5.) Chapter 6 will discuss holistic/analytic and field-independent/field-dependent constructs of cognitive style and their implications for cross-cultural teaching. That chapter will conclude with a discussion of cognitive style theory's implications for theological education.

FIGURE 4.1

Five dimensions of culture's influence on teaching and learning

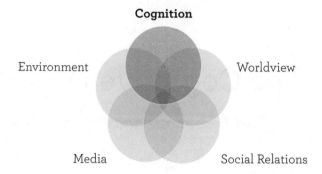

Cognition

Environment   Worldview

Media   Social Relations

What Is a Cognitive Style?

Cognitive style describes the ways an individual perceives, organizes, and processes information. Riding and Rayner define it as "an individual's preferred and habitual approach to organizing and representing information" (1998, 8). Peterson, Rayner, and Armstrong provide this more comprehensive definition: "Cognitive styles are individual differences in processing that are integrally linked to a person's cognitive system. More specifically, they are a person's preferred way of processing (perceiving, organising and analysing) information using cognitive brain-based mechanisms and structures" (2009, 11).

Cognitive style is often confused with learning style. Learning style, as discussed in the previous chapter, tends to be a more comprehensive umbrella concept, whereas cognitive style describes more narrowly perception and information processing. As understood in this volume, cognitive styles are, for the most part, not innate but malleable and developmental.

Understanding Cognitive Development

Cognitive style is among the most extensively researched constructs and has been a focus of numerous cross-cultural studies. How people develop their cognitive styles and abilities is influenced by many factors, such as environment, literacy, formal schooling, socialization, and cultural values. These influences come together in complex ways that researchers are only beginning to unravel. One review of the literature concludes that "cognitive styles are not simply inborn structures, dependent only on an individual's internal characteristics, but, rather, are interactive constructs that develop in response to social, educational, professional, and other environmental requirements" (Kozhevnikov 2007, 477). For example, An and Carr cite studies showing that "in the case of the concrete/abstract dichotomy, the dichotomy is not a set of attributes but reflects the level of development of expertise and an individual's educational experiences" (2017, 411). In chapter 6 we will look more closely at the role of schooling and everyday life in the development of cognitive abilities.

Research into cognitive styles began in the 1940s, and by 1992 it could be said that "in no other area of cross-cultural research have tests been used more than in the area of cognition" (Berry et al. 1992, 111). Thus, even devoting three chapters to the cognitive dimension of learning we can only attempt to summarize the most important insights and their implications for teaching across cultures. Cognitive style research has faced many of the same difficulties that learning style theory in general has faced (as discussed in chapter 3). In 2007 one researcher wrote, "At the present time, many cognitive scientists would agree that research on cognitive styles has reached an impasse. In their view, although individual differences in cognitive functioning do exist, their effects are often overwhelmed by other factors, such as general abilities and cognitive constraints that all human minds have in common" (Kozhevnikov 2007, 464). But research into cognitive style is gradually moving forward, and many are seeking to integrate various approaches (see Zhang, Sternberg, and Rayner 2012; Kozhevnikov 2007).

Is Cognitive Style a Preference or an Ability?

There is debate regarding the extent to which a cognitive style describes more an individual preference or an ability. Zhang and Sternberg are probably correct in claiming that "a style is not an ability, but rather a preference in the use of the abilities one has" (2001, 198). But the line between a cognitive ability and cognitive style is not always clear. Ability describes functions such as perception, memory, and speed of mental processes related to specific learning tasks or subject content. Most researchers also differentiate between cognitive style and cognitive strategy: a cognitive style is less self-conscious, whereas a cognitive strategy is an intentional choice about how to process a learning activity or solve a problem (Sternberg and Grigorenko 2001, 3). Though many experts believe that a person's cognitive style is relatively stable across learning tasks and domains, research indicates that it may change through influences such as literacy and education. Riccardo Viale concludes from various studies,

> These data seem to support the image of a human being genetically endowed with concepts and universal principles of inference. It is likely that there are

not fixed irreversible cultural differences in cognition that stem from relative culturally different and fixed metaphysical and epistemological theories about the world. On the contrary, the cognitive abilities develop from universal type inferential principles that are genetically inherited. They can follow different paths of development depending on different cultural contexts. However, their diversity is reversible, and the cognitive styles are dependent on knowledge, expertise, and pragmatic needs. These factors are able to reduce and, in some cases, neutralize the cultural diversity of the cognitive abilities. (2006, 22)

In this sense, cognitive style theory is no basis for racial or ethnic prejudice; all humans are endowed with basic cognitive reasoning abilities. Nor may we assume that people cannot change in their ways of thinking, perceiving, and reasoning. One's cognitive style may change and develop.

Concrete and Abstract Orientations

How people conceptualize their world is largely determined by their culture. In some cultures people tend to understand the world more in terms of concrete relationships and experiences, and others more in abstract categories and principles. Early anthropologists such as E. B. Tylor spoke of a development of cultures from "primitive" to advanced, cultures with more abstract conceptualization being categorized as the most advanced. Lucien Lévy-Bruhl described non-Western cultures as "pre-logical"—not differentiating the natural from supernatural and unconcerned about logical contradiction. Such theories have since been demonstrated to be inaccurate and misleading. Others have highlighted the Greek emphasis on discovering universal principles and the philosophical tradition that has led to Westerners' preoccupation with abstract concepts (e.g., Nisbett 2003). Platonic idealism proposed that abstract forms and ideas are more real than the experienced world—that an abstract universal truth exists independently from particulars. Perhaps more importantly, modern scientific method found that by discovering the underlying laws or principles governing the visible material world, we could solve all sorts of problems, from curing illnesses to putting a man on the moon. Consequently, the quest for understanding abstract principles has become foundational to the Western worldview, epistemology, and way of life. However, many Majority World theologians regard much of Western systematic theology as too abstract and rationalistic (see sidebar 6.4 on p. 130). Chinese philosophers have tended to be more Taoist and intuitive, and distrustful of formal logic (Norenzayan, Choi, and Peng 2007, 585–86). From a more practical point of view, remote nonindustrialized societies have less need for abstract conceptualization in their daily lives and occupations. There are, no doubt, many other contributing factors. For our purposes, the origins of cognitive differences are less important than how they play out in real life and their implications for teaching.

Of course, people everywhere are capable of thinking and expressing themselves both concretely and abstractly. Another way of describing this cognitive difference is in terms of pragmatic and academic orientations (e.g., DeCapua and Marshall 2010). The difference hinges on the level of importance that context plays in speech and thought. More concrete cognitive styles are best characterized as *high-context thought*, and more abstract thinking as *low-context thought*. This is because concrete language and thought are more dependent on having a specific context of things, people, places, and actions to be meaningful, whereas abstract, decontextualized thinking can meaningfully formulate language and thought independent of such specific contextual references. J. Peter Denny (1991) has argued that decontextualizing is the key, distinctive feature of Western thinking compared to more contextualized thinking in non-Western cultures.[1] (Although the contrast of Western versus non-Western is problematic, the underlying concept is accurate.) He demonstrates that "characteristic of all human thought, are rationality, logic, generalizing abstraction, insubstantial abstraction, theorizing, intentionality, causal thinking, classification, explanation, and originality" (1991, 81). Thus, people in all cultures think logically, express insubstantial concepts, and utilize certain abstract categories, but some do so in ways that are more context-specific. In more context-dependent thinking, principles and abstract concepts are likely to be expressed with proverbs, parables, metaphors, or similar conceptual tools of a more concrete, highly contextual nature, and less in terms of universal laws or axioms.

As with all such dichotomies, either-or differentiation between concrete and abstract orientations must be avoided. One cannot conclude that all remote, preliterate societies are necessarily concrete and high-context in their cognitive orientation. Conversely, a study in the UK and US found that people consider causal explanations that include concrete details as better than explanations that are strictly abstract. For example, explaining the cause of a traffic accident by recounting that the driver drank "eight vodka shots and three glasses of

---

1. Denny makes a nuanced distinction between abstract and decontextualizing thought: "Western thought, to which literacy is a big contributor, is widely believed to be more reflective, more abstract, more complex, and more logical than thought in preliterate agricultural and hunter-gatherer societies. The available research, however, shows that these beliefs are wrong and that Western thought has only one distinctive property separating it from thought in *both* agricultural and hunter-gatherer societies—decontextualization" (Denny 1991, 66). For our discussion the concepts of abstract and decontextualized will be used more or less synonymously. This will also avoid confusion with the very different concept of field dependence and independence to be discussed in the next chapter.

gin and tonic at Joe's bar" was found better than the abstract explanation that an excessive amount of alcohol reduced his concentration and reaction time (Bechlivanidis et al. 2017, 1456).

Language, Literacy, and Cognition

The way people conceptualize their world and process thought is closely related to language, which is the primary tool of thought. Language and literacy are perhaps the most fundamental factors influencing cognitive processes and reasoning.

Language, Worldview, and Reasoning

One of the most influential and controversial theories about the relationship of language and cognition is the so-called Sapir-Whorf hypothesis, based upon Edward Sapir's work in the first half of the twentieth century and later elaborated upon by Benjamin Whorf. It claims that the structure of language affects cognition by providing categories and concepts of thought (Whorf 1956). According to this theory, called linguistic determinism, languages do not merely give expression to thinking but determine perceptions, logical functions, and ultimately a people's worldview. This hypothesis has been contested at a number of levels. Empirical research has demonstrated that although language may influence minor aspects of cognition, such as categorization tasks, it does not determine worldview or cognitive ability (Chiu, Leung, and Kwan 2007; Berry et al. 1992, 101–5). It can also be easily observed that ethnic groups with very different languages can have very similar worldviews, relativizing the influence of language. Noam Chomsky (1965; 1968) and Robert Longacre (1976) argued that linguistic differences are primarily at the surface level and that the deep structure of all languages are in fact similar.

Russian developmental psychologist Lev Vygotsky emphasized the social origins of mental functioning. It is through social interaction that a child acquires cognition, memory, attention, and logic (Wertsch and Tulviste 1992). Craig Christy sums up Vygotsky's work this way: "He believes language and thought work together as a dynamic coupled system to enable the thought process: 'Thought is not merely expressed in words; it comes into existence through them'" (2013, 202). Thus language, culture, and cognition mutually influence each other.

This is illustrated by ways that grammar and worldview are related. Chinese, for example, does not require use of a pronoun to indicate the subject of a sentence, even when the verb inflection does not indicate person or a subject-verb agreement rule. "Consistent with the idea that language encodes cultural conceptions of the self, groups whose language allows pronoun drop tend to stress the importance of being interdependent with the social world" (Chiu, Leung, and Kwan 2007, 671). John Mbiti's classic study *African Religions and Philosophy* (1969) revealed that many East African languages have no idiomatic expressions for distant future. In the cultures of those language groups, life is primarily oriented to the past and present, and this is reflected in language. The distant future has not yet occurred and is therefore not considered a part of "time." This, however, does not mean that the *concept* of the distant future is inconceivable to them.

The claim that certain concepts are untranslatable from one language into another has often been overstated. The meaning content of language usually can be translated, although it may take a sentence or paragraph to convey the idea of a single word. More difficult to translate are nuanced meanings and connotations—such as those expressed in poetry, metaphors, or literature—and meanings associated with contextually specific experiences. But this is no indication of inherent cognitive limitations due to language alone. The debate continues regarding the extent to which language influences thought, or thought influences language, and whether language limits or empowers thinking (e.g., Zlatev and Blomberg 2015). The best evidence seems to indicate that linguistic differences do not necessarily limit or empower cognitive *ability* but are more likely evidence of differing cognitive styles or preferences that are culturally conditioned.

A language can be understood in terms of its orientation toward concrete relational (high-context) or abstract conceptual (low-context) expression. More abstract languages tend to decontextualize meaning from concrete relations and expressions. English, for example, easily turns attributes into abstract entities: "friend" or "friendly" is decontextualized and reified, becoming "friendliness." A quality becomes objectified, and "friendliness" suddenly has meaning fully independent of a specific friendly action or friendly person. Most languages, even if they are more context-dependent, can express insubstantiality; Cree uses a morpheme *-win*, as in *naapwin* ("maleness") derived from *naapew* ("man") (Denny 1991, 76). But not all languages are capable of this. Thus, in those languages abstract concepts depend on context for meaning. Take the word *friendly*: the concept it expresses has little meaning apart from a person, nation, animal, spirit, or agent of some kind that has a friendly disposition. One may speak of a friendly person or friendly gesture, but not *friendliness*. "Friendly" does not exist independently of embodiment as an actual behavior or attitude, and meaning is bound to that concrete relationship.

A more concrete language is more dependent on context because it communicates primarily in terms of specific actions, objects, experiences, and observations. Abstract concepts may be expressed through narrative or metaphor, using the observable to describe the unobservable. Chinese, for example, expresses the abstract concept of "essence" with the Zen *yenmu*, "eye," and *yen-ching*, "the pupil of the eye" (Hesselgrave 1991, 380). Denny points out that "the contextualized thought of non-Western societies can be highly theoretical; traditional myths express theories about the origins and structure of human society, but do so in the context of dramatic stories about individual characters and events" (1991, 77). Walter Ong gives this example: "Navaho narrators of Navaho folkloric animal stories can provide elaborate explanations of the various implications of the stories for an understanding of life from the physiological to the psychological and moral, and are perfectly aware of such things as physical inconsistencies" (1982, 57).

Nermi Uygur (1988) compares Turkish, a quite concrete language, to German, which is more abstract. Turkish tends to use concrete or metaphoric expressions to convey concepts that in German are entirely abstract. (English equivalents are given here.) For example, in Turkish the single concrete word *yol* ("way" or "path") is used to express a whole collection of abstract concepts including "order, method, or system." The Turkish word for "to marry" is *evlenmek*, literally "to build a house," and the word for "mourn" is *karala giymek*, "to be clothed in black." "To be bored" in Turkish is *Canim sikiliyor*, "my mind sinks." Hesselgrave, citing Eugene Nida, describes several examples from other languages:

> When a Valiente speaks of "hope in God," he says "resting the mind in God." . . . The Navajos use "My mind is killing me" for the word "worry." . . . The root of [the Cuicatec] word for "worship" is the same root used for a dog wagging his tail, and the pronoun subject, included in the verb, indicates that the reference is to a human and not to an animal. The Cuicatec Indians have recognized that the attitude of worship is similar to that of a dog before his master. (1991, 378)

It would be a mistake to draw an extremely strong dichotomy between concrete and abstract languages, but these orientations are clearly observable and reflect cognitive orientation.

Over a century ago, pioneer anthropologist Franz Boas argued that the reason some languages are more concrete than others has little to do with cognitive ability per se. He suggested that in remote traditional societies, people simply have little need to discuss abstract matters because they are primarily occupied with daily tasks such as farming, herding, fishing, hunting, and cooking. Boas conducted experiments among the indigenous people of Vancouver Island, who spoke a concrete language, and found that after some discussion they could make good sense of an insubstantial, decontextualized adjective or verb such as "love" and "pity." However, such expressions were not idiomatic (1911, 151). Therefore, speakers of a more concrete language are capable of understanding and expressing abstract concepts, but such thinking may be deemed impractical or linguistically awkward. Indeed, some studies demonstrate that non-idiomatic formulations of concepts translated from another language can be a source of misunderstanding and incorrect assessments of cognitive ability (e.g., Au 1983). Furthermore, experiments have shown that bilingual children can develop cognitive skills and acquire the linguistic tools for more abstract tasks (e.g., Greenfield 2005, 78–79). Such evidence supports the view that language may influence cognitive style but does not necessarily limit the ability to reason, nor reflect innate cognitive ability. As we shall see below, all people have similar fundamental reasoning abilities that include a certain level of abstraction. In summary we can conclude with Chiu, Leung, and Kwan that

> the availability of certain structural properties in a language is *important but not sufficient* for it to affect cognitions. Instead we suggest that the vocabulary of a language provides its speakers with some *linguistic tools* for encoding experiences and expressing thoughts, and that these tools may influence cognitions *only when they are used*. . . . Language is also a tool for negotiating shared meanings in the context. (2007, 669)

Language is the primary tool not only for communication in general but also for conceptualizing the world. Long-term cross-cultural teachers will thus want to give every effort to learning the primary language of their students. This can go a long way toward learning to think and communicate in ways that seem natural to and are more easily comprehended by the learners. Short-term teachers who cannot learn the local language should not depend solely on translators to make difficult concepts understandable. Rather, they should determine whether learners are more concrete or more abstract in their orientation and adapt their teaching content accordingly, for which suggestions are given in the next chapter. More specific guidelines for teaching in another language will be discussed in chapter 11.

Literacy and Abstract Thinking

Approximately 750 million adults, two-thirds of whom are women, cannot read or write (UNESCO 2017). As of 2020, approximately 35 percent of adult sub-Saharan Africans and 27 percent of adult South Asians were illiterate.[2] The number of people who have learned to read and write but

---

2. World Bank, "Literacy Rate, Adult Total," data as of September 2020, https://data.world bank.org/indicator/SE.ADT.LITR.ZS.

for practical purposes are unable to perform simple literate tasks is much higher, although definitions of functional illiteracy are debated and reliable data is difficult to attain (Vágvölgyi et al. 2016). By some estimates as many as 80 percent of the world's people are oral-preference learners, "who can't, don't, or won't learn through literate means."[3] According to one international study, "between 4.9% and 27.7% of adults are proficient at only the lowest levels in literacy and 8.1% to 31.7% are proficient at only the lowest levels in numeracy" (OECD 2013, 23).

Ong claims in his classic *Orality and Literacy* that "more than any other single invention, writing has transformed human consciousness" (1982, 78). Literacy alters the architecture of cognition in a variety of ways. Oral communication is highly context-dependent (Greenfield 1972). "Spoken utterance is addressed by a real, living person to another real living person or real, living persons, at a specific time in a real setting which includes always much more than mere words. Spoken words are always modifications of a total situation which is more than verbal. They never occur alone, in a context simply of words" (Ong 1982, 101). Written texts, however, decontextualize communication by separating the message from the messenger and from the context of the communicative act. Because the message is no longer linked to a speaker in a social setting, and no longer retained or transferred by persons, a change takes place in the way that knowledge is stored and examined. "Literacy does not cause a new mode of thought, but having a written record may permit people to do something they could not have done before—such as look back, study, reinterpret, and so on" (Olson and Torrance 1991, 1). At the same time, there is also something that you cannot do that you did before: you can't ask a text for clarification; the text can't answer you as a person could. Texts thus become subject to analysis and interpretation apart from the original speaker (or author), entirely unlike oral messages. "Decontextualization" becomes "the main style of thought encouraged by literacy" (Denny 1991, 81). Written language must become more precise to compensate for the loss of context for interpreting the message; consequently, written languages develop large vocabularies. Oral communication is often repetitive to ensure that the listener does not miss important points. Written communication, on the other hand, can be very concise, since underlining, boldface, or italics can emphasize important points and the reader can reread the text if something is missed. Because written texts are difficult to change, especially once they are mass produced, they have a certain finality about them. A speaker who is questioned about an orally communicated message can add nuance when replying, and

3. Lausanne Movement, "Orality," accessed November 5, 2020, https://www.lausanne.org/networks/issues/orality; International Orality Network, "Oral Learners: Who Are They?," https://orality.net/about/oral-learners-who-are-they.

a message can be changed in the next telling of a story, but written texts do not have this flexibility. Thus, analysis of written texts is possible in ways that oral communications are not. In sum, literacy tends to promote more analytical and abstract thinking because written ideas and messages take on a life independent of specific experiences, people, and contexts. Research indicates that formal schooling promotes more abstract, decontextualized reasoning because of literacy and the presentation of information apart from its natural context in symbolic medium (Greenfield 1966; Bruner 1966; Scribner and Cole 1981, 12–13). However, some studies indicate that it is not literacy per se that fundamentally alters cognition; rather, formal Western style schooling has a greater impact (e.g., Berry et al. 1992, 123–24). Some people from more oral cultures reject this kind of analysis by cultural outsiders (e.g., Archibald 2008).

There has been growing interest, especially among those involved in missionary work, in better understanding orality. An oral culture is not necessarily an illiterate culture; rather, it is a culture in which the preferred method of communication is not in written form but in oral forms such as speech, drama, and music. Some writers now speak of "high orality reliance" and "low orality reliance" cultures to avoid the literate/illiterate dichotomy (e.g., Madinger 2017). Oral cultures typically are also high-context cultures in which concrete, contextual thinking predominates. Because oral learners depend on non-written, mostly verbal, often face-to-face communication of information, the social dimension of learning becomes more prominent. The relationship between teacher and learner can be a critical factor in the learning process (Thigpen 2016). The two examples in sidebar 4.1 illustrate how concrete learners may struggle to make sense of texts that communicate hypothetical situations without a real-life context. One example describes observations of preliterate Hmong adults in an English language and literacy class, and the other describes an experience developing a literacy text for the Tarahumara people (or Ralamuli, as they call themselves) in Mexico. Confusion resulted even though texts were narratives describing familiar situations. Although these examples may appear extreme, the experience is not unusual among preliterate or semiliterate people. Much of written communication is fictional, hypothetical, or descriptive and seeks to communicate principles or concepts abstracted from concrete cases or contexts; this may present challenges for more context-dependent thinkers.

In preliterate cultures, numeric concepts and counting may be very concrete. For example, the Yale people of the West Papua highlands—100 percent of whom were nearly illiterate in the 1990s—used body parts for counting. They would begin counting with the little finger as 1, ring finger as 2, and so on. After the first five fingers they proceeded to count up parts of the arm to the head, and then back down the other side again, ending with the other little finger at 27. Twenty-seven of something is called a *teng*. Any amount more than two *teng* was difficult for the Yale to comprehend (Steinbring 2010). Denny studied Ojibway and Inuit hunters' mathematic words and found that "number concepts could not be expressed in isolation, that is, there was no equivalent for purely numeric words such as English *one, two, three*" (Denny 1991, 69; 1986). They would express the numeric concepts

---

SIDEBAR 4.1

Concrete Thinkers' Understanding of Fictional Texts

Although certainly not characteristic of all oral learners, the two examples below illustrate that fictional stories are unfamiliar or confusing to people in some cultures. In their cultures, stories are always about real people and events.

Example 1. Christina Hvitfeldt (1986, 71) describes Hmong students in an English language and literacy class:

> One of the classroom readings . . . features a man named Tim who works as a janitor in a large office building. Upon completion of the reading of the paragraph, one of [the] students who cleans office buildings at night asks, "Where he work? Same place me?" The teacher replies, "Tim isn't a real man. He doesn't live. He doesn't work. He is only in the story." When the paragraph is reviewed the next day, however, the student tries again, asking "Where Tim work? He work same place me?"
>
> Context dependent interpretation of classroom material is also apparent in the course of oral language practice. When the teacher uses fictional Hmong names in sentences for oral drill, the students invariably stop to ask one another who the person is, where he or she lives, and to whom the person might be related. This unwillingness to accept fictional people, places and

events and the subsequent imposition of a known context appears to reflect an orientation which is both personal and concrete.

Example 2. Ted Wingo (2010) describes developing a literacy text for the Tarahumara in northern Mexico:

> One friend Rosa was working with my wife Sharon on a literacy booklet. Sharon was making up a story using only the letters already taught. She related the story to Rosa about "Juana going to the store to buy corn." When Sharon tried to interact with Rosa about the story, Rosa wanted to know *which* Juana went to the store. "Was it Bakibo ajtigame? Or, maybe Osachi ajtigame?" That is, "The one who lives at Bakibo? Or, maybe the one who lives at Osachi?" (They identify people by their first name and the name of their ranch.) Rosa and Sharon discussed this for a long time and my wife, who is very good in the language, explained that this Juana was just a "make believe" Juana. But Rosa would have none of it! She literally could not imagine an imaginary person. We learned their world doesn't have a slot for imaginary people—only real ones. Even dreams, to them, are not imaginary but are the spirits of real people really interacting.

with suffixes: *pinguasut*, "three (elements)," or *pinguasit*, "three (sets)," or *pinguasuiqtaqtuq*, "he did it three times."

The characteristics of oral learners are similar to the characteristics of learners with a more concrete cognitive style. Thus teaching methods most suitable for oral learners are similar to those for concrete learners (discussed in chapter 5).

Concrete Thinking and Critical Analysis

Concrete thinkers may struggle to formulate abstracted principles from specific situations. For example, they may have difficulty sorting out relevant from extraneous details and may lack analytical skills that are central to Western education and course assignments. Higher levels of schooling place emphasis upon critical thinking and inductive reasoning that develops theories based upon evidence. Also emphasized and valued is deductive reasoning that draws specific conclusions based upon abstract, universal axioms. The ability to compare and evaluate competing theories or arguments is one of the chief goals of much of Western higher education. But all of these approaches may be unfamiliar to concrete thinkers, especially when assignments involve situations, relationships, or objects that are foreign to them.

In a course taught in Germany on intercultural communication, students were given an assignment to interview individuals who were raised in Africa, Asia, or Latin America and ask them to describe what they considered "typically German." The idea was to identify stereotypes and impressions non-Germans have of Germans. However, the students found that the people they interviewed who had little formal education often could not answer the question or were confused by it because the concept of "typical" was too abstract. But when the question was reformulated—"Describe things you have observed about Germans that show how they are different from people where you come from"—interviewees gave rich, revealing answers. In another setting, a person who worked among a nomadic ethnic group found that the people had difficulty answering discussion questions based upon a Bible story. For example, if God was not explicitly described in a particular text, they could not answer the question, "What does this story tell us about God?" They also had difficulty drawing principles from a text, so struggled to answer a question such as, "What could this story mean for our lives today?"

Lest we think that more analytical approaches are always superior, more abstract thinkers may become so preoccupied with theoretical questions that they have difficulty moving from the hypothetical and theoretical to specific application to real life. I recall one of the first Bible discussions I attended in Germany. The topic was highly practical, based upon James 1:1–8 regarding the need for perseverance and wisdom in "trials of various kinds" (v. 2). The discussion droned on for nearly thirty minutes as participants attempted to define what qualified as a "trial." The demand for precision of definition and consideration of a host of hypothetical situations fully overshadowed concrete personal experiences or applications. Apart from perfect clarity at the theoretical level, there was little point in moving on to the practical. In a similar situation related by Uygur (1988, 197–98), an informal conversation among German friends became an exercise in dialectic as the discussion circled around and around trying to define the term *dialectic*. If irrelevant detail can be a distraction for concrete thinkers, a predisposition for abstraction can be a distraction for abstract thinkers!

Approaches to Reasoning

We turn now to alternative ways of reasoning, different forms of argumentation, and different plausibility structures. Research has demonstrated that all children are endowed with innate reasoning abilities like "little scientists," irrespective of their environment or culture (Viale and Osherson 2006). However, these abilities develop in culturally conditioned ways over time.

Persons with high-context, concrete cognitive styles tend to reason more in terms of experienced reality, whereas those with low-context, abstract thinking styles will tend to favor formal, axiomatic logic. At the outset of this discussion we must be clear that "cross-cultural differences in thought concern habits of thinking, not capacities for thought" (Denny 1991, 66). Similar patterns of logic are at play in all cultures, but the relationship to context is often the primary difference in the manner in which logic is employed (Mercier 2011). It is therefore better to speak of different ways of reasoning, not of "different logics." In the strict sense, the law of noncontradiction applies everywhere,[4] much in the way that mathematics is the same everywhere. No people would survive very long if they had *no* logic. Thus, we must distinguish between formal logical reasoning (such as mathematics and noncontradiction), which is universally employed by all people, and informal argumentation or procedural norms that are culturally conditioned (and thus not universal). "Procedural norms, being based on social conventions, may be expected to vary across cultures. In contrast, epistemic norms, being based on, presumably universal, mathematical laws, may be expected not to vary between cultures" (Karaslaan et al. 2018, 359). For example, the basic idea that a claim or thesis is supported by arguments is universal, but the *kind*

---

4. The law of noncontradiction is the principle that a statement cannot be both true and false at the same time.

of evidence that is considered relevant, or the kinds of arguments deemed plausible, may vary from culture to culture.

In real life, individuals' reasoning is rarely as clean-cut as formal logic and mathematics. Not only are people context-specific in their informal reasoning; some cultures have a higher tolerance for ambiguity. They don't live in terms of either-or dichotomies and strict logical inferences; a more dialectical approach to reasoning is employed. Conversely, people in some other cultures have a lower tolerance for ambiguity—less space for mystery. In such cultures people have a greater need for closure. It has been argued that "Westerners reason about contradiction by applying a folk form of formal logic that aims to eliminate contradictions. East Asians reason about contradictions by emphasizing the 'middle way' between contradictory propositions or by tolerating opposites" (Norenzayan, Choi, and Peng 2007, 581). Nobuhiro Nagashima claimed that in Japan, "to argue with logical consistency is thus discouraged, and if one does so continuously one may not only be resented but also be regarded as immature" (1973, 96). However, these claims and the research behind them have been challenged, and even contradicted, in more recent research (e.g., Mercier et al. 2015). To the extent that they do exist, such cultural differences are very nuanced, and we must expect considerable variation within a culture.

Formal/Abstract versus Concrete/Functional Reasoning

Numerous experiments have examined culture's influence on inferential reasoning. Alexander Luria discovered in the 1930s that people in different cultures do not always give formally correct responses to straightforward syllogisms. Take for example the following syllogism:

> Major premise: In the far north all bears are white.
> Minor premise: Novaya Zemyla is in the far north.
> Question: What colors are the bears there?

Luria found that unschooled Uzbek farmers were unable or unwilling to answer. One said, "But I don't know what kind of bears are there. I have not been there and I don't know. Look, why don't you ask old man X, he was there and he knows, he will tell you." Another said, "I don't want to lie" (Luria 1971, 271). Persons from the same town who had some formal education had no difficulty in drawing the formal logical conclusion. One could jump to the conclusion that the rural farmers were incapable of simple logical reasoning. However, as Scribner and Cole state, "Today most psychologists would agree that the tendency to respond empirically to syllogisms (and thus often give incorrect answers) is not so much a sign of inability to reason logically

as it is an indication of how people understand this particular verbal form"
(1981, 155).

A distinction can be made between "theoretic" and "empiric" answers
(Scribner 1979). Theoretic answers are based on the information contained
in the syllogism (context-independent reasoning), and empiric answers more
upon experience (context-dependent reasoning). Persons who reason more
concretely and contextually approach the problem differently. As noted above,
hypothetical premises may make little sense to some concrete learners. Or if
the premises are believed to be unlikely, untrue, or contrary to experience, the
formally "correct" answer makes little sense to them. The respondent may have
observed a brown bear in the far north, which he may take as a contradiction
of the premise of the syllogism. Or he may feel that without having actually
seen the situation in reality, an answer would be dishonest or meaningless.
Respondents may not even engage the logical process at all if the content of the
syllogism is unfamiliar (Luria 1971). Hugo Mercier explains the willingness of
schooled persons to reason with abstract, hypothetical syllogisms in this way:

> Used that we are to empty school exercises, we take for granted something that
> is, as a matter of fact, utterly strange. Creating random facts out of the blue and
> trying to draw inferences from them is not what you would otherwise expect
> of a rational individual. . . . Moreover, by accepting—however temporarily—
> something that has no reasonable grounding, these participants run the risk of
> being perceived as gullible. (2011, 90)

Seen this way, the response of the uneducated Uzbeks is the more reasonable
one.

The more a syllogism deals with real-world subjects, the less likely it is that
a person with more concrete reasoning will employ strict syllogistic reasoning.
But when the syllogism deals with a subject that clearly is fictitious, such as
flying dogs, they are more likely to give the correct answer (playing the game)
using syllogistic reasoning. Such reasoning is clearly more context-dependent
in contrast to context-independent syllogistic reasoning, but it is not illogical.
Das and Dash conclude:

> Performance on syllogistic reasoning tasks depends largely on the subject's
> willingness to treat the problem as a self-contained logical unit from which
> inferences can be drawn without recourse to any external source of knowledge.
> In these tasks, the subject must clearly separate the knowledge in the premises
> from his or her knowledge from other sources. (Das and Dash 1989, 235)

Thus "empiric" reasoning is not based upon a truly alternative logic; rather,
the same logical functions are at work, but in a culturally conditioned manner.

Studies by James F. Hamill (1991) have demonstrated that the same underlying reasoning processes are usually at work, even when an answer is incorrect according to formal, textbook logic. He gives examples of how, due to semantics and taxonomy of categories, respondents sometimes interpreted the meaning of syllogisms differently and reformulated the premises (in their minds) to make sense. Once the premises had been changed, those respondents' argument were valid according to textbook logic. Syllogisms operate as a form of deductive logic, which everyone—irrespective of culture or education—intuitively uses in daily life (e.g., *I need money to buy food; I have no money; therefore I cannot buy food*). Yet even this statement could be contextually qualified (e.g., *Later today I might find money, or someone might lend me money, and then I can buy food*). In such reasoning, inferential logic is still at work while allowing for contextual factors not included in the premises. Hamill concludes,

> The structure of logical reasoning is the same regardless of language or culture. The results of all research into syllogistic reasoning have shown that when people reason with syllogism, they draw conclusions validly. Furthermore, the pattern of valid and invalid syllogisms is the same from culture to culture and from language to language. This pattern differs from the one defined in logic textbooks. (1991, 103)

Researchers have not reached a consensus about the role that schooling and literacy play in the likelihood that respondents will follow the rules of syllogistic reasoning (Segall et al. 1999, 115–22; Burnett and Medin 2008). As one survey of the research concludes,

> this preference for concrete reasoning is not limited to illiterate societies. Highly educated, industrialized East Asian samples in China and Korea also are more likely than comparable Western samples to favor concrete, intuitive, knowledge-based reasoning. Thus, the preference for formal logical reasoning prevalent in Western cultures may be only partly the result of the introduction of modern institutions such as industrialization. Other cultural factors that historically have been tied to the Western intellectual tradition, such as adversarial debate, contractual relationships, theoretical science, and formalization of knowledge, may account for the development of formal logical reasoning as a rhetorical system central to these activities. (Norenzayan, Choi, and Peng 2007, 575–76)

A study by Das and Dash (1989) in rural India found that unschooled children actually outperformed schooled children in solving certain types of syllogisms, such as those contrary to experience[5] or describing artificial conditions.[6] In such cases, context or experience did not interfere with the "pure" abstract logic of the syllogism. Thus, unschooled children were found to possess the same basic reasoning abilities. Age, not schooling, was the more important factor in their ability to solve syllogisms according to textbook logic.

To quote Denny once again, "Although all humans can do logic and evaluate and criticize logical reasoning, it is the job of the literate specialist to make a consciously formulated account of the various patterns of reasoning that humans carry out unconsciously" (1991, 81). The cross-cultural teacher must explore the way in which learners reason, and not assume that people are illogical or ignorant when their thinking does not conform to expectations that are based upon more abstract approaches to reasoning.

In contrast to formal logic and the law of noncontradiction, some cultures reason more dialectically. The principles of East Asian dialectical reasoning have been described as follows:

1. *The principle of change:* Reality is a process that is not static but rather is dynamic and changeable. A thing need not be identical to itself at all because of the fluid nature of reality.
2. *The principle of contradiction:* Partly because change is constant, contradiction is constant. Thus old and new, good and bad, exist in the same object or event and indeed depend on one another for their existence.
3. *The principle of relationship or holism:* Because of constant change and contradiction, nothing either in human life or in nature is isolated and independent, but instead everything is related. It follows that attempting to isolate elements of some larger whole can only be misleading. (Nisbett et al. 2001, 301)

Here we see how the predominant world view of a culture and its understanding of the nature of reality can influence people's approach to reasoning and plausibility.

In conclusion, we must remember what Wu and Rubin state in their analysis of argumentation by Chinese and Americans: "Logic is a cultural artifact rather than an inherent psychological capacity. The syllogistic reasoning of Aristotle has been part of the Anglo-European tradition for such a long time that English speakers tend to assume that it is a natural phenomenon of the human mind rather than an invention of the human mind" (2000, 168).

5. If the horse is well fed, it cannot work well. Ramu Babu's horse is well fed today. Can it work well today or not?
6. Those having wings can fly. If dogs would have wings, would they fly?

Categorization

Another way in which reasoning is influenced by a culture is in the way that items are categorized. Language itself creates categories to identify and associate items, and these categories vary in different languages and cultures. For example, terminology socially categorizes people by what kind of person they are, what roles they may assume, and what expectations others have of them. People may be categorized on the basis of age, kinship, occupation, ethnicity, and so on. Kinship terminology in some Asian languages does not merely describe consanguinity; it has social meanings, such as defining potential marriage partners (Medin, Unsworth, and Hirschfeld 2007, 630–35).

The way that culture and categorization relate to reasoning was investigated in Luria's early research that examined the ways people in rural Uzbekistan group and classify items. Subjects were shown pictures of four objects—a saw, ax, shovel, and log—and asked which three items belong together (fig. 4.1).

Literate persons tended to use the abstract category "tool," and group the shovel, saw, and ax together because the log is not a tool. But illiterate farmers of the same village consistently grouped items according to functionality: the log belongs together with the saw and ax, while the shovel does not belong because it cannot be used to cut the log. The objects were considered "similar" because they were "suitable for each other." When it was suggested that one man had grouped the shovel, saw, and ax because they could be described by a single word, *tool*, they consistently rejected that as a possible correct response, saying such things as, "No, that man was not correct; he does not know his business; he is a fool" (Luria 1971, 268). The abstract concept of "tool" was of familiar, of course, but the illiterate farmers did not consider it a reasonable or useful basis for categorization.

FIGURE 4.2

Categorization and culture

Of the items below, which three belong together?
Why do they belong together?

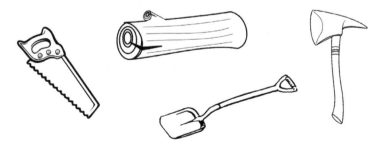

Later experiments consistently reveal the same underlying pattern. For example, when asked which two things belong together when shown pictures of a chicken, cow, and grass, American children grouped the cow and chicken, while Chinese children grouped the cow and the grass. When college students were asked the same of a panda, monkey, and banana, the panda and monkey were paired by American students, but the monkey and banana were paired by the Chinese. Concrete thinkers tend to group items on the basis of their relationship to one another or observable attributes, whereas abstract thinkers tend to group items based upon less obvious qualities and by applying rules (Nisbett 2003, 140–42). For example, the abstract category "mammal" is defined not by readily visible attributes but by use of rules: e.g., mammals bear live offspring, nurse their young, and have hair. It follows that a whale would be categorized not with a shark but with a monkey. Most studies indicate that formal education increases abstract categorization and that this effect of schooling does not wear off over time (e.g., Plueddemann 1990), although there are some counterexamples. Segall and his colleagues perhaps summarize it best:

> What was once thought to be a difference across ethnic groups in the *capacity* to process information is better thought of as a reflection of the experiences people have, and of the cultural appropriateness of the way their skills are assessed. Given the right opportunities to learn to play the Euro-American psychologists' sorting games, people anywhere can come to play them well! (Segall et al. 1999, 168)

Argumentation and Rhetoric

In the 1960s, Robert Kaplan was the first to introduce the idea of contrastive rhetoric, comparing rhetorical styles, discourse structures, and argumentation forms that he observed among students learning English as a second language. Kaplan generalized that unlike most Westerners, students from many cultures do not use a linear form of argumentation in their writing. The Western academic tradition generally prefers structuring arguments according to what's sometimes called Aristotelian logic. The discussion is linear, beginning with an introduction and thesis statement, then describing supporting arguments or evidence, and concluding with a summary statement supporting the thesis. Or alternatively, but still linear: *situation*, *problem*, *solution*, and *evaluation*. Creative thinking, challenging of ideas, and self-expression are valued. Deductive rhetoric begins with a thesis statement and then gives evidence and arguments supporting the thesis, whereas inductive rhetoric does the opposite, presenting evidence or arguments and then formulating the thesis as the logical conclusion drawn from the evidence. Both, however, are more or less linear in structure.

Kaplan contended that non-Westerners, particularly East Asians, often employ a different rhetoric whereby "circles or gyres turn around the subject and show it from a variety of tangential views, but the subject is never looked at directly" (1966, 10). Such rhetoric is sometimes called spiral, indirect, or "doodling." Deron Walker summarizes: "Simply stated, the researchers contend that from a western perspective East-Asian academic writing 1) features a delayed thesis statement; 2) turns more to unrelated subjects or other angles than proceeding in a linear fashion; 3) contains fewer topic sentences but incorporates more topic changes; 4) uses more metaphor and 5) employs fewer transition markers" (2011, 72). There has since emerged a considerable body of literature and research on comparative rhetoric, some contesting Kaplan's ideas, and others adding nuance to them and refining ways of describing culture's influence on writing style.

Much of the research on contrastive rhetoric has focused on the writing styles of native and non-native speakers of the target language. Initially such differences were thought to be related to linguistic differences between the first and second languages. Now differences are more commonly attributed to cultural convention. Students are taught what is proper writing style; what is considered aesthetic, persuasive, and socially appropriate (e.g., assertive versus restrained). For example, here is how a group of African students described their rhetorical style: "Whereas the Western style of writing is polemical, the African system is more of a negotiation with the audience so as to make them 'accept' our work." Another group said, "African communication is mostly implicit. When a speaker is too explicit, he is perceived by the audience as trying to undermine their intelligence" (Black 2018, 2833–35, 2840–41).

Cultural values are reflected in the classical Chinese form of the "eight-legged essay,"[7] which includes parallelisms and harmonious contrast. This has been simplified with the more contemporary *qi-cheng-zhuan-he* pattern. The four parts are:

> *qi*—"beginning," an introduction to the topic
> *cheng*—"hook up"; development of the topic
> *zhuan*—"turning" to another viewpoint
> *he*—"coming together" or "closing," summary of conclusion (Chen 2007, 140).

On the surface the structure appears similar to the Western *problem-solution* rhetoric. "However, in the Chinese four-parts, it seems that the arguments

---

7. The eight elements are: "1 breaking open the topic (poti), 2 receiving the topic (chengti), 3 beginning discussion (qijiang), 4 initial leg (qigu), 5 transition leg (xugu), 6 middle leg (zhonggu), 7 later leg (hougu), 8 conclusion (dajie)" (Elman 2009, 696).

are often delayed, and that arguments, statements and narration seem unconnected to the rhetoric patterns of the Western readers" (140). The claim or thesis statement is also delayed, as the speaker or writer considers it inappropriate or too bold to present the thesis without first examining the subject from various angles. Confucius mentions that one must first state the condition of a matter before advancing one's own idea. The thesis is arrived upon gradually as the case is made. Rhetorical questions are answered indirectly. Chinese students are encouraged to quote proverbs, poems, famous sayings, and idioms as elements of an argument, and doing so is rewarded by a good grade (Wu and Rubin 2000, 156). Yang and Zang (2010) argue that actually, *qi-cheng-zhuan-he* and *problem-solution* rhetoric have much in common, except in the manner by which the problem is introduced, "resulting in seemingly abrupt English beginnings to the Chinese reader and rather lengthy and irrelevant Chinese details at text beginnings to the English reader" (77). They suggest that contemporary Chinese writing sometimes deviates from the conventional *qi-cheng-zhuan-he* pattern (77). Lin Yang and David Cahill's (2008) analysis of Chinese student essays, textbooks, and contemporary writing manuals found that their rhetorical style does often depart from this pattern in favor of more directness.

In each of these approaches to argumentation, cognitive style differences play some role, but cultural values and communication conventions are more significant factors. Different logics are not at play, but rather different ways of structuring arguments. In general, Americans tend to be more direct in communication and assertive in voicing their individual opinions or position, especially in academic writing. Asians, in general, tend more toward indirect, less assertive communication. As we will see in chapter 10, collectivism and individualism can influence such features of writing style (see table 10.2 on p. 222). These different expectations in writing style can create difficulties for both student and teacher. Western readers, especially teachers, may have difficulty clearly identifying an author's standpoint and may fail to see where an essay is headed. They may suspect that the author himself is unsure of his position and lacks clarity of thought. This has resulted in lower grades for Chinese studying in the West (Chen 2007, 137).

Cross-cultural teachers need to become familiar with alternative rhetorical styles, and avoid mistakenly viewing them as a sign of inferior intelligence. They are not. One can become aware of potential differences without adopting sweeping stereotypes about the rhetoric style of East Asians or other populations that are neither helpful nor entirely accurate. For instance, Lin Yang and Cahill's analysis of two hundred essays by Chinese and American students found that "Chinese students also prefer directness in text and paragraph organization, but they are significantly less direct than American students.

The result of this study seems a compromise between the view that Chinese and English writing differ fundamentally and the view that there is no difference between the two" (2008, 124). One must also remember that cultures and norms for writing can change. Commenting on Korea, Eun-Young Julia Kim warns, "Stereotypical notions of non-linearity and reader-response prose, which were introduced during the heyday of contrastive rhetoric by researchers of Asian writing, now seem to be losing ground as the writing instruction clearly emphasizes the same features including a linear structure and audience awareness, as those emphasized in the West" (2017, 10–11). She nevertheless remarks that features such as digression and indirect style may still often be present. There is considerable variability of style even within Western cultures. Ágnes M. Godó (2008) compared American and Hungarian academic writing styles and concluded that Hungarians place more value on all-encompassing knowledge and complexity of issues, while Americans place more value on personal expression and viewpoints.

Wain-Chin Chen suggests "that teachers and learners together could explore the contrastive discourses on which writing is based and work at these and at the process of writing and not just look at the final product" (2007, 145). The cross-cultural teacher must take care to understand the conventional approaches to argumentation and rhetoric of the host culture. For example, an American teacher could easily misread such stylistic conventions as evidence that the writers are unclear, confused, lack confidence, or are unable to get to the point. American teachers would do well, under many circumstances, to adopt the host culture's forms of rhetoric in their own teaching and writing so as to not be misread by students as arrogant, simplistic, or tactless.

In the next chapter we will consider the practical implications of these understandings of cognition for teaching and learning across cultures.

The Cognitive Dimension

Part 2: Teaching Concrete Thinkers

Having laid the conceptual foundations of concrete and abstract cognitive styles in the previous chapter, we now come to the practical implications of these understandings for teaching and learning. Because most readers of this book are more familiar with Western pedagogical approaches that favor abstract thinking, this chapter will discuss teaching methods that resonate with concrete thinkers and oral cultures. There can be distinct advantages to helping learners develop new learning strategies and expand their cognitive abilities through mismatch in teaching and learning preferences. Evidence points to the ability of learners to develop new approaches to learning and processing information. While we may not want to speak of concrete thinking as less advanced than abstract thinking, the reality is that abstract thinking is important for engaging the modern world. Abstract reasoning is required not only in technical fields of learning such as mathematics, the sciences, and engineering, but also in advanced biblical studies such as hermeneutics and contextualization. Yet in theology and hermeneutics, oral methods are being explored, and the value of more concrete approaches to biblical studies is being increasingly recognized.

Especially for short-term teaching assignments and in more informal or non-formal teaching settings, it will be most effective to adapt teaching to the more concrete thinking style of learners. It should be noted that even in societies with high levels of formal education, oral or concrete forms of

CHAPTER OVERVIEW

- Oral and Concrete Features of Biblical Literature
- Teaching with Stories
- Use of Metaphor and Object Lessons
- The Wisdom of Proverbs
- Case-Based Instruction
- Other Methods and Media
- Advantages of Decontextualized, Abstract Teaching

communication may still be preferred. Many, if not most, persons with more concrete cognitive styles are also oral learners:

> Many groups transmit their beliefs, heritage, values and other important information by means of stories, proverbs, poetry, chants, music, dances, ceremonies and rites of passage. The spoken, sung, or chanted word associated with these activities often consists of ornate and elaborate ways to communicate. Those who use these art forms well are highly regarded among their people. Cultures which use these forms of communication are sometimes called "oral cultures." (LCWE 2005, 12)

As what follows will make clear, teaching methods that are especially effective with concrete thinkers are also valuable for more abstract thinkers.

Oral and Concrete Features of Biblical Literature

Lest we are tempted to think that concrete approaches to teaching are suitable for children but inferior to more analytic and abstract approaches when teaching adults, we should remember that the Bible employs a wide range of genres: poetry, law, wisdom, epistolary discourse, prophecy, apocalyptic, and historical narrative. Historical narrative comprises over half the pages of the Bible. The most profound truth revealed to humanity, the story of redemption, is not an abstract ideal but the story of God's concrete intervention in history in creation, miracles, the exodus, and most of all in the incarnation as God himself enters history in the person of the Son. The prophets often used object lessons, Jesus taught in parables, apocalyptic uses vivid imagery, and proverbs formulate wisdom in pithy, real-life language. Unfortunately, these forms suited for concrete and oral learners are often neglected in Western-style adult education. Adapting teaching to utilize this range of communicative forms must be rediscovered by many Western teachers. Even the Epistles of the apostle Paul included oral patterning and rhetoric (Harvey 1998).[1] Recently, some have called for "oral hermeneutics" as a way to read Scripture with greater attention to the oral nature of the biblical texts (e.g., Steffen and Bjoraker 2020).

This chapter's emphasis on more concrete teaching methods should not be understood as a rejection of more abstract approaches. The apostle Paul "reasoned" when he proclaimed the gospel in the synagogues (Acts 17:2, 17; 18:4, 19). His writing in general, and particularly his message in Athens

---

1. In the New Testament era only about 10 percent of the Greco-Roman population was literate (Harris 1989; Hezser 2001), although some have argued for considerably higher levels (Wright 2015).

(Acts 17:22–31), employed the rhetorical argumentation familiar to educated Greeks (Sampley and Lampe 2010; Witherington 1998, 517–21). Culturally compelling, rational arguments and logic were part of his communication repertoire. Theology teachers often gravitate to the more abstract teaching and reasoning of the Epistles. Yet even the Epistles address specific (concrete) issues facing the young churches. For example, the high Christology of the Epistle to the Colossians is a theological response to the local struggle against syncretism, which was related to mixing Jewish and folk religious beliefs with Christian faith (Arnold 1996). Thus, even though the theology of Colossians might be considered abstract, understanding the context can make it accessible to concrete learners.

Teaching with Stories

Stories, oral history, legends, and myths all are concrete narrative ways of describing life and the lessons of life. Stories not only entertain but also preserve traditions and create cultural identity. Stories are used in legal cases to convince juries and by politicians to win votes. Stories can create a vision for the future. In traditional cultures, stories reinforce cultural values (Lawrence and Paige 2016). But stories can also challenge traditional thinking, as Jesus did by telling parables.

In stories the message is easily visualized and principles are embedded in the actors and actions that are context-specific. There is often a moral behind the story, but that moral has meaning because of the story. Of course, stories are effective teaching tools for all learners, not just concrete or oral learners. Consider what you remember from a sermon you may have recently heard: it's the stories and illustrations. This is in part because the listener can visualize the message and connect with the message on a personal level. Stories connect the idea or lesson with the familiar.

Furthermore, stories help learners organize information in a meaningful context. Instead of simply memorizing facts, principles, or dates as isolated pieces of information, embedding them in a larger, unfolding narrative helps learners establish their meaning and identify logical connections. In the book *How Learning Works*, Susan Ambrose and her colleagues give the example of the difference between simply memorizing 1588 as the date that the British defeated the Spanish Armada, and being able to place that event in the context of a host of historical developments leading up to it (2010, 44). The same might be said about learning theological truths or confessional statements. By teaching them in the context of biblical history, biographical narratives, or prayers, truths that in isolation seem abstract can take on deeper meaning and practical significance.

In cultures that lack television and modern technology, storytelling is still a primary form of entertainment. But in most Western cultures, the art of verbal storytelling has been largely lost. Hollywood films and television tell the stories, and the visual can overshadow the spoken word. Americans, however, can learn much about good storytelling from such personalities as the late Studs Terkel or, more recently, Garrison Keillor.

Oral Literature

The term "oral literature" may sound like an oxymoron until we realize that "literature" may be passed on not only in written form but also by oral transmission. Jane Nandwa and Austin Bukyena describe oral literatures as those "whose composition and performance exhibit to an appreciable degree the artistic characteristics of accurate observation, vivid imagination and ingenious expression" (1983, 1). Ruth H. Finnegan emphasizes that performance is a significant feature of oral literature, writing, "Oral literature is by definition dependent on a performer who formulates it in words on a specific occasion—there is no other way in which it can be realized as a literary product" (2012, 4). Even when oral literature has been put into writing, the enactment or delivery remains essential to the full impact. Interaction with the audience is another feature of oral literature absent from transcriptions. The World Oral Literature Project has advanced the study of the topic, providing numerous fascinating resources from around the world, including publications and online written, audio, and video materials.[2] In Kenya oral literature has become its own field of study and has been introduced into school curriculum (Okombo and Nandwa 1992).

Storytelling Traditions

Different cultures can have different storytelling traditions; thus the teacher should become familiar with the local method. Sidebar 4.1 in the previous chapter (p. 76) illustrated how some cultures are unfamiliar with fictional or hypothetical stories; in those cultures, stories are expected to relate the events of real people and places. Sometimes stories are to be told with specific gestures as a performance, whereas in other places the storyteller is to remain somewhat aloof. In some oral traditions stories should be passed on with great precision and accuracy. Listeners may quickly correct the storyteller if he veers from the correct telling in the slightest detail. But other traditions allow for considerable creativity in retelling of familiar stories. "There are some cases when the performer introduces variations on older pieces or even total new

---

2. See www.oralliterature.org.

forms in terms of detailed wording, the structure or the content" (Finnegan 2012, 10). Joseph Grimes and Barbara Grimes (1974) describe how the Huichol people in Mexico may even change the lead character when retelling a story. This would obviously create problems when retelling Bible stories: for example, if Judas became more important than Jesus in the stories of the Gospels! In chapter 11 we will examine the use of various media for telling stories.

Research on Learning and Storytelling

Jerome Bruner underlines the power of narrative when he writes,

> It has been the convention of most schools to treat the art of narrative—song, drama, fiction, theater, whatever—as more "decoration" than necessity, as something with which to grace leisure, sometimes even as something morally exemplary. Despite that, we frame our accounts of our cultural origins and our most cherished beliefs in story form, and it is not just the "content" of these stories that grip us, but their narrative artifice. Our immediate experience, what happened yesterday or the day before, is framed in the same storied way. Even more striking, we represent our lives (to ourselves as well as to others) in the form of narrative. (1996, 40)

Stories are a vehicle to embody and illustrate truth and to motivate moral action. "A substantial body of evidence attests to the power of narratives to change attitudes, beliefs, and behaviors" (Nabi and Green 2015, 138). Stories have persuasive power beyond that of cool, disembodied, rational arguments and nonnarrative or rhetorical messages (139). (See sidebar 5.1.)

It is well established that an emotional connection facilitates learning, and stories are one of the most effective ways to establish that connection. Robin Nabi and Melanie Green demonstrate that the emotional connection with narrative communication "enhances its persuasive potential. Further, the emotion and emotional shifts created by a story may have implications for a range of post-message involvement activities, including repeated consumption, message and topic elaboration, and social sharing" (2015, 138). Friederika Fabritius and Hans W. Hagemann argue that the default mental network of our brain is a *narrative* network, and this may be why stories so effectively engage us. They further maintain that for stories to be effective, there must some level of common connection and relatability. This is why cross-cultural teachers need to become immersed in the local culture and experiences of the people and use stories with which everyone to some extent can relate.

Recent cognitive research has revealed another fascinating aspect of storytelling. We are drawn to stories that we think will be emotionally relevant to others in

SIDEBAR 5.1

Dimming the Stars?

Rubem A. Alves describes the impact of storyless truth in *The Poet, the Warrior, the Prophet.*

"Please, tell us your stories," the villagers said to the newcomers. The villagers were all silent and smiled as the Enlightened began telling the truth. But they did not tell stories. They opened thick books, treatises, commentaries, confessions—the crystallized results of their work. And it is reported that, as they spoke, the stars began to fade away till they disappeared, and dark clouds covered the moon. The sea was suddenly silent and the warm breeze became a cold wind.

When they finished telling the truth of history and interpretation the villagers returned to their homes. And, no matter how hard they tried, they could not remember the stories they used to tell. And they slept dreamless sleep.

As to the members of the order, after so many years of hard scientific work,

they had their first night of sound sleep, also without dreams. Their mission was accomplished. They had finally told the truth. (1990, 71, quoted in Steffen 2005, 41–42)

Tom Steffen relates this to his own early ministry.

The Ifugao wanted stories; I gave them systematic theology. They wanted relationships, I gave them reasons. They wanted a cast of characters, I gave them categories of convenience. They wanted events, I gave them explanations. While I succeeded initially in dimming the stars, covering the brightness of the moon, calming the churning sea, and turning warm winds into cold, cutting ones, unlike the people mentioned in the quote, the Ifugao would have no part of it—*they did not want dreamless nights.* Fortunately, they refused to take part in the mental gymnastics in which I had inadvertently asked them to participate. (Steffen 2010, 147–48)

our social group. So when we listen to a story, a part of our brain is deciding if it is a story worth retelling. If we decide that it is, our attention intensifies and our learning and memory increase. If you convey information in a story that people want to share, whether that sharing takes place in person or via social media, then you have succeeded, not only as a story teller, but as a teacher. (Fabritius and Hagemann 2017, 199)

In addition to being an important pedagogical tool, stories can provide the cross-cultural teacher with a tool to facilitate worldview change, which will be discussed in chapter 8.

Stories embody values, inform identity, and shape worldview. Common narratives and stories—be it in oral literature, folk tales, bestselling paperback novels, or Hollywood and Bollywood films—can be discussed to discern the deeper messages and contrast them with biblical teaching. This heightens the relevance of teaching and raises awareness of the messages being communicated. Students become the critics of their own culture. In recent decades missionaries have rediscovered the value of storytelling and oral methods. Narrative has been found to be a useful communication tool in health education (Fitzgerald et al. 2020). Sidebar 5.2 gives an example of using storytelling to train caregivers of traumatized children in high orality reliance cultures. Sidebar 11.5 (p. 252) describes how a narrative approach using audio dramatizations increased loan repayment in a grain bank co-operative in Bangladesh.

SIDEBAR 5.2

Training Caregivers through Drama

Susan Vonolszewski trained caregivers of traumatized children living in rescue homes and orphanages. Because these caregivers had limited formal education and were from high orality reliance cultures of Africa and Asia, Vonolszewski adopted an orality-appropriate approach by creating dramatized training materials, described here by Chuck Madinger (2017):

> Her solution was to develop a radio-drama (*Holding Esther*) about children caught in the grips of loss and exploitation. She tenaciously pursued the best script writers, production managers, and actors in African media outlets. They composed seven episodes around learning goals, objectives, and outcomes agreed upon by several thought leaders and practitioners in the field. After the final editing, her team adapted the program to forms that could be used as standalone radio broadcasts or used in small groups and training.

The training approach was then field-tested in workshops to determine its effectiveness. Madinger continues:

> The results of the study showed a dramatic change in knowledge and attitudes about how to think of the children and the common attitudes that must change in their culture. They recognized the harsh words spoken when a child seemed "rebellious" or the harmful physical responses (slapping or pointed blaming finger) they used. They learned more gentle ways of helping the children through their momentary or recurring outbursts. Those in the test group (workshop) demonstrated a far deeper awareness of the principles of good care as well as better intentions to put them into practice than those who did not listen to the programs.

> The radio/drama workshop was then implemented, resulting in markedly better care of the children and widespread adoption.

Chronological Bible Storying

The chronological Bible storying approach to evangelism and discipleship is one of the most significant rediscoveries in modern missionary methods. A good overview of the background, history, and practice of biblical storytelling in recent cross-cultural mission work is found in Paul F. Koehler's *Telling God's Stories with Power* (2010). Although biblical storytelling has always been part of the communication of the gospel and church teaching, one of the more significant developments in the chronological Bible storying approach came through the work of Trevor McIlwain, a missionary among the remote Palawano people in the Philippines. He was frustrated by their seeming inability to grasp central truths of the gospel. Instead of attempting to organize and present biblical teaching in a systematic, thematic, nonsequential manner of isolated doctrines, he determined to simply tell the Bible story beginning with Genesis and ending with the ascension of Jesus, including teaching regarding the patriarchs, the Old Testament sacrificial system, and other elements of

---

SIDEBAR 5.3

Resources for Bible Storying and Oral Learners

Online Resources

International Orality Network: www.orality.net

Orality Journal: www.orality.net/library/journals

Ethnos360: www.biblestudy.ethnos360.org

Storying the Scriptures: www.storyingthescriptures.com/category/resources

GoodSeed: www.goodseed.com/tools.html

God's Story Project: www.gods-story.org

International Mission Board (Southern Baptist): www.imb.org/give/project/orality-and-bible-storying-development

Recommended Books

Bowen, K. Carla, with James Bowen. *Building Bridges to Oral Cultures: Journeys among the Least-Reached.* Pasadena, CA: William Carey, 2017.

Chiang, Samuel E., ed. *Orality Breakouts: Using Heart Language to Transform Hearts.* Hong Kong: International Orality Network / Lausanne Committee for World Evangelization, 2010.

Chiang, Samuel E., and Grant Lovejoy, eds. *Beyond Literate Western Practices: Continuing Conversations in Orality and Theological Education.* Hong Kong: International Orality Network, 2014.

De Neui, Paul H., ed. *Communicating Christ through Story and Song: Orality in Buddhist Contexts.* Pasadena, CA: William Carey, 2008.

Koehler, Paul F. *Telling God's Stories with Power: Biblical Storytelling in Oral Cultures.* Pasadena, CA: William Carey, 2010.

Sessoms, Rick, with Tim Brannigan. *Leading with Story: Cultivating Christ-Centered Leaders in a Storycentric Generation.* Pasadena, CA: William Carey, 2016.

Steffen, Tom. *Reconnecting God's Story to Ministry: Cross-Cultural Storytelling at Home and Abroad.* Rev. ed. Downers Grove, IL: InterVarsity, 2005.

SIDEBAR 5.4

Chronological Bible Storying and Leadership Development

In a North African Muslim-dominated country, 17 young men (many of whom could barely read and write and some not at all) underwent a two-year leader training program using chronological Bible storying. At the end of two years, students mastered approximately 135 biblical stories in their correct chronological order, spanning from Genesis to Revelation. They were able to tell the stories, compose from one to five songs for each story and enact dramas about each of the stories. A seminary professor gave them a six-hour oral exam. They demonstrated the ability to answer questions about both the facts and theology of the stories and showed an excellent grasp of the gospel message, the nature of God, and their new life in Christ. The students quickly and skillfully referred to the stories to answer a variety of theological questions. (LCWE 2005, 8–9)

the larger narrative of salvation history. He discovered that when he taught the Bible this way, the message was more readily understood and a biblical worldview was constructed because the telling provided background information essential to grasping the significance of Christ's death and resurrection. Local people understood the gospel in a new, more profound way. McIlwain compiled a system of Bible storytelling—not only for evangelism but also for discipleship—in the multivolume *Building on Firm Foundations*.

Such chronological Bible storying has since been adapted by others, and used with remarkable effectiveness in countless contexts around the world. Some story sets are geared to the needs of specific non-Christian worldviews. Tom Steffen, in his book *Worldview-Based Storying* (2018), recounts how various approaches to Bible storying have developed in recent decades and provides a helpful resource for teachers wanting to explore this approach further. These approaches present the biblical message in a compelling narrative format and are easily retold and passed on to others. Theological doctrines are addressed in the context of the narratives as they arise. Today, hundreds of resources in numerous languages have become available for Bible storying and discipling oral learners (see sidebar 5.3).

Sidebar 5.4 gives an example of how chronological Bible storying has been used not only in evangelism but also in leadership development.

Use of Metaphor and Object Lessons

Until recently, the Western philosophical tradition dating back to Aristotle has viewed metaphor with disdain, if not contempt (Ricoeur 1977). All teachers, but especially cross-cultural teachers, would do well to rediscover the power of metaphor in their teaching. Metaphor and simile are ways of transferring characteristics from the familiar to the unfamiliar by way of analogy or likeness. "Metaphor enables a movement from an abstract concept to a concrete image; it triggers affect and/or experience; it bridges logical gaps, it relates parts to a larger whole, and it maps out nonverbal phenomena or behavior" (Kimmel 2004, 276). Often, though not always, metaphor is employed where literal language is either unavailable or can only with difficulty describe the matter at hand. Metaphors are often more than simple analogies or colorful illustrative aids, but rather communicate a whole complex set of meanings, relationships, dynamics, and emotions. Furthermore, metaphor plays an important part in cognitive functions. According to Raymond Gibbs, research on cognitive linguistics "has demonstrated that metaphor is not merely a figure of speech, but is a specific mental mapping that influences a good deal of how people think, reason, and imagine in everyday life" (1999, 145). Metaphors structure cultural models in linguistic communities, "shaping what people believe, how they act, and how they speak about the world and their own experiences" (154). Cultures typically have so-called dominant metaphors. For example, Americans and Hungarians may speak of life as *war* or as a *journey*, but the Hmong speak of life as a *string* (Kövecses 2004, 265). Studying the dominant metaphors of a culture can reveal much about their worldview.

An object lesson is an enacted metaphor or real-life example employed to illustrate a point. Because the object lesson is often more involved than a single metaphor, its illustrative power is greater. An object lesson typically uses a physical object as a visual aid, thus involving more senses than merely hearing. Simulation games can be a form of object lesson that activate the learner, increasing the impact of the lesson.

However, the use of metaphor in cross-cultural teaching is not without pitfalls and potential for misunderstanding. Different cultures may assign different metaphoric meanings to the same object. Jeannette Littlemore's research on the experience of international students found:

> Metaphors have been shown to be a stumbling block for overseas students when trying to follow lectures at university. An inability to understand the metaphors used by lecturers can lead students to misinterpret not only the information conveyed in the lecture, but also the attitude of the lecturer toward the information that he or she is presenting. (Littlemore 2001, 273)

She also found that

> students were most likely to interpret the metaphors in ways that supported, rather than contradicted their own value systems and schemata. Furthermore,

> even when they understood the more "factual" content of the metaphors, the students appeared to interpret their *evaluative function* in terms of their own value systems and schemata, rather than that of the lecturer. (282)

Thus, even when the intended meaning of the metaphor is understood, the metaphor may carry connotations unintended by the communicator. One must always examine how a metaphor is specifically used in cultural discourse and not underestimate how it may embody whole systems of thought, beliefs, values, and emotions.

The Bible is full of metaphors that are not only linguistic conventions but also describe spiritual realities such as kingship, redemption, slavery, cleansing, and adoption (see Ott 2014). Because of metaphoric language's vivid, concrete nature, which conveys rich layers of meaning, relationships, and emotions inaccessible through naked abstract formulations, this type of language is most appropriate to describe the profound mysteries of God and his dealings with humanity. However, Bible teachers should be cautious not to interpret a biblical metaphor in a manner foreign to the originally intended meaning. For example, in Western cultures we typically think of the heart as the seat of the emotions, whereas in Hebrew the heart is more the seat of the will. Among the Chuis of Guatemala, the abdomen is the seat of the emotions, and among the Totonacs of Mexico it is the spleen (Nida 1960, 190). When Jesus calls Herod a fox in Luke 13:32, what does he mean? To the Cuicatecox in Mexico it might mean he is homosexual; to the Maxakali of Brazil it would mean that he has red hair (Shaw 1988, 213).

Cross-cultural teachers will do well to study the host culture's use of metaphor and make the most of utilizing metaphor and object lessons in their teaching. Not only will metaphor add color to instruction, but understanding will also be enhanced, especially when instructing concrete learners.

The Wisdom of Proverbs

A proverb is difficult to define, but you know it when you hear it. It is usually a short, pithy, memorable statement embodying some insight, wisdom, or moral. Proverbs may be in rhyme or meter and often employ metaphor. They are usually concrete and rooted in familiar daily experience, even when describing a moral principle. For example, "The fear of the LORD is the beginning of knowledge" (Prov. 1:7) does not contain a concrete metaphor but speaks to a familiar disposition. On the other hand, "The fear of the LORD is a fountain of life, turning a person from the snares of death" (Prov. 14:27) contains two familiar metaphors—a fountain and a snare—making the concept more imaginative and visual. The message of such proverbs, especially biblical proverbs, is no less true or less profound than more abstract theological statements. But they are more accessible to concrete thinkers and more memorable for everyone.

Because proverbs often include wit or irony, they touch the emotions, and the humor disarms resistance to the message. Consider, for example, Proverbs 27:15: "A quarrelsome wife is like the dripping of a leaky roof in a rainstorm." Proverbs also provide shorthand in daily conversation to express complex relationships or to emphasize a moral lesson to be learned from a specific situation. In the words of one writer, "a great deal of proverb mind work can be accomplished in a brief moment" (Honeck 1997, 1). The proverb quickly connects an individual experience or event with a universal principle. The statement or judgment it conveys is distanced from the individual quoting it, since the proverb invokes the voice of collective wisdom, not personal opinion. An entire argument or an analysis of a situation can be summarized with a single proverb, such as "The grass is always greener on the other side of the fence."

As a genre, proverbs should be understood as expressing general principles of wisdom, not as immutable, scientific laws of life admitting no exception. Take, for example, Proverbs 15:1: "A gentle answer turns away wrath, but a harsh word stirs up anger." There will be situations in which the soft answer actually kindles the wrath of the listener, but as a general principle, the soft answer is the wise response and certainly better than a harsh one. In fact, proverbs may be self-contradictory or paradoxical, as in Proverbs 26:4–5, "Do not answer a fool according to his folly, or you yourself will be just like him. Answer a fool according to his folly, or he will be wise in his own eyes." Such a proverb highlights the enigmatic nature of life or the quandaries we face—in this case, the dilemma of trying to deal with a fool. A culture may possess proverbs that contradict each other, such as "Absence makes the heart grow fonder" and "Out of sight, out of mind." But this is not viewed as a logical dilemma, for life itself is full of contradictions. Rather, the appropriate proverb can be cited depending on the situation and what the speaker wants to emphasize.

Proverbs reflect on the one hand the universal human desire to express ideal truths and wisdom about life in simple, memorable formulas, while on the other hand they embody specific cultural values and mores. The proverbs that are most often quoted tell us much about what a particular culture values and how people understand their world. Thus the cross-cultural teacher can discover much about a culture by noting the most commonly used proverbs. Consider, for example, how American culture is reflected in these proverbs: "The early bird catches the worm" and "No pain, no gain." Compare them to this oft-quoted African proverb: "If you want to go fast, go alone. If you want to go far, go together."

Educated Westerners sometimes dismiss proverbs as trite, folksy, and insufficiently nuanced to be useful for serious discourse. But this is a mistake. Plato used proverbs, and Shakespeare provided us with some of Western culture's most memorable proverbs. In many Asian cultures, proverbs are viewed as authoritative expressions of collective wisdom and may even be cited in academic writing or invoked in valid argumentation (Wu and Rubin 2000; Günther 1990). In quoting a proverb, one taps into traditional wisdom, borrowing the voice of the group and making it one's own; their use is considered elegant and a sign of being well educated (Günther 1990). In some African contexts, proverbs have persuasive power cited by judges and lawyers in legal argumentation. "Among the Anang Ibibio [of Nigeria], for instance, proverbs are often skillfully introduced into speeches at the crucial moment and are influential in the actual decisions reached" (Finnegan 2012, 396).

Richard P. Honeck provides one of the most thorough and fascinating discussions of the nature of proverbs in his *A Proverb in Mind: The Cognitive Science of Proverbial Wit and Wisdom* (1997). Comprehension of proverbs requires complex brain functions, and laboratory experiments reveal that a healthy brain cannot begin to understand proverbs until at least age seven (214–46). Honeck argues that proverbs reflect "pancognitive processes" (43) that are common features not just of language but of all human thought. In other words, proverbs resonate with universal mental functions and can thus be a powerful communication and instructional tool for anyone. What distinguishes proverbs from other forms of speech, such as metaphor, aphorisms, and slogans, is that one of their purposes is didactic and their structural features "facilitate memory, teach, and persuade" (13, 29). They have proven valuable in treatment of addictions, as anyone familiar with Alcoholics Anonymous can attest (T. Rogers 1989).[3] "Proverbs also provide a more subtle lesson in thinking. They are verbal puzzles that engage conscious components of remembering, reasoning, problem solving, and communicating. They might therefore promote these skills in other domains" (Honeck 1997, 274).

Honeck proposes that proverbs could prove an especially helpful tool in developing more abstract reasoning skills.

> Proverbs could teach children abstract thinking and reasoning in several ways. First there is the matter of meaning levels. As for all proverb comprehension, a child must move off the literal level. . . .
>
> Second, there is a mental flexibility factor. The child learns that the same utterance can mean different things in different contexts. . . .

---

3. For example, a favorite AA proverb is, "If you hang around the barber shop long enough you're going get a haircut." This is a warning not to enter a bar or situation where alcohol is consumed. When the temptation arises, the recovering alcoholic repeats the familiar proverb to herself as a reminder to stay away.

Finally, the process of mapping proverb, topic, and general ideal provides implicit instruction in analogical thinking. It is possible, therefore, that direct instruction in the use and comprehension of proverbs could provide valuable lessons in critical thinking. (274–75)

Honeck cites evidence that use of proverbs has, in fact, facilitated critical thinking skills. In this regard, the use of proverbial sayings has long been a feature of traditional African culture and pedagogy (Reagan 2000, 25–55). One African writer describes the importance of proverbs in traditional Yoruba education this way:

> Proverbs which constituted an important mode of communication were used to develop the child's reasoning power and skill, and in expressing the deeper thoughts most essential in settling disputes and in decision-making processes. They had to be mastered if the child was to be fully developed and be able to cope with the various occasions when they had to be used. (A. Fajana 1986, 45, quoted in Reagan 2000, 31)

The pedagogical value of proverbs, especially in teaching concrete learners, should be self-evident. Real-life application is never far from the meaning of a proverb. Mejai B. M. Avoseh (2012) sees connections between the use of proverbs in the Ogu and Yoruba contexts and Western adult learning theories

---

SIDEBAR 5.5

Carrying the Hound to the Hunt

I have taught in numerous cultural settings about the importance of self-motivation in Christian ministry. I frequently quote a German proverb: "You shouldn't have to carry the hound to the hunt." In other words, a good hunting dog should be eager to hunt, and the master should not have to prod the dog to get it moving. The irony of a hunter having to carry, pull, or kick the dog to get it to hunt is never missed. Such a dog might make a friendly companion, but it is worthless for hunting. So too a minister must be a self-starter, "champ-ing at the bit" to plan, work, meet people, and see results, and should not have to be prodded or motivated by others. He should be more like the single-minded hunting dog, nose to the ground, not distracted to the left or the right, because it is doing what it was bred to do: hunt. Although this is a relatively minor point as part of many hours of training, at the conclusion of several days of training, participants frequently mention in their feedback how memorable and impactful that proverb was.

FIGURE 5.1

The reasoning process in the use of proverbs

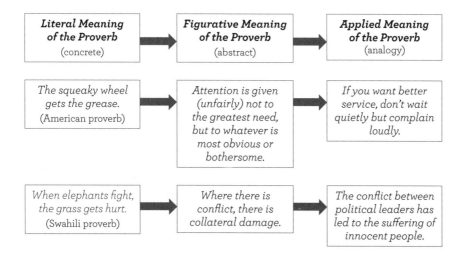

that build on experience and praxis, such as the learning theories of Malcolm Knowles and Paulo Friere. Also, the persuasive logic of a proverb is readily grasped by concrete learners.[4] For that reason they are powerful pedagogical tools that are memorable and have affective impact (see sidebar 5.5).

The memorable quality of proverbs is particularly important in oral cultures in which communication is primarily verbal and messages are not retained in written form. Proverbs often appear in poetic form for memorability and use familiar, picturesque language to covey meaning. The listener must move from the literal image or relationship conveyed in the metaphor or simile and apply the concept in an entirely different, nonliteral, context—in other words, must exercise analogical reasoning. The abstract relationship or message must be understood for the proverb to have meaning beyond the literal; then that meaning must be applied appropriately in the new concrete situation (see fig. 5.1). The truth (or wisdom) of a proverb rests not on linear, inferential logic of abstract propositions but rather on analogical logic of relationships familiar in daily life. Thus, formulation of abstract figurative meaning (as in the examples in the middle column of fig. 5.1) is usually implicit, since an intuitive sense of the analogical meaning is readily grasped and applied.

Sometimes the analogy is explicit, as in this Ashanti proverb: "A wife is like a blanket; when you cover yourself with it, it irritates you, and yet if you

---

4. An Akan proverb states, "When a fool is told a proverb, the meaning of it has to be explained to him" (Finnegan 2012, 402).

SIDEBAR 5.6

A Learning Activity Using Proverbs

This group activity is designed to help learners make connections between the folk wisdom expressed in their most common proverbs and biblical teaching on morals, ethics, and wisdom. By reflecting upon proverbial teaching, they become more aware of their cultural values. Then they can critically evaluate those values by comparing their teaching with the teaching of the Bible.

1. Have learners write a list of the ten most commonly cited proverbs in their culture. Then have them discuss the central teaching of each proverb and the contexts in which it would be cited. What values are expressed? What ethical or moral standards are reflected? How is life depicted? What attitudes are endorsed or discouraged?

2. For each proverb, have learners find biblical proverbs that have similar or contradictory teaching. Other biblical passages speaking to the given principle can be cited.

3. Then have learners describe the ways in which cultural values are being affirmed or challenged by biblical teaching.

4. Bring all discussion groups together and discuss each group's findings. Where is there consensus? Where do the findings differ, and why? What can be done to address cultural values that are inconsistent with biblical values? How can proverbs (both cultural and biblical) be used to help people become more faithful followers of Jesus?

cast it aside you feel cold" (Finnegan 2012, 385). Sometimes the analogy is tacit, as in this Zulu proverb: "No polecat ever smelt its own stink" (386). Because the metaphor appears in verse and in some kind of relationship, the communicative power of the metaphor is heightened. In moral development, learners can not only reflect upon the meaning of the proverb but also consider hypothetical or real experiences to which the proverb speaks. Biblical parallels can be discovered that illustrate or reinforce the teaching of a traditional proverb. For example, the Swahili proverb "When elephants fight, the grass gets hurt" can be compared to biblical history when evil kings brought suffering upon the people.[5] Numerous similar examples, including biblical parallels, can be found at www.afriprov.org. Sidebar 5.6 offers a model for using proverbs to launch a discussion with adults in order to stimulate critical reflection on cultural values and worldview.

5. These ideas are taken from http://www.afriprov.org/african-proverb-of-the-month/27-2001proverbs/172-nov2001.html.

SIDEBAR 5.7

Use of Proverbs in Evangelism

Jay Moon relates how a Meru proverb from Kenya became an effective evangelistic tool. A visiting pastor shared this proverb with theological students: "When a man is in love, he doesn't count how long and steep the road is to his fiancée's house." Moon writes, "He recalled how he walked a long and dangerous path to visit the home of his fiancée and did not even consider staying at home—his love compelled him to go. As he shared, smiles came across many faces as the other pastors began to picture their own journeys to visit their fiancées" (2009, 118). The pastor went on to share how God's love for the church led him to embark on the long and steep road from heaven to earth in the person of Jesus, facing rejection and the suffering of the cross. Upon hearing this, one student became enthusiastic and returned to his home to use the proverb in sharing the gospel. This resulted in hundreds of people becoming Christians. He later explained, "I used many proverbs at home, and the people became very excited when I told them the proverbs. The young people were taught in the past to leave the old things behind, but the messages were very foreign. Now, they see me as a wise man and I speak wisdom in a way they can understand" (119).

Jay Moon has argued that the use of proverbs among the Bulisa people of Ghana could be a key to contextualizing Christianity. "Proverbs function as symbols in the Bulisa culture and have been created within the culture. As such they can be used as building blocks to construct a Bulisa Christian worldview, and then communicate this within Bulisa culture" (Moon 2009, 196). Interestingly, Moon found that the attempt to use nonindigenous proverbs, such as those from the biblical book of Proverbs, did not have the same affective impact on the Bulisa as did their indigenous proverbs, *yam umagisma*, which seem to be a distinct subset of the larger genre of proverbs (9). Cross-cultural teachers who become thoroughly acquainted with local proverbs will grasp nuances not evident to a cultural newcomer and can make frequent use of the proverbs in teaching. Bible truth can be connected with folk wisdom. Peter Unseth (2013) advocates the use of proverbs in evangelism, preaching, counseling, discipling, and theological teaching (see sidebar 5.7).

Case-Based Instruction

Case-based instruction is particularly suitable for more concrete learners because it begins with concrete situations, usually of the kind that the learner is likely to encounter in real life, and moves from there to more abstract analysis and understanding. The learning exercise is thus more interesting and engaging, and the practical usefulness of instruction more readily recognized. Learners participate actively in the learning process through their own analysis of the case and discovery of the dynamics at play. As an instructional methodology, case study is perhaps one of the best-known approaches to strengthening learners' problem-solving and analytical skills, and it has been widely used in teaching business, law, medicine, the social sciences, and even theology (Wendland 1998). Entire academic courses have been taught using only case studies. Furthermore, case-based instruction has been used effectively in numerous cultural contexts. A case analysis can be done as a group or individual activity.

In ministry training or instruction, case method is well suited for learning objectives related to leadership, counseling, conflict resolution, evangelism, and strategic planning, to mention just a few. Numerous collections of case studies have been compiled for various learning objectives such as counseling (Swetland 2005; Collins 1991), ethics (Milco 1997), and cross-cultural ministry (Neeley 1995; Hiebert and Hiebert 1987). Ideally the cross-cultural instructor selects cases from the host culture so that conditions are familiar to the learners. Cases from an unfamiliar culture can be problematic because learners may not understand the cultural dynamics at play. However, sometimes a cross-cultural teacher can adapt a foreign case to fit the cultural context of instruction.

Case-based instruction is among various inductive approaches to learning and reasoning that begin with the concrete and move to the abstract. The case method begins with the presentation of a specific historical or hypothetical scenario, often a problem, which leaners then analyze or attempt to solve. Learners are typically asked, "What would you do in this situation?" or "How would you solve this problem?" Learners then propose a course of action. Often the actual outcome of a real-world case is given only after learners have completed their analysis or suggested solutions. Lessons may be drawn from the case and principles discussed that might be applied analogically to other situations. Connections are made to how the particular case illustrates various theories from the literature.

Research has found that such inductive approaches foster a deep approach to learning, intellectual development, problem-solving skills, and improved learning retention (e.g., Prince and Felder 2007; Bennal, Taklikar, and Pattar 2016). Instructors often first present a principle and then use a case to illustrate the principle. But research on case-based instruction suggests that learning may be better promoted by presenting principles after cases have first been discussed (Alfieri, Nokes-Malach, and Schunn 2013, 110), which underlines the value of the inductive approach. Use of various media in the case presentation—as opposed to exclusively text-based sources—also enhances effectiveness (Krain 2010).

A particular feature of case method is that the learner is forced to examine a case in its real-life complexity. Because a wide variety of factors are typically at play in any given case, the learner must thus discern how various factors interact and how interventions will affect the case in terms of those factors. Instructors may need to help learners identify the case's key issues and make connections to more generalizable theories or principles. This can be accomplished by providing a list of questions learners might ask as they analyze the case, or by drawing attention to important details of it that might be overlooked. If the instructor is writing her own cases, adequate detail must be provided to make the case realistic, provide adequate information for analysis, and challenge learners.

Learning by use of case method, however, is not automatic. Learners may fail to identify the concepts appropriately or be tempted to draw simplistic conclusions; they may formulate cookie-cutter solutions to problems ("if this happens, always do that"). Thus, instructors need to carefully facilitate discussion and the learning process. One strategy to overcome some of the method's weaknesses is to have learners study multiple cases, compare their similarities and differences, and consider how principles might be applied in new situations using analogical reasoning. Studies by Gentner, Loewenstein, and Thompson "show that learners cannot be counted on to spontaneously draw appropriate comparisons, even when the two cases are presented in close juxtaposition" (2003, 403). Studying two cases increased learning transfer only to the degree that instructors increased their support of learners in making comparisons. For example, Alfieri, Nokes-Malach, and Schunn found that "asking learners to find similarities between cases, providing principles after the comparisons, using perceptual content, and testing learners immediately are all associated with greater learning" (2013, 87). Thus, the process of case analysis and cross-case comparison is most effective when guided by the instructor.

Other Methods and Media

In chapter 11 we will explore the use of media as one of the five dimensions of how culture influences teaching and learning. Here, we will focus on media in the context of teaching methods suitable for more concrete learners. The use of film, drama, role play, simulations, and other instructional methods that help learners visualize or enact real-life situations will be especially useful. The advantage of their usage is similar to that of case-based learning because they are more immediately related to praxis and employ inductive or analogical reasoning.

Repetition and memorization are among the easiest ways for oral learners to recall and internalize information. However, attention must be given to memorization with meaning—that is, that learners genuinely understand what they are learning. Beat Strässler (2005a) discovered in teaching students in Papua New Guinea that the formulation of questions made a considerable difference in the student's ability to understand and answer correctly. For example, the question "Name three points that James teaches about sickness" is relatively abstract, and it often confused Strässler's students. He reformulated the question in a more narrative and concrete manner: "You are sick and want to do what is biblical. What will you do? What did James teach us about sickness?" With this formulation the intent of the question was better understood and more often answered correctly.

A simple object lesson can sometimes be used similarly to a simulation game to help learners grasp abstract concepts. Lingenfelter and Lingenfelter relate this example of a mathematics instructor teaching addition to indigenous people in Brazil: "The written numbers did not mean anything until she used turtles in two basins and moved them back and forth according to the equations she was trying to teach. Using any object such as blocks or balls would not have sufficed. These men needed to connect the abstract numbers to something concrete in their world" (2003, 38). One teacher in Cameroon taught Daba children arithmetic by counting sacks of sorghum in the local

---

SIDEBAR 5.8

CHIMES for Oral Learners

Jay Moon recommends the adaptation of instruction for oral learners, even in formal theological education, by designing learning experiences around the acronym CHIMES:

- *Communal*—Students learn best through social interaction such as discussion.
- *Holistic*—Projects and topics are relevant to their context.

- *Images*—Use of images, object lessons, symbols, and mind maps helps students visualize concepts.
- *Mnemonics*—Use of proverbs, songs, rituals, dance, storyboards, and so on helps students recall information.
- *Experiential*—Exercises and activities engage learners through participation.
- *Sensory*—Multisensory media are used, such as audiobooks, music, and visual arts. (Moon 2018, 5334–87)

market. She found that children were unable to work with abstract numbers before they had reached the third grade (Giger 1991). Sidebar 5.8 memorably summarizes six ways to adapt instruction for oral learners.

Advantages of Decontextualized, Abstract Teaching

Up to this point the discussion has focused on ways to adapt teaching to concrete cognitive styles. Linking new concepts with familiar concepts or experiences has long been considered fundamental to facilitating understanding and memory for all learners. But does it lead to the ability to transfer what is learned to other contexts outside the classroom and in unfamiliar situations? Day, Motz, and Goldstone surveyed numerous related studies and conducted their own experimental research, which found:

> Despite these compelling benefits, more recent evidence suggests that concrete instructional examples may also come with some significant costs. For example, any extraneous detail in the presentation of information tends to distract learners from the relevant content, leading to poorer recall for that material. . . . More insidiously, even those concrete details that are integral and relevant to the examples may harm learning by impairing transfer to new situations. . . .
>
>   Perversely, then, it is those very same qualities that are so beneficial in the learning of new material—concreteness, familiarity, personal relevance—that appear so detrimental to the generalization of that knowledge. (2015, 2)
>
>   . . . The more contextualized a training case, the more difficulty learners can have in recognizing and applying its principles in new and dissimilar situations. (10)

If learners are to move beyond merely imitating behaviors, memorizing facts, and mastering cookie-cutter solutions, they must learn how to discover and apply principles to unfamiliar situations and problem-solving. Using familiar narrative material leads students to supplement the learning content with additional previously known facts and personal relevance, enhancing conceptual grasp and memorability. But such familiarity reduces learning transfer. Research demonstrates that such learning transfer occurs best when decontextualized teaching methods are also employed. Because acquisition is a prerequisite to generalization and transfer, it may be best to integrate concrete (contextual) and idealized (decontextual) methods (Day, Motz, and Goldstone 2015). Chapter 6 will further address cognitive development of analytic abilities that facilitate learning transfer.

   Although many of these studies were conducted with Western students and did not involve cross-cultural teaching, it is reasonable to assume that non-Western, concrete learners would also benefit from such an approach.

Such findings support the contention described in chapter 2 that there can be advantages to mismatching teaching and learning styles, so long as the mismatch is not too severe and unfamiliar methods are introduced with care. Cross-cultural teachers can help concrete thinkers expand their cognitive skills and reasoning strategies by presenting learning material both in concrete/familiar forms and in more abstract, context-independent forms. This can help students to conceptualize learning content, and also to develop theoretical skills to apply concepts and principles to new situations. The ability to transfer learning is increasingly important, especially for church leaders, in a rapidly globalizing world in which leaders are continually confronted with new ideas and unfamiliar challenges. Leaders must be able to apply biblical principles and truths wisely in situations foreign both to the Bible and to their own cultures.

The Cognitive Dimension

Part 3: Holistic and Analytic Cognitive Styles

Our discussion of cognition so far has focused on factors related to language, literacy, orality, concrete versus abstract orientation, and reasoning processes. We now turn to factors related to how a person perceives and organizes information: holistic and analytic cognitive styles, and the related construct of field articulation. Although research findings are not always consistent and are variously interpreted, "the main message of this research is that styles represent relatively stable individual differences in preferred ways of organizing and processing information that cut across the personality and cognitive characteristics of an individual" (Kozhevnikov, 2007). Cognitive style is among the most extensively researched constructs and has been used in numerous cross-cultural studies. Recall that cognitive style is understood in this volume as a description of how people perceive and process information; characteristics that are not innate but malleable and developmental. For example, An and Carr cite studies showing that "in the case of the concrete/abstract dichotomy, the dichotomy is not a set of attributes but reflects the level of development of expertise and an individual's educational experiences" (2017, 411).

CHAPTER OVERVIEW

- Holistic and Analytic Cognitive Styles
- Field Dependence and Field Independence
- Culture and Field Articulation
- Cognitive Development and Culture
- Implications for Instruction
- Implications for Theological Education

Holistic and Analytic Cognitive Styles

Some researchers believe that virtually all cognitive styles can be subsumed under the bipolar dimensions of analytic versus holistic orientations (e.g., Miller

1987; Riding and Cheema 1991). Sometimes the term *serial* is used to describe analytic, and *global* to describe holistic, but the underlying concepts are the same. The central difference between analytic and holistic cognitive styles is the way in which learners perceive and organize information: holists perceive and process information more as an integrated whole and "organise information into loosely clustered wholes, while analytics are inclined to organise information into clear-cut conceptual groupings" (Riding and Rayner 1998, 141).

SIDEBAR 6.1

Holistic Learners and Language Learning

Christina Hvitfeldt (1986) drew these conclusions from her study of Hmong adults in English literacy classes.

> In language drills involving the manipulation of grammatical endings and verb tenses, the students are able to focus on the significant word or ending only if the teacher continually draws their attention to the item being emphasized. When their attention is not so directed the students tend to focus on the meaning of the whole rather than the form of the subpart. When the teacher asks for the past tense of *She's walking*, for example, the entire class answers *she went*.
>
> This difficulty with the categorization of vocabulary and language structure seems to be the result of the Hmong students' generally holistic approach to classroom work. Attending to the whole rather than the part, the students tend to focus on meaning rather than category or form and respond to content rather than to the relationship between the parts or of the part to the whole. (72)

A similar experience described below by Michaela Bekaan (2009) illustrates the difficulty that an oral learner with a global cognitive style can have with typical grammar exercises in a foreign language class.

> A sixty-year-old woman from Somalia who had already lived twelve years in Germany enrolled voluntarily in an entry level German as Foreign Language class. She had no formal schooling and came from a very poor, rural region. She had taken several literacy courses, but demonstrated little progress and made serious mistakes with even the simplest exercises.
>
> It's noteworthy that this student had good oral skills and command over a relatively large vocabulary. However, she struggled with written assignments that required primarily abstract understanding and that lacked exact instructions. For example, she could not master simple written fill-in-the-blank exercises for inserting the correct verb form into a given sentence. However, when the teacher worked with her on the assignment orally, she made no errors. Written assignments that were especially challenging for her included filling out tables, all kinds of fill-in-the-blank texts, multiple choice questions, and classification assignments. Interestingly, producing freely written texts presented no problem.

Examples of Holistic and Analytic Cognition

This difference between holist and analytic cognitive styles is manifested in a variety of ways. For example, holistic learners pay greater attention to social cues and the broader environment in which events take place. Objects are perceived as more bound or embedded in their environment. Persons with a more holistic cognitive style have better recall of details and background elements of photographs than persons with a more analytic style. Analytic persons, on the other hand, tend to focus on the salient or focal features of a photograph, attending less to larger contextual details (Nisbett 2003, 86–102; Masuda and Nisbett 2006).

Another difference between holistic and analytic cognitive styles is the ability to separate the parts from the whole. For example, foreign language instruction often gives attention to rules of grammar and uses written fill-in-the-blank exercises to reinforce or assess learning. As illustrated in sidebar 6.1, more holistic learners often have difficulty with such exercises because they require the learner to break down a sentence into its component parts and understand how the part functions on the basis of abstract rules. Yet the same students may excel in formulating grammatically correct, full sentences as complete thought units. Holistic learners may also have difficulty isolating relevant details of a story or phenomenon from irrelevant details, as the example in sidebar 6.2 shows. For holistic learners, an event, phenomenon, story, or visual image is experienced as a whole, whereby the various elements or impressions flow together.

Although analytic learners tend to outperform more holist learners in schooling, there are disadvantages to an overly analytic orientation. "For example, at a manufacturing firm, engineers are being taught how to be creative. They were initially so analytical in their thinking that when asked to brainstorm creative new products for the firm, they could only concentrate on the details of why their ideas would not be feasible. They had to be shown how to see the forest instead of the trees" (Flannery 1993, 18). As we will see in chapter 7, persons with highly analytic cognitive styles may be reductionistic in their analysis of an issue or problem, focusing on only a single or a few causal factors while overlooking multiple factors that may contribute to the phenomenon.

Culture's Influence on Cognitive Style

Extensive research conducted by Richard Nisbett and his associates comparing East Asian and American students reveals that East Asians tend to be more holistic and Americans more analytic. In short, "Asians view the world more through a wide-angle lens, whereas Westerners have tunnel vision"

SIDEBAR 6.2

Discerning the Relevant from the Irrelevant

I once had a graduate student from rural Kenya who was given a course assignment to write a case study of a specific church plant. The methodology for the assignment was described in detail and included visiting a newly established church, interviewing the church planter and congregants, making field notes, and so on. These findings were to be compared with principles discussed in the course lectures and readings. Given the practical nature of the assignment, I assumed that it would present no major difficulties for a concrete, holistic learner. However, the student turned in a paper that was a running narrative beginning with how he and his family (each member was introduced) were on the way home from their home church (describing the sermon of that day), and how their car was low on fuel and that, while searching for an inexpensive gas station (according to his wife's directions), they found the church plant that would be studied. In narrative style he proceeded to describe every detail observed upon visiting the church, down to the clothing and teeth of the pastor. Social commentary on race relations and morality in the US, and explanation of differences between African and American culture, were interspersed in the storyline. The narrative continued in the same style page after page. No analysis followed, and connections to concepts presented in the course were absent. The student clearly had difficulty discerning relevant information from extraneous details for the purpose of the assignment.

It would be a mistake to assume that the difficulty in analytically separating irrelevant from relevant information is a cognitive style describing only non-Westerners. A Swiss student once submitted a case study on teaching across cultures that included details of a flight en route to the village where the case occurred, including the number of times one airsick person vomited!

(Nisbett 2003, 89). Although the research by Nisbett and others is impressive, we must be cautious about making such sweeping statements. Asia is far too diverse a region to speak of an "Asian learner" (see Marambe, Vermunt, and Boshuizen 2012).

San Martin, Schug, and Maddux examined the relationship between cognitive style and relational mobility in the US, Spain, Israel, Nigeria, Morocco, and Japan, whereby relational mobility is "the opportunity of individuals to form new relationships and terminate existing ones" (2019, 495). They found that in cultures where there is greater relational mobility, persons tend to be more analytically oriented, and in cultures with lower relational mobility, they tend be holistic. Exposure to greater diversity of contexts, ideas, and relationships promotes more analytical cognition.

One study suggests that thinking style is a predictor of university students' classroom behavior. Chinese students, who were found to be more holistic, tended to ask fewer questions and be less active in class discussion. American students, who were more analytic, tended to be more active in this regard. The explanation the researchers suggest is that holistic students want to obtain the big picture and make connections before expressing themselves in class, whereas analytic thinkers respond more quickly to units of information (Cheng, Andrade, and Yan 2011).

While culture clearly influences a person's cognitive style, there is evidence that one's style can be expanded; more specifically, a holistic learner can become more analytic. Marambe, Vermunt, and Boshuizen compared learning strategies of Sri Lankan, Indonesian, and Dutch university students and found differences regarding various learning strategies. But contrary to expectation, they also found no difference between the groups' use of analyzing strategies (2012, 311). They believe that this points to the ability of learning environments to have a greater influence than culture on development of student learning strategies (314). Stated differently, though culture may influence the holistic/analytic cognitive style of a learner, culture is not determinative in an absolute sense. Cognitive style can develop in different directions.

Field Dependence and Field Independence

We turn now to one of the most widely researched approaches to cognitive style: field articulation, which describes a person's way of perceiving and processing information. It is one of the most significant and widely researched notions in cognitive psychology (Evans, Richardson, and Waring 2013; Zhang and Sternberg 2012, 137). Field-dependent (FD) persons tend to perceive a field as a whole and have difficulty isolating individual items from the larger context of that field.[1] A field-independent (FI) person has greater ability to isolate individual items from the larger perceptive context. FDI will be used as shorthand for the construct as a whole. Strictly speaking, FDI is a measure of perception; however, studies have made significant correlations between FDI and cognitive style and other personality characteristics. FD persons evidence similar cognitive processes as holistic learners, and FI persons are similar to analytic learners.

Background

FDI research was pioneered and developed by Herman Witkin in the 1950s. Others, such as John Berry, used it widely in cross-cultural research. At first

---

1. Here *field* refers to the entire perceptive experience as a whole. For example, a whole situation or experience; an entire photograph or diagram; or a social interaction, such as a conversation.

FIGURE 6.1

Rod-and-frame test

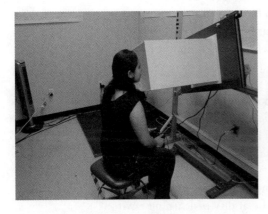

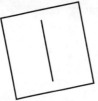

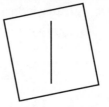

Field Dependent   Field Independent

Source: Vincent Koppelmans, Burak Erdeniz, Yiri E. De Dios, Scott J. Wood, Patricia A. Reuter-Lorenz, Igor Kofman, Jacob J. Bloomberg, Ajitkumar P. Mulavara, and Rachel D. Seidler, "Study Protocol to Examine the Effects of Spaceflight and a Spaceflight Analog on Neurocognitive Performance: Extent, Longevity, and Neural Bases," *BMC Neurology* 13, no. 205 (2013), https://doi.org/10.1186/1471-2377-13-205.

Witkin researched the extent to which a person in a darkened room could adjust an illuminated rod to the vertical position when an illuminated frame surrounding the rod was not positioned vertically. This was called the rod-and-frame test (see fig. 6.1 for a modern example of this test).

A body-adjustment test was then developed that tested the ability of a person seated in an adjustable rotating chair to adjust the position of their body to a vertical position independently of the room, which could be rotated. Persons with greater ability to adjust the rod or their body to the correct vertical position, independently of the surrounding field, are considered more FI; those less able to do so are more FD. Embedded figures tests were developed that tested the subject's ability to visually identify a geometric figure that is embedded in a larger, more complex geometric pattern (see figs. 6.2 and 6.3).

Persons who need less time to locate the embedded figure are considered more FI. This test was adapted using natural figures embedded in natural

FIGURE 6.2

Group embedded figure test

Here is a simple form, which we have labeled "X":

This simple form, named "X," is hidden
within the more complex figure below:

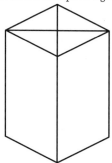

FIGURE 6.3

Leuven embedded figure test

Find the simple figure above in one of the complex figures below:

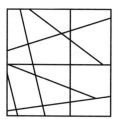 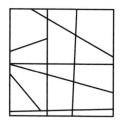 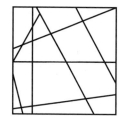

Source: Lee de-Wit, Hanne Huygelier, Ruth Van der Hallen, Rebecca Chamberlain, and Johan Wagemans, "Developing the Leuven Embedded Figures Test (L-EFT): Testing the Stimulus Features That Influence Embedding," *PeerJ* 5 (January 2017). https://peerj.com/articles/2862.

settings to be used with persons unfamiliar with geometric shapes. Other tests were developed for various ages and contexts that measured the same ability.

Extensive research began to make correlations between FDI measures and other personal traits. For example, FD persons were found to be more socially oriented, more sensitive to interpersonal interaction, and have greater perception of nonverbal social cues in the environment. FD persons are often better liked and perceived as warmer and more tactful and caring than FI persons. They are more drawn to people and seek out more socially oriented occupations, such as teaching. FI persons tend to be more analytical and are more likely to restructure information or organize it in small categories than FD persons. FI persons gravitate toward more impersonal and analytical occupations related to mathematics and science, such as engineering. FD therapists trended to be less directive than FI therapists. Studies have identified a correlation between FD and collectivism, and FI and individualism (e.g., Kühnen et al. 2001; Nisbett et al. 2001; Konrath, Bushman, and Grove 2009; Kitayama et al. 2009; Peng, Hu, and Guo 2018), although this correlation has been challenged (e.g., Bagley and Mallick 1998; Marquez and Ellwanger 2014). Here again, one must be cautious about stereotyping or pigeonholing.

By 1988 nearly 400 education-related dissertations and over 550 academic articles had researched FDI (J. K. Davis 1991, 149). Between 1988 and 2020 an additional 268 academic articles were published.[2] Although research on FDI has since peaked and further nuance is needed in understanding the concept (Evans, Richardson, and Waring 2013), it remains a useful construct for understanding cognitive processing differences among learners and between cultures.

Field Articulation and Learning

FDI does not describe a learning style as such, but because it describes how a person perceives and organizes information, the construct has many implications for how people learn. Summarized below and in table 6.1 are some of the most important and consistent findings of the extensive research on the educational implications of FDI as reported in several literature reviews (e.g., Witkin et al. 1977; J. K. Davis 1991; Pithers 2002; Tinajero et al. 2011). FD persons were found to be more attuned to learning social material. They are more positively or negatively influenced by feedback and reinforcement such as praise or criticism. FI learners tend to give structure to information that is disorganized (e.g., a lecture) or randomly presented (e.g., lists). This

2. Results of searching "field dependence-independence" on EBSCO Academic Search Complete.

ability gives FI learners better long-term recall with higher-order learning skills, such as analysis and application of factual material (e.g., Kiewra and Frank 1988).

FD learners, on the other hand, are less able to give structure to information and thus have greater difficulty learning such material, especially when larger amounts of information are involved. FI learners tend to be better in both reading skill and comprehension than FD learners, although differences are minor. When learning from material presented in texts was compared with learning through video presentation, FD learners benefited more from video material, whereas FI learners learned equally well from both. In programmed learning, FD and FI learners retained information equally well with small-step sequences of material, but FI had better retention of large-step sequences. In concept attainment experiments, FI learners tended to prefer hypothesis testing while FD learners preferred a spectator approach—yet with the same number of trials, both were equally able to discover the concept. Examining studies related to overall academic achievement, J. Kent Davis concludes, "research shows that field-independent students perform significantly better than field-dependent students, not only in math, science, and technology . . . but also in virtually every curriculum area that has been studied" (1991, 158). FI students are generally better at problem-solving, in part because they are better able to discern relevant from irrelevant information and can better organize the data (Tinajero et al. 2011, 504). For most school-related learning tasks, FD learners need greater assistance to attain achievement equal to that of FI learners. FI students also perform better in distance learning courses. Some of these findings may be explained by the fact that much of school instruction and testing uses methods less suitable for concrete and holistic learners.

Only in skill learning do FD learners have an advantage. The more social orientation of FD learners leads them to attend more to social aspects of a field or learning material, sometimes at the expense of others (Nisbett et al. 2001). One of the more controversial early findings of FDI research was that apart from a few locations in rural Africa, women were consistently found to be slightly more FD than men (e.g., Berry 1991). However, subsequent studies have found no significant difference based upon gender alone (Pithers 2002, 120; Drążkowski et al. 2017).

Not surprisingly, when characteristics of teachers were studied, FD teachers were found to be more socially oriented, to use more two-way communication, and be more student centered in their instruction than FI teachers. FD teachers are somewhat more dependent upon authority than FI teachers. FI teachers were more direct in giving feedback to students, more directive, and more often used one-way communication in their instruction. They are also

TABLE 6.1

Influence of Field Dependence and Field Independence on Learning

Field-Dependent Learners	Field-Independent Learners
More attentive to social indicators in learning material and environment	Less attentive to social indicators in learning material and environment
More influenced by positive or negative reinforcement and feedback	Less influenced by positive or negative reinforcement and feedback
Information perceived as a whole; greater need for external structuring	Information given structure by the learner; less need for external structuring
Need for smaller learning steps	Able to learn well with larger learning steps
Better concept attainment by observation	Better concept attainment by hypothesis testing
Prefer more people-oriented subjects and occupations	Prefer more analytical subjects and occupations
Perform best with example instruction	Perform best with deductive instruction
Tend to be more collectivistic	Tend to be more individualistic

more interested in the abstract than FD teachers and are perceived as more distant and aloof. However, teachers' FDI orientation did not seem to impact student achievement.

Field Articulation: Style or Ability?

Because FI students consistently outperform FD students in nearly every school subject, researchers have investigated whether FDI tests measure a value-free style or an ability, and whether FI is associated with higher intelligence. Sternberg and Grigorenko assert that "the preponderance of evidence at this point suggests that field independence is tantamount to fluid intelligence" (2001, 7; see also Zhang, Sternberg, and Rayner 2012, 6–9; Richardson and Turner 2000). Furthermore, although research confirms that FD persons are more socially oriented, there is no compelling evidence that they have greater interpersonal *skills* (Messick 1994, 127). Witkin and Goodenough (1981) argued that children become more FI until their mid-teens, and beyond that time there is no further development. This seems to indicate that FI is a developmental characteristic, at least to a point. However, subsequent research has demonstrated that adult learners can become more FI and analytic as they progress in a course of study, and that it is even possible to train people to develop more analytical and FI skills (Pithers 2002, 121–22). This all seems to indicate that FDI is not a bipolar construct but a developmental and directional ability, moving from FD to FI. FDI is thus not as fixed and persistent as initially assumed, but is at least somewhat malleable and influenced by environmental factors (Zhang, Sternberg, and Rayner 2012, 5–6). This in turn means that instructional interventions have the potential for helping FD learners to become more FI, which could improve their academic performance. A study of Hong Kong nursing students found that participation in online learning can increase FI (Ching 1998). Evans, Richardson, and Waring reviewed the research and rightly conclude that "whether FI is just a cognitive ability or a cognitive style is not the central issue, as both can be developed" (2013, 210). Because in the West academic ability is highly valued, and FI is associated with higher academic ability than FD, the FDI construct is considered by some not to be value-free (Messick 1994; 1996). Of course, such valuing reflects a cultural bias in favor of school performance as a measure of intelligence and overlooks other forms of intelligence. (For alternative ways of understanding intelligence, see Sternberg 2007.)

Culture and Field Articulation

We know from numerous cross-cultural studies that average measures of FDI can greatly differ between ethnic groups. For example, one study that tested for FDI among students in Nigeria and Kenya found that, compared to average scores for Americans, 84 percent of Kenyans tested and 100 percent of Nigerians tested were more on the FD side of the spectrum (Bowen and Bowen 1991). Another similar study in Kenya found that 80 percent of college students and 90 percent of theological students were more FD (Buconyori 1991). African American students were found to be more FI than black South Africans (Engelbrecht and Natzel 1997), and East Asians more FD than Americans (Ji, Peng, and Nisbett 2000). Another study found American and German university students (who are more individualist) to be more FI than Russian and Malaysian students (who are more collectivist); the Malaysians were found to be the most FD (Kühnen et al. 2001). Americans have been found to be more focused than Western Europeans (Germany and UK), and Western Europeans more focused than Japanese (Kitayama et al. 2009). However, other research has been unable to consistently confirm a connection between FDI and cultural features such as emphasis on conformity or collectivism. This may be due in part to changing norms of American children (to whom others are compared) and increased exposure to new cultural and educational experiences elsewhere (Bagley and Mallick 1998).

The above examples demonstrate that, as previously noted, all such national profiles must be given nuance. For example, a study of FDI among
Chinese college students found regional differences (Peng, Hu, and Guo 2018).
This makes international comparisons problematic. Any given individual may
not correspond to the national average. The age or educational level of the
subjects may not be representative of the nation as a whole. Also, to simply
describe a group as "80 percent FD" does not tell us where on the spectrum
between FD and FI this 80 percent is, nor is the standard deviation (variation
within the group) always stated. Some countries—Kenya, for instance—are
very diverse, composed of many different ethnic groups in different environmental settings and with differing access to educational resources, all of which
impact cognitive style and development.

Furthermore, international comparative studies face the numerous difficulties of psychometric testing across cultures, including tests related to perception. For example, one study compared the memory ability of Moroccans
and North Americans and found no structural difference in memory. But this
was determined only by using culturally appropriate tests, such as the Moroccans' ability to remember rug patterns which were familiar in their daily lives
(D. Wagner 1978). People develop the perceptive and cognitive skills necessary
to function in their environment or that are valued in their social context.
These concerns notwithstanding, it can generally be said that Majority World
learners tend to be more holistic/FD, and North American and European
learners comparatively more analytic/FI. As long as we do not stereotype,
or attribute such differences to inherent intelligence, these generalizations
needn't be considered condescending.

Cognitive Development and Culture

Culture's influence on cognitive development has been a subject of great interest and the research is voluminous. Michael Cole and his colleagues conducted
extensive research related to cognitive development and culture and concluded
that a "context specific approach" is the best way to understand differences. In
short, it proposes that specific abilities are related to specific contexts. Activities
and abilities that a culture values or that are important to everyday life shape
the direction of cognitive development (LCHC 1983). Swiss developmental
psychologist Jean Piaget's theory of cognitive development in children has
been one of the most widely used constructs in research on the influence of
culture on cognitive development. Numerous literature reviews (e.g., Mishra
2014) document that cognitive development is influenced by factors such as
socioeconomic status, parents' education and occupation, urban/rural environments, and schooling, with schooling perhaps the most significant.

Environmental Factors

Early research on cultural factors influencing FDI was conducted by John W. Berry, who focused numerous studies upon environmental factors. He and others found, for example, that hunters and gatherers were more FI than agriculturalists, nomads more FI than sedentary peoples, dense populations more FI than low-density populations, and groups with assertive socialization more FI than groups with high compliance socialization (Berry 1991; Mishra 2001, 123–25). Even the type of agricultural work can make a difference in cognitive style and development. For example, large-scale differences were found in China between rice farmers in the south, who are more interdependent and holistic-thinking, and wheat-growing farmers in the north (Talhelm et al. 2014). Similarly, southern Chinese were found to be more FD than northern Chinese (Peng, Hu, and Guo 2018). Upper-middle socioeconomic status is associated with greater FI than lower socioeconomic status (Forns-Santacana, Amador-Campas, and Roig-López 1993). The influence of modernization and economic development upon FDI is inconclusive, although numerous studies, such as that of Gruenfeld and MacEachron (1975) comparing FDI in twenty-two countries, point to a strong connection.

As with all such conceptualizations we are cautioned against oversimplification. As Ramesh Mishra's concludes his review of the literature, "the diversity of the findings does not allow us to draw an easy conclusion about the relationship between culture and cognition. As a matter of fact, recent research has added elements of complexity to this relationship" (2001, 131).

Schooling and Cognitive Development

As noted above, schooling is one of the most significant factors in promoting cognitive development. Numerous early studies consistently demonstrated that whether comparing children from different cultures or from within the same culture, schooling affects the cognitive development of children across cultures in similar ways (Bruner, Oliver, and Greenfield 1966). For example, in the 1960s Patricia M. Greenfield examined the cognitive development of Senegalese Wolof children, testing their progress in Piaget's stages of cognitive development (Greenfield 1966). She describes her intention:

> Contrary to Piaget's notion of universal cognitive development that was independent of learning processes, the goal of my research was to show that learning opportunities, which should vary in different ecocultural environments, would affect developmental processes. In other words, cognitive development was not just a joint function of universal maturational processes and universal opportunities to interact with the physical environment, as Piaget had posited; it was also a function of culture-specific learning opportunities. (Greenfield 2005, 73)

She found that the age at which children achieved Piaget's conservation and categorization stages depended upon schooling (Greenfield 1966).[3] In Western cultures, conservation is achieved at around age seven, but in other cultures it may be delayed by several years. She tested children with three different backgrounds: rural unschooled, rural schooled, and urban schooled. She found that a rural or urban setting made no difference in the children's development, but on certain tasks children with schooling (whether from the bush or from the city) outperformed children without schooling. She also found that schooling promoted more abstract thinking. Gay and Cole (1967) made similar discoveries regarding the influences of formal schooling in their research among the Kpelle of Liberia. They found that the culturally foreign methods of Western schooling had positive effects on children's performance on mathematical tasks, though it did not improve performance on familiar tasks such as estimating the volume of rice.

Such studies have been critiqued for neglecting indigenous forms of learning or for using culturally inappropriate testing methods. Various other studies have questioned the influence of schooling on the age that Piaget's stages are attained (e.g., Das and Dash 1989). Mishra concludes from his review of the research:

> It is quite likely that the time lag often found in cognitive development of Indian children in comparison to Piaget's norms may be due to the complex interplay of socio-cultural factors with cognitive operations rather than low cognitive potential. . . .
>
> These findings suggest to us the possibility that lack of certain cognitive operations in children in some cultures may not be due to the low cognitive competence (potential), but it may be simply a result of inadequate experiences or absence of experiences, which are necessary for the actualization of the latent cognitive structures. (2014, 216–17)

Nevertheless, we should not underestimate the value of schooling to develop cognitive skills that are necessary for more abstract functions, higher levels of analysis, and critical thinking abilities. For example, "schooling teaches a broad range of skills that create, facilitate, and strengthen associations between information from different contexts. In contrast to learning in school, everyday learning is geared toward participation in a unique setting"

---

3. Conservation is the ability to make judgments about mass, length, volume, etc. For example, picture two rows of coins, with five coins in each row. But in one row they are placed closer together than they are in the other, so that the row appears shorter. The child who has not attained conservation will say that the longer row has more coins because it appears longer (although it actually has the same number of coins). The child who has attained conservation will see that although the length of the rows are different, both have the same number of coins. For a video demonstration of this, see https://youtu.be/YtLEWVu815o.

(Brouwers, van de Vijver, and Mishra 2017, 310). In other words, schooling promotes the ability to transfer learning from one context to another.

Everyday Cognition

The concept of *everyday cognition* has been introduced as a way of describing cognitive skills that develop in everyday activities apart from schooling. Studies of cognitive development often focus on abstract skills that formal schooling promotes, whereby the testing is conducted in culturally unfamiliar laboratory settings. But this can lead cross-cultural researchers to overlook other important cognitive abilities. "Studies of cognition reveal that people may perform well on reasoning tasks in natural settings despite the fact that they fail to solve what appear to be similar tasks in laboratory or testing settings" (Schliemann and Carraher 2001, 137). Culturally relevant cognitive abilities that are developed in everyday life may be overlooked because they are not reflected in typical tests of cognitive development. As we saw above, even using culturally familiar test objects, such as Moroccan rug patterns, can make a difference in test results (D. Wagner 1978). Schliemann and Carraher's review of the extensive literature on the subject concludes, "Researchers have been aware for the last few decades that, to understand cognition and learning better, we need studies of cognition in everyday settings" (2001, 140).

Everyday cognitive abilities are developed in activities such as farming, weaving, shopping, carpentry, cooking, and commerce. Everyday mathematics is used to estimate or calculate quantities, volumes, and measurements. For example,

> Street vendors seem to develop the basic logical abilities needed for solving arithmetic problems in their work settings; their difficulties with school arithmetic seem to be related to the mastery of particular symbolic systems adopted by schools. Given the emphasis on fixed steps to manipulate numbers in the solution of any problem, school algorithms set meaning aside. In contrast, arithmetic oral strategies developed at work preserve meaning throughout the solution of problems, thus avoiding nonsense errors. (Schliemann and Carraher 2001, 142)

Here we see how a more concrete cognitive style plays out in everyday life. To cite another early example, Greenfield and Childs (1977) looked at Mayan boys' and girls' analytical representation of indigenous weaving patterns. The boys, who had received schooling, were more abstract; the girls, who had not received schooling, were more concrete—but both were analytical. Thus, indigenous learning also develops analytical skills, though they may be different from those developed through Western schooling. The reasons why schooling promotes cognitive development in certain ways are complex. But the simple point here is that culturally foreign learning opportunities such as Western schooling may stimulate more abstract forms of cognitive development, but other forms of cognitive development relevant to daily life should not be overlooked.

Everyday learning is limited in that it is normally specialized to a specific context or task, and difficult to transfer to other contexts. School learning, by providing exposure to different contexts, develops the ability to transfer learning to new contexts, to generalize, and to discriminate. As Fleer and Ridgway put it in their summary of Lev Vygotsky's theory of everyday concepts and what he calls scientific concepts, "Developing everyday concepts in the context of children's everyday world is important for living. However, everyday concepts cannot be easily transferred to other contexts. Knowing only about everyday conceptions may locate children's thinking into embedded contexts and reduce their opportunities to apply these concepts to new situations" (2007, 25). Brouwers, van de Vijver, and Mishra argue from a review of the literature and their own research of Kharwar children in India, "Learning based on everyday life is typically not geared to generalizability of solution strategies. Schooling, however, is typically more focused on the generalizability of learned skills; much instruction explicitly focuses on the transfer of learned skills to new contexts" (2017, 317). However, they conclude that "cognitive development is typically the net result of the increase of everyday skills grounded in daily participation and the increase of skills that are associated with school practice and instruction" (317–18). In other words, both everyday learning *and* school learning contribute to cognitive development, but they do so in different ways.

The socialization of children is significant in cognitive development. In many cultures adults rarely converse with children or read books to them. Such social interaction teaches children verbal skills, and asking them questions teaches them to form their own opinions and express them. Asking them what they see in a book ("What's the doggie doing?") or when taking a walk ("Do you see the bird in the tree?") also develops observation skills. Children who build puzzles or play with geometric figures, such as placing a round peg in a round hole, develop spatial, reasoning, and problem-solving skills. All of these activities stimulate cognitive development and prepare children for school learning. Children from homes or in cultures where they do not experience these kinds of stimulation are less prepared for schooling. Such children may have learned more through observation and imitation: for example, how to hunt, fish, cook, or weave. But such activities develop cognitive abilities that are less analytical. Studies of early childhood cognitive development have found that "a stimulating atmosphere, sufficient nutrient and social interaction with caregivers are necessary for optimum development of the brain in young children" (Khatib et al. 2020, 1). Parental communication with children is especially important because "responsive parenting can avert early inequalities and encourage cognitive and socio-emotional development in young children" (1). Programs that promote such stimulation in early childhood have been found to have long-term positive outcomes. Early childhood education programs, such as preschool, have been also found to promote cognitive development (e.g., Rao et al. 2019). Though most readers of this volume will not be involved in early childhood education, awareness of these factors can help explain the trajectory of cognitive development into adulthood.

Implications for Instruction

The discussion thus far has established that there are clear differences in the cognitive styles of learners, and that culture greatly influences cognitive development and the dominant cognitive style of a people, but that these styles are malleable. We now turn to the practical implications for cross-cultural teachers, who in many cases have a different cognitive style from that of their learners. In chapter 5 we examined implications regarding concrete and abstract cognition. Here we focus mainly on FDI and holistic/analytic cognitive styles.

Matching and Mismatching Cognitive Styles

To what extent should teachers adapt their teaching to the cognitive style of learners? Will learners simply struggle if there is a mismatch, or are their possible advantages to a mismatch? In chapter 3 we saw that in some cases there are advantages to a mismatch of learning and teaching styles. Does this apply to cognitive style?

Witkin's early research on FDI seemed to indicate that matching teacher and student cognitive styles could improve learning (Witkin et al. 1977, 32–38), but subsequent research has been less conclusive. FI learners seem to be less negatively impacted by teacher mismatch than FD learners, and FI outperform FD learners regardless of matching or mismatching (J. K. Davis 1991, 159). Davis sums up the ambiguity: "Research suggests that matching on the basis of cognitive style can influence achievement. Sometimes it is beneficial, sometimes it is detrimental, and sometimes it is inconsequential" (161). A later review of research, however, concluded that "the only matching type studies to examine learned performance in educational settings have found the process led to improved performance for only the field-independent learners. Nevertheless, mismatching led to improved performance for more field dependent individuals" (Pithers 2002, 128). In other words, matching can help FI learners, though not FD learners; but mismatch can help FD learners. FD learners benefit from the fact that FI teachers provide more structure in their teaching than FD teachers. FI learners are less impacted by match or mismatch because they are better able to provide their own structure for information, whereas "field dependent teachers fail to provide the sort of explicit organisation of material and well defined structure that is needed by field dependent learners" (128).

If the goal is to improve school performance and cognitive abilities that require analytical skills, then teachers will want to help learners expand their cognitive style. Mismatch of teacher and learner cognitive styles is one way to accomplish this. Though there is some limited evidence that FDI matching produces some short-term gains, such as learner satisfaction, R. T. Pithers cites studies that demonstrate that "in the longer term, there are considerable benefits for the learner in developing a flexible approach to information processing or cognitive style. That is, when the situation demands it, the individual is able to adopt or adapt more FD or alternatively, more FID attitudes, characteristics and teacher leadership behaviour" (2002, 125). He further points out that matching can have disadvantages because

> the individual learners are not exposed to a range of styles during training. They, therefore, do not develop a degree of cognitive style flexibility; rather, they are more likely through further practice and feedback, to have their own predominant approach strengthened and this may not be the one later needed to solve the range of problems they face in the work place. In short, the homogeneous cognitive style approach to teaching and learning simply tends to strengthen stereotypic thinking and problem solving. . . . The learners may then become defensive to anyone else, including another teacher, who challenges their attitudes, beliefs and strategies. (126)

Thus, *over the long term* there are advantages to helping students develop new cognitive strategies and skills, which can in part be developed through teacher-student mismatch. However, mismatch alone is not likely to achieve the desired development. Rather, initially the teacher will need to meet the students where they are and then over time introduce them to new learning strategies and skills, helping them to understand the process. This is not to undervalue the more social orientation of holistic/FD learners or overlook individuals' other cognitive abilities, but rather to expand their cognitive abilities and learning strategies, improve their ability to transfer learned material to new situations, and develop additional problem-solving skills.

Teaching Field-Dependent Learners

Holistic learners may need assistance structuring learning material.

- Provide structure through learning materials such as outlines, handouts, course overviews, or mind maps.
- In the course of a lesson, state frequently where the material fits into the larger outline, and point out progress through the outline.
- Explicitly draw learners' attention to logical connections between points.
- Clearly identify main points and the most important content.
- Demonstrate how parts relate to the whole or how details fit into the larger picture.
- Eliminate unnecessary detail.
- Consider structuring the course according to the structure of the primary textbook.
- Use tables that logically organize content.
- Provide images and diagrams that visually illustrate how concepts relate to each other.
- Give instruction in how to take lecture notes.

Holistic learners may have difficulty with self-guided assignments.

- Give assignments with small and explicit steps.
- Break down larger assignments, such as seminar papers or research projects, into various components.
- Explain not only the expectations of the assignment but also methods to be used or the process of completing it.
- Provide samples of exemplary student work.
- Give explicit reading assignments.
- State clear, firm deadlines for completion of work.

Holistic learners are more influenced by the social climate of the learning environment and tend to be more collectivistic. (See also chap. 10 on teaching collectivistic learners.)

- Make efforts to promote harmonious relationships among students and a friendly class atmosphere.
- Demonstrate personal interest in students' well-being.
- Consider appropriate group social activities outside the classroom such as meals, field trips, or recreation.
- Consider assigning group projects or assignments.
- Avoid situations or feedback that might shame a student.

Holistic learners are more positively or negatively influenced by feedback.

- Give frequent feedback and positive reinforcement.
- Give correction or critique with great care and tact.
- Attend to students who seem discouraged or lack motivation.

Probably the single most important way to improve learning for FD learners is to provide structure or advanced organizers to the learning content, such as outlines, overviews, and diagrams. Numerous studies have demonstrated that providing adjunct questions, embedded headings, diagrams, and illustrations improves the recall of FD learners (Tinajero et al. 2011, 499; see also sidebar 6.4). However, too much detail can prove confusing for FD learners, who have difficulty in identifying relevant information, which would undercut the benefit of adding structure (Angeli and Valanides 2004).

SIDEBAR 6.4

Providing Structure for Holistic Learners

Jude Carroll (2015, 122) recommends these ways of giving more structure to lectures.

Sign posting—e.g., "I will now illustrate that point about x by ... "
"I made the point that x, but here is some of the evidence that supports it."
Naming the parts—e.g., "This is an introduction ... "
"So, in a summary of the last section ... "
Providing a one-page summary—One lecturer used an overhead projector to show an outline of the lecture alongside the main PowerPoint slides screen. At various points, he showed students where he was on his one-page outline.
Signaling importance explicitly—e.g., "The evidence which was used—that is what is important. The evidence. It was important because ... "
Implying importance—e.g., by stressing a word ("It's the evidence from the controlled study that ... ") or raising an index finger at its mention. Both of these signals are culture and language specific, and thus they may not be universally understood. Lectures can also be careful not to have too many key points.

However, the reality is that more analytic/FI teachers who are on *short-term* assignments are probably better off adapting their teaching style to the needs of more holistic/FD learners by adopting some of the instructional strategies described below. Sudden, stark mismatch during a teaching assignment of just a few weeks or months is likely to produce more frustration than positive cognitive development, and ultimately may be detrimental to student learning.

Teaching Learners with a More Holistic Cognitive Style

Especially on short-term teaching assignments, teachers need to meet holistic/FD learners where they are. Sidebar 6.3 summarizes ways more analytic/FI teachers can adapt their teaching for the needs of holistic/FD learners (see also Bowen and Bowen 1991; Flannery 1993).

Perhaps more important than providing structure is to teach FD learners, over time, how they themselves can structure and organize information. Studies have shown that such approaches help FD learners perform certain tasks at a similar level as FI learners (Tinajero et al. 2011, 500). FD learners who are given written assignments or research projects will be more successful at completing the task if the teacher breaks larger tasks into smaller steps, provides clear instructions and expectations, and suggests ways to structure the report. Positive feedback is helpful, too; it not only increases FD learners' motivation but also improves their academic performance and reduces the gap between them and FI learners (502).

Implications for Theological Education

How might these understandings of cognitive style influence the way we understand and teach theology? In the previous chapter we saw how orality methods are increasingly being used in development work, public health settings, and Christian ministries such as evangelism and discipleship. But what about for formal theological reflection and education? Much of Western systematic theology is concerned with abstract concepts and propositions on matters such as the nature of God. Often, concepts and forms of argumentation are borrowed from the world of philosophy. Questions and concerns are sorted into neat categories such as soteriology, eschatology, Christology, and pneumatology. Doctrines are timelessly formulated independent of specific, concrete biblical-historical contexts, and often using a synchronic and encyclopedic approach. Although this is a caricature of systematic theology, it is nonetheless the impression that many Majority World learners and theologians have (see sidebar 6.5). Logic and rational thought cannot be entirely cast aside if it is to remain comprehensible, but it can be expanded upon (M. Lee 1999).

Cross-cultural teachers of theology will need not merely to be aware of these critiques; they will need to go further to help learners forge a theology that is biblical and relevant to the learners' context. The method, content, and teaching of theology must give attention to more concrete ways of thinking and learning. Since the mid-twentieth century, narrative theology has become an important topic of discussion in biblical studies, and many have argued for a more narrative representation of the Christian faith (e.g., Hauerwas and Jones 1997; Lodahl 2008). Authors such as Maarten Wisse (2005) have answered criticisms leveled against the narrative approach. For example, narrative is not necessarily as ambiguous as often thought. Wisse distinguishes between the different functions and outcomes of narrative and doctrinal theology, with a wise caution:

> Narrative theology aims to connect the faith with the real life context of the believer, whereas doctrinal theology attempts to provide an overall description of what Christian faith amounts to in the most precise terms possible. Arguments along these lines may then include a word of caution against uses of either narrative or doctrinal theology that amount to a replacement of all the different ways of doing theology with just one type. Narratives will probably

not be optimal bearers of precise overall descriptions of faith; on the other hand, an overall description of the Christian faith may not be directly located in the everyday experience of the believer. (2005, 246)

At the popular level, fictional works such as C. S. Lewis's Chronicles of Narnia and Space Trilogy embody much theology in narrative form. Mark Shaw's *Doing Theology with Huck and Jim: Parables for Understanding Doctrine* (1993) is a great example of how short stories can launch discussions on theological topics and relate theology to everyday life.

Understandings of orality are not important only for evangelism and discipleship; they also hold potential for deeper theological reflection. In their

---

SIDEBAR 6.5

Perceptions of Western Theology in the Majority World

The following critiques illustrate the negative assessment that many Majority World theologians have of "Western theology," and are evidence of the difficulties of a theology that is one-sidedly abstract.

Theology that is captive to individualism and rationalism. In 1982 a consultation organized by the Asia Theological Association, the Theological Commission of the Association of Evangelicals in Africa and Madagascar, and the Latin American Theological Fraternity issued "The Seoul Declaration: Toward an Evangelical Theology for the Third World." While affirming the importance of sound biblical exegesis for theology, it states,

> Western theology is by and large rationalistic, moulded by western philosophies, preoccupied with intellectual concerns, especially those having to do with the relationship between faith and reason. All too often, it has

reduced the Christian faith to abstract concepts which may have answered the questions of the past, but which fail to grapple with the issues of today. It has consciously or unconsciously been conformed to the secularistic worldview associated with the Enlightenment.

> We have recognized that if Evangelical theology is to fulfil its task in the Third World it must be released from captivity to individualism and rationalism of Western theology in order to allow the Word of God to work with full power. Many of the problems of our churches are, in part, the result of this type of theology. (Asia Theological Association 1982, 64)

Danger of reductionism. Ruth Padilla DeBorst comments:

> Extremely valuable areas of research and discovery have come as a fruit of the modern scientific endeavor. However, when this means of knowledge is absolutized, it runs the risk of reducing reality to its constitutive material elements, it becomes intolerant of paradox

book *The Return of Oral Hermeneutics*, Tom Steffen and William Bjoraker raise a question in regard to biblical interpretation: "Has our fascination for a fixed printed text that brings precision and exactitude blinded us to other hermeneutic possibilities? Is there something beyond cerebral-cognitive documents, outlines, words, standard and stock phrases, series of editions of printed versions of texts, grammar, semantics, and ideas?" (2020, xii). Their answer is yes. While not fully rejecting more literate approaches to biblical interpretation, they argue that approaching the Bible in terms of orality will "offer a fuller understanding of not only the cognitive but also the effective/cultural/psychological/motivational context the author had in mind" (xiii).

To teach primarily oral learners well, the way that theology is formulated and the way that theology is taught in higher education both need to be

and ambiguity, and it demands that processes be reproduced independent of context.... When the tendency is to frame everything in either-or terms and airtight categories, the integrated whole is often lost. (Padilla DeBorst 2016, 141)

Specialization and professionalization of theology. Ismael Amaya from Latin America writes about how theology can become an overly specialized and professionalized exercise:

This profound sense of "specialization" and "professionalism" has led the theologian to develop an "ivory-tower" theology, produced mostly in the office and in the library. This type of theology, which is a mere academic exercise and is usually out of touch with reality, is destined to be short lived. (Amaya 1983, 32)

Irrelevance to praxis. Hwa Yung includes this critique in his book *Mangoes or Bananas? The Quest for an Authentic Asian Christian Theology*:

Western theology is often perceived as being built on an idealistic conception

of truth which sharply distinguishes it from its practice. This leads to a theology which is "unengaged" and, therefore, lacks the power for human and social transformation....

The perceived unengaged nature of Western theology leads to the related perception that it often fails to be pastorally and missiologically relevant. (Yung 1997, 8–9)

Moonjang Lee notes a common criticism that even Westerners themselves perceive Western theology as an ivory-tower exercise disconnected from daily life: "It is perceived as an abstract theology being discussed only within the confined academic guild system" (1999, 258).

These critiques are admittedly harsh and are themselves gross generalizations. Lee states, "The Asian critiques of Western theology are only partially right in that they fail to deliver a true picture of Western theology" (262).

But they should nevertheless give theology teachers pause, and stimulate fresh thinking about how to teach theology and develop future theologians.

reconsidered. This is difficult to imagine for teachers trained in Western-style seminaries. However, creative approaches are possible. For example, Kiki and Parker have proposed for Papua New Guinea and the Asia Pacific region a holistic *Wokabaut-karikulum* for theological education that "fosters the human relationships and obligations, and seeks by this integration to develop the physical, emotional, mental, and spiritual components" (2014, 117). Its constitutive components are community, relationship, and sharing (120; see also Kiki 2010). The book *Beyond Literate Western Practices: Continuing Conversations in Orality and Theological Education* (Chiang and Lovejoy 2014) offers case studies and practical suggestions for training professors in the use of oral methods, reframing the task of theological education in oral cultures, and implementing more oral methods, such as storytelling, in the teaching of theology.

The Western theological tradition is known for its more analytical and abstract approach and for systematization of biblical teaching. This can, however, lead to such a fragmentation of understanding that learners can no longer see the theological forest for the analytical trees. David Wells expresses the challenge when he writes of the typical seminary curriculum:

> Subjects and fields develop their own literatures, working assumptions, vo-cabularies, technical terms, criteria for what is true and false, and canons of what literature and what views should be common knowledge among those working in the subjects. The result of this is a profound increase in knowledge but often an equally profound loss in understanding what it all means, how the knowledge in one field should inform that in another. This is the bane of every seminarian's existence. The dissociated fields—biblical studies, theology, church history, homiletics, ethics, pastoral psychology, missiology—become a rain of hard pellets relentlessly bombarding those who are on the pilgrimage to graduation. Students are left more or less defenseless as they run this gauntlet, supplied with little help in their efforts to determine how to relate the fields one to another. In the end, the only warrant for their having to endure the onslaught is that somehow and someday it will all come together in a church. (1993, 244–45)

In terms of reasoning and theological reflection, Peter Chang argues that in biblical interpretation one should not rely solely upon analysis of grammar, word studies, authorship, context, and so on, but look also to a more intuitive, holistic approach. "The Bible communicates something through our imagina-tion that it does not communicate through our reason" (P. Chang 1984, 118). Marlene Enns argues that "theological education also needs to take seriously diversity of reasoning represented in the body" (2005a, 264). Analytical and holistic approaches to theology should be viewed as complementary, not as competing approaches. She sees parallels of the torah tradition with more expository (non-Western) pedagogies emphasizing authority, and parallels of the prophetic tradition with analytical and constructive (Western) pedagogies whereby questioning is central. She then proposes greater emphasis on the wisdom tradition, or torah tradition, over the prophetic tradition in theological education. Wisdom emphasizes appreciation before questioning and can bridge the holistic and the analytical, interfacing Eastern and Western ways of reasoning. Enns writes, "Theological education needs to recover the unity between reason and spirituality, between knowing and fearing God, between knowing as a human effort and as a gift of God, between searching out and reverently accepting mystery, between inquiry and doxology" (2005b, 23).

The Worldview Dimension

Part 1: The Influence of Worldview on Learning

Behind the observable and explicit aspects of teaching and learning are the less obvious convictions that undergird those practices. As renowned cognitive psychologist Jerome Bruner has stated it, "Teaching, in a word, is inevitably based on notions about the nature of the learner's mind. Beliefs and assumptions about teaching, whether in a school or in any other context, are a direct reflection of the beliefs and assumptions the teacher holds about the learner" (1996, 46–47). A person's worldview influences not only their understanding of teaching and learning but also their conception of reality as a whole and how the world works. When a teacher and a learner hold different worldviews, teaching will be a challenge. The challenge is even greater if an objective of teaching is to promote worldview change.

We now come to the second dimension of how culture influences teaching and learning: worldview. This chapter will examine the characteristics and fundamental nature of worldview. How a worldview affects learning and how teachers can facilitate worldview change will be taken up in chapter 8.

> **CHAPTER OVERVIEW**
> - The Nature of a Worldview
> - Epistemology: How We Know What We Know
> - Causal Attribution: Why Things Happen
> - Understanding Time

The Nature of a Worldview

Imagine for a moment that from the time you were born, pink contact lenses were permanently placed in your eyes (these are not normal contact lenses). You have never seen the world without them, and you are not even aware that you are wearing them. Everyone else in your family also wears pink contacts.

FIGURE 7.1

Five dimensions of culture's influence on teaching and learning

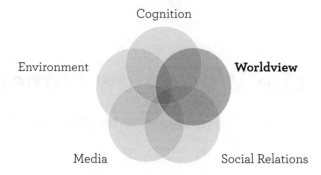

Your world is pink; it is all you know, and you don't even know it is pink. But then one day you go to school and meet a schoolmate who says the world is really blue. Naturally, you protest. But after further debate you determine that he is wearing blue contact lenses and doesn't realize it. When you attempt to explain this to him and help him remove the lenses, he objects and insists that you are the one wearing lenses—pink ones. At this point you reach an impasse and complain that some people just don't see the world as clearly as you.

A worldview is, so to speak, the lens through which we see the world and make sense of it. The term *worldview* captures that collection of learned values, beliefs, and understandings that inform our interpretation of how the world works, what is important, what is good or beautiful, and what is ultimate. It is core to human nature to attempt to give meaning to our experience and perceptions of reality. But that lens through which we see the world is colored by the culture in which we were raised, and we are seldom aware of it. We believe that people who see the world differently are just wrong. Conflict, confusion, and miscommunication are inevitable.

People everywhere experience similar phenomena in life, such as birth and death, sickness and health, prosperity and poverty. But we do not all interpret those experiences through the same lens. Look, for instance, at the drawing in figure 7.2: every reader will see the same ink on the page when examining the picture, but some recognize a young girl, while others see an old woman. So too we give meaning to the experiences and mysteries of life, but these meanings are learned and are by no means universal. What appears obvious in one culture may not be in another. Much the way it is difficult to see an old woman in the picture if you first saw a young girl (or vice versa), so too it is difficult to understand why people of another culture see the world so differently than you do.

Paul Hiebert defines worldview as "the fundamental cognitive, affective, and evaluative presuppositions a group of people make about the nature of things, and which they use to order their lives. Worldviews are what people in a community take as given realities, the maps they have of reality that they use for living" (2008, 15). A worldview serves to organize one's experiences and knowledge and make some sense of life. "The way people organize their knowledge tends to vary as a function of their experience, the nature of their knowledge, and the role that knowledge plays in their lives" (Ambrose et al. 2010, 47). Cross-cultural teachers will likely encounter learners with a very different worldview from their own. This experience can be baffling and frustrating. The cross-cultural teacher will need to have some understanding of their own worldview and the worldview of others to be effective.

A worldview may be consciously explicit or unconsciously implicit. Justin Barrett speaks of reflective and nonreflective beliefs. "*Reflective beliefs* are those beliefs we consciously hold and explicitly endorse" (2011, 47). "*Nonreflective beliefs* map closely onto what might be called tacit or intuitive knowledge. . . . [They] are representations that we have whether or not we know we have them" (48). These nonreflective aspects of a worldview are the colored lenses that we look *through*, not *at*; which is to say that most people are not really aware of much of their worldview. To illustrate this, consider two Christians from two very different cultures. They may share similar reflective beliefs based upon the Bible—about God, humanity, the course of history, and so on. But they may have very different nonreflective beliefs about causality. One may have a deep-seated assumption that everything in life has an entirely natural explanation: for example, seeing sickness as strictly biological. The other Christian has the sense that everything in life has a supernatural cause: for example, seeing sickness as the result of a curse, sin, or unseen powers. How these individuals approach a solution to the problem of sickness will differ greatly.

FIGURE 7.2

The young girl/old woman

Most aspects of a worldview are nonreflective; they are "primary founda-tional commitments," or presuppositions. "They are what we come to when we can no longer explain why it is we are saying what we are saying" (Sire 2015, 18). These commitments are not proven or demonstrated; they are the assumptions upon which most beliefs, values, and behaviors are based. *Worldview* will be used in this chapter to refer to both reflective and non-reflective beliefs.

The very concept of worldview has been contested and debated in aca-demia.[1] Nevertheless, it remains a helpful explanation of why people act and think differently in different cultures—if we heed a few warnings. First, worldview should not be defined in strictly cognitive, idealistic categories. It must embrace cognitive, emotive, and behavioral dimensions of life. Second, one should not overpromise the extent to which worldview change will change society.[2] As Hiebert reminds us, "Worldviews are not the engines that drive culture. Rather they are repositories of deep corporate assumptions and ways of looking at reality" (2008, 324). Furthermore, in much the way that no cul-ture is static, but virtually all cultures change over time, so too the worldview of a people evolves. As always, we must be cautious about stereotyping and assuming that everyone in a particular culture shares the same worldview or acts consistently with the dominant worldview. Individuals still differ. As a society becomes more pluralistic, members of that society will tend to share a common worldview less and less. Finally, as we shall discuss below, one must be self-reflective and critical about one's own worldview. We must all be open to learning and changing, bringing our own worldview ever nearer to conformity with the teachings of Scripture.

How a person views the nature of reality shapes the way they approach learning. Cross-cultural teachers will need to devote considerable effort to enter their learners' world and see the world through their eyes. It is impos-sible to explore in this brief chapter all the dimensions of a worldview and all that is involved in worldview change.[3] We'll consider only those aspects of worldview that most directly influence teaching and learning: epistemol-ogy, causality, and time. We will then address the question of teaching for

---

1. For a full discussion of the debates, alternatives, and dangers and benefits of the con-cept of worldview, see David K. Naugle's 2002 book *Worldview: The History of a Concept* (especially 331–44).

2. See, e.g., James Davison Hunter's discussion in *To Change the World* (2010) of how societies change, and of various views of the relationship between faith and culture.

3. Dimensions of a worldview include (but are not limited to) ontology, epistemology, se-miotics, axiology, causal attribution, and teleology. For fuller discussions, readers should con-sult works such as Hiebert's *Transforming Worldviews* (2008); David K. Naugle's *Worldview: The History of a Concept* (2002); and James W. Sire's *Naming the Elephant: Worldview as a Concept* (2015).

worldview change. The descriptions that follow are admittedly very simplified. They are intended merely to alert readers to some aspects of a worldview and illustrate the challenges of teaching persons whose worldview is different from one's own.

Epistemology: How We Know What We Know

Fundamental to most learning is our epistemology: our understanding of what it means to learn, what is worth learning, and how we know whether knowledge claims are reliable and true. These understandings are especially important for teachers, who impart knowledge, help learners discover knowledge, and develop learners' critical skills in discerning knowledge claims. As Charlene Tan comments,

> Knowing the epistemological foundation of belief system enables comparativists to understand why some indigenous beliefs are regarded as more important than others by a group of people, why these beliefs are more likely to persist over time and resist revisions or replacement, and why they play an influential role in helping the believers to make sense of, interact with and modify foreign ideas and practices. (2015, 197)

Epistemological differences in learning models are illustrated in a comparative study of American and Chinese students:

> Taken together, the US learning model (representing Caucasian middle- and upper-class members) basically presents a view of learning as a process by which individual minds acquire what is out there. Knowledge exists as a more or less neutral body (as embodied by the large number of school subjects) that the minds of individuals can acquire. . . .
>
> Members of the Chinese culture may view learning as a personal relationship that the individual builds to knowledge. Unlike the Western construal, the Chinese regard knowledge as something that is indispensable to their personal lives—something that creates meaning for their lives, without which human lives would be unthinkable. . . . Knowledge includes not only the externally existing body but also social and moral knowing. The scientific agenda of knowing the world is not the ultimate purpose. (J. Li 2002, 55–56)

Thus, what constitutes knowledge and how one attains it is culturally conditioned. Cross-cultural teachers who fail to take this into account may actually miss opportunities to place factual knowledge in a larger context of social and moral reasoning, which is often a primary concern of Christian cross-cultural workers.

What Is the Source of "Knowledge"?

There is a wide range of sources through which we believe knowledge might be obtained. Our worldview determines which sources we consider reliable. Before discussing possible sources of knowledge, it is important to note an underlying conviction about how one even obtains knowledge. In the Western tradition, it is believed that individuals are able to critically assess truth claims, or gain knowledge by reflecting upon experience. An individual constructs knowledge through this process. One of the primary goals of education is to help learners develop those discernment skills. This conviction leads to pedagogical methods that emphasize discovering, processing, and evaluating information, with less stress on mastery and reproduction of information. Socrates needed only to pose the right questions and his students would discover truth.

But other cultures do not share this underlying conviction. They believe that knowledge is not discovered or constructed by the learner, but rather that it is passed on from generation to generation, usually through authoritative persons who have in some way been qualified to teach. In this way of thinking, learners are not like a bud of latent wisdom and knowledge waiting to blossom with a little stimulation from the teacher; they are like empty containers that are to be filled with knowledge by the teacher. Swathi Nath Thaker describes, for example, the Hindu understanding of acquiring knowledge this way: "Though Western belief teaches that an individual is empowered through himself or herself, Hinduism argues that true empowerment emerges through an understanding of the sources of knowledge, not just its components, which in turn leads to unity with the universe" (2007, 58).

In many cultures, it is considered arrogant for a learner to suppose that they could arrive at knowledge and understanding on their own. For example, Stephanie Black relates her experience with graduate students in Kenya:

> They felt that as younger members of their communities it could be inappropriate to put themselves forward as sources of new knowledge. One group . . . suggested that "the risk of appearing 'too pompous and overconfident' haunts us." They further explained, "We still see ourselves as the little boys and little girls of our villages. Despite our academic level, we still want to be self-effaced in our communities." Others agreed that "the writer needs to portray himself not as one providing the solutions, but the one who is privileged to lead the discussion of coming up with solution(s) for the problem(s) addressed." Along these lines I observed how regularly African students and colleagues took the first few moments of a presentation to express humility about the opportunity to speak, along with appreciation of those who had gone before them, to whose work they hoped to add "some small thing." (2018, 2748–56)

From a biblical perspective it could be said that truth about God is revealed in Scripture and, in this sense, is not constructed by the learner. Yet in another sense the apprehension, appreciation, and application of that truth is seldom arrived at by *telling* it to learners but rather by the learner personally reflecting upon and engaging that truth.

Furthermore, Westerners tend to be more dichotomizing, giving less attention to the holistic nature of the universe and its components. Nisbett and his colleagues note that the way one defines the object of knowledge will in turn shape the way one organizes that knowledge and what is considered useful knowledge.

> People who believe that knowledge about objects is normally both necessary and sufficient for understanding their behavior will believe it is important to find the appropriate categories that apply to the object and the appropriate rules that apply to the categories. The search for categories and rules will dictate particular ways of organizing knowledge as well as procedures for obtaining new knowledge about rules. . . . Abstractions will be the goal. (Nisbett et al. 2001, 306)

Americans are particularly known for their pragmatic orientation: knowledge is valued if it has some demonstrable, practical usefulness. Wisdom is considered a different category of knowing.

Now we will examine just three approaches that some might accept, but others might reject, as valid sources of knowledge: science, tradition, and the supernatural. How a person views them will influence what information that person considers compelling and who the person considers to be a legitimate teacher.

SCIENCE

Western cultures tend to look to modern science as one of the most reliable source of information, if not *the* most reliable. Advancements in technology, medicine, engineering, and countless other areas of life have been the result of rigorous scientific inquiry that is governed by agreed-upon methods of empirical research. The West's high regard for science is rooted in the worldview conviction that reality is rational and is governed by natural laws. Thus, the key to understanding and problem-solving lies in discovering those laws. Nature is less a mystery than a machine. Scientific knowledge is always progressing with new discoveries, which means the "knowledge" of today may be the myth of tomorrow. We experience this, for example, in the world of health and diet: a food that was once considered healthy is now, on the basis of new research, found to be harmful. People living in such a culture have no difficulty with a steady stream of discoveries of this sort that lead to new knowledge that corrects, or even contradicts, old knowledge. Science has, in fact, solved so many challenges—from putting a man on the moon to developing the polio vaccine—that this modern worldview has evolved: "With enough research and time, science can solve any problem." Truth claims that are not rooted in scientific evidence are generally considered less reliable and are relegated to the categories of opinion, speculation, or myth. Creativity and experimentation are often valued, because even though there may be many failures along the way, in the end they can lead to new breakthroughs in understanding and efficiency. Truth claims that are not subject to empirical investigation or falsification, such as religious claims, are relegated to the category of opinion or superstition. The postmodern critique of this modern worldview has not really unseated these convictions in the lives of average people. However, even in societies that place high value on scientific knowledge, the claims of science may be challenged on the basis of ideology or a fundamental suspicion of science.[4]

TRADITION

Other cultures look not to science but to tradition for the most trustworthy and credible knowledge. Tradition represents the collective wisdom passed down through generations. This has been called *indigenous knowledge* shared by the community. Unlike scientific knowledge, Sharan Merriam describes indigenous knowledge as being generated in people's daily lives, and being typically passed on orally from generation to generation (2007, 11). Knowledge based in tradition is rooted in history and generations of experience; it is not independently discovered or evaluated by the learner. This accounts in part for the emphasis upon memorization, as opposed to critical thinking skills, in so many parts of the world.

Traditional knowledge tends to value wisdom more than facts. For example, as noted in chapter 5, proverbs are an expression of traditional wisdom. Thus, in Asia even academic writing may cite proverbs as valid support of an argument (Wu and Rubin 2000; Günther 1990). They may be cited by judges and lawyers in Nigeria in legal arguments (Finnegan 2012, 396).

Methods for hunting, fishing, cooking, farming, child-rearing, healing, managing the environment, and the like have been honed through the ages. Because such traditional knowledge has led to the survival of the society, often under harsh living conditions, societies with subsistence economies can be very resistant to change. This can be particularly frustrating for development workers who seek to introduce new methods to increase productivity

4. This is evident in the West, for example, in the rejection of scientific arguments in favor of evolution, immunization and vaccination, and global warming. Although scientific counterarguments are sometimes posed, they are often ideologically motivated.

or improve health care. However, from the perspective of a traditionalist living in a context of poverty or subsistence farming, experimenting with new methods can entail great risk. A crop failure is not just one experiment gone bad; it can threaten the livelihood of whole families. Therefore, creativity is not a value. New ideas and methods are not only risky but can be seen as disrespectful of parents, ancestors, and communal values. What right does a person, especially a young person or outsider, have to challenge time-tested methods and wisdom? Arguments that begin with "But science has demonstrated . . ." are likely to be viewed with suspicion or skepticism. In some cases, traditional practices and knowledge are rooted in religious beliefs that are not to be questioned under any circumstances.

THE SUPERNATURAL

In most Western cultures, claims of divine revelation, supernatural phenomena, and mystical experiences are written off as superstitious and scientifically unverifiable. In many other cultures, however, they are considered valid sources of knowledge to be taken most seriously. For example, astrology is a formal subject in some reputable Indian universities including PhD-level study.[5]

An important source of knowledge in many cultures is dreams or visions. In most Western cultures, dreams are understood as involuntary mental images during sleep. Dreams are believed to be entirely imaginary with no connection to reality, other than perhaps a subconscious processing of one's real-life experiences or emotions. By contrast, many cultures believe dreams have meaning and need interpretation. They may be considered a supernatural source of prophetic information. Such an understanding is found in numerous passages in the Bible, such as Pharaoh's and Nebuchadnezzar's dreams (Gen. 40; Dan. 2). In Judaism, the Talmud describes dreams from God and their interpretation (Berekhot 55). Other religions, such as Islam (Sirriyeh 2015), Buddhism, and Hinduism (Young 2003), as well as many so-called folk religions see dreams as meaningful or as sources of supernatural revelation today. For example, "many herbalists in the past and even today in Botswana claim that the secrets of their medicines and how they should be administered were communicated to them mainly through dreams" (Ntseane 2007, 120). Among the Guarani of Brazil, conflicts arose between the *Paje* (traditional shaman) and the public schools because the schools introduced scientific thinking and questioned traditional teaching as superstition. In some villages this led to the ostracism of families who sent their children to the schools (Gerstetter 1999).

5. BBC World Service, "Indian Astrology vs Indian Science," May 31, 2001, http://www.bbc.co.uk/worldservice/sci_tech/highlights/010531_vedic.shtml.

Before moving on it should be noted that although these different sources of knowledge may seem to be in conflict with one another, in many cultures they exist side by side and are valued variously depending on the situation and issue at hand.

What Makes a Teacher Credible?

Establishing the authority and qualifications of a teacher is important if learners are to take the teacher seriously. The following factors related to worldview will influence a teacher's credibility to varying degrees.

FORMAL CREDENTIALS

In many Western cultures, formal credentials are the primary qualifications that overshadow all others. Life experience and demonstrated expertise play secondary roles. A teacher is considered qualified primarily on the basis of earned diplomas, certifications, or degrees that conform to publicly recognized and monitored standards, and such qualifications are required for teachers in all formal schools. The teacher has credibility because he has demonstrated mastery of the subject matter or skill. That mastery has been assessed and recognized in the granting of the degree. The more prestigious the educational institution, the greater the respect and credibility.

TITLE OR POSITION

In some contexts, simply having a title such as "professor" or holding an office such as "director" establishes the authority and credibility of a teacher. The assumption here is that the credibility of information lies more in the person communicating it than in the original source of or evidence for the information. A title is indication that the teacher or communicator is qualified to assess the value of the information. Thus, in some cultures, once a teacher has acquired the requisite academic position, students may believe her blindly, whatever she teaches (see sidebar 7.1). Islam sees the student-teacher relationship as sacred: "Just as the Prophet is venerated in the Islamic tradition, the position of teacher is revered in a society for that person is following in the footsteps of the Prophet for becoming a keeper of God's treasure; that is, knowledge" (Kamis and Muhammad 2007, 30).

If you trust the person, you trust the information. It is impossible for the average person to have enough background knowledge to accurately assess highly specialized information, so people everywhere depend on experts to make judgments on their behalf. We more or less take their word for it on the basis of their title or position. What source would you believe for reliable information about a rare disease: the director of the United States

Centers for Disease Control and Prevention or the online blog of Joe's Home Remedies?

AGE AND LIFE EXPERIENCE

In cultures that place high value on tradition, life experience often has the place of honor. Life wisdom is valued above factual knowledge. A person with poor character would not be considered qualified to teach any subject, irrespective of formal qualifications. Experience is particularly important in most cultures. Short-term cross-cultural teachers often arrive in a new culture and attempt to introduce to their hosts new methods and ideas. If the teacher draws a blank when someone asks, "Have you done this yourself?" or "Has it been done in our location?" for all intents and purposes the lesson is over. One of my German students went to South Sudan to instruct midwives in practices that could help reduce infant and maternal mortality, a great concern in the region. However, when she sought to instruct the older, more experienced

---

SIDEBAR 7.1

Teacher Knows Best?

Brian Arensen relates his experience teaching in Tanzania:

> While teaching a course on the Minor Prophets at a Bible school in Tanzania, I discovered a decided difference in my students' understanding of truth. The discovery began when I assigned each student one book to research and then teach to the class.
>
> As the first student taught, no one took notes. I blamed it on poor teaching. However, when the top student taught the next week with a thesis, outline, and other notes on the blackboard, still not one of them put pen to paper.
>
> Now I suspected a pattern. I spoke up and told everyone to take notes. At this, they took sparse, sporadic notes, but with no great enthusiasm.
>
> After class, I asked one of my students: "What is the problem with taking notes?"

> "He is just my fellow student," he said. "How do I know he is saying the right thing? I don't want to write something down which may be wrong."
>
> "How do you know that what I teach is correct?" I asked.
>
> He replied, "You are a teacher and were taught by other teachers."
>
> The light dawned—we understood biblical truth to come from different sources. (Arensen 1995, 338)

- How was this teacher's approach to knowledge and learning different from that of the students?
- How does this difference reflect different worldviews about knowledge?
- If you were the teacher, how would you respond to the students? Would you change anything in the way that you teach?

Sudanese midwives, they quickly discovered that she was unmarried and had never given birth herself. Although she had years of experience, knew the most up-to-date medical practices, and had successfully delivered many babies, she had no credibility in the eyes of the Sudanese midwives.

These differing understandings can create frustration, confusion, or rejection. Western teachers may be baffled by their students' readiness to believe whatever they say, yet hold to seemingly contradictory viewpoints without blinking. Non-Western teachers may be frustrated by Western students' impatience with mysteries or insulted by their unwillingness to accept the knowledge and authority of the teacher merely on the basis of their position.

Knowledge as Power

Today, for people with access to the internet and libraries, all kinds of information is readily available. Because of its ubiquity, most information is not considered a particularly valuable or rare commodity. However, in cultures with limited access to information of any kind, knowledge is valuable and powerful because few people have it. A person with more knowledge has higher status and often knows how to get more things done than less knowledgeable people do. Thus, people with more knowledge or more formal education may be reluctant to share that knowledge with others. Teachers from cultures with universal education and easy access to information may find this rather selfish or petty. However, they should remember that industrialized nations also have powerful knowledge that is not openly shared: for instance, insider information about the stock market, proprietary information about new products, and military secrets. It has been argued that economies and societies are shifting from being based on commodities to being based on knowledge (Kefela 2010). Education (knowledge) is regarded as the key to prosperity. This notion can lead to competitive situations in which students are unwilling to collaborate or share knowledge with fellow students because they want to achieve a higher class ranking than their peers and thus attain better job prospects (see sidebar 10.1 on page 206). Because a teacher not only possesses valuable knowledge but is also willing to share that knowledge with students, the teacher is highly respected and may receive signs of appreciation in various forms.

Causal Attribution: Why Things Happen

The question of why things happen is one of the most fundamental elements of a worldview. Can events be explained on the basis of natural laws? (In other words, does the world function like a machine?) Or are benevolent or malevolent unseen powers at work? (Does the world function like a person?) Are humans more or less free to shape their futures, or are they prisoners of fate or deterministic forces? Is the world a rational place governed by reason and logical consistency, or is it full of mystery and seeming contradictions? How one answers these questions will influence one's outlook, motivation, and behavior as a learner in countless ways.

Holistic-Complex versus Analytic-Reductionistic Causality

The natural-science approach to knowledge looks for cause-and-effect relationships and logical explanations. According to Occam's razor (or the law of parsimony), the simplest explanation of a phenomenon is most likely correct. Alternative hypotheses are verified or eliminated through rigorous experimentation and observation. That process is much easier if the number of variables can be kept to a minimum. This can lead to a reductionistic view of life and causality that seeks a single explanation for any given event. Nisbett cites numerous studies that support his contention that "consistent with the complexity of the world they live in, Westerners see fewer factors as being relevant to an understanding of the world than Easterners do" (Nisbett 2003, 129). This leads to Westerners' tendency to exclude data or information as irrelevant, information that Easterners might regard as possibly important. For example, one study asked physics students to read a story about a murder and a list of one hundred related information items. Korean physics students considered 37 percent of the items irrelevant, while Americans thought 55 percent were irrelevant. The more holistic the participant's worldview, the fewer items were eliminated (Nisbett 2003, 129). Another study, this one just of Americans, found that persons with a more mechanistic worldview were less likely to use complementary and alternative medicine for treatment of chronic pain (Buck, Baldwin, and Schwartz 2005).

The more holistically a people see the world, the more they see everything as somehow related to everything else.

> For example, most who have addressed the question hold that European thought rests on the assumption that the behaviors of objects—physical, animal, and human—can be understood in terms of straightforward rules. Westerners have a strong interest in categorization, which helps them to know what rules apply to the objects in question, and formal logic plays a role in problem solving. East Asians, in contrast, attend to objects in their broad context. The world seems more complex to Asians than to Westerners, and understanding events always requires consideration of a host of factors that operate in relation to one another in no simple, deterministic way. In fact the person too concerned with logic may be considered immature. (Nisbett 2003, xvi)

Nisbett is no doubt oversimplifying the difference between Asians and Westerners in the above quote, but these two contrasting approaches can be observed often enough. The desire to reduce all true knowing to rules, natural
laws, and observable phenomena is inflexible, leaving little room for mystery;
it excludes other forms of knowing such as tradition, intuition, and divine
revelation. Though this is a broad generalization, at the popular level most
Westerners prefer thought systems that are logically consistent and have some
sense of coherence and closure.[6] In chapter 4 we saw that Westerners tend to
prefer more formal/abstract reasoning that views reality in terms of rules and
principles, whereas others use a more concrete/functional reasoning that takes
into account many real-world factors beyond axioms and laws. Westerners
tend to be uncomfortable with mystery, conundrum, and paradoxes. Most
non-Western worldviews more readily embrace mystery and see life more
holistically (see sidebar 7.2).

Non-Westerners are also often more comfortable accepting seemingly
contradictory claims. Because they tend to be less reductionistic and see all
objects as complex and interrelated, "Contradiction will seem inevitable,
since change is constant, and opposing factors always exist. . . . Logic will
not be allowed to overrule sensory experience or common sense" (Nisbett et
al. 2001, 306). Life is viewed as more than a series of cause-and-effect events
or natural laws. Indeed, reducing life to rules and natural laws can be seen
as simplistic and childish. Daniel Wildcat writes of American Indians' more
experiential, less rationalistic cause-and-effect approach to knowledge, "where
explanation is often discussed in terms of experiential correspondence and
understood as irreducible to simple mechanical causality" (2001, 49). Thus
"rationalistic explanation is unnecessary if one depends on experience. . . .
Indigenous people depend on experiential verification, not logical proof" (53).
Not only do many cultures have a more holistic view of the natural world that
allows for mystery or contradiction, but this can be especially so in questions
of religion and the supernatural. David Hesselgrave speaks of what he calls
"multireligion" whereby in places such as Japan, Shintoism and Buddhism
coexist side by side without contradiction, each occupying its own domain
of life and each with its own temples, rituals, and festivals. "In their homes
the Shinto god-shelves and the Buddhist god-shelves coexist, each claiming
attention that is appropriate to its domain. And beneath the surface is found
Confucianism" (Hesselgrave 1991, 283). In such contexts, the truth claims of
one religion are not necessarily understood as invalidating the truth claims
of another. Sometimes a pragmatic approach is taken; one may participate in

6. In the Western philosophical tradition, Hegelian dialectic, existentialism, and postmodernism reject strictly rationalistic understandings of reality. But these views have had relatively
little influence on how most Westerners view daily life and how the world works.

SIDEBAR 7.2

A Holistic Melanesian Worldview

Gwayaweng Kiki and Ed Parker describe the worldview in Papua New Guinea (PNG):

> PNG religion, culture and theology are built upon a Melanesian (traditional tribal) worldview that is cosmic, and in which everything, including deities, spirits, animals, humans, plants and natural phenomena, are linked together into a cosmos. In other words, it is the unity in which everything exists together in an inextricable mix, cementing the natural and supernatural world together into a single system, an ordered whole without which nothing can exist. The deep-felt value called "life," as seen in this Melanesian reality, is a religious experience, a biocosmic religious experience for Melanesians where both biological existence and cosmic renewal stand together. PNG Melanesian life is an interrelated experience, in which religious and non-religious experiences are not differentiated. Such a world view shapes their perception of reality and one that implies that knowing and existence or knowing and being are interrelated; an integrated whole for knowing that has a holistic outlook on life. (2014, 111)

---

practices of various religions, seeking to reap the benefits of each in its own way. We see a close connection here between holistic and analytic cognitive styles discussed in chapter 6.

Role of Unseen Powers and Natural Causes

Whereas materialist approaches look for causes based entirely on natural law, other worldviews often look to unseen forces behind the visible event. Natural explanations may explain the *what* of a phenomenon, but supernatural causes are often behind the *why*. This is particularly so regarding sickness, fertility, misfortune, or good fortune. For example, Paul Gerstetter (1999) observed in his work among the Guarani of Brazil the belief that sickness may be caused by a virus, but the virus was sent by an evil spirit; a synthesis of traditional beliefs and natural science is evident. In cultures with worldviews of this sort, people look to blessings and curses, taboos, demonic powers, the jinn, angels, or other unseen powers to explain why something occurred. They believe events of life are influenced by unseen forces that may be personal, such as spirits and demons, or impersonal, such as astrology or magic. Although a medical doctor may be able to physically cure a disease with medication based solely upon biology and chemistry, persons with more supernatural worldviews may not feel truly healed or safe without knowing that the underlying spiritual cause has been dealt with. Must a local god be appeased? Did someone break a taboo? Did a witch cast a curse? This is why often even Christians when sick will visit a medical doctor and also consult a shaman. Two modes of causality are being addressed.

While such views of unseen powers may be inconsistent with a biblical worldview, so also is the overly rationalistic and materialistic view of many Western Christians, which sees little, if any, influence of unseen powers, apart from an occasional answer to prayer. Both worldviews must be examined and corrected in light of Scripture. Malaysian Hwa Yung describes how his worldview evolved as a result of his theological education in the West:

> I grew up in a thought world where ancestral spirits, demonic powers, "gods," and miracles of all kinds abounded. Modern education, the most powerful force behind secularization, almost succeeded in getting me to toss out everything as superstition. Some of these supernatural elements clearly are, but not all. A careful reading of the Bible and the sheer weight of empirical evidence eventually brought me back to a supernatural Christianity. In this, I found myself out of sync with much of Western theology. (Yung 2010)

The failure of Western missionaries and development workers to address the dimension of unseen powers in a people's worldview can have several negative consequences. If Christianity is perceived as a foreign religion unable to address the people's deepest fears, it may be rejected altogether—or people may remain Christian but continue harmful or syncretistic practices in secret. This can also explain why development projects sometimes face resistance by the local people. Even when new methods are visibly more productive, if they violate sacred taboos, the people may fear some form of spiritual retribution. Hiebert described this problem in a classic essay, "The Flaw of the Excluded Middle" (1994, 189–201), that is still worth reading.

Innate versus Acquired Intelligence

Motivation is an important factor influencing why some students perform well and others poorly. Is performance a result of natural giftedness or of hard work? The answer is no doubt a combination of both, but most cultures emphasize one factor more than the other. Culturally different approaches to causal attribution are evident not only regarding student ability but also in explaining a person's behaviors, why historical events took place, or even why a sports team won or lost a game. Americans tend to attribute behavior to individual personality traits such as disposition and character, which are viewed as relatively fixed and unchangeable. Asians, on the other hand, tend to attribute behavior to more contextual factors, such as the social environment. They also tend to see personal traits as more malleable and less fixed than do Americans (Nisbett 2003, 111–35; Burnett and Medin 2008, 949). This difference can be explained in part by the tendency of Americans to be reductionistic in their causal explanations (as noted above), leading them to overlook other factors contributing to a particular behavior.

In our discussion of learning styles, we saw that it is common in many cultures to attribute learning success to the student's innate abilities. A student does poorly in math because he is "just not good at math." The cultural assumption is that the ability to perform well in math is inborn and has little to do with the student's effort. To expect more of the student would be like expecting an elephant to climb a tree. As Catherine Scott describes it,

> People conceptualise human attributes as either entities (stable, universal—that is, fixed traits probably present from birth) or processes (malleable—that is, unstable, qualities that can be influenced and shaped by effort and experience). . . .
>
> The Western cultural tendency is to use entity theories to explain human behavior, for example, IQ models of human potential, which imply that children are born with a fixed quantum of ability that is resistant to environmental influences. In contrast, many Asian cultures favour a model that emphasises the process of developing personality and ability, and explanations for how people act and perform are more likely to feature observations about the interaction between individual characteristics and the context in which the person was acting. (Scott 2010, 12)

Viewing a learner as innately able or unable, or viewing all learners as having potential if they only work hard enough, makes an enormous difference both in a learner's motivation and in a teacher's attitude toward the learner. "Those in the entity mold tend to make judgments about people very quickly, based on very limited interactions with them, and to expect that people's behaviour will be stable; that is, that how people are first perceived will be an indication of how they will act in all contexts" (Scott 2010, 12). This view tends to pigeonhole learners as "one of those." Also, "teachers and parents in the West often make unrealistically positive appraisals of their students' and children's performance and set lower expectations of their achievement" (Salili 1996, 100).

Because in the West student success tends to be attributed to student ability, John Biggs comments, "teaching becomes not so much educative in intent as *selective*. The classroom becomes an arena in which students display their ability to learn, assessment the instrument for sorting out those that learn well from those that don't" (2001, 304). Other cultures view learning as more a result of controllable factors such as hard work and persistence and less a matter of innate ability. Effort attribution locates learning in student activity. In cultures that place more emphasis upon student effort, all students tend to be treated equally and with the same expectation of performance. Numerous studies point to this as a key reason that Asian students so often outperform other ethnic groups in subjects like mathematics and science, even when they are from disadvantaged family backgrounds (Salili 1996; Jerrim 2015; Liu and Xie 2016). Furthermore, American parents tend to blame the teacher, the school, the curriculum, or poor testing for a student's low grades, whereas Asian American parents tend to blame the child (Brislin 1993, 152). The picture is actually more complex than this dichotomy suggests (Elliot and Bempechat 2002). Wing On Lee sees the source of this conviction in the Confucian tradition: "Because there is strong belief in attainability by all, there is also a strong belief that one's failure is not due to one's internal make-up or ability, but one's effort and willpower. A weak-willed person making no effort is doomed to failure. On contrast despite your level of intelligence, if one tries and keeps trying, one will certainly 'get there' sooner or later" (1996, 39).

In the words of one Chinese student, "Learning is hard work. If you're not a good student, your immediate reaction is like you didn't put enough effort and hours into it" (Wan 2020). Although educational reforms in China have moved more in the direction of Western approaches, the underlying epistemological basis remains Confucian (C. Tan 2017; Meng et al. 2017). The downside of this view is that students may feel extreme guilt or shame upon failure, and parents or teachers may exert extreme pressure on struggling students to just work harder. Students in Hong Kong may repeat exams numerous times, unwilling to concede that they just may not have the natural intelligence or ability necessary to successful study in the discipline (Salili 1996, 100).

Self-Efficacy and Learner Motivation

The concept of self-efficacy (or self-competence) refers to the sense of control that one has in life—in the context of education, a student's sense that they can do well in school or life on the basis of hard work (Bandura 1997). In other words, success is dependent less upon innate abilities or outward circumstances and more on effort. Although the very term *self*-efficacy seems to emphasize a bias toward individualism, there can also be a sense of collective self-efficacy. For example, a study of managers from collectivistic cultures judged themselves most efficacious and productive when working in a team versus working alone or in culturally diverse groups (Bandura 1997, 470–72).

We have just seen that a worldview emphasizing innate ability can negatively affect a learner's sense of self-efficacy. Environmental factors also influence worldview and self-efficacy. People who have grown up in a context of relative security, moderate affluence, freedom to make many life choices, and educational opportunity tend to believe that hard work pays and anyone can get ahead in life if they only try hard enough. Life is somewhat predictable and one can afford to take risks. Even when a crisis hits there are economic and social safety nets. But most people of the world have not grown up under those conditions. For many people, very little in life is predictable: their lives may be disrupted by power outages, strikes, storms, drought, epidemics, political turmoil, wars, and ethnic conflicts. Plans seldom pan out as expected, so planning for the future seems futile. That sense can be compounded by limited educational opportunity and corruption or nepotism in schools and social institutions. Very little is under one's control, and one has very few choices in life. Under such circumstances people often develop a more fatalistic view of reality: hard work may not be rewarded; much more depends upon one's birth family, who one knows, and luck. In the words of one person from sub-Saharan Africa,

> Usually, you'd like to think if you go to college and graduate with a good GPA it will transition into you finding a good job. But it doesn't work that way in my country. . . . There is always a push to know someone in the workplace who will get a job for you. I know networking is important in America, but my country is not as much of a merit-based system as the US. It's hard to make it on your own merit. This is very bad because it's a sign of a corrupt system. People will do well in school, but then not get a good job because they don't know the right people. This is the main thing that hurts student motivation. (Kenworthy 2020)

Another person from the same country describes her experience:

> Someone who is less qualified will get a job either because they know the right person or because they will work for less money. My family has experienced this. . . . My brother studied at the University of Nottingham in the U.K. He studied artificial intelligence. He's very gifted. But he graduated in 2016 and still [in 2020] has no job in his field. He takes random jobs here and there. So, why should a student want to work hard in school, if hard work makes them less employable in the long run? (Kenworthy 2020)

The benefits of schooling are deferred at best and may seem very far away and uncertain. Whereas the affluent tend to have an overly efficacious view of their ability to control the future, others may have an overly fatalistic and resigned outlook.

Affluence is not the only social factor that can contribute to a student's sense of self-efficacy. Take, for example, a study comparing Thai, Singaporean, Austrian, and German university students. Thailand is generally considered a

collectivistic culture with high power distance (acceptance of unequal distribution of power) and status awareness. The study found that Thai students tend
more than the others to hold professors more responsible for their success and
failure. Singapore, one of the most affluent countries in the world, is known
for its strong work ethic, and Singaporean students were least likely to hold
professors responsible for their success, even less so than the Austrians or
Germans in the study (Apfelthaler et al. 2007).

It is not difficult to imagine how the sense of self-efficacy can impact learners' aspirations and motivation. "The stronger the perceived self-efficacy, the
higher the goals people set for themselves and the firmer their commitment
to them" (Bandura 1997, 116). Numerous comparative cross-cultural studies
confirm the positive correlation between student self-efficacy and academic
performance; indeed, across cultures, "it is the single most important predictor
of academic achievement" (Salili, Chiu, and Lai 2001, 244). If learners believe
that they are fundamentally inferior or that hard work will not bring rewards,
teachers will need to be encouragers and create alternative narratives. Cross-
cultural teachers and development workers need to instill a spirit of hope and
realistic optimism in those who are resigned to simply accepting their fate
in life or who have crippling self-doubt regarding their ability. Salili and his
colleagues conclude from their research and review of the literature, "In order
to promote self-efficacy, educators should design the content, instructional
approach and assessment techniques in a way that would enhance students'
interest, engagement and sense of competence" (244).

If new, unfamiliar methods are being introduced, some safety net may
need to be created in case the experiment fails. Teachers may need to help
students appreciate the benefits of learning, even if they do not result in immediate rewards or a better job. One of the keys to the famous success of
Paulo Freire's literacy program in Brazil, where other programs had failed,
was *conscientização*—critical consciousness or consciousness raising—and
the ability to instill in learners a sense of empowerment to change their world
(Freire 2005; Roberts 2000). Conversely, if teachers believe that some students,
or the whole class of students, is inferior and no amount of hard work will
bring positive results, then teachers can become resigned and lack motivation.
They will need to acknowledge this worldview and look for alternative stories
that give hope and inspire a vision for human potential.

Understanding Time

Is time linear or cyclical? A commodity to be spent, wasted, or invested? Is a
person more oriented on the past, the present, or the future? How does one
measure time? Time is one of the least reflected upon aspects of a worldview.

Measuring Time

In many nonindustrial societies, days are measured by the position of the sun, not by minutes. Months are measured in moons or seasons, not calendars. Some people may not know the year in which they were born, because large spans of time are not carefully counted in years but are counted by major events such as a drought. In fact, some people may change their name after some dramatic personal life event. A medical worker in a remote region of Mozambique found this particularly challenging in attempting to determine the identity of patients, track their health, and prescribe medications. Will the patient know what it means to take a medication every three hours or to return for a follow-up treatment in four weeks? In some cultures large time spans are counted not in decades or centuries but in generations or reigns of a clan.

A teacher was lecturing in Guinea-Bissau on Martin Luther and the Reformation, which took place in the sixteenth century. Because the teacher was from Germany, he was asked by a student, "Have you ever met Martin Luther?" In amazement, the teacher replied, "But that was hundreds of years ago." To which the student responded, "But you are from Germany, you could have known him." Especially when teaching history, one must give attention to people's understanding and measurement of time. Another teacher of young adults from a remote indigenous people in Bolivia was asked by a student if Martin Luther lived before or after Jesus. Not only are concepts like "sixteenth century" unfamiliar, but further confusion can be caused by the tendency of Western teachers to deal with subjects topically and not chronologically. In Western-style education, subjects are typically organized conceptually and systematically, not chronologically and holistically as embedded in historical events as really experienced.

Monochronic and Polychronic Time

An even more fundamental difference in how different cultures view time was conceptualized by Edward Hall (1983) with the idea of monochronic and polychromic time. Most industrialized cultures are *monochronic*; they approach time as a commodity not to be wasted but to be invested as one would invest money. Time is carefully measured and portioned out. Managing time well has much to do with increasing productivity and efficiency. Thus people measure time in minutes, make precise appointments, and wear wristwatches. "For them, time is an active, physical commodity that they think they can control in some way. While it is true that they cannot actually control it, they nonetheless use vocabulary that indicates that somehow then can 'tame' it for their purposes" (Moreau, Campbell, and Greener 2014, 142).

Many other cultures are *polychronic*; they experience time not as a commodity but as an event. They measure time not in minutes but in the rhythms of life or simply in terms of however long it takes to complete a task. Because life is unpredictable, tasks cannot be measured in minutes or even hours. One manages one's life not according to the clock but according to relationships and events. Time belongs to the community, not to the individual.

Punctuality

It is easy to see why culture conflict is inevitable with such divergent understandings of the very nature of time, especially when it comes to punctuality—a concern to many teachers. What counts as punctual or late, and does it even matter? For some, an event begins when nearly everyone is present, and it ends when nearly everyone has left. Wristwatches are worn less as a timepiece and more as a piece of jewelry. In one culture, failing to arrive at the appointed time can be a sign of disrespect, but in another culture it can be a sign that the relationship is one of friendship, not about business. In some cultures arriving ten minutes late to an appointment would require an apology; in other cultures that might only be necessary after thirty minutes or even an hour. It may even be expected that high-status persons, as a matter of principle, will always arrive late. Then again, what counts as late for one type of occasion, such as a business meeting or class lecture, does not count as late for another kind of meeting, such as a family gathering.

Cross-cultural teachers will need to adjust their social sensibilities about punctuality accordingly. What a teacher may interpret as wasting her time, her student may interpret as building the relationship. Students may feel frustrated that a teacher is impatient, is too businesslike, and lacks appreciation for the local pace of life. They may perceive the teacher as always in a rush and more concerned about an agenda than people. This can block students' ability to learn. The cross-cultural teacher will need to be flexible and determine what is acceptable in the given context or institution, to what extent tardiness should be an issue, and how to deal with it if it is. Students not accustomed to planning ahead may have difficulty completing assignments on time, and to improve their study habits they may need assistance such as coaching or help breaking assignments into smaller segments.

The next chapter will explore various approaches to teaching that can lead to change in a learner's worldview.

The Worldview Dimension

Part 2: Teaching for Worldview Change

CHAPTER OVERVIEW

- Worldview Change and Worldview Changers
- Cognitive Approaches
- Spiritual Approaches
- Communal Approaches
- Conclusion

Paul G. Hiebert relates the following experience from living in India:

> In a South Indian village all the Christians painted big white crosses on their houses. I thought this was good witness to their new faith, but they explained that the cross was a powerful sign to defend them from the evil eye. . . . People had reinterpreted Christianity as a new and more powerful form of magic that enabled them to gain success and harm enemies through right formulas. . . . It is one of the most common and greatest dangers in the church. (2008, 11)

We read of similar experiences in the New Testament. For example, Simon the sorcerer, who had become a Christian, attempted to purchase the power of the Holy Spirit (Acts 8:9–24). When Paul and Barnabas entered Lystra and healed a lame man, people interpreted the miracle as a sign that they were gods, and so the people wanted to bring sacrifices to them. The apostles clarified that they were but men and then explained to them about the true Creator God. But, "Even with these words, they had difficulty keeping the crowd from sacrificing to them" (Acts 14:11–18). Even a miracle was interpreted though the people's worldview, and one short sermon did not change that.

Such observations and incidents highlight the fact that conversion and growth in the Christian faith entails a change of worldview, and that such change is not usually immediate.

Most Christian cross-cultural teachers do not want to just see learners accomplish tasks, develop skills, or master content; they also want to help them see the world more biblically and lead lives more consistent with those teachings. This is what we mean by teaching for worldview change. This is a challenge when making disciples of Jesus anywhere, but it is especially difficult when the teacher and the learner are from different cultures.

This chapter will focus primarily on practical approaches to facilitating such change. But before describing teaching methods, two concerns must first be addressed: (1) the legitimacy of worldview change as a teaching objective and (2) the disposition of the teacher approaching such an objective. We'll then look at three approaches to worldview change: cognitive, spiritual, and communal.

Worldview Change and Worldview Changers

In a postcolonial era, the thought of a cultural outsider being involved in culture change can be particularly offensive. The legacy of colonialism and its many abuses has created a healthy skepticism toward outside influences. To be sure, cultural outsiders are often insensitive to local cultures, and some have sought to import or impose foreign values and ways of thinking without having first sought to at least understand the local people and their culture. But such negative examples should not blind us to the realities of culture change in the modern, globalizing world. Intentionally or unintentionally, a cross-cultural teacher will be an agent of culture change, so we need to reflect carefully on how such change occurs.

Worldview Change as a Teaching Objective

There are several reasons why from both a sociological and a Christian point of view, culture change is inevitable and even necessary. First, as discussed in chapter 1, all cultures change. This is an age of technological advancement and globalization, and all but the most remote peoples experience outside influences. Because all cultures evolve and change, the only question is whether they will change for the better. A cross-cultural teacher will inevitably be a part of that culture change, so it then becomes more a matter of intentionality and desired outcome.

Second, local people who are most affected by change should be the ones most directly involved in decisions about change. There is no place for manipulation, coercion, or hegemony by cultural outsiders. However, because sojourners often bring an additional perspective or new information, they can be a part of that decision-making process. Often this occurs by asking questions, pointing to resources, and helping to think through the consequences of change. An example of this was a series of colloquia in Nairobi, Kenya, in 2013 and 2014 on witchcraft accusations. African and non-African leaders engaged together in biblical-theological study and empirical inquiry, which resulted in a series of publications, audio recordings, and ongoing research.[1] Africans were the primary presenters, but outside experts provided additional perspective and input.

Third, all worldviews have elements that can lead to harmful behaviors and injustice. It is right to seek to change aspects of a worldview that contribute to such evils. The aforementioned witchcraft accusations against defenseless widows and children is only one example. Countless others could be mentioned, such as racism and casteism, exploitation of the poor, extreme hedonism, harmful rituals, and discrimination against the disabled, to name just a few.

Finally, from a Christian point of view, God has revealed in the Bible his perspective on creation, human dignity, life and afterlife, history, good and evil, unseen powers, and the foundational elements of a worldview.[2] If our goal is to develop disciples of Jesus Christ, then we should look neither to the teacher nor to a specific cultural narrative but to the Bible as our authority and guide to shape our worldview. As we shall see below, humility is required from all parties in this process. Maturing in one's Christian faith, the process of discipleship, and loving God and neighbor with all our heart, mind, and strength requires a transformation of the way we see the world and the deepest level of beliefs and values (Rom. 12:2). Such worldview change is necessary in all cultures, including those with a long Christian heritage. No culture can claim to have perfectly embodied a biblical worldview. All cultures remain fallen and have blind spots. This leads us to the attitude of the cross-cultural teacher.

The Disposition of the Teacher

Cross-cultural teachers who seek to facilitate worldview change must begin with a spirit of humility and take a careful, self-critical look at their own worldview. James Sire writes, "For any of us to be fully conscious intellectually we should not only be able to detect the worldview of others, but be aware of our own—why it is ours and why in the light of so many options we think it is true" (2015, 14). It is natural to think that one's own worldview is correct—it's just "the way things are." We acquire our worldview unconsciously, usually without questions or reflection. We are quick to assume others are just wrong.

---

1. See https://henrycenter.tiu.edu/witchcraft-accusations.
2. For a discussion of the basic contours of a biblical worldview, see "Toward a Biblical Worldview," chapter 10 in Hiebert's *Transforming Worldviews* (2008, 265–305).

Humility entails awareness that our worldview, like others, is shaped by many positive and negative factors, and the lens through which we see the world is also tinted. No worldview is perfect. We must have the humility to learn from others the distortions and imbalances in our own worldview.

Christians look to the Bible to form a worldview and attempt to see the world as God sees it. However, we read the Bible in part through our culturally tinted lens; our understandings are imperfect. Examples of this are given in books such as *Misreading Scripture with Western Eyes* (Richards and O'Brien 2012) and *Misreading Scripture with Individualist Eyes* (Richards and James 2020). We must continually allow the Bible's teaching to correct our worldview. Listening carefully to those from other cultures, who often read the Bible differently than we do, can be a corrective that uncovers our false assumptions and blind spots. Due to our fallen human nature, on this side of heaven no one group of Christians will arrive at the perfect Christian worldview. Although Christians may differ in the details of their interpretation of the Bible and its implications, the basic contours of a biblical worldview are there for all to discover.[3]

The pursuit of growth in wisdom, understanding, and worldview change must proceed in a spirit of humility on the part of both teacher and learner. Not only must the teacher begin in a spirit of humility, but she must also be patient to first understand the worldview of the people she is teaching. Countless examples could be told of the failure of missionaries to understand the worldview of a people before attempting to communicate the gospel. The people then interpret the message through the grid of their worldview, which leads not only to misunderstanding but also to syncretism: elements of the Christian message are embraced but then mixed with non-Christian beliefs and practices in ways that compromise the biblical message. Facilitating worldview change among learners will surely miss the mark if the worldview of the learners is not first understood from their perspective.

The Process of Worldview Change

Logical arguments alone seldom alter a person's deeply held convictions about reality and what matters in life. A holistic approach to effecting worldview change must be taken that touches on a person or people's mind, emotions, and experiences. For this reason, the following discussion of cognitive approaches, spiritual approaches, and communal approaches draws convenient, but admittedly somewhat artificial, distinctions. The approaches clearly overlap in practice.

3. For a response to the argument that the Bible contains multiple worldviews and there is no unified biblical worldview, see Hiebert 2008, 265–68, and Naugle 2002, 253–90.

Worldview change occurs most often in one of two ways: incrementally or abruptly. Incremental change takes place over time as people become exposed to new information, new technologies, and social change. Such change is often subconscious. For example, rapid economic development in China has weakened Confucian values regarding teaching (Meng et al. 2017). Global migration brings people into contact with others who have different values and perspectives on life. Abrupt worldview change is often prompted by a dramatic experience, whereby a person comes to realize that the way they have understood the world so far can no longer account for their present experience. They become aware that their worldview must change. A Copernican revolution in perspective occurs. The experience of conflict or tension between an existing worldview and the need for a new one can be described as disequilibration, which will be discussed below.

Because a worldview provides a sense of security in making sense of our lives and validating our cultural norms, worldview change can feel threatening and is often resisted, at least at first. The gap between teacher and learner in this regard is sometimes extremely difficult to overcome. Learners may dismiss the teacher's approach as naive or uninformed (see sidebar 8.1).

Facilitating worldview change is thus a sensitive process that must be approached with humility, wisdom, and patience. A starting point is to help learners become more aware of their worldview, particularly their nonreflective beliefs. But most teachers will want to go further and help learners explore alternatives and help them discover a more biblical worldview. What

---

SIDEBAR 8.1

Enlightened or Clueless?

I received this email from a German instructor teaching at one of West Africa's leading theological seminaries:

> A problem has arisen this week that appears impossible to manage. We discussed the animistic worldview, explaining everything with examples from our region, and contrasted it with theistic and secular worldviews. We also worked through the relevant literature.
>
> At the end a group of future pastors said to me, "You are simply a European.

You can say what you want, but behind everything that occurs is either a good or evil spirit. Nothing is without this cause-effect relationship."
>
> When I pointed to the Bible and various examples of spiritual powers being defeated by Christ, they did not appear convinced. They replied, "Africa is just different. Whoever says otherwise is simply clueless."
>
> So, there I was: stuck and speechless. Not all of the students were of this opinion, but one could sense that these were entirely new concepts for them.

is essential in this process is that learners themselves become aware of the need for change and work through the alternatives without coercion or the teacher providing quick answers.

Cognitive Approaches

Cognitive approaches are those that appeal to the mind, such as logical reasoning, the critical examination of competing truth claims, and most importantly, understanding biblical teaching.

Biblical Instruction

The Bible teaches, "Do not conform to the pattern of this world, but be transformed by the renewing of your mind. Then you will be able to test and approve what God's will is—his good, pleasing and perfect will" (Rom. 12:2). There is no substitute for the study of Scripture and meditation upon it to transform the mind and lifestyle. Scripture addresses the great questions of God, creation, humanity, good and evil, life, death, suffering, the course of history, and more. Perhaps most importantly, it connects us with God, as the Holy Spirit speaks to us through that living Word, applying it to our hearts and minds.

In the words of David K. Naugle, "'Worldview' in a Christian perspective implies the objective existence of the trinitarian God whose essential character establishes the moral order of the universe and whose word, wisdom and law define and govern all aspects of created existence" (2002, 260). It is from such biblical premises that we move forward together in humility, seeking as both teacher and learner to grow in the knowledge of God and the world and to conform our thoughts, heart, and actions to his will. As noted above, our interpretation of the Bible will be influenced by our tradition, history, experience, and reason, but this does not mean that the central contours of the biblical worldview are inaccessible or entirely constructed by the reader. A global conversation will help us to read the Bible from multiple perspectives and come to a fuller understanding (Ott and Netland 2006; Greenman and Green 2012). To stimulate worldview change, a dialogical approach, whereby learners themselves wrestle with the implications of biblical teaching for their daily lives, is essential.

The Bible is composed of diverse literary genres: history, law, poetry, prophecy, epistolary, apocalyptic, and so on. It is thus able to speak to a variety of cultures. Cross-cultural teachers should be sure to include the fullness of biblical literature in their teaching. Tom Steffen found in his work with the Ifuago people in the Philippines that even the genealogies were an important element in establishing the credibility of the Bible (Steffen 1993b, 193; 2018, 69).

Narrative: The Power of Stories

It's often been said that humans are storytelling creatures. Recent understandings of worldview have come to see that they are nearly always embodied and passed on in stories.

In chapter 5 we discussed the importance of narrative teaching for concrete learners. Here we examine narrative a means of stimulating worldview change. Grand narratives give our world meaning and our lives direction. They tell us what really matters and how life works. Grand narratives tell us who is a hero and who is a villain; who is a victim and who is a victor; whether life is fundamentally fair or unfair; what is worthy of praise and what is not; how to cope with life's challenges, victories, and defeats, and more.

As we have already seen, storytelling is one of the most powerful communicative methods; it captures heart and mind. Stories stimulate the imagination, touch the emotions, underscore values, emulate behaviors, and interpret human experience, all of which are core to reinforcing a worldview, influencing attitudes, and directing behaviors. The events of life are understood by placing them in the larger narrative of life. Community health workers and environmentalists, among others, have discovered the value of storytelling to tap into indigenous worldviews and influence behavior (e.g., Hodge et al. 2002; Fernández-Llamazares and Cabeza 2017).

Cultures with a more abstract or rationalistic approach to understanding life can easily overlook the power of stories to shape worldview. But even in the most rationalistic societies, stories are impactful in ways that rational arguments cannot be. We see evidence in the popularity of paperback novels, television dramas, and Hollywood movies. They have exercised enormous influence in shaping public discourse and opinion on a host of issues from gay rights to defining the "good life" (see sidebar 8.2). "The mythical structures of images and behavior are widely used by mass media to affect the society as well as certain groups" (Issina and Serebryakova 2013, 165). *Harry Potter*, *Star Wars*, and *The Lord of the Rings* provide modern mythic narratives and archetypal images. Precisely because they are fictitious and make no factual claims, their depiction of ideals (such as heroes, values, and cosmology) is more readily accepted and often subconsciously assimilated. Implicit or nonreflective narratives influence our opinions and sense of justice—for example, our views on whether capitalism is a liberating or an oppressive economic system (Haidt 2014).

If we want to facilitate worldview change, then storytelling will be one of the most powerful means. Social psychologist Jonathan Haidt is not entirely exaggerating when he says,

> You can't really convince people on moral and political issues by giving them facts. And the reason is because human reasoning does not take place in a logical

SIDEBAR 8.2

The Power of a Story to Change Society

The PBS *American Experience* film documentary *The Poison Squad* recounts the story of the battle for food safety in America. Until 1906 there was no government regulation of food production in the United States. Poisonous chemicals, including copper sulfate, salicylic acid, and formaldehyde (known as an embalming fluid), were used as preservatives. Not only was milk heavily diluted with water, but plaster of Paris or chalk was added to keep it white, formaldehyde was added as a preservative, and it was often laden with bacteria. This resulted in the deaths of thousands of children.

Food safety advocates, led by chemist Harvey Washington Wiley, attempted for decades to raise public awareness and see legislation passed to protect consumers. There was even a widely publicized "poison squad" of volunteers who participated in human trials to document the health hazards of commonly used food preservatives. Despite this, the food manufacturers' lobby was too powerful, and Congress could not be persuaded to pass legislation. Overwhelming scientific evidence of the dangers was not enough to make a difference.

What finally turned public opinion so powerfully that Congress was compelled to act? A story. In 1906 Upton Sinclair released the novel *The Jungle*, which told the story of meat-packers in Chicago and the horrific conditions of the slaughterhouses.

The purpose of the book was primarily to raise public awareness of working conditions and worker's rights, advocating for socialism. But the real impact

Poster advertising *The Jungle*

Source: Library of Congress, https://www.loc.gov/resource/ppmsca.13488

was to alert the public to the unsanitary conditions of food production. Within six weeks the book sold 25,000 copies. Public outrage was so great that by the end of the year Congress had to act, passing the Meat Inspection Act and the Pure Food and Drug Act in 1906.

What simple facts, scientific studies, and even human tragedy were not able to accomplish, a compelling and heart-wrenching—or better, stomach-wrenching—story was able to accomplish, ultimately saving lives and improving the health of an entire nation. That's the power of a story well told.

Source: www.pbs.org/wgbh/americanexperience/films/poison-squad/#part01 and www.pbssocal.org/programs/american-experience/the-poison-squad-5sf93j.

world based on facts; it takes place in an emotional world based on stories. And we don't even write these stories. We imbibe them; we drink them in as we grow up. We may not even be able to tell them ourselves. (2014)

Stories may be implicit, but more often they come in the form of explicit myths, legends, biographies, histories, literature, film, dreams, or symbolic actions that embody, illustrate, and reinforce the worldview. Tom Steffen states,

> Stories create, maintain, and change world views. People express beliefs and behavior based on stories from parents, relatives, strangers, friends, enemies, and for some, animals. Stories influence how a person views and participates in the world. . . . Stories are much more than fiction. They are symbols and metaphors of reality because they create and shape reality; they are the articulated values and philosophies of communities. (Steffen 2005, 13)

Take, for example, Neville Bartle's experience as a missionary in Papua New Guinea. In his book *Death, Witchcraft and the Spirit World in the Highlands of Papua New Guinea*, he writes about how myths play an important role in forming a worldview:

> Myths are multi-functional. They explain the universe, nature and the customs of society in ways people can easily remember and understand. Stories are entertaining. They are told around the fire at night. The glow of the fire reflects off the face of the story teller, and the faces of the listeners. They do not hurry, for the sweet potatoes roast slowly in the depths of the accumulated ashes. The stories stretch out to fill in the evening, with no breaks for commercials. . . . Told and retold, they endure because they provide meaning and hope to life. (2005, 165)

Hiebert also writes of myths, calling them "the language not only of thought but of the imagination. They speak of things too hard for humans to bear by telling them these things indirectly. . . . It is because root myths are archetypes of human existence, told in story form, that they are so important in our attempts to understand worldviews" (2008, 83).

Stories not only reinforce cultural beliefs and values but also can challenge and transform them. In contemporary societies, stories have served as a powerful means to change social narratives of oppression. So-called counter-storytelling has been widely used as a pedagogical tool in education, psychology, and law to promote cooperative action and challenge racism and prejudice (e.g., Solórzano and Yosso 2002; Salter and Adams 2013; Brescia 2018). Alternative narratives can reframe one's perspective on reality, which can in turn reshape one's identity and sense of personal efficacy.

The Bible is first and foremost a story. It does not begin with philosophical axioms, ethical principles, or creedal formulations, although we find elements of this in the various genres of the Bible. Not only is approximately three-quarters of the biblical text narrative (story), but the thrust of the overall message of the Bible is framed in terms of a grand narrative that moves through creation, fall, redemption, and consummation. Human history has a starting point and an end. At the center of this story is a loving, righteous, sovereign God who gives all things meaning, to whom all creatures will give account, and who is carrying out a plan of redemption. That plan climaxes in the incarnation and work of Jesus Christ. Within this grand story are embedded many smaller stories, symbols, metaphors, poems, laws, rituals, discourses, miracles, visions, and exhortations. If our goal is greater conformity of our worldview to a biblical worldview, the use of stories must be central, not only because the Bible is full of stories but also because it presents a unifying grand narrative behind them. We saw in chapter 5 how Bible-storying has become an important approach not only in oral cultures but with all people to shape a grand narrative of God. In the telling of this story, a biblical worldview is vividly crafted, describing God's nature played out in creation, in his sovereign action in history and redemption, and ultimately in human lives.

We need to tell not only the biblical story but also new stories that reinforce and compellingly illustrate a biblical worldview. Fantasy stories such as Tolkien's Lord of the Rings trilogy or C. S. Lewis's Chronicles of Narnia series have become especially powerful in addressing the themes of worldview. Popular fiction, such as Frank E. Peretti's *This Present Darkness* and William Paul Young's *The Shack*, despite their questionable literary quality and theological accuracy, have influenced millions of readers, stimulating their imaginations to reconsider many aspects of life and spirituality. Bartle writes,

> If we Christian communicators want to change a people world-view so that it reflects Christian values, then we will have to tell them a life changing story . . . that links the power of God with human problems. It must be a story that is cosmic and yet relates to local issues. It must be a story that people can identify with, remember and which will have a life changing impact. (2005, 185)

Terry Schultz, missionary among the Chayahuita people in Peru, created comics to address in story form topics such as white magic (see fig. 8.1). Lesson plans consist of simple drawings that illustrate a familiar plotline in a contemporary setting. The lesson concludes with relevant Bible passages that stimulate reflection on the worldview behind the issue. In this way, lived reality and worldview are addressed in a way that is accessible, relevant, and interesting for the readers.

FIGURE 8.1

A sample comic used to address white magic among the Chayahuita people in Peru

Photo courtesy of Terry Schultz

Above is a sample page from the comic book "What's Wrong with White Magic?" The caption reads: The Christian father is thinking, "The gifted shaman is helping me. He's involved in my problem. He's healing my son! *God seems so distant and uninvolved*; otherwise he would have answered my prayers and healed my son! The only one who responded to my need to save my son was the gifted shaman." Tangoa pointed out, "The Christian father forgot what the Bible teaches in Psalm 125:2: 'As the mountains surround Jerusalem, so the Lord surrounds his people both now and forevermore.' God is never distant or uninvolved with his children!"

Enacting stories in the form of drama, dance, film, or visual arts can increase the impact of the story. "Storytelling need not be a strictly oral process. . . . Just as our ancestors created stories on skins and on rock walls, we can tell our stories in visual or embodied ways. Artistic expression can unlock a part of the brain where stories reside but are not in our immediate conscious awareness" (Lawrence and Paige 2016, 69). Music and ballads that tell a story also have affective impact.

Disequilibration and Worldview Change

Disequilibration is a term for the upsetting of equilibrium. Picture a gymnast walking on a balance beam: suddenly the beam shifts under her feet. She then loses equilibrium and either falls to the ground or adjusts her equilibrium to the new position of the beam to stay on it. Jean Piaget used the term to describe how a child develops cognitively when she encounters experiences that do not fit her mental structure of understanding the world. She must modify or replace that mental structure with one that can better explain the phenomenon and restore mental equilibrium. For example, let us say that this child believes that the height of a glass determines its volume; the taller the glass, the more water it holds (former scheme). But she begins to notice that a shorter glass might actually hold more water than a taller glass. This experience creates a cognitive disequilibrium. Equilibrium is reestablished by adopting a new interpretive scheme that assimilates and makes sense of the conflicting information. In this case, eventually the child realizes that both diameter and height need to be taken into account to determine the volume of a glass (the new scheme).[4]

Similarly, worldview change often occurs when a person encounters information or experiences that contradict his worldview. That person's former worldview will be found inadequate to explain the world in which he lives. This is why people often become more open to questions of faith when they face life crises. Hiebert describes the process this way: "Normal transformations in worldviews are precipitated by surface contradictions, life's dilemmas, and new experiences that cannot be resolved by simply acquiring more information, enhancing problem-solving skills, or adding to one's competencies. Resolution to these dilemmas requires a change in our worldviews" (2008, 316). Thomas Kuhn's "paradigm shifts" (1996) and Jack Mezirow's "transformative learning theory" (1991) describe, in different terms, a similar phenomenon.

Educators James Foster and Glenn Moran (1985) make a fascinating connection between disequilibration and the teachings of Jesus. They point out that Jesus's parables were seldom simple illustrations; rather, they typically had a surprise element: the settings and characters of the parables were familiar to his listeners (a vineyard, day labor, shepherds, etc.), but the story line presented a situation that challenged their "common sense" understandings. For example, it was a disdained Samaritan, not a priest or Levite, who demonstrated love of neighbor in the parable of the good Samaritan (Luke 10:25–37). In the parable of the workers in the vineyard all the laborers were paid the same amount, although some had worked many hours and others only a few (Matt. 20:1–16). These parables disequilibrated and sometimes angered the listeners. The intended effect was to expose the flaws in a legalistic religion and prompt hearers to reconsider what it means to truly love one's neighbor or how they understood God's grace.

4. For a demonstration of this, see https://youtu.be/YtLEWVu815o.

Sometimes people deal with disequilibration by reinterpreting new information or experience to fit their scheme or worldview. For example, because Jesus's opponents were not willing to accept that he was sent by God, they posited that he cast out demons by the power of Beelzebul. Despite Jesus's exposure of the flaw in their logic, they stubbornly refused to change their minds (Mark 3:22–27). This is common: people everywhere naturally to attempt to fit new information into their existing scheme or worldview. To foster worldview change, the cross-cultural teacher must develop creative teaching methods that expose learners to ideas and experiences that cause them to reconsider their assumptions. One suggestion is to present the learner with a series of problems of increasing difficulty that cannot be solved on the basis of the person's worldview (Foster and Moran 1985, 100). Writing new parables, designing experiential learning exercises, and exposing learners to diverse opinions are just a few ideas. Whatever method one employs, it is important for the learners themselves to wrestle through the dilemma and arrive at their own conclusion that their current worldview is inadequate. At that point alternatives can be presented and explored. If learners do not sense the need for change, the alternatives will be either rejected or adopted at only a superficial level, while the nonreflective aspects of their worldview remain unchanged.

Spiritual Approaches

Of course, teaching the Bible is itself a spiritual approach, but focusing more intentionally on the spiritual dimension brings the supernatural working of God in a person's heart and mind more into view. A biblical worldview must take the spiritual dimension of life seriously. God is active in the world and in people's lives. The kind of worldview change we are discussing is one that ultimately only the Holy Spirit can accomplish. The previous discussion noted the importance of teaching the Bible as God's supernatural revelation. Here we will briefly discuss the role of prayer and encounters with spiritual power as ways in which God supernaturally enlightens people's eyes to new realities and opens the window of their minds to see reality as God sees it.

Prayer

The transformation of heart and mind so central to worldview transformation begins with forgiveness and renewal through faith in Jesus Christ and grows through the work of the Holy Spirit. This cannot be humanly manufactured or manipulated. Therefore, prayer for ourselves and the people we teach, calling upon God to transform our worldviews, will be essential. This is evident in the apostle Paul's prayers, such as his prayer for the Colossian believers: "We continually ask God to fill you with the knowledge of his will through all the wisdom and understanding that the Spirit gives, so that you may live a life worthy of the Lord and please him in every way" (Col. 1:9–10a). Ironically, it no doubt belies a flaw in many modern Christians' worldview who pray so little and depend so heavily upon human means in developing spiritual growth in themselves and others. One may superficially acknowledge the importance of prayer, but one's lack of actual prayer and lack of faith that God will be at work through it evidences that this truth has hardly taken hold at the deeper worldview level.

Power Encounters

Sometimes so-called spiritual *power encounters* precipitate worldview change. When Boniface, the eighth-century missionary to Germany, cut down the sacred Oak of Thor, the pagan Hessians believed he would surely be struck dead by lightning. When that did not occur, their beliefs about Thor were shattered; in Piagetian terms, they experienced disequilibration. Their worldview about the gods collapsed. Boniface even went on to build a church from the wood of that oak![5] This led to their conversion to Christianity. We are reminded of the prophet Elijah challenging the prophets of Baal and the apostles casting out demons. Alan Tippett (1967, 100–118) documented how such power encounters have often been an important part of conversion and worldview transformation among adherents to traditional folk religions. However, Tippet notes, missionaries rarely initiated the encounters; rather, local people themselves destroyed their fetishes and sacred objects in ritual manner, symbolically marking a new day (106). He contends that the public nature of such acts is particularly important, which leads us to the next point.

Communal Approaches

Because most Western teachers come from more individualistic cultures and have a more cognitive way of looking at life, they easily overlook the importance of community in forming a people's worldview. Communities provide common experiences, social reinforcement, and role models that exemplify the beliefs and behaviors of a worldview. All cultures have rituals, symbols,

---

5. Willibald, *The Life of St. Boniface*, in *The Anglo-Saxon Missionaries in Germany, Being the Lives of SS. Willibrord, Boniface, Leoba and Lebuin Together with the Hodoepericon of St. Willibald and a Selection from the Correspondence of St. Boniface*, trans. C. H. Talbot (London: Sheed and Ward, 1954), chap. 6, available at https://sourcebooks.fordham.edu/basis/willibald-boniface.asp.

and ceremonies that visually or physically embody such beliefs and behaviors. They serve to solidify a social bond and act as instructional aids.

Experiencing Community and Observing Role Models

One way that learners can become more aware of their own worldview is to expose them to others—not merely in theory, but by meeting people with different worldviews. The Christian church is a community of believers seeking to come to a greater understanding of a biblical worldview and its implications for daily life. As Christians live together, discuss together, and read Scripture together, a mutual learning and transformation takes place. Remember, a worldview is more than a philosophy or belief system; it involves the whole of life: thought, emotions, and behaviors. In all cultures, but especially in collectivistic cultures, a community of peers is a powerful context for personal change. It can be especially helpful for concrete learners to experience what it means to view the world biblically and live accordingly.

In the community there will be also role models of people living out a Christian worldview. Ideally the teacher is such a role model. Christian liberal arts colleges often claim to teach all subjects from the perspective of a Christian worldview. But what does it mean to teach history or biology or literature from the perspective of a Christian worldview? (See Dockery and Thornbury 2002.) Too few teachers have carefully thought this through. By cognitive modeling and explaining more explicitly their thought processes and the underlying reasoning, teachers can help students begin to see what a difference a biblical worldview can make in all aspects of life.

Empowerment through Encouragement and Hope

In the previous chapter we saw how learner motivation is stifled by a worldview that claims that hard work does not pay, that fate alone will determine one's future, or that one is fundamentally incapable of learning. Along with a biblical view of human potential, the encouragement of a supportive community with regular affirmation will go a long way in creating a more hopeful outlook and a shift in worldview.

The film *Freedom Writers* is based on the true story of high school teacher Erin Gruwell, who bridged cultural and social gaps and overcame countless obstacles to reach her urban ethnic minority students. Many of them were involved in street gangs, came from broken families, had experienced violence, saw little hope for a brighter future, and were convinced that they could not succeed in school. Dropout rates were high. Remarkably, Gruwell was able to motivate her students to learn and even to excel. She didn't accomplish this by merely developing creative teaching methods. She built trust, created hope, instilled a sense of dignity and value, and changed the dominant narrative of pessimism and failure. Many went on not only to graduate from high school but also to attend college, some even completing graduate degrees.[6]

Schools and churches can be places of hope and encouragement, creating an environment of empowerment and affirmation: a living contradiction to defeatist narratives that dominate many learners' worldviews and cultural expectations. Such change does not come through words alone but must include practical support, exposure to personal testimonies of change, sacrifice, and the opportunity for incremental successes.

Rituals, Symbols, and Ceremonies

Hiebert (2008, 322–24) has argued that creating "living rituals" is another way to facilitate worldview transformation. These rituals are typically shared and practiced by the community. As described by Kathleen E. Fite and John L. Garcia,

> Ritual is one of the ways individuals make sense of the vastness and awe-evoking nature of the world in which we find ourselves; establish a symbolic connection with our ancestors and something greater and more universal than ourselves; feel soothed and validated by the constancy of human experience; ameliorate our isolation; and play a personal role with others in human and civil anthropology. (2006, 77)

All societies have rituals that embody cultural values. Think, for example, of saluting the national flag and singing the national anthem to instill patriotism and reinforce national identity. Or consider how school graduation ceremonies underscore the value of education, serve as a rite of passage, and are an occasion to affirm family solidarity. All societies have rituals related to birth, marriage, and death that mark key transitions in life. Baptism is such a Christian ritual, marking new life in Christ. The Lord's Table is another ceremony that regularly underscores the nature of the salvation that Christ purchased on the cross. These and other Christian rituals reinforce and illustrate beliefs and values of a worldview. Rituals are "social performances" that embody values and beliefs (Alexander, Giesen, and Mast 2006). "Ritual performance encourages personal-collective transformation through physical and emotional elements, often underestimated and overlooked by

---

6. I had the privilege of mentoring a PhD student who was one of the original "freedom writers" depicted in the film. Growing up often homeless and in a violent environment, he nearly dropped out of school. But eventually he graduated from the University of California (Berkeley), completed a master of divinity degree, and eventually entered a doctoral program.

SIDEBAR 8.3

A Kenyan Burial Ceremony

David Kimiri Ngaruiya describes here a traditional burial ceremony of the Luo people of Kenya and its potential use in churches of Kenya. By planting a tree, the memory of the deceased is kept alive.

> A tree symbolically conveys deep meaning of rootedness and life. Ecologically, tree planting is healing to a deforested and eroded environment. In this connection, one can draw some parallels between a life shattered by bereavement and earth depleted by erosion due to tree loss. Erosion worsens a deforested earth just as bereavement worsens the life of the bereaved. A deforested earth looks bare just as the life of a bereaved person is bare from the relationship lost. A deforested earth is "healed" by tree planting just as the loss of a human life can be "healed" by cultivation of a new relationship as would be appropriate in a given situation. It requires a worker to nurture a tree to grow, just as it should take a mentor or an encourager to help the bereaved person nurture a relationship. Thus, the church can utilize tree planting as a healing ritual for the bereaved Christian.
>
> A church tree planting ritual can also be an idea that the church can export to the wider Kenyan culture. Among the Luos, for example, the family plants a banana tree on the grave of a barren woman. Luos shun barrenness and the banana planting is a ritual to protect the life of those bereaved from angry spirits. The church, too, can export helpful rituals to surrounding communities. (Ngaruiya 2008, 248–49)

researchers more focused on cognitive interpretations" (Steffen 2018, 166). Matthias Zahniser has argued that most cultures see symbols and ceremonies as indispensable parts of life. He boldly proposes a contextualized use of symbols and ceremonies, writing: "Christian Scripture contains a rich heritage of symbols. These can be associated with appropriate symbols familiar to believers from traditional religious cultures and used to integrate their world and that of Scripture into a holistic Christian application of faith to life" (1997, 13). (For a discussion of the use of rituals in disciple making, see Moon 2017, 90–110.)

Many cultures have rites of passage: for example, when boys become recognized as men and girls become recognized as women. In the West we think of school graduations and wedding ceremonies as ritualized life transition markers. Many non-Western societies have coming-of-age rituals that are infused with occult rituals or harmful practices such as female genital cutting. By creating a Christian substitute for such rites, the new ceremony can become a teaching tool (e.g., to instill biblical understandings for manhood and womanhood). For an example of this, see sidebar 8.3.

Conclusion

Because both teachers and learners are consciously and subconsciously influenced by their worldviews, it is essential for both to take worldview into consideration for learning. This chapter has only scratched the surface of this complex topic. One's worldview affects the goals, motivation, style, and content of learning. Especially when teacher and learner are from different cultures, confusion or conflict will be inevitable if worldview factors are not accounted for. This will be all the more important when teaching has as its objective worldview change. Although teaching for worldview change is perhaps one of the most challenging tasks a teacher can face, it is not impossible. Effectiveness will depend in part on utilizing some of the teaching methods described here, but also must proceed in a spirit of humility and dependency on God's supernatural working in everyone's hearts and minds through the Word of God and prayer.

The Social Dimension

Part 1: The Influence of Social Hierarchy

Teaching and learning are all about teachers and learners interacting with one another. Whether that interaction is formal or informal, in class or out, culture dictates which kind of interactions are appropriate and which are not. When those cultural norms for social intercourse between teacher and learner do not match, there is a strong likelihood of irritation or misunderstanding at best, catastrophe or disciplinary action at worst. Consider these examples:

> An American teacher at a foreign-language institute in Beijing exclaimed in class, "You lovely girls, I love you." Her students, according to a Chinese observer, were terrified. An Italian professor teaching in the United States complained bitterly about the fact that students were asked to formally evaluate his course. He did not think that students should be the judges of the quality of a professor. An Indian lecturer at an African university saw a student arrive six weeks late for the curriculum, but he had to admit him because he was from the same village as the dean. (Hofstede, Hofstede, and Minkov 2010, 393)

Navigating relationships between teacher and student is perhaps *the* most essential skill the cross-cultural teacher needs to be effective. Many missteps and misunderstandings can be reconciled when relationships are healthy and strong. But where relationships are strained and expectations unmet, and the sojourner doesn't know how to correct them, then the consequences can be

<aside>
CHAPTER OVERVIEW

- The Importance of Social Relations for Effective Teaching
- The Nature of Status, Hierarchy, and Authority
- The Role of Status
- Authority and Student-Teacher Interactions
- Patron-Client Relationships
- From Authority-Based to Critical-Reflective Learning
</aside>

FIGURE 9.1

Five dimensions of culture's influence on teaching and learning

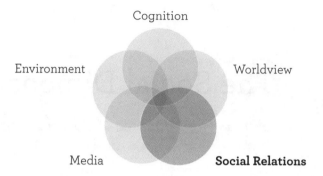

Cognition

Environment   Worldview

Media   **Social Relations**

dire. In this chapter and the next one we will look at the ways social relations and expectations shape the teaching/learning experience—the third dimension of how culture influences teaching and learning.

In this chapter we will examine how various expressions of social hierarchy, status, and authority influence teaching and learning. In chapter 10 we will take up how collectivism and individualism have an influence, which will include the related topic of shame and honor.

The Importance of Social Relations for Effective Teaching

Teachers who are more task oriented and individualistic can easily overlook how important harmonious and amiable social relationships are to student learning. Students who feel uncomfortable with the teacher or with each other will be distracted at best, and perhaps even blocked from learning altogether. Field-dependent and collectivistic learners are most impacted (positively or negatively) by the social environment. Furthermore, culture largely defines what relationships are considered appropriate, and what people find to be a comfortable, safe social atmosphere. A cross-cultural teacher may not even realize that she is creating a relational learning environment that is disadvantageous for effective teaching and learning.

In more individualistic cultures there is a tendency for students to rate teachers as "good" on the basis of classroom competencies such as the ability to explain clearly and answer questions, while more collectivistic cultures place high value on qualities such as being friendly and a good moral example (Cortazzi and Jin 2001). In some cultures, a harmonious classroom atmosphere and warm teacher-student relationships are imperative to learning. Delbert Chinchen describes his experience and research with college students in Liberia and Malawi:

> The student with a relational cognitive style needs to determine if the facts known by the teacher are also owned by the teacher before genuine learning can take place. A relationship with the teacher is necessary in order for the student to ascertain this. The student without a relationship with the teacher may learn facts, but the learning will often be void of meaning. Linking up with the teacher through a personal relationship enables the student's knowledge to be translated into learning. (1997, 324)

A study of how Chinese undergraduate students describe their best and worst professors found that although competence in knowledge and instruction were important, the relational aspects were no less important.

> Over one-third of the students specify care as one of the key teacher qualities. Favorite teachers are regarded as those who demonstrate concern and patience, are encouraging and responsible, and relate well with students. . . . Least favorite teachers are those who do not show any care or concern for students and are perceived as being irresponsible. . . . Almost three-quarters of the students describe the personality of their favorite or least favorite teachers. (Tam, Heng, and Jiang 2009, 152)

Favorite teachers were also viewed as "role models with heart." The comments of one of my Korean students in a note to me reflect a similar attitude: "You have been my pastor before becoming my professor. I want to resemble you in life and in ministry. I will pay back your love and grace by serving God's kingdom and loving God's people as you have lived and taught. Thank you!!!"

Among the first things that the cross-cultural teacher must discern are the various social expectations and obligations of the teaching context. This can be done initially through observation and conversation with local people. As always, every cross-cultural teacher will need to discover the specifics of the context in which they work. General descriptions of national profiles may not apply to the specific institution of work and may even be misleading. A helpful list of context-specific questions should be asked to determine local expectations. Here is a sampling of Jude Carroll's excellent list of such questions:

- How did students show respect to teachers?
- What titles and names were used?
- What place, if any, did gifts play?
- What was the purpose of gift giving?

- How were disagreements or difference of views between students and teachers managed? (2015, 32–33)

This is not to suggest that in every situation the cross-cultural teacher should conform 100 percent to the hosts' expectations. As we saw in chapter 3, as a teacher, Jesus did not meet the expectations that his contemporaries had of a Jewish rabbi. At times, Christian character calls one to a humble, serving posture and to relate to learners in ways that are countercultural. However, before naively attempting to be countercultural, the teacher should be sure that she properly understands the cultural norms for social interaction and has carefully weighed the costs and benefits of nonconforming behavior.

One's cultural bias influences which biblical ideals one emphasizes. Persons from more egalitarian societies prefer to quote Jesus's words in Matthew 20:25–26, "You know that the rulers of the Gentiles lord it over them, and their high officials exercise authority over them. Not so with you. Instead, whoever wants to become great among you must be your servant." But persons from more hierarchically oriented cultures prefer to quote 1 Timothy 5:17, "The elders who direct the affairs of the church well are worthy of double honor" and 1 Peter 5:5, "You who are younger, submit yourselves to your elders." As

---

SIDEBAR 9.1

A Question for Miss Yoshikawa

Theresa: "That was an excellent presentation. You and Dr. Nagai must have worked very hard on this."

Miss Yoshikawa: "I was very honored to be asked by Dr. Nagai to assist him on this project. He's my thesis advisor, you know."

Theresa: "Well, you were very good. He's lucky to have found you. I had a question about a point you made at the end."

Miss Yoshikawa: "Yes, of course. Let me just get Dr. Nagai."

Theresa: "Oh, don't bother him; he's talking to some other people. Anyway, it's about a point that you made."

Miss. Yoshikawa: "I see. Can I get you some tea?"

- How would you explain Miss Yoshikawa's behavior?
- How would you explain Theresa's behavior?
- What different expectations of social interaction and status are at play?
- How is each person coping with the failure to communicate?

Source: Craig Storti, *Cross-Cultural Dialogues: 74 Brief Encounters with Cultural Difference*, 2nd ed. (Boston: Intercultural Press, 2017). Reproduced by permission of Nicholas Brealey Publishing © 2017 Craig Storti.

a cultural outsider, it is easy to misjudge social norms of the host culture, not because they are contrary to biblical norms, but because their meanings are simply not understood in context. In any case, the good of the other person should be the highest priority (Phil. 2:3–4).

The Nature of Status, Hierarchy, and Authority

One of the most common sources of frustration in intercultural social relations regards the nature of social status, hierarchy, and authority. Showing too little deference to a person's status may be interpreted as disrespect or insubordination; showing too much deference may be interpreted as flattery or creating unnecessary social distance. In the reverse direction, *expecting* someone to show more respect may be interpreted as being prideful, authoritarian, or socially distant, while attempting to remove all social distance can be interpreted as undignified or inappropriate (especially when interacting with persons of the opposite gender). Sometimes an encounter can be just bewildering for both parties (see sidebar 9.1).

The Role of Status

All cultures have ways of differentiating between persons with high and low status. However, cultures differ in the marks of status, the characteristics that increase or decrease status, and the extent to which outward expressions of status are considered appropriate. Persons with higher status often have more privileges in society and generally receive more respect (though they may be resented by persons of lower status). Persons with lower status often face discrimination and other disadvantages in society. It has been demonstrated that "one's relative status has profound effects on attention, memory, and social interactions, as well as health and wellness" (Koski, Xie, and Olson 2015, 527). Very egalitarian societies may attempt to downplay the importance of status out of a desire to treat all people as equals. But Judith Lingenfelter and Sherwood Lingenfelter warn, "Some western teachers embrace the idea of building relationships but mistakenly conclude that the appropriate way of relating is as a peer or a friend" (2003, 42).

Status remains a feature of social life, even in the most egalitarian societies. In chapter 7 we considered how worldview relates to teacher credibility. The way that status is ascribed is often a key factor. Egalitarian societies tend to emphasize *achieved status* based upon a person's performance or accomplishments, whereas more hierarchical societies tend to emphasize *ascribed status* based upon inherent qualities over which the person has little control, such as age or being born into a certain family (see sidebar 9.2).

SIDEBAR 9.2

Exercise: Qualities That Determine a Person's Status in a Society

Read the following list of human characteristics and then complete the exercise below.

- education
- birth family
- income or wealth
- public awards
- skin color or tone
- occupation
- attractive bodily appearance
- clothing
- membership in certain clubs
- language, dialect, or accent
- titles
- religion
- place of residence
- age
- athleticism or bodily strength
- gender

- size of family (children or wives)
- diplomas or certificates
- width of hips (for a woman)

1. List the characteristics that would increase a person's status in your home culture.
2. Now list the characteristics that would increase a person's status in the host culture where you serve.
3. Read the two lists and note which qualities are forms of achieved status and which are forms of ascribed status.
4. What does this tell you about the nature of status attribution in your home culture and host culture?
5. Comparing the two lists, where do you see potential conflict or misunderstanding?

Cultures that are strongly hierarchically structured expect persons with lower status to show signs of respect to higher-status persons by use of titles, formal language, or grammar; performing services; and deference in decision-making. Lower-status persons may also be expected to use bodily postures that demonstrate recognition of status, such as bowing, standing up when the teacher enters the classroom, and certain forms of greeting. For example, young Malay students may avoid walking in front of their professors, bow slightly when walking past them, or kiss the teacher's hand when greeting them (Kamis and Muhammed 2007, 30; see also sidebar 9.3). On one occasion I spoke to a group of over one hundred Indian students. After speaking I took my seat, and the moderator dismissed the audience. I was preoccupied for a few minutes organizing my papers and then noticed that not a soul in the auditorium had moved. My host then leaned over to me and said, "They won't get up until they see you get up first." I promptly rose, and within seconds the auditorium was empty!

The Thai Experience

A person who grew up in rural Thailand described her school experience there this way:

> Buddha reigns above all, then comes the Emperor, and after that come parents and teachers. These four groups demand reverent respect. Practically, that means that when children approach a teacher, they must bow down deeply before him or her. Should they refuse to do so, they will later be brought before the entire class and struck with a bamboo rod. The parents do not interfere with such discipline, and often support it. (Klotz 2000)

Although this may not be the case everywhere in Thailand today, corporal punishment is not uncommon in many parts of the world. Parents typically side with the teacher out of respect for the teacher's authority. It would be unthinkable for parents to file a complaint against a teacher in support of their child. A deep reverence for the person of the teacher is instilled in children, which remains through adulthood.

Such respect can carry on even into university study. An American professor teaching in Thailand recounts this experience with the *wai khruu* ceremony:

> Today, Thai students paid homage to their professors. It was a symbolic celebration which after teaching American students for fifteen years, I found astonishing. In a large room students crawled up, in the "kowtowing" manner of supplication, and gave beautiful floral offerings to their professors. Their choral chants asked for blessings and expressed gratitude. Their speeches asked forgiveness for any disrespect or non-fulfillment of expectations. They promised to work diligently. (George 1995, 6)

In certain situations, eye contact is particularly confusing. In the West, direct eye contact is generally considered respectful and a sign of paying attention. But in many Asian cultures, direct eye contact can be considered disrespectful, prideful, or a sign of defiance. The body language of a professor can be a huge distraction to learners if he is acting in a way considered undignified—for example, if he walks around the classroom during a lecture, sits on a desk, puts his foot on a chair, or uses his left hand to point something out.[1] This was the experience of Teri McCarthy teaching in China: "She initially believed that as a teacher she needed to walk around the classroom, moving among the students to make connections and to hold their attention. She had always been taught that way. . . . Little did she know that her students were completely unable to

1. Showing the underside of one's feet is considered an insult in some cultures. Shoes are often considered very dirty, and should never touch furniture. In some places shoes should be removed, even in a classroom. Some cultures consider the left hand unclean and suitable for only one use. This can be a challenge for left-handed teachers who gesticulate naturally with the left hand.

learn because they were so uncomfortable with their teacher roaming around the classroom" (Romanowski and McCarthy 2009, 61–62).

Charlene Tan sees the Confucian worldview reflected in students' respect for the teacher, attention and discipline in class, and the importance of practice. This is expressed in a classic Chinese text, *Xueji* (Record of Learning). Accordingly, "the 'teacher dominated' pedagogy is believed by many Chinese educators to be indispensable for 'good' teaching" (C. Tan 2015, 197).

> It follows from the Chinese's notion of learning that a teacher is not just a content expert; he or she is also and should be respected as, a role model and moral guide. The cultural script of the students' respect for the teacher is manifested in daily classroom rituals (a reflection of Confucian propriety or *li*) such as standing up to greet the teacher, waiting to be called by the teacher before speaking in class, and sitting down only when instructed by the teacher. (200)

Tan continues, "The epistemological basis of the teacher as the transmitter and exemplar of the 'way,' coupled with a view of knowledge as residing in the canon and acquired through systematic tutelage, explains why teachers continue to be respected and play a prominent role in modern Chinese classrooms" (205).

Needless to say, cross-cultural teachers disregard such conventions at their own peril. Refusing to receive learners' gestures of respect may place the learners in an awkward situation and actually block learning (Chinchen 1997). One American professor teaching in India insisted that his students address him by his first name, without any title. This placed his students in a dilemma: to respect their professor, they must do as he requests; but the professor was requesting that they treat him disrespectfully (in their eyes)!

Status-related expectations extend to all kinds of matters of which the sojourner is often oblivious. One American professor in Korea had been using a very worn leather briefcase that was like an "old friend" to him. But when his hosts saw it, they gave him a very expensive new briefcase. The old one was not only undignified but gave the appearance that he was not being adequately paid. Or take the example of clothing. Some cultures expect high-status persons to dress differently: for example, a male teacher should wear a coat and tie, or a female teacher should wear a dress. This not only emphasizes the status of the teacher but is a sign of respect toward learners. Failure to dress formally might be judged as not taking one's role seriously or simply having little self-respect. Conversely, overdressing might be considered inappropriate in a more egalitarian setting. A Kenyan graduate assistant insisted on wearing a white shirt, tie, and dark suit for weekly lectures in an introductory course in a US college. This struck some American students as a mix of arrogance and taking himself too seriously, and it unnecessarily distanced him from the students. Improper attire can undermine a teacher's credibility and create too much or too little distance between teacher and learner. One study found that even the dress of a professor as he appears in an icon of an online course makes a difference. Americans preferred the image of the most casually dressed professor, but Sri Lankans and Moroccans preferred the image of the most formally dressed professor, stating their reasons as "professionalism," "seriousness and respect," and "appearance is key," factors that to them increased the professor's status and credibility (Knight, Gunawardena, and Aydin 2009, 28). Especially teachers on short-term cross-cultural assignments should inform themselves in advance of the appropriate attire for their role and save themselves the embarrassment of being over- or underdressed for the occasion.

One often challenging aspect of more hierarchically structured societies regards the appointing of leaders or promotion of workers: Should a person be promoted on the basis of competency or on the basis of attributed status, such as age or length of employment? In Western cultures, competency is generally seen as most important. But in more hierarchical cultures, if a more competent person is promoted over others who have higher status, that promoted lower-status person may not be respected by the others and thus be unable to function effectively in the new role. Team cohesion may also be threatened. Therefore, ways need to be found to honor those who have higher status, while allowing more competent but lower-status persons to also exercise their abilities. Here the advice of experienced cultural insiders is essential.

Authority and Student-Teacher Interactions

A widely used construct describing different cultural expectations regarding authority is *power distance*. The idea was developed and researched by Geert Hofstede, who defines it this way: "the extent to which the less powerful members of institutions and organizations within a country expect and accept that power is distributed unequally" (Hofstede, Hofstede, and Minkov 2010, 61). Hofstede's work was originally based upon a study of over 116,000 employees of IBM in seventy nations, and it is among the most widely cited source for cross-cultural comparisons. Hofstede's research and country profiles have been critiqued (e.g., Jones 2007; Signorini, Wiesemes, and Murphy 2009), and as discussed in chapter 2, we must avoid thinking in terms of homogenous national characteristics. Nevertheless, we know that in all societies power is distributed unequally and that some cultures consider such inequality more acceptable than others do. The perception of the use of authority also varies greatly in different cultures (e.g., Zhou, Lam, and Chan 2012). One study compared how American, Indian, Japanese, and Hong Kong Chinese working groups responded to authoritarian versus democratic leadership styles. It found that authoritarian leaders created a poor working atmosphere, lower motivation, and lower productivity with the American group. But the opposite was true of the other groups (Mann 1980).

Social Distance

Although teachers in many cultures are highly respected authority figures, this does not mean that students necessarily perceive them as cold or distant. While that might be the case in a Western setting, Asian students often speak of the great respect and honor that they have for their teachers, but in the same breath speak of their teachers as having had a motherly or fatherly relationship with them. Korean students have frequently remarked that although Korean professors are more formal in class, outside class they often take great personal interest in the students; whereas American professors are often more approachable in class but more distant outside of class. One study compared Hong Kong teachers with Australian teachers and found that in the classroom, Hong Kong teachers were more authoritarian than Australians, but outside the classroom they were more caring. For example, Hong Kong teachers often contact the student at home, which Australian teachers rarely do.

> Such contrasting relationships could be explained in terms of the complex nature of social roles and relationships in collectivistic cultures: in the formal class situation, the more formal and hierarchical relationship is in operation, which enables the teacher to be authoritarian and thus facilitates the teaching and learning process, whereas outside the classroom relationships are informal and the social climate could be warm. (Ho 2001, 108)

As an assignment for a course I was teaching, international students were interviewed about how they experience American professors. A Taiwanese student related that despite the high power distance between student and professor in Taiwan, the relationships between them often go deeper than in America: "For instance, students and professors may play games, go to eat, share dreams, and discuss future careers." A Nigerian student studying in America commented on the relationship between students and professors, declaring, "Too formal, too official!" He often had conversations with his Nigerian teachers about his family, children, and even dogs, but he reported that professors in America were more concerned about "What's your question?" He felt that American professors tended to "compartmentalize their relationships with students." He also lamented that in order to speak with an American professor, an appointment had to be booked in advance. Thus, despite the desire of many American professors to be informal, in fact they are often perceived as very professional and less approachable outside of class.

Class Participation

One facet of deference to the status or authority of a teacher can be that learners are reluctant to express contrary opinions or ask questions in class. A student speaking up in class can be viewed as disrespectful, assertive, or arrogant. For example, in a study of Arab Gulf State students in America, "a female participant could not explain Americans' eagerness to participate in the classroom. She felt they were 'showing off' or trying to appear 'smart'" (Al-Harthi 2005). This reluctance to speak up in class can be a challenge to teachers wanting to stimulate class discussion and critical thinking. A tutor attempting to guide group discussion with students in a Middle Eastern country experienced this:

> Every time they want to say something or to discuss anything, they look at me. I try to tell them not to look at me. I am not the center of the session, they are the center of the session. . . . But they still feel that the teacher should be the center of everything, should be the one to give the answers, and should be the one who has the upper hand on them. (Frambach et al. 2014, 1103)

"Critical thinking" is a somewhat foreign concept to many learners from high power distance or very traditional cultures. A Chinese graduate student in an English online course expressed it this way: "We have been asked to write several critical analyses. But, what does the word 'critical' mean here? Although I knew this term is very popular in the Western higher education, I never really catch what it exactly means, because in our country, such term seldom appears in the circle of education" (Dillon, Wang, and Tearle 2007, 165). Sidebar 9.5 at the end of this chapter illustrates how one teacher provocatively taught students to challenge his authority by intentionally teaching something contrary to an explicit teaching of the Bible. Students then needed to choose the authority of the Bible over the authority of the teacher.

We have already seen how Asian students are often perceived by Western teachers as passive because they are reluctant to speak up in class. Sometimes this is because the class is being conducted in a language that they are less comfortable speaking. In other cases the students are actually taking time to think about their answer. The teacher then becomes impatient and simply moves on. But in many cases it is in deference to the teacher. In the words of one Chinese student,

> If the teacher has already given his opinion in class, then I express mine, which I believe other students will buy because I experienced the similar situation before. What would happen to the teacher? It could put him in an embarrassing situation. Students would think he hasn't prepared his lessons well enough. This would jeopardize his image of an authoritative figure a teacher is supposed to have among the students. (Wu 2009, 100)

Western teachers should not think that seemingly passive behavior means that learning is only at surface level. As noted earlier, in international comparisons Asian students consistently outperform American students in science and math. "It appears that Chinese teachers are able to achieve good results in both student achievement and behavior with their authoritarian approach, and this raises doubts about the universality of humanistic approaches to education as advocated in the West, while at the same time making many Western theories appear irrelevant in the training of Asian teachers" (Ho 2001, 99). On the other hand, in the more egalitarian settings of most Western schools, an authoritarian approach is unlikely to have the same effectiveness.

Foreign-language teachers working with students to increase their vocabulary sometimes ask students what topics they want to discuss. The idea is that this will make instruction more relevant and increase student motivation. Often, however, students are bewildered by the question. They expect the teacher to know what the students need to know (Kleppin 1987). James Plueddemann relates this story of conflicting cultural expectations of students and a teacher.

> One of my American friends taught for many years at a theological seminary in Africa. When students asked him a question, he gave them ideas for how they could look up the information for themselves. He wanted to help them learn how to learn, while the students assumed his role was to give them answers. The teacher decided that the students were immature, and the students thought the teacher was not very competent. (2018, 14)

Students may feel that extended class discussions are just too informal and chaotic. One teacher, herself an Indian educated in England, attempted to use frequent class discussion when teaching in India. She was told that her class was like a coffee shop! Asking the teacher questions in class can be perceived negatively in several ways. For example, it may be construed as an admission that the student did not pay close attention or as an attempt to show off one's knowledge to other students. Sometimes it is considered out of place for students to ask questions of a teacher, because it could be understood as an indirect accusation that the teacher has not communicated clearly. It could embarrass the teacher if he is unable to answer the question, and the teacher would lose face. Romanowski and McCarthy write, "In some cultures it is inappropriate for the teacher to say, 'I don't know.' If asked a question that you don't know the answer to, respond this way: 'Great question. I want to give that question a full and meaningful answer. Let's not take time out today, but let's address it first thing tomorrow in depth.' Then go home and study like crazy to find the answer" (2009, 121).

Studies have demonstrated that Chinese classrooms are generally more teacher-centered and authoritarian than in the West. "The teacher, with the whole learning blueprint in mind, decides what to teach, and how to teach. . . . Teachers are expected to be actors, spending years preparing for the final stage performance in the classroom" (M. Li 2002, 16). One-way communication is the norm, and teachers control the learning. However, the same study found that Chinese students liked collaborative learning, even though they seldom experienced it. Thus, in such settings, the cross-cultural teacher might experiment with more participative methods that are less common, but appreciated.

Countless interviews with students from high power distance cultures in Africa, Latin America, and Asia consistently find that they generally prefer the more participative approach of Western teachers and professors who have a less strictly lecture-oriented approach. They value student discussion and the contributions of students. Students report that they felt that they learned the material better. At the same time, intensive discussion during which the teacher may ask students to answer questions can be experienced as very stressful.

Beware of Stereotypes

Here again stereotypes can be deceiving. For example, according to Hofstede's data, Singapore has a somewhat higher power distance value than Thailand, and Austria and Germany have much lower power distance values than either of the other countries. A comparative study of university students from these four counties is enlightening. Consistent with expectations, the Thai and Singaporean students had a higher preference for memorization than the Austrian and German students. But Thai students on average saw a greater status difference between themselves and their professors than did Singaporean students. In fact, Singaporean students saw less status difference in relation to professors than did German and Austrian students. These findings are inconsistent with expectations. And even more surprising, in spite of the higher perceived status difference, Thai students considered it more acceptable to criticize their professors than did students from Singapore (Apfelthaler et al. 2007). Two takeaways emerge from this study. First, country values for power distance may not be applicable to specific learning contexts. Students from an Asian country (in this case, Singapore) emphasized status less than students from supposedly more egalitarian European countries. Second, there is not always a direct correlation between perceived status difference and willingness to criticize a professor. The cross-cultural teacher will need to assess each context on its own merits and refrain from depending on stereotypes or broad generalizations in the literature.

Patron-Client Relationships

Patron-client relationships are a social system of interdependency whereby the patron is a resource person, provider, and protector to whom the client offers services in return. The patron is clearly in the position of power and authority but cannot conduct his business or achieve goals apart from the services or support of the client. Unlike an employer-employee relationship or other arrangement that is purely business, the patron is often in somewhat of a parental role, providing for personal needs of the client, and the client is in somewhat of a child role, giving loyalty to the patron. This concept of patronage, sometimes called clientelism, is most often applied to political or economic arrangements, but it can also be seen in educational contexts in both positive and negative ways.

Due to the unequal power distribution, the system is subject to abuse or corruption. Teachers can abuse their power over students, giving unfair preferential treatment to some, soliciting bribes, withholding or granting recommendations, or otherwise taking advantage of their role. Students may expect such favors when they perform services for the teacher. For example, the student may give the teacher a small gift—say, a jar of honey. The cross-cultural teacher may interpret this as a kind gesture of gratitude, but the student may be expecting the teacher to raise the grade on an exam in return. In contexts where teachers are poorly paid, such gifts or services may be an informal means of remuneration, but they can also place the teacher in a compromised position. However, gifts from students to teachers can also be an innocent gesture of gratitude. Korean students have been known to give lavish gifts to their professors without expecting anything in return.

The patron-client arrangement, when rightly understood and navigated in educational settings, can have a positive side. Chinchen's research involving Liberian and Malawian students underscores the importance of reciprocity in the teacher-student relationship, reflecting patron-client understandings. The teacher provides not only information but encouragement and personal care. Malawian university students describe their expectation of teachers in these statements:

"The teacher has the feeling of success on every pupil."
"My whole academic life is in his hands."
"He is the one upon which our success and brighter future dwells."
"He is determining my future."
"What we are is because of teachers."
"The teacher is the one who takes us out of our ignorance." (Chinchen 1997, 324)

One student said, "My parents said to me, as I was leaving home to go to school: 'You are no longer in our hands because you will spend much time with your teachers. Respect them as you do us because they are your second parents'" (326). Another Malawian said, "The teacher will gain respect from the student if he assumes the role of the father" (327). The consensus among the students was that the more the student respects the teacher, the more they are able to learn. Half of Liberian and Malawian students expected teachers to visit them if they were sick, and 90 percent expected teachers to discipline them if necessary. In such a setting, teachers who view their role as merely that of in instructor, limited to formal, professional interactions, will likely disappoint students and hinder learning. Teachers from cultures that value independence and student self-direction may view such attitudes as unhealthy, but this reflects an unexamined cultural bias and a confusion of categories.

In patron-client relations reciprocity is important. In student-teacher relations, the teacher has the power and gives the student not only the gift of knowledge but also various other benefits such as encouragement, networking,

TABLE 9.1

Tangible Gifts from Patron	Intangible Gifts from Patron
Money, credit	Counsel
Employment	Influence, status
Dining, companionship	Time, visits
Phone calls, letters, internet	Advancement, recommendation
Clothing	Interest, concern
Books	Protection, support
Scholarships, grants	Mediation of conflict
Partnerships	Relationships, networking
	Knowledge, wisdom

Tangible Gifts from Client	Intangible Gifts from Client
Labor, service	Submission, respect
Chickens, fruit, food	Protection, risk of life
Token money or gifts	Display of affection
Visits	Life-long loyalty
Carry books or briefcase	Language assistance, translation
Comfortable seat	Friendship

Source: Adapted from Lingenfelter and Lingenfelter (2003, 85).

and recommendations. The student seeks to reciprocate by giving the teacher respect, performing small favors, and the like (see table 9.1). Some teachers feel that they do not need such gifts and refuse them. But Chinchen contends that this blocks the cycle of reciprocity, leaving the student feeling indebted and perhaps disrespected. The student has no way to establish his dignity and bring his part to the relationship.

> When the teacher (usually a foreigner) does not understand or participate in the collective system, the teacher blocks the student's goal of involving the teacher in his or her learning endeavor. The teacher not only rejects this precious collective value of society, but also, unwittingly, rejects the student. A negative attitude toward this teacher ripples across the entire student body (due to their aggregate nature). The individualistic teacher is considered to be selfish, uncaring, and unconcerned. (328)

It may take some experience for the cross-cultural teacher to discern which gifts from learners are appropriate and which are not. In any case, the teacher should not trivialize such gifts, however small, and should resist a condescending attitude or the impression that the student has nothing of value to offer the teacher.

For over twenty years I have regularly given students the assignment to conduct interviews with people of different nationalities, asking them to describe the best teacher they ever had in their home country. A consistent picture emerges: the best teachers are ones who really *cared* about the student (not just student success). Good teaching is not just about pedagogy in the narrow sense but also about caring and healthy relationships. Ken Bain's insightful study of *What the Best College Teachers Do* in American colleges and universities found, among other characteristics, that "the best teachers we studied displayed not power but an investment in students. Their practices stem from a concern with learning that is strongly felt and powerfully communicated" (2004, 139).

From Authority-Based to Critical-Reflective Learning

We have seen that students in many cultures feel it is not their place to develop their own creative ideas or to critically evaluate what they are being taught. Rather, they desire to receive the knowledge and wisdom that the qualified teacher offers. Sometimes this leads to an emphasis on memorization. We have seen that, contrary to Western preconceptions, memorization can lead to understanding (Kember 2000; Kennedy 2002; Marton, Dall'Alba, and Tse 1996). International comparisons that indicate stronger academic performance by students in more teacher-centered cultures are evidence that Western teaching methods are not necessarily better.

But memorization does not *always* lead to understanding, especially in educationally under-resourced contexts where rote learning with only surface understanding is often the norm. I've heard firsthand reports of students memorizing answers to catechism questions, which they could reproduce verbatim—but if the teacher merely changed the order of the questions, the students could no longer give answers. Children who do not speak Arabic, but are involved in Islamic instruction, can often recite from memory Qur'anic verses in Arabic—but because they do not speak the language they do not know what they are memorizing. Most teachers in higher education want students to develop more reflective learning and critical thinking skills. Students will one day face questions and challenges for which the teacher and textbooks have no answers. Problem-solving skills and abstract analytical skills are increasingly important in navigating rapid social change. Students should come to a place where they do not merely take the teacher's word for something but are able to evaluate the information or truth claims on their own merits. Bible teachers will want students to be able to read and apply the Scriptures themselves in new situations and to be able to critically assess new teachings or ministry models that they encounter. Developing such abilities can be a challenge in a culture where learners expect clear answers from teachers and are so deferential to the authority of the teacher that they are unwilling or unable to engage teaching content critically.

Traditional Learning

Isolde Demele (1988) describes a developmental process of educational forms through which she believes most societies move, progressing from traditional learning to rote learning, and ultimately to critical-reflective learning (see table 9.2). Traditional learning involves mastery of basic life skills such as hunting, farming, cooking, and simple task-oriented problem-solving. The primary instructional method is observation and imitation, usually by parents or family members. Sometimes initiation rites, rituals, and religious instruction play important roles. All societies have such learning, especially in the early years of life, which includes everything from learning how to tie one's shoes to table manners. Traditional learning also includes moral education and wisdom. Rural, nonindustrial societies that have little formal schooling depend almost entirely upon such traditional learning, which is authority-based and rooted in traditional methods of accomplishing life tasks. It requires relatively little verbal instruction. Trial and error is more important than explanation; practice is more important than theory. Literacy is not essential.

TABLE 9.2

From Authority-Based Learning to Critical-Reflective Learning

Traditional Learning	Rote Learning, Memorization (intermediate stage)	Critical-Reflective Learning
Observation and imitation	Authority oriented, hindering independent thinking	Liberal society a precondition (criticism possible)
Moral education	Often due to deficient teacher knowledge and training	Qualified and trained teachers necessary
Use of senses and everyday problem-solving in context	Literate, content oriented, out of context	Conceptual learning; languages with abstract expression

Source: Based on Demele (1988).

Rote Learning and Memorization

Demele argues that a society seldom moves directly from traditional learning to reflective learning and critical thinking. An intermediate phase that is based largely on rote learning usually comes with formal schooling and literacy. With schooling, children in virtually all societies acquire some basic knowledge through memorization, be it spelling, arithmetic, history, or geography. The learning content is decontextualized information received in a classroom, not in the field, the workshop, or the kitchen. It is not learned by direct observation but is mediated through a teacher and thus based largely upon the authority of the teacher: something is so because the teacher says it is. A great challenge in many under-resourced locations is that teachers are poorly trained. It was estimated that in 2016 only half of primary-school teachers and only a quarter of secondary-school teachers in sub-Saharan Africa were qualified, having received minimal formal education and little, if any, pedagogical instruction (UNESCO 2016a, 331). In some regions, teachers may have less than a total of ten years of elementary and secondary education. Thus, teachers themselves do not always understand the content of the curriculum that they are teaching. Because the teachers too often do not understand the material, they dictate it or write it on a blackboard, and students merely memorize the information with or without understanding it. Teachers do not encourage discussion or questions because they may not know the answers themselves. This typically goes hand in hand with a more authoritarian, high power distance culture in which it is considered inappropriate for children to question adults. That is the situation in many under-resourced parts of the world. The challenge is aggravated where class sizes are unmanageably large with only one teacher (see chap. 13).

Needless to say, such conditions are not conducive to highly interactive instructional methods and depend heavily upon the teacher as a strong authority figure and dispenser of knowledge. The cross-cultural teacher working in such regions is likely to encounter students, even in tertiary educational levels, who have never been exposed to learning approaches beyond authority-based rote learning and who have minimal experience of learning with textbooks.

Critical Thinking and Reflective Learning

For students and educational institutions to move beyond rote learning to reflective learning, according to Demele (1988), several conditions must be met. Teachers must be adequately trained so that they understand the content of the curriculum and are not threatened by student interaction in the classroom. Class sizes must be reduced to facilitate more student interaction and discussion. But more importantly, the broader society must be liberalized so as to allow for the open exchange of ideas, including ideas that are critical of traditional knowledge. Because open criticism may reap severe consequences in the many countries ruled by authoritarian governments, there is not a culture of critical thinking and open communication. Authority, including that of a teacher, is simply not questioned. As noted in sidebar 9.3, corporal punishment is not uncommon, even for questioning a teacher's authority. In other words, some level of social emancipation is a condition for open exchange of ideas and the development of critical thinking.

At least in the higher grades, there must also be the freedom for students to adopt a more constructivist approach to learning: not merely accepting the teacher's or the textbook's viewpoint but exploring alternative ideas and explanations, evaluating arguments and evidence, and arriving at their own conclusions. Teachers should not be threatened by such exploration but rather value and encourage the development of critical and evaluative skills.

Problem-Based Learning

The critique has often been raised that more participative student interaction in teaching reflects Western values and should not be imposed upon learners in other cultures. While it is true that silence does not necessarily mean that a student is not processing and reflecting upon class content, there remain good reasons to introduce more interactive and student-centered approaches to instruction—even if countercultural.

But how well can participative instructional methods be introduced in traditional, teacher-centered learning contexts? Educators' use of problem-based learning (PBL) serves as a well-researched example of how more student-directed learning (SDL) might be introduced with positive results.

> In contrast to teacher-centered, lecture-based educational approaches, PBL places students at the center of the educational process by encouraging them to direct their own learning processes, construct knowledge actively, and develop problem-solving and team communication skills. . . . Tutorials take a central role in PBL, during which a small group of students collaboratively discusses a learning issue presented as a problem case, aided by a tutor who acts as a facilitator rather than a knowledge transmitter. (Frambach et al. 2014, 1003)

PBL has many similarities to the case-study method and other discussion-oriented, problem-solving, and knowledge-building pedagogies.

In recent decades Hong Kong, where education has been traditionally very teacher-centered, has introduced educational reforms including PBL. PBL was received with some success (Biggs 2001, 296; Burton 2010; Tam, Phillipson, and Phillipson 2016). The students had some initial difficulty adopting PBL due to conflict with cultural values such as politeness, harmony, and conformity, which would hinder critical exchange and debate. Yet other aspects of PBL can appeal to Asian values, such as a more holistic approach to life (Khoo 2003). By adapting PBL to allow for more student collaboration, in the end it was rated overwhelmingly positive by the students. In the words of one student, "Problem-based learning gives me a sense of release for I will no longer be like a clammed duck" (cited in Biggs 2001, 310). Similar positive responses to PBL, after initial adjustments, have been documented in other Asian countries, too (Khoo 2003). Such liberalizing educational reforms have been held by some to be responsible for student protests in Hong Kong against government policies (Fung and Su 2016; Yeung 2016). If that is true, then it may be less a matter of society liberalizing so that learning can become more reflective, and more a case of reflective learning *leading to* the liberalizing of society.

Another study similarly found that Middle Eastern students initially experienced more uncertainty with PBL than students in Hong Kong or the Netherlands, but they eventually embraced it.

> Rather than feeling motivated, many students felt lost and unable to find appropriate information to address their learning objectives. Uncertainty was related to experiences of traditional, teacher-centred secondary education, but also to a culturally determined focus on tradition. Middle Eastern respondents referred to their society's respect for the "old ways" and wariness regarding innovations. As they became used to PBL, however, their attitudes changed significantly. Students came to support the principle of SDL [student-directed learning] and information seeking became less problematic, although students still felt PBL was not easy and wanted more guidance. (Frambach et al. 2012, 742)

The authors conclude that in cultures with more authority-oriented learning,

> Gradual exposure to SDL, with relatively strong guidance and support in the first year, might ultimately yield the development of more SDL skills. . . . Thus, although PBL may not be cross-culturally applicable in a straightforward way, it would be wrong to conclude that it cannot be applied across cultural contexts as practice continues to prove. (745)

Numerous other examples with similar results could be cited, including Singapore, Pakistan, India, Japan, the Philippines, and other locations (Khoo 2003; Biggs 2001, 300–303). Carol Chan (2009) studied the introduction of classroom innovation and of knowledge-building approaches (learning how to learn) in Hong Kong. She found that such methods can increase student participation and collaboration, and improve test scores, without reducing content learning. Learning content and learning cognitive metaskills, such as learning strategies and problem-solving methods, are not contradictory approaches.

These examples illustrate that even though more participative, student-directed learning that is countercultural may be resisted at first, if it is introduced with cultural sensitivity students will embrace it and feel empowered. Students who only are familiar with teacher-centered learning can feel insecure if they are uncertain of exactly what the teacher wants and what the "correct" answers are. Teachers introducing alternative methods will need to take such student uncertainty into account and alleviate their fears by creating a safe environment for learning and encouraging students to experiment with new approaches. Sidebar 9.4 summarizes recommendations for introducing PBL that would apply also to other participative methods.

SIDEBAR 9.4

Introducing Problem-Based Learning in More Teacher-Centered Learning Contexts

- PBL implementation requires training of teachers/tutors/facilitators and students.
- Trigger problems [clinical or case problems presented to the student to stimulate self-directed learning and problem-solving skills] must be carefully designed to make them relevant and interesting.
- PBL sessions must use language that students are comfortable with.
- PBL sessions should take place in non-threatening, comfortable surroundings.
- PBL implementation should incorporate ongoing group monitoring and evaluation of the PBL process.

Source: Khoo (2003, 402)

Unfamiliar teaching methods are not inherently wrong because they are "foreign." When rightly employed without entirely replacing more traditional pedagogies, they can stimulate higher cognitive processes and release greater student potential. And that is the ultimate goal of the cross-cultural teacher.

SIDEBAR 9.5

Learning to Contradict the Teacher

Trevor McIlwain worked among the Palawano people of the Philippines, who were very authority oriented in their learning and reluctant to contradict a teacher. So that they would be able to identify false teachers who were entering the region, he wanted them to look to the Bible as their sole authority and to correct a teacher if necessary. Here's how he described his rather unorthodox approach.

I would first teach them the truth and then contradict the truth by teaching error. In the Palawano culture, it is improper to "lose face" and become embarrassed. This, in turn, would cause the person who had contradicted the teacher to also become embarrassed. Even so, these church leaders needed to be taught to stand for God's Word, regardless of the cultural discomposure caused by confronting a teacher with the truth. . . . Of course, I only used this method after months of teaching these men. This method would not have been effective if used in the beginning of my association with the Palawano leadership. They would have verbally agreed with me in spite of what they actually believed in their hearts.

I had taught for many hours from the Scriptures on salvation by grace through faith alone. Then, without warning or explanation, I began to teach faith plus works as the way of salvation. Abruptly, I pointed to one of the men and asked him, "Is what I have just said correct? Is it true that sinners are saved, not only by faith, but by their good works?"

The tribal teacher hesitated and then finally answered, "No, it is wrong. We are saved by faith alone."

Feigning surprise, I continued to question him, "Do you mean to say you are telling me, the missionary, that I am wrong?"

Hesitatingly, he said, "Yes, you are wrong."

Still not giving them any clue to my real thoughts, I turned to another man and said, "He says that what I said was wrong. Do you agree or disagree?"

He answered, "What you said is wrong."

I then asked him, "How long have you been a Christian?" His answer indicated that he was a much younger Christian than I. "Oh!" I said, "I have been a Christian for many years. I have also been to Bible college. Do you still think that I could be wrong?"

Again, he answered that I was wrong.

Even then, I did not show agreement or disagreement but turned to a third man and asked him what he thought. Much to my surprise, he said, "You are right!"

Thinking he had misunderstood, I repeated what I had said previously, stating that we are saved not only by faith but also by our good works.

Again, he said that my statements were correct.

I then asked him, according to my usual procedure, to give scriptural proof for this statement. To my even greater surprise, he turned to Ephesians 2:8, 9. Hoping he would understand his mistake once he read these verses, I asked him to read them to all present. He did so and concluded by saying, "There it is. We are saved, not only by faith, but by our good works also."

Many of the men were now smiling, but I was looking to the Lord for wisdom in what to say to avoid embarrassing him.

I, therefore, asked Perfecto, for that was his name, to read Ephesians 2:8, 9 once again. He did but still maintained that these verses were teaching salvation through faith plus good works. I knew simply to tell him he was wrong would not establish the truth in his mind. It was important that he see for himself what these verses actually teach.

I said to Perfecto, "Those verses do not seem to be saying what you claim they do. Read them once again very slowly to yourself so you will understand what they really mean."

While we waited, Perfecto read the verses through slowly. Finally, he looked up at me with a look of great surprise and said, "No, I am wrong! We are not saved by faith and works, but by faith alone through God's grace."

Source: McIlwain (1987, 15–17). Used by permission.

The Social Dimension

Part 2: The Influence of Individualism and Collectivism

Social interactions can be among the most perplexing aspects of living and working across cultures. This is true not only regarding the role of social status and hierarchy, as we saw in the previous chapter, but also in terms of how one's sense of individual and group identity play out in everyday settings. The following situations illustrate the challenge:

CHAPTER OVERVIEW

- Characteristics of Individualism and Collectivism
- Limitations of the Individualism/Collectivism Construct
- The Role of Shame and Honor
- Learner Motivation
- Social Interactions in Instructional Contexts
- Writing Style
- Academic Integrity: Plagiarism and Cheating
- Conclusion

- A Swiss teacher in Rwanda expressed anger over the extent to which students were cheating and helping one another during examinations. But the students couldn't understand why a seemingly minor offense would evoke such an extreme response from the teacher, and they lost all respect for him.
- A Filipino student in America was baffled that American students dislike group projects and prefer to work alone.
- A school in Papua New Guinea requested that an expatriate teacher manage the school funds. The expatriate teacher felt that she was being placed in an inappropriate and awkward situation.
- A Japanese student had been studying for several years in America when he became engaged to marry a Japanese woman also studying abroad. However, he had not first received approval of the engagement from his parents or his pastor (who were all still in Japan).

Because of this, his relationship with them became so strained that
he fell into a severe depression, broke off his study, and returned to
Japan, although he was only months away from graduation.

- When a German teacher spontaneously called upon a Chinese student to answer a question in class, she sat in silence staring down at
her desk. The teacher waited. After what seemed like an eternity to
the student, she suddenly bolted from the classroom, never to return.

Each of these scenarios can be explained, at least in part, by understanding
the dynamics of individualism and collectivism (I/C): a well-developed social-
science construct describing the way individuals interact with others and con-
ceive of themselves in relation to the larger social group to which they belong.

To survive and thrive in life, we all need others. But to what extent is a
person willing to submit their individual goals to the collective will of their
group? How important is the opinion of others in determining one's behavior?
How does group "belongingness" influence one's personal identity and sense
of well-being? Why are people in some places so strongly motivated by the
shame or honor they experience before their peers? Each of these factors will
influence the social interactions that take place in teaching and learning. I/C
can be a helpful tool in sorting out these and many other questions. Before
exploring the implications of I/C for teaching and learning, we must first
consider carefully the complex nature of these concepts.

Characteristics of Individualism and Collectivism

Individualism and collectivism (I/C) is one of the most widely researched
constructs in attempting to understand cultural differences. In fact, it has
been argued that "no construct has had a greater impact on contemporary
cross-cultural psychology than individualism and collectivism" (Triandis
2001, 35). Geert Hofstede (1980), Harry C. Triandis (1995), and other early
researchers developed this concept, which has since been the basis of literally thousands of studies. As used in this book, *collectivism* refers not to a
particular political or economic system such as communism but to a social-
psychological orientation. The contrasting elements of I/C have been defined
this way: "Individualism pertains to societies in which the ties between individuals are loose: everyone is expected to look after him- or herself and his
or her immediate family. Collectivism as its opposite pertains to societies in
which people from birth onward are integrated into strong, cohesive in-groups,
which throughout people's lifetime continue to protect them in exchange for
unquestioning loyalty" (Hofstede, Hofstede, and Minkov 2010, 92). Whereas

Hofstede's research focuses more on work-related collectivism, the approach taken by GLOBE focuses more on family-related collectivism (Brewer and Venaik 2011). Broadly generalizing, the differences between individualism and collectivism are summarized in table 10.1.

These descriptions are painted in black-and-white, either-or categories only to illustrate the fundamental differences. The reality is much more nuanced, complex, and mixed. We can only scratch the surface here of the vast research and debates related to I/C.

Numerous studies reveal correlations between I/C and other cultural differences. For example, the more collectivistic a society is, the greater the power distance tends to be; and the more individualistic, the lower the power distance (Hofstede, Hofstede, and Minkov 2010, 103). Also, based upon data from the World Values Survey in sixty-five societies, Ingelhart and Baker note that "economic development is associated with shifts away from absolute norms and values toward values that are increasingly rational, tolerant, trusting, and participatory" (2000, 19). Individualism tends to increase with increase in

TABLE 10.1

Characteristics of Individualism and Collectivism

Individualism	Collectivism
Personal identity is loosely associated with group belonging	Personal identity is tightly associated with group belonging
How one is different or special matters	What one has in common matters
Personal freedom and expression are highly valued	Social obligation and solidarity are highly valued
Personal goals take priority over group goals	Group goals take priority over personal goals
Loose conformity to group norms is allowed	Tight conformity to group norms is expected
Creativity and innovation are important	Tradition and history are important
Greater guilt orientation	Greater shame/honor orientation
Egalitarian; low power distance	Hierarchical; high power distance
Low in-group/out-group distinction	High in-group/out-group distinction
Independence: *"Stand on your own two feet!"*	Interdependence: *"Together we go further"*
Direct communication style	Indirect communication style
Self-actualization is the goal	Social harmony is the goal

per capita income, as does the value of self-expression (Hofstede, Hofstede, and Minkov 2010, 132–33; Brewer and Venaik 2011, 441–42). One explanation for affluent societies tending to be more individualistic is that people are less immediately dependent upon family or the larger social group to provide for basic needs. Each person or nuclear family tends to earn and manage its own income, is responsible for meeting its own needs, and is independent of assistance from others. Personal savings and insurance are available to provide for emergencies. With affluence usually comes more education, more career options, and more freedom for self-expression because not as much time and resources are consumed for basic survival needs.

In low income settings, people are more dependent on the larger social unit, such as extended family or clan, to provide for basic needs. The larger group is the only "safety net" for emergencies such as medical expenses. Income and housing may be shared among the larger social unit. Thus it is important in collectivistic societies to demonstrate solidarity with the group and not to act too independently. The collective well-being of the group takes priority over personal goals. Interdependence is a high value because individuals are aware that "others need me, and one day I will need others." The importance of social solidarity can lead to greater in-group and out-group distinctions among collectivists—that is, individuals relating differently to persons who are members of the primary social group for which they have mutual obligations, versus how they relate to persons who are outside that group. As a society becomes more affluent, however, it may retain many aspects of collectivism.

For collectivists, one's personal identity is more closely bound to belonging to the in-group. Isolation or excommunication from the primary social group not only makes a person more vulnerable but also can create an identity crisis. The terms *independent self* and *interdependent self* (Markus and Kitayama 1991) express this aspect of I/C, which emphasizes identity in relation to others. Harmony is important to group solidarity; thus it is no surprise that numerous studies find that (1) indirect communication and indirect conflict resolution strategies tend to be preferred in collectivistic societies and (2) individualists tend to be more direct and confrontational. The reality is more complex. Research has shown that although differences in conflict management style exist between individualists and collectivists, simplistic, binary typology of "avoidance versus confrontation" is inadequate and misleading (Cai and Fink 2002). Indirect communication can be understood as disingenuous by more individualistic persons, while more collectivistic persons may consider individualists' more direct communicative style rude and abrasive. We shall discuss below the associations of collectivism with face-saving and shame/honor orientation.

Many collectivistic societies emphasize honoring or venerating ancestors, which is expressed in rituals. Although the understandings of the exact role an ancestor plays in the society vary greatly from culture to culture, they have this in common: ancestors give the group a strong sense of collective identity through a common lineage and history—be it for the family, clan, ethnic group, or nation. Participating in such ancestor practices expresses group solidarity and loyalty, reinforcing the collective values of the community. Individualistic societies place less emphasis on a common heritage and more on individual expression and identity in the present. They give comparatively little attention to ancestry.

Limitations of the Individualism/Collectivism Construct

Before discussing the implications of these distinctions for teaching, a few caveats must be noted regarding the use of I/C. First, as noted in chapter 2, one should not depend heavily upon national profiles such as those provided by Hofstede's work. A nation is not a culture, and most nations are composed of numerous cultures and subcultures. Furthermore, all cultures are evolving and changing with increasing speed as a result of technology and globalization. China, for example, is often considered a predominantly collectivistic society, but there is evidence that through industrialization, urbanization, and globalization it has become more individualistic (Yu and Yang 1987).

Second, collectivism and individualism are not necessarily polar opposites (Schwartz 1990; M. Kim 2007). They are not either-or human characteristics (like eye color) but exist to different degrees in everyone. People of the same culture may behave more collectivistically in some situations, but more individualistically in other situations. For example, Koreans are generally considered very collectivistic in relationship to family, community, and nation. But in the context of competing for high exam scores necessary for admission to a university, they can be very individualistic.

Numerous studies show "that the concepts of collectivism and individualism are far more complex than is generally thought, as for example is evidenced by studies in Hong Kong, in which participants scored high on both individualism and collectivistic [face-saving] concerns" (Frambach et al. 2014, 1018; see also sidebar 10.1). The specific social grouping or institutional setting must always be taken into account. Triandis argues that I/C behaviors "should be conceived as 'tools' that individuals utilize in different combinations, depending on the situation" (2001, 39), though a person may have a predominant orientation. Either-or categorizing of an individual or culture must be avoided.

SIDEBAR 10.1

Hypercompetitive Collectivists? Not an Oxymoron!

Although persons from more collectivistic cultures are generally described as less competitive and more committed to social harmony, one should not assume that they cannot at times also be very competitive. The Chinese Singaporean concept of *kiasu*, common also in other Chinese heritage cultures, illustrates this. *Kiasu* describes the fear of missing out and not wanting to be disadvantaged. According to national profiles, Singapore is considered a more collectivistic culture. But Singaporean students motivated by *kiasu* work extra hard, even to the disadvantage of fellow students. It has been interpreted by some as hypercompetitiveness. Even in group projects students may "act in a manner that is detrimental to the group effort in order to subtly benefit themselves" (Hodkinson and Poropat 2014, 437). This illustrates that national profiles can be misleading and that concepts such as collectivism are complex. Characteristics such as collectivism and individualism must be understood in terms of the specific context of each educational setting.

Third, these characteristics should not be construed as deterministic. While they may help explain certain behaviors, this does not mean that people cannot change their behavior or adopt new social and learning orientations. Just as cultures change, so do individuals. Furthermore, the causal relationship between I/C and learner cognitive processes is ambiguous. In other words, the fact that persons who are more collectivistic or individualistic tend to learn or behave in certain ways does not mean that I/C is the cause behind those behaviors. Other cultural factors may be responsible (Oyserman and Lee 2008). Cross-cultural teachers should not make I/C (or any other construct) the single explanatory tool for understanding their students.

Finally, there is a temptation for Westerners to make the value judgment that individualism is more advanced than collectivism. Individualism is a more common characteristic in industrialized nations, but that does not warrant a value judgment. Dividing the world into "developed and modern" (more individualistic) versus "traditional and backward" (collectivistic) is a feature of colonial discourse that is both ethnocentric and inaccurate (Fougère and Moulettes 2007).

Despite these caveats and the longstanding debates over the validity of Hofstede's work, one should not entirely dismiss the I/C construct. "Overwhelming evidence indicates differences in basic psychological processes between members of individualistic and collectivistic cultures" (Darwish and Huber

2003, 49). Decades of impressive research has demonstrated that it is a helpful way of describing cultural differences when properly applied. "Hofstede's largely positivistic approach, despite its flaws, is widely accepted because it provides the 'best available explanation' for many cross-cultural issues, especially for practice. Critics should also appreciate what the framework explains, rather than focus on what it is unable to explain" (Venkateswaran and Ojha 2019, 425). I/C is only a tool, and like any conceptual tool it should be used with discretion to shed light on otherwise perplexing behaviors. First, teachers need to meet students where they are and respect their values and preferences, and then they can consider how to proceed.

The Role of Shame and Honor

Closely associated with collectivism is shame/honor orientation, which is often contrasted with guilt orientation. Research suggests that persons from collectivistic and individualistic cultures experience guilt and shame differently (Wallbott and Scherer 1995, 474–81). Anthropologists Ruth Benedict and Margaret Mead, working in the early twentieth century, were among the first to make a distinction between cultures that are more guilt oriented or more shame oriented.[1] In recent decades missiological literature and conferences have given increased attention to the theme (e.g., Wiher 2003; Georges and Baker 2016).[2]

There is some debate as to the precise difference between the psychological feelings of shame and guilt. Some researchers describe guilt as being centered more on the negative behavior—"I *did* something bad"—versus shame being focused more on the self—"I *am* bad" (e.g., H. Lewis 1971). Others focus more on the notion that guilt and shame are related, respectively, to internal versus external sanctions (e.g., Wallbott and Scherer 1995, 474). In other words, shame is more related to a person's conformity to norms or expectations of others, while guilt is more related to one's own internal sense of right and wrong. Yet still others see the central difference in shame being the result of the public exposure of one's bad behavior, versus guilt as a negative feeling of remorse or self-blame apart from public exposure (e.g., Smith et al. 2002). Each of these distinctions has limitations and has been contested. Nevertheless, there is little doubt that some persons are more motivated by the avoidance of shame than others, and that culture plays a role in the importance of shame avoidance. Our concern here is how that influences learners' behaviors and motivations.

---

1. See Wiher 2003, 103–32 for an overview of the development of anthropological views on guilt and shame cultures.

2. For an excellent theological discussion of the topic, see Lau 2020.

Although the language of guilt and shame may be psychologically imprecise, the terms *shame orientation* and *guilt orientation* are used here merely as a convenient way to describe observable differences in learners' desire to avoid public exposure of weakness or unacceptable behavior. *Shame orientation* generally describes a person who is heavily influenced by the desire to avoid shame or, conversely, to protect honor. What is in view here is more than mere embarrassment; it is a deep sense of moral failure or inferiority. It is experienced most acutely when the behavior is exposed to other persons who may judge one to be of poor character (e.g., Bedford 2004, 45–46). Avoiding shame is thus a strong motivational factor. *Guilt orientation* describes a person for whom avoiding feelings of guilt is a stronger motivational factor. *Guilt* is not used here in the legal sense, but rather to mean the feeling of moral culpability or remorse for having violated one's own moral or ethical norms, apart from public exposure or the opinion of others.

When we speak of a culture being more shame oriented or more guilt oriented, we are speaking of the way a society collectively shapes these feelings and their relative importance to a person's sense of well-being. People in collectivistic cultures tend to be more shame oriented because social solidarity is more central to their personal identity and sense of well-being. Behavior that has been exposed as violating that solidarity threatens their sense of belonging and acceptance by the group. Shameful behavior may bring dishonor not only to the individual but also to the group, and thus has a stronger collective dimension. This does not mean that shame-oriented people do not have a sense of guilt if wrong behavior is not exposed, but for them that sense of guilt typically is overshadowed by the discomfort of being shamed. As Bedford sums up in the context of comparing Taiwanese culture with most Western cultures,

> Every person's self-concept includes a picture of how the self fits into society, and what kind of society the self is a part of. This sense of connectedness with others is much stronger for Chinese than for Westerners (Hwang 1999). This means that Chinese, to a greater extent than Westerners, are sensitive to being personally shamed by actions (or lack of action) on the part of others. (2004, 48)

However, we must keep in mind that just as individualism and collectivism are not bipolar opposites, so too shame and guilt orientations are not opposites, and some writers have challenged the distinction altogether (e.g., Cozens 2018). Western cultures are experiencing what has been called a "great renaissance of public shaming," particularly through the use of social media (Ronson 2015, 11). There are also serious limitations to Western conceptions of guilt and shame that do not reflect the experience of people in other cultures (Wong and Tsai 2007). Other languages have many terms that express more nuanced and differentiated feelings of guilt and shame that do not translate well into English.[3] All people experience feelings of both shame and guilt; indeed, the feelings may often overlap. For example, the Japanese are generally considered to be a more shame-oriented people. But one study found that most Japanese who engage in a socially deviant or immoral behavior experience feelings of both guilt and shame (D. Lewis 1993, 230–31), and it has been argued that Japan is actually more guilt oriented than shame oriented (Lebra 1983). In fact, it may not be possible to say which is the stronger feeling or motivation, even in so-called shame-oriented cultures (Bedford 2004, 46–47). One international study of nearly 3,000 subjects from 37 countries found that people do experience a difference between guilt and shame, though "no differences were found with respect to the felt intensity of the two emotions" (Wallbott and Scherer 1995, 472). There is enough empirical evidence to warrant maintaining a distinction between more shame-oriented and more guilt-oriented cultures, but the distinction should be viewed only as a very imperfect tool to make some sense of behaviors that may otherwise seem mystifying. As always, the cross-cultural teacher will need to study the given local culture carefully to obtain a more accurate understanding of such complex emotions and motivations.

The Concept of "Face"

Chinese or so-called Confucian heritage cultures serve as good examples of shame orientation in terms of *face*, many of whose features can be found elsewhere. In most Asian cultures one speaks of *saving* or *losing face*. Losing face has been defined as "a damaging social event, in which one's action is publicly given notice and negatively judged by others, resulting in a loss of moral or social standing" (Ho, Fu, and Ng 2004, 70). Often it is not merely a matter of personal embarrassment but can have consequences for one's social standing, job advancement, and mental health. In Chinese there are two aspects: *mianzi* relating to prestige and honor, and *lian* relating to moral integrity. One can gain or lose face in both senses (Hwang, Francesco, and Kessler 2003; Wu 2009). In the words of Xiaoxin Wu, "The central theme or the Chinese concept of face is the positive respectable public self-image that a person, a family or a community claims for themselves in social interaction. It is a public property and is hierarchical, reciprocal and interdependent in

---

3. For example, see Bedford (2004) for a nuanced description of three different Mandarin terms used in Taiwan to express "guilt" and four different terms to express "shame." "Common aspects of these shame experiences include exposure, inadequacy and concern with identity. They differ with respect to transgression issues and function" (45). Another study found over 113 Chinese ways of expressing shame (Li, Wang, and Fischer 2004). Japanese has similar terminology to Chinese (Ho, Fu, and Ng 2004).

nature. The protection of face is an important mechanism in maintaining harmony" (2009, 91). *Diu lian* (loss of face) may represent the feeling of a loss of personhood (Bedford 2004, 37). "*Bie diu za jia de lian* (Don't make our family lose face), an expression often used in daily conversation within Chinese-speaking cultures, indicates the collective nature of 'face' in Chinese culture" (Wu 2009, 95). "For those with traditional Chinese beliefs, much behavior is directed at avoiding the loss of *lian* because it entails withdrawal of community acceptance and support" (Bedford 2004, 37).

Negotiating Relationships

Concerns about shame and the high value placed on harmonious relationships can affect even the use of the word *no*. Its use is avoided in some cultures because of its negative connotations. For example, answering no to an invitation or saying no to someone asking for help could be interpreted as being unfriendly, inhospitable, or antisocial. It may seem rude. Consequently, even if the real answer is no, one answers yes. This can be frustrating for more direct communicators who understand *yes* as yes! This is sometimes interpreted by them as dishonesty or outright lying. But in most cases it's only a social convention, much like answering "fine" when asked "How are you doing?" Highly indirect discourse can be a way of protecting the honor of both persons in the communicative exchange. One must learn from body language and other indicators whether a *yes* really means yes. Cultural insiders know how to read those signs, but they can be difficult for cultural sojourners to discern.

SIDEBAR 10.2

Exercise: From Direct to Indirect Communication

Reformulate the following direct (and possibly shaming or confrontational) statements into indirect statements that are less shaming or confrontational. For example, *Who is responsible for this problem?* could be reformulated as *How can we avoid this problem next time?*

- That is not a good idea.
- Why are you late for class?
- My impression is that you are just not trying hard enough.

- Something doesn't add up with the numbers.
- You didn't complete the assignment properly.
- You are approaching this the wrong way.
- The majority of people in the group disagree with you about that.
- Your answer is incorrect.

Although people everywhere want to avoid conflict and criticism, in more shame-oriented cultures expressing any kind of critique, dealing with conflict, and other negative social interactions are especially discomfiting. Consequently, cultures and individuals develop indirect ways to communicate negative messages, such as silence, using indirect language, engaging a third person as a mediator, or simply removing oneself from the situation (see Elmer 1993). Face-to-face confrontation or reconciliation is typically avoided. Sometimes an issue can be resolved through symbolic actions, such as by giving a gift with a personal note or by publicly praising the offended person to restore honor (Georges and Baker 2016, 134–41). Persons from cultures where more direct communication is the norm may view the use of a mediator as going behind one's back: "If you have a problem, then talk to me about it, not to someone else!" But in a more shame-oriented culture, direct confrontation might be viewed as extremely shaming or disrespectful and could possibly destroy the relationship altogether (see the exercise in sidebar 10.2). Sometimes indirect language such as a proverb or story is used to address a problem (see sidebar 10.3). However, the reluctance of persons in shame-oriented cultures to address conflict can lead to social dysfunction, passive-aggressive behavior, and other problems.

No one likes to have their vulnerability exposed, but in more shame-oriented cultures the fear of exposure can be acute. In some Asian countries, exam scores are publicly posted for all to see. No student wants to be shamed

---

SIDEBAR 10.3

A Reprimand and a Thirsty Horse

The following true incident illustrates how a student in a shame-oriented culture used indirect communication in an attempt to express frustration or criticism to a teacher.

Missionary Ted Veer of Ethiopia recounted how on one occasion he reprimanded two students who came to class over an hour late. The incident passed without further discussion until the last day of class at which time one of the two students stood to ask a question. One began by telling the story of a horse that had worked hard and then went to a waterhole to drink. Somebody had so muddied the water, however, that it was impossible for the horse to drink it. The student concluded by asking, "Now what should be done about the situation?" (Hesselgrave 1991, 326)

- What is the student attempting to communicate to the teacher by telling this story?
- If you were the teacher, how would you respond or answer the question posed by the student?

by appearing low on the list, so shame is "shamelessly" exploited by schools as a negative motivation! Sometimes if students suspect that they will perform poorly on an examination, they may simply not appear or drop out of a class. For example, in a course at Zhejiang University in China that prepared students for a qualifying exam to study abroad, if students feared that they would fail the exam they would drop out of the course or become "sick," even though it meant abandoning their hopes of studying abroad (Mitschian 1991, 346). "A Micronesian student would rather not take an exam than take it and fail, or would prefer to not turn in a written assignment than to demonstrate an inability to write" (Lingenfelter and Mayers 2016, 94). Describing the situation in China, Biggs and Watkins report that "guilt and shame of not being able to cope academically has led to depression and suicide of even pre-teen age children" (1996, 277).

The shame factor can be especially difficult if a student has gone away to school or university only to flunk out and have to return home to family and friends as a failure. Face-saving ways need to be created that allow a student lacking ability to graciously exit without the shame of failure. One approach is to offer all students a certificate after the first semester or year of study, but only the better students are invited to continue study. In this way no one appears to be a failure.

Learner Motivation

Learner motivation is clearly affected by a student's I/C orientation. Although everyone is affected to some extent by the opinion of others, collectivists are affected more so than individualists. Public recognition increases honor, the opposite of shame. Learners in individualistic cultures often are motivated by a sense of self-realization, personal fulfilment, and the intrinsic value of learning. Of course, diplomas and recognitions are also an important factor, but participation in continuing education and non-formal programs such as adult evening classes are a popular approach to personal enrichment and may have little practical value for job advancement or public recognition.

Because learners in collectivistic societies experience a greater sense of well-being when they act in the interest of the larger group and are publicly recognized, motivation may be more extrinsic. Avoiding loss of face, as described above, is a negative motivation. Achieving honor or higher status, which is symbolized through public awards, certificates, diplomas, and formal recognition of accomplishment, is a powerful positive motivation. In Liberia, Argentina, Nepal, and Hong Kong (and the list could continue), church-based educational programs that may involve just a few days of instruction often conclude with a celebrative ceremony in which each participant is called

FIGURE 10.1

In many cultures, completion of even a non-formal seminar is celebrated with the granting of a certificate

forward by name to receive their certificate. Group photos underscore the collective nature of the event.

In more collectivistic cultures, shaming sometimes is intentional. Shaming a student in front of the whole class may be used by a teacher as a way to deal with inappropriate student behavior (Ho 2001). A Nigerian student reported that in her high school, "Each year during the awards ceremony, the headmaster would not only award the top three students in each class, he would name the three worst students and the whole student body would boo them" (Kenworthy 2020). Fear of being shamed or ashamed of oneself can be a strong negative motivation. Teachers from more individualistic cultures can easily underestimate how deeply a student from a more collectivistic culture may feel shamed at the slightest correction in the presence of others. Students who have felt shamed in front of their class may never return.

Asian university students are often financially supported by parents or family at great sacrifice, reinforcing collectivistic bonds and obligations. "Collectivistic cultures emphasize filial piety and family cohesion. Achieving excellence would not only make their parents proud, but also is an indication that the family's financial help is not wasted. Hence the students are highly motivated" (Salili, Chiu, and Lai 2001, 241). This often obligates the student to study in a field such as medicine or engineering that brings the prospect of a well-paying job. That person can then finance other family members' studies and provide for parents in their old age. Zhiwei Chen and Ying Liu (2019) conducted a study comparing learning motivations of Chinese and American adults. They found that for the Chinese, learning and other decisions were made more by parents, whereas Americans made more individual decisions with little family influence. Financial obligations in the home and fulfilling parental expectations were a strong motivation for Chinese, as illustrated by this comment: "My parents had already set up a goal for me to climb up to since my childhood" (16). Americans, on the other hand, experienced less economic or parental pressure, exemplified in the statement, "I am not driven to work, although I could get well paid, but the most learning motivation is still dependent upon me, say, my own free will" (18). Studies of Sri Lankan and Indonesian students have found high percentages of students who had no choice in their career path, which was determined by parents or other family members (Marambe 2007; Ajisuksmo and Vermunt 1999).

A teacher's evaluative feedback of a learner can be perceived very differently in different cultures and, in turn, may impact learner motivation differently. Some child-rearing traditions believe that praise will spoil a child and it is rarely given, but criticism is frequent. In other cultures there is the conviction that children need frequent praise to develop in a healthy manner and that criticism will damage their self-esteem. This means that the experience of praise or criticism in a learning situation is culturally conditioned through the socialization of the child. In collectivistic cultures, individual praise— singling out the individual from the group or indirectly emphasizing how the individual is better than peers—can be experienced as embarrassing. A well-known Japanese proverb says, "The nail that stands out gets hammered down." No student wants to be the nail that stands out!

> An example of this group-oriented thought is the experience of a white teacher among the Hopi. In class she assigned a task and told students to raise their hands when they completed the work. When no student did so, even though they had completed the work, she became angry. She did not realize that the first one to raise a hand would put the others to shame and would be treated by them as arrogant. (Hiebert and Meneses 1995, 129)

In one cultural setting, praise for an easy task may be construed by the learner as an indication that the teacher has low expectations of the student's ability. Criticism may be construed as the teacher viewing the student as having more ability. But in another cultural setting, the learner's reaction may be the opposite. "These findings suggest that praise, often given for reinforcement, may have negative consequences on students' perception of ability" (Salili 2001, 83). Studies found that Chinese students are less dependent on praise than Western students, but because they receive it so seldom, it is considered a higher honor when they do receive it (94).

Social Interactions in Instructional Contexts

Group Work versus Individual Work

In Western, more individualistic settings, great emphasis is placed upon individual performance. To get ahead in life, one must learn to "stand on one's own two feet" and not depend on others. Starting in the early grades, American schools grade students individually, and the emphasis is on students learning to study, write papers, and learn on their own in other ways. In more collectivist societies, it is a cultural value to learn to cooperate in life and help one another. In school, students should be less competitive and more supportive of one another. There is often a strong sense of class solidarity. Collectivistic learners typically enjoy common experiences and group activities (see sidebar 10.4).

Observations by Christina Hvitfeldt (1986) of classroom behaviors of adult Hmong language and literacy students illustrate characteristics of certain highly collectivistic learners:

> Individual students are continuously in touch with those around them, maintaining interpersonal interaction through verbal and nonverbal checking of each other's books, papers, and worksheets. The weaker students look around for assurance; the stronger students maintain a constant check on the work of the weaker students in order to make certain that they are progressing correctly. Help is freely given and, even when not requested, accepted as a matter of course. . . .
>
> Classroom achievement is never personal but always considered to be the result of cooperative effort. Not only is there no competition in the classroom, there is constant denial of individual ability. When individuals are praised by the teacher, they generally shake their heads and appear hesitant to be singled out as being more able than their peers. (70)

In light of this highly collectivistic orientation, Hvitfeldt recommends avoiding exhortations such as "do your own work." One should allow for more group cooperation on worksheets and quizzes, avoid the praise of individual students, and focus teaching content on personal and social topics (74–75).

SIDEBAR 10.4

A Visit to the Ice Cream Parlor

German language teacher Helga Saa-thoff recounts this story about language students from Russia and Kazakhstan, which illustrates what might be considered typical behavior of a strongly collectivistic group of students.

> On a warm Friday afternoon in July instead of the regular class instruction, I decided to give the students a change of pace and make an excursion to a local ice cream parlor. There they could practice their newly acquired German language skills socializing, reading the menu, ordering, discussing the various ice cream flavors, and then paying the bill.
>   After arriving and dividing the students into four table groups, to my surprise soon there was silence. What had happened? Within moments they had decided that everyone at the same table would order the same flavor of ice cream. At one table everyone ordered strawberry ice cream, at another table only chocolate, and so on. My teaching plan for conversational practice literally melted away, as each group enjoyed the same ice cream selection! This became a cross-cultural learning experience for me.
>   Upon noticing my visible disappointment that they had all ordered the same flavor at each table, and had missed the opportunity to discuss all the different ice cream options, they explained to me what was important to them: not the wide array of flavors, but having the same pleasurable experience in common; not explaining each individual choice, but group harmony. Not the long consideration of what to order, but the quick consensus to all order what the recognized leader at each table preferred. (Saathoff 2007)

American individualism illustrates characteristics opposite those of collectivistic learners. For example, the principal of an American middle school that one of my children attended had studied educational practices abroad. He introduced group projects for which all students in the group would receive the same grade. Upon discovering this, the parents were aghast and protested vehemently, claiming that their children would need to learn how to succeed in life in general, and in college in particular, *on their own* without depending upon others. Furthermore, one lazy student in the group could bring down the grade of the other diligent students.[4] The experiment had to be abandoned. As one study of American college students concluded, "Individualists who

---

4. *Social loafing* is the tendency for one group member to rely upon the work of other group members to complete a task. The phenomenon is not only evidenced in American workgroups, but is nearly universal. However, studies have shown that in some collectivistic cultures, in group settings members may actually work harder, a phenomenon called *social striving*. See the discussion in Segall et al. 1999, 211–12.

feel independent and self-reliant are less apt to engage in cooperative behavior, and collectivists who feel interdependent and reliant on groups are more likely to behave cooperatively" (J. Wagner 1995, 167). Furthermore, the larger the group, the less cooperative individualists tended to be.

An international graduate student studying in America was perplexed by the social environment of his daughter's American high school. For a research methods course, he wrote an ethnography of that school, which involved interviewing the school principal. He asked why there was no sense of class comradery or cohesion, observing that students changed classrooms and classmates every hour and were left to fend for themselves and find their own friends and social circle. To his astonishment, the principal replied that this is the way to prepare students for success in life. Social skills and learning about teamwork might be considered valuable, but they are secondary compared to the importance of individual academic performance and self-reliance. It is no surprise that studies find the United States to be the most individualistic country in the world.

China is generally considered a more collectivistic culture where teaching is very teacher-centered and learning in groups is generally not practiced. A German automobile organization introduced a training concept that included collaborative and self-regulated learning approaches. The firm found that the transition to collaborative approaches was unproblematic, though learners felt somewhat overtaxed. However, to adjust to self-regulated learning that calls on the learner to solve real problems, learners needed the support of a trainer who assisted with comprehension of the problem and feedback on their solution. A study of the effort concluded that unfamiliar instructional methods can be introduced and be well received, but there was a caveat: "Learners should be gradually introduced to the different teaching and learning culture to avoid problems and the potential for reduced acceptance. This includes that the teacher explains the purpose and process of the use of new methodologies and that he offers adequate instructional support" (Fischer and Kopp 2007).

Preferential Treatment

More collectivistic cultures draw stronger distinctions between in-group and out-group, which means that persons belonging to one's primary social group (the in-group) are treated differently from persons who belong to another group (the out-group). Because group solidarity is important to collectivist learners *and* teachers, this can create problems regarding the equal and fair treatment of diverse students. For example, if various ethnic groups or clans are represented in a class of students, the teacher may treat students from his in-group preferentially by grading those students' assignments more favorably or by giving them other advantages over their peers. Teachers may actually assist certain students during exams because it would not be acting in solidarity with the in-group to allow a student of one's own group to fail. For this reason, in some places expatriate teachers—who belong to none of the groups and are likely to be more impartial—have been called upon to proctor and grade exams. In individualist groups, grading and treatment of students should be as impartial as possible. Students will complain bitterly if they suspect that they have not been treated equally.

Student Participation in Class Discussions

Western pedagogy emphasizes a dialogical approach to learning with discussion and question and answer to stimulate student reflection. Through this process, learners themselves construct knowledge. Other cultures tend toward a more didactic approach, whereby students receive the knowledge delivered by the teacher. Of course, this shapes student expectations of teachers. In rural Brazil, the Guarani are unfamiliar with rhetorical questions and uncomfortable with a teacher asking a question for which he already knows the answer. For a

---

SIDEBAR 10.5

Blank Stares

Susan Willhauck describes her attempt to stimulate discussion among her theological students in Yucatan, Mexico.

I asked my class for examples of how their communities do [spiritual formation]. There was some whispering and glancing around; I waited, but there was no answer. I asked them another question that often generates lots of discussion and energy, "What is a Christian and how do we know when one is being formed?" The room was deadly quiet. One of the older men in the group crossed his arms and said gruffly, "A Christian is somebody who believes in Jesus Christ and is saved." Okay, I thought, one answer. Do I want to tackle that one? His body language indicated that the case was closed. Next question: "What does it mean to be saved?" The unspoken answer

in the tense atmosphere was "Well, if you don't know that, sister, why are you here?" I continued further down into the pit. "Is being a Christian just about a person's individual relationship with Jesus? Is there more?" Students looked down at their hands. No one else spoke. It was as if the question had been answered and it was time to move on. I then asked, "How do you do Christian education, or how are Christians formed in your ministry settings?" Once again, blank stares.... Very tentatively, one of the young women spoke as if to try to break the ice. She said that she led a Bible study, but shrugged as if it was just a mundane thing. I probed for more, but no one else followed. It was not going well. I decided to dispense with the questions and to tell a story. (Willhauck 2009, 225) teacher to do so is considered dishonest. One teacher was excitedly told by a Guarani student, "You should not ask a question when you already know the answer! That is forbidden among us. Never do that again!" (Gerstetter 1999).

Western teachers in non-Western classrooms are often frustrated by the seeming lack of student participation in discussion or asking questions in class (see sidebar 10.5). One American professor teaching in China writes,

> I would say, "What about this?" And then I'd wait. I'd sit there and sip my tea. . . . Nothing. Then I'd call on somebody, "Chung, what do you think?" He would look down at his book . . . [silence] . . . [silence]. I have no experience with this—the experience of calling on a student and the ability of the student to outwait me! (George 1995, 14)

We saw in chapter 9 that in more authority-based cultures students may be reluctant to ask questions or engage in discussion, out of deference to the teacher. Factors such as collectivism and shame orientation also contribute to such behavior.

We must underscore again that such seemingly passive behavior does not mean that students are not learning or are not deeply processing the information that the teacher is presenting. Sometimes the reluctance of students to answer questions is due to the short amount of time teachers give them to answer. Studies have found that on average, Western teachers wait less than one second for an answer before repeating the question or giving their own answer! As one Chinese student put it, "I wanted to contribute my ideas to the discussion in class on many occasions. But my attempt was often blocked by the insufficient time I needed to find the right words or expressions and to think about how to express my idea in understandable and appropriate English" (Wu 2009, 93–94). Although Western teachers usually like students to engage in lively, spontaneous discussions, the reality is that often such student contributions are rather impulsive reactions and not always well informed or based on reflection. Teachers' short wait times for answers almost eliminate that very possibility. But by increasing the wait time to just three seconds, cognitive achievement can be increased (Tobin 1987). Western teachers may be overestimating the value of rapid-fire class discussions. However, in some settings longer wait times reduce students' confidence in answering (Ingram and Elliott 2016). Culture influences at what point longer wait times can cause student boredom or discomfort.

Hodkinson and Poropat describe well the influence of *face* on student participation in classroom interactions:

> One way in which *face* is expressed is when a student who is uncertain about the answer to a question posed in public by a tutor, avoids answering for fear of

losing *face* by giving an irrelevant answer. In their mind, it is safer not to answer knowing that the tutor will inevitably have to pass on to another student. This is so even if the non-respondent does not understand and would benefit from attempting an answer. Similarly, students who are uncertain of a concept are unlikely to ask a related question in class for fear of losing *face* because that could lead to judgements of a lack of diligence on the part of those asking. (2014, 434)

If a teacher asks shame-oriented students whether they have understood the class material, they almost always hear the answer yes. To publicly admit to not having understood something would entail loss of face either for the student (for admitting lack of understanding) or for the teacher (for not explaining the material well). Shame-oriented learners typically do not want to be called upon individually in a class, because if they answer incorrectly they would be shamed in front of their peers. A Bible school student in Papua New Guinea who was once asked a question in class by the teacher was so ashamed that he could not answer that he hid his head under the desk. The teacher learned to ask relatively simple questions and would read students' facial expressions. If a student appeared uncertain, a hint would be given to help him answer correctly and not lose face. This alleviated anxiety and built trust between the students and the teacher. Over time the students came to participate more freely in class interactions (Strässler 2005a). In China, even when students know the answer, the majority will not volunteer to answer in class for fear of losing face (Wu 2009). One solution is to present a short-answer question to a class and request that all the students answer *in choir*—that is, aloud together. Uncertain students can "lean" on the response of the rest of the class and not stand out if they don't know the answer. In Western settings this may seem somewhat childish, but I have found that with adult learners in many parts of the world, this approach is welcomed and common.

Students' willingness or reluctance to ask questions in class may also be related to *face*. For example, American students often feel that they can gain recognition (or *face*) by asking questions in class.[5] Why is this? "One possibility

5. Ironically, "In the United States, InAsk [asking questions in class] had a negative effect on grades, whereas OutAsk [asking the professor out of class] had a positive effect. . . . However, in contrast, InAsk had a positive impact on grade performance in Hong Kong. The opposite effect of InAsk on grade performance in the United States and Hong Kong implies that in-class questions in Hong Kong led to the desired grade-performance knowledge, whereas this was not so in the United States." Furthermore, "because the general level of in-class question asking is higher in American classes, the frequency of questions need not necessarily be correlated with the importance of those questions. Apart from taking up time, the greater number of questions may lead to loss of focus on the really important information in each lesson and, consequently, affect grades in a negative way (as shown in our data)" (Hwang, Francesco, and Kessler 2003, 87). "In the Singapore sample, it was neither InAsk nor OutAsk that had an impact on grades

is that questioning behaviors provided opportunities for individuals to show their depth of knowledge through profound questions that others may not have thought of. In so doing, students who raise these questions may gain the admiration of others for their deep knowledge" (Hwang, Francesco, and Kessler 2003, 87). But Hong Kong and Singaporean students may fear that they could lose face by asking questions in class. Singaporeans who need help to understand material presented by the teacher prefer to ask other students outside of class, which does not make them lose face. This points to the need, especially in more shame-oriented societies, to provide informal channels outside of class, either with peers or the teacher, for students to have their questions answered. Students in shame-oriented cultures may also be reluctant to ask questions in class because they want to avoid implying the teacher did not explain the material clearly or embarrassing her should she not know the answer. Neither the teacher nor the student should lose face. Even when speaking privately with another person, directly addressing a problem or complaint with that person can be experienced as extremely shaming or disrespectful.

One way to stimulate greater learner participation in more collectivistic cultures is through small-group discussions. As Hodkinson and Poropat state,

> Chinese students tend to respond better to small group activities because they provide a lower risk of loss of *face*. Thus, small group discussions could be used to develop consensus views which would be delivered by a group spokesperson who would be more comfortable contributing, because they would be delivering a group's collective view. (Hodkinson and Poropat 2014, 439, citing Holmes 1997)

The group's spokesperson is not perceived as putting herself forward in an immodest or *face*-threatening manner; she speaks for the group as a whole. The small group size also encourages maximum participation without any individual being at risk of losing face before the entire class. In my experience and the experience of others, this has been found to be an effective approach in many collectivistic settings (e.g., Apfelthaler et al. 2007, 32). Furthermore, intergroup competition can be a motivational factor improving student performance and offsetting negative aspects of *kiasu* (Hodkinson and Poropat 2014, 441).

Writing Style

A fascinating study by Wu and Rubin (2000) surveyed the literature and conducted a study comparing academic writing styles of Taiwanese and North

---

but rather OutCheck with a negative impact on grade performance. The implication was that checking with fellow students for desired knowledge is not a good move in Singapore; presumably, the knowledge so acquired is inadequate or wrong in its substantive content" (88).

American students to investigate the influence of collectivism and individualism. Table 10.2 summarizes their findings (remembering that Taiwanese students are not uniformly collectivistic). Some stylistic features considered collectivistic were evident in the writing of Taiwanese students who scored as more individualistic on the I/C test. This indicates that many of these features are linked less to collectivism per se than they are to the writing conventions students are taught in Taiwan that dictate good writing style in that culture. There is also considerable variability in these features, and some Taiwanese writers evidenced some of the same stylistic marks as the North Americans,

TABLE 10.2

Collectivistic and Individualistic Writing Styles

Taiwanese Students *Collectivistic*	North American Students *Individualistic*
Harmonious values: do not challenge prevailing ways; deference, cooperation, conformity.	Assertive values: establish arguments, then defend or refute them; creativity.
Indirect: • Circle around the main point; delay claims or purpose until the end • "From surface to core" • Use of metaphors and implication	Direct: • Set forth the main point or claim from the start • Lead with a topic sentence or thesis • Straightforward arguments
Deductive, inductive, and mixed reasoning	Deductive reasoning
Arguments based upon intuition and analogy	Arguments based upon postulation and syllogism
Humble, nonaggressive tone; use of hedge words (e.g., "might")	Confident, aggressive tone
Low self-disclosure of emotion, autobiographical information, accomplishments, etc.	High self-disclosure of emotion, autobiographical information, accomplishments, etc.
Emphasize collective wisdom, citing proverbs, idioms, maxims, poetry, etc.	Emphasize originality, using their own words and current sources
Preference for first-person plural and passive voice	Preference for first-person singular and active voice
Appeal to collective virtues, benevolence, group or family solidarity	Appeal to personal rights, gratification, and experience

Source: Summarized from Wu and Rubin (2000)

such as assertiveness. For students writing in a language other than their native language, lack of assertiveness may be related to the student's lack of confidence in their language skills.

What are the practical implications of this study and similar findings? It is not unusual for North American teachers or professors to give lower grades to assignments written in the more collectivistic style because it does not meet the kind of linear logic and structure of argument that is expected of good North American writing. "Why can't they just state their point and quit beating around the bush?" Conversely, a collectivistic teacher or professor may find the writing of individualistic students to be simplistic or arrogant. "Who do these students think they are? They're so critical of others and so confident in themselves!" In either case, teachers should help students understand the stylistic norms that they expect, and students should learn to adapt their writing styles to those norms. Cross-cultural teachers will, in many cases, need to adapt their stylistic expectations to those of the host culture. What constitutes good writing and a persuasive argument is culturally conditioned.

Academic Integrity: Plagiarism and Cheating

One of the most common and disconcerting experiences of teachers everywhere is the matter of plagiarism and cheating by students. Western educational institutions place a high value on academic integrity; violations are considered absolutely unacceptable. Of course, it still occurs all too often in the West, with 50 to 80 percent of students admitting to cheating[6]—but it is generally not tolerated and students are disciplined when discovered. Most other cultures also consider such behavior inappropriate, but international studies reveal cultural differences in the seriousness with which cheating is regarded. One team of researchers even developed a "tolerance of cheating index" based upon international comparisons (Magnus et al. 2002). Higher levels of cheating are sometimes associated with collectivism (e.g., McCabe, Feghali, and Abdallah 2008). Standards for plagiarism also vary greatly. For example, at Shantou University in China, up to 50 percent of an essay can be plagiarized without severe penalty (Slethaug 2007, 167). In many cases, students simply do not understand what plagiarism is or why it is a problem.

Students are especially tempted to plagiarize when attempting academic writing in a foreign language. A study of graduate linguistics students in Iran found that 94 percent believed that they had intentionally or unintentionally

---

6. Josephson Institute of Ethics, "2012 Report Card on the Ethics of American Youth," 2012, https://b3vj2d40qhgsjw53vra221dq-wpengine.netdna-ssl.com/wp-content/uploads/2014/02/ReportCard-2012-DataTables.pdf.

plagiarized (Babaii and Nejadghanbar 2017). The following reasons for plagiarism were discovered:

- students' unfamiliarity with plagiarism
- students' low academic writing skills
- teachers' carelessness and leniency
- students' lack of time
- students' laziness and deceitfulness
- educational system and its policies
- students' low language proficiency
- students' unfamiliarity with the subject of writing
- teachers' high expectations

A study of German and Slovene students found that easy access to information-communication technologies and the internet was the main reason for plagiarism (Jereb et al. 2018).

When entering a new educational setting, a cross-cultural teacher must learn the standards for academic integrity and how violations are normally dealt with. It is unlikely that the sojourner will be able to change the standards and procedures, so it's best to accept them and work within the system. If

---

SIDEBAR 10.6

What Is *Real* Cheating?

Judith Lingenfelter relates two stories that illustrate how "cheating" is viewed in different cultures.

An SIL colleague teaching in Ghana illustrated the idea of the social struggle vividly for me. She was teaching two adult literacy classes. The first time she gave an exam, she discovered at lunchtime that all the morning class members who had just taken the test were sharing the questions and their probable answers with the afternoon class who would take it next. She was aghast because to her that was cheating, whereas to her students that was expected behavior. Another colleague defines cheating in the "patron" context quite differently from my pedagogical one; he says Africans told him cheating was withholding information from those who needed it! (Lingenfelter 2001, 445)

- If you were the teacher in the first incident described above, what would you do?
- What would you say to students who told you that real cheating is withholding information from those who need it?

as a matter of conscience one absolutely cannot agree with the institutional policies, then that conflict needs to be addressed early along so that students are not caught in the middle. As discussed above, dealing with such unpleasant matters is a particularly sensitive issue in more collectivistic and shame-oriented cultures.

My first experience with different cultural mores regarding cheating came when I was studying German as a foreign language in Munich. There were only two other Americans in the course. Most of the other students were from Eastern Europe and Turkey. During quizzes, if the teacher left the room even for only a moment, students openly exchanged answers without the slightest compunction. As an American, I had been taught that this is inappropriate and that each student should do their own work. I was rather shocked at such boldfaced cheating. However, my lack of participation in the "exchange" made me appear disloyal to the group, failing to demonstrate solidarity by helping struggling fellow students. Here we see collectivistic behavior in action. In the hierarchy of values, which is worse: not helping a fellow student, or cheating on a test? In collectivistic cultures, the former is often the greater evil (see sidebar 10.6).

Cheating on a quiz may seem like a relatively small offense. But cheating on major exams, including college entrance exams and qualifying exams for government employment, is quite problematic in some cultures. Bribing teachers to receive better marks on such major exams is not uncommon in many places (e.g., Rahman 2011). Legal action had to be taken against government

---

SIDEBAR 10.7

Homework Cartels

An ESL teacher in Kazakhstan describes his experience this way:

Copying classmates' homework was routine. One of my students explained that there was too much busywork for students to do all of it themselves, so they made a pragmatic decision to take turns. The rest would copy from the appointed homework doer. A professor in Thailand experienced a similar "homework cartel" (George 1995, 10). The name is appropriate due to the level of organization and sophistication I witnessed. During midterms and finals, students could be seen in the cafeteria and hallways carefully creating and photocopying *shpargalki* (cheat sheets) to be surreptitiously used during exams. As they walked through the halls, professors would laugh, scold, or simply turn a blind eye. A colleague who taught Kazakh in the United States described her surprise when her American students would not "help" each other on a quiz, even after she encouraged them do to so.

officials and schools in India for tolerating cheating, where, for example, family members could be seen openly passing cheat sheets through schoolroom windows to students taking qualifying exams (e.g., Pratap 2015). Students may share exams with other students, allow written assignments to be copied and used by a student taking the class at a later time, prepare cheat sheets for

---

SIDEBAR 10.8

Tips for Teaching Collectivistic Learners

These tips are intended for teaching learners who are strongly influenced by collectivistic social behavior and identity. This is not to suggest that these learners cannot develop other ways of learning. However, introducing more individualistic approaches to learning may require time and patience.

- Learn students' names and promote a positive social atmosphere through informal social contact with the group outside of the classroom.
- Avoid competitive activities and comparing students to one another.
- Assign small group projects and assignments, mixing stronger and weaker students, thus encouraging social learning, group solidarity, mutual assistance, and group accomplishments.
- Praise the group as a whole. Do not praise individuals in the presence of the class.
- Realize that learner motivation is likely to be greatly influenced (positively or negatively) by grading and feedback on assignments. Frame negative comments with care.
- Avoid calling on individual students to answer questions in class. Allow students to answer in choir. Avoid di-

rectly critiquing a learner's viewpoint in class discussions.
- Promote class discussion by first having students discuss the topic in groups of three or four. Then have a spokesperson for each group share the group's findings with the class.
- Value tradition and history; don't overvalue creativity and change. Help students appreciate judiciously their traditions and history.
- Inform students of the standards for academic integrity and the consequences for violating those standards. It is equally important to make clear the rationale for the standards.
- Learn the culturally appropriate ways to resolve conflict and address problems. This often entails indirect communication and/or use of mediators.
- Discern, if necessary, face-saving ways to discipline or dismiss poorly performing students.
- Accept that students probably look to you as an authority figure and expert. Do not insist that students address you familiarly, such as by first name. However, also know that you can have close relationships with students in a fatherly or motherly manner. They may expect this.

exams, or form "homework cartels" in which students collaborate on assignments intended to be individually completed (see sidebar 10.7).

Of course, in real life if someone doesn't know the answer to a question, there is nothing wrong with asking someone else for help. Why should it be different in school? Teachers who want to impress upon their students the importance of not cheating or plagiarizing should explain that the purpose of exams and written assignments is not only to assess student ability but also to be a learning tool.

Conclusion

Positive relationships are foundational to effective teaching and learning everywhere, be it the relationship between teacher and learners or learners with one another. But cultural norms and expectations make navigating these relationships a challenge for the cross-cultural teacher. A cross-cultural teacher can bring some sense and guidance to what might otherwise be baffling behavior by taking steps to understand the underlying values of the host culture regarding status and social hierarchy, individualism and collectivism, the experience of shame and guilt, and various other dimensions of intercultural relations. These categories and dimensions are imperfect and complex, and must be applied in a nuanced manner. How they play out in any given culture or in the life of any individual must be discerned on a case-by-case basis. There are no easy formulas. But with patience, attentiveness, flexibility, and a sense of humor, a cross-cultural teacher can grow in appreciation of her students and improve instructional effectiveness. Sometimes this will mean conforming to the social norms and expectations (sidebar 10.8 summarizes how one might adapt teaching for collectivistic learners). But at other times it will entail introducing new, unfamiliar approaches to learning and social relations. As always, we must first understand the culture well before introducing change and be aware that how we introduce change can be as important as the desired change itself.

The Media Dimension

Part 1: Instructional Methods

I n this chapter we come to the fourth dimension of how culture influences teaching and learning: use of instructional media and modes.

How do learners in different cultures respond differently to various instructional media, learning exercises, and assignments? Because in previous chapters we already discussed topics such as orality, literacy, narrative teaching, and teaching methods for holistic and concrete learners, they will not be readdressed here. The focus here is on how various media can be utilized in cross-cultural instruction and the possible misunderstandings that arise by virtue of the medium itself. Instructors who have grown up in a world of books, television, computers, video games, and the like may assume that learners in other cultures are equally familiar with such media and share the same background of how messages in such media are to be understood.

Cross-cultural teachers often also depend heavily on verbal forms of instruction dominated by lecture, discussion, reading, and writing assignments. They will do well to expand their pedagogical toolbox and employ teaching tools and learning experiences beyond the verbal. Numerous resources can be consulted to discover the wide variety of teaching methods (e.g., Svinicki and McKeachie 2014; B. Davis 2009; LeFever 2004). To utilize a particular method effectively, the teacher must assess its instructional advantages as well as the potential pitfalls and misunderstandings due to cultural differences. In this chapter we will consider various instructional tools, types of learning

CHAPTER OVERVIEW

- Observation and Traditional Learning
- Teaching and Learning in a Foreign Language
- Reading and Writing Assignments
- Lecturing
- Use of Visual Media
- Song, Drama, and Other Arts

FIGURE 11.1

Five dimensions of culture's influence
on teaching and learning

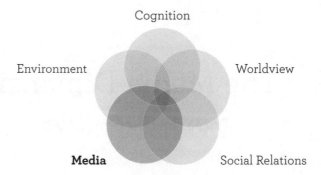

Cognition

Environment   Worldview

Media   Social Relations

assignments, and how they are received in different cultural settings. Chapter 12 is devoted to the cultural factors influencing online learning.

Observation and Traditional Learning

In societies with little formal schooling, observation is the primary mode of teaching children how to learn an occupation, develop life skills, and assume their role as responsible adults in the society. Of course, all children imitate the people around them and learn countless skills informally, from tying their shoes to table manners. Observation is central to enculturation everywhere. However, in many nonindustrial societies most learning is observational: girls learn to cook and sew by watching and helping their mothers, and boys learn to hunt or fish by accompanying their fathers. Verbal explanation is minimal, and the children seldom ask, "Why do we do it this way?" Take the example of Dalib, an Ethiopian son of an automobile repairman. At age six he began accompanying his father to the auto shop. There he observed his father, with no explanations given about the work. By age eleven Dalib could on his own fully remove and replace an automobile motor (Rose 1999).

Children who grow up almost exclusively exposed to such observational learning can face challenges when entering more formal schooling. As one study in Samoa concludes,

> Children who grow up in a family and community environment that emphasizes observational learning may be at a great disadvantage in a Western classroom that emphasizes active participation and dyadic instruction. . . . Children growing up in a non-Western cultural environment might not be prepared to

benefit from the intensive social scaffolding, lengthy dyadic interactions between teacher and student, as well as other forms of cognitive acceleration approaches to teaching that are valued and promoted in Western classrooms. (Odden and Rochat 2004, 47)

Cross-cultural teachers entering such a context must be cognizant of this limitation and seek to accommodate for it.

Apprenticeships are typically a more observational and experiential approach to learning a trade. They usually employ instructor modeling, trial and error, "shadowing," and similar methods of learning on the job. At the popular level there has been increasing attention given to observation as a way to train Christian workers for relatively simple tasks. Approaches are suggested describing modeling steps, such as MAWL—"model, assist, watch, leave"—or "I do, you watch / we do together / you do, I watch / you do alone / you teach another." Such approaches are easily reproduced and are suited for tasks that can be imitated. They require less verbal instruction or theory and are particularly effective with oral and concrete learners. They are, however, less suitable for instruction in more complex tasks that require theory and problem-solving. Nevertheless, observation can be an important supplement for developing practical skills that require more theory-based learning.

Teaching and Learning in a Foreign Language

Language is the most basic tool of teaching, and in many, if not most, cross-cultural teaching situations language presents the first big challenge to effectiveness. Language ability has an impact on teacher-learner interactions in the classroom and the ability to find suitable resources, such as textbooks and video material. When the teacher's native language is not the native language of the learners, there are several possible scenarios how instruction will occur, and each has its own particular advantages and disadvantages.

The teacher gives instruction in the native language of the learners. This is in many ways ideal for the students, but of course it requires that the teacher have a high level of proficiency in the language of instruction. This is normally only possible for long-term sojourners who have become fluent in the local language and is not an option for most short-term teaching assignments. If the teacher is not reasonably competent in the language, but attempts instruction in it anyway, the likely results will be teaching marred by grammatical errors, diction limitations, a foreign accent that is difficult for learners to understand, or outright incomprehensible sentences. Needless to say, this will reduce the teacher's credibility and distract from learning. It is better to use a translator than to attempt to speak broken or "baby talk" in the foreign language. In such a case, it's better to keep the use of the local language to a few friendly greetings or simple conversations, which the learners will appreciate.

The teacher gives instruction in her native language (e.g., English) without translation, and students are expected to have adequate proficiency to learn in that language. This is easiest for the teacher but the most difficult for most learners, especially if they are expected to write lecture notes or complete written assignments. Providing handouts or using slide presentations can alleviate this problem to some extent. Sometimes a visiting teacher or professor will be told that the learners are proficient in English. But the reality is that all too often student language proficiency may be adequate for casual conversation but not for learning at the level necessary for the course content. If comprehension is limited, real learning is minimal. Even when students are reasonably proficient in the language of instruction, teachers should intentionally speak slowly, articulate clearly, avoid slang and colloquialisms, and explain advanced vocabulary. It may take time for learners to adjust to the teacher's accent and style.

Instruction is translated into the native language of learners by an interpreter. In this case effectiveness depends heavily on the translator's proficiency. Countless stories can be told of teachers whose interpreters translated course content incorrectly or even reached an impasse and were unable to translate a concept at all. I've experienced interpreters who misconstrued or reinterpreted my message (as I later found out). In more than one of those cases, students who knew English disagreed with the interpreter's translation, and the teaching was interrupted by a debate over the correct translation or meaning.

Sequential translation—the teacher pausing after each sentence to allow the interpreter to translate—cuts the lecture length almost in half. However, pauses are not all bad: they give learners more time to process each sentence, and the teacher can gather his thoughts or reformulate material. Ideally, after a few sessions the teacher and interpreter can develop a comfortable rhythm and the translation process becomes less of a distraction. However, this approach makes class discussions between teacher and students difficult, since interactions must be translated in both directions.

Despite these limitations, if a competent interpreter is available, this approach is probably the best alternative for most situations. If the teacher is confident that the translator is competent and understands the subject matter, then it is wise to follow Pamela George's recommendation: "Make it known to your translator that you want her to elaborate on the concepts and add her own ideas" (1995, 188). Sidebar 11.1 describes ways to increase accuracy of translation and improve clear communication when teaching through a translator.

Whichever approach one adopts, it may be helpful to prepare a simple glossary of key terms. This can be translated into the native language of the students and distributed to them. They can then refer to it during lectures or when reading textbooks. Cross-cultural teachers are sometimes surprised at how much of the basic terminology and concepts essential for their subject

---

SIDEBAR 11.1

Maximizing Effectiveness When Teaching through a Translator

- Send lecture notes, handouts, or slide presentations to be translated well in advance of your visit. This will allow translators the time to look up difficult terms or concepts, ask for clarification, and prepare for translation. However, know that such materials may not in fact be ready upon your arrival. In one case my slides were translated, but out of order, and some slides were even located in the wrong lesson. If possible, check through them prior to teaching.

- Meet with your interpreter prior to teaching to clarify any difficult vocabulary and unfamiliar concepts.

- If you know of books using the concepts of your teaching that have been translated into the language of instruction, recommend these to your interpreter, so that she can acquaint herself with the vocabulary and ways of expressing the concepts.

- Ask the interpreter to give you ideas on how to make your content clearer. Give her the liberty during translation to explain your ideas to the students in her own words or to ask you for clarification before translating.

- When lecturing, keep sentences short and use simple language whenever possible. Explain key terms. Do not assume that the learners will associate the same meanings with them that you do.

- Use visual aids such as photos, diagrams, and video to support your teaching.

- Check Bible translations. If you are quoting a Bible verse and the exact wording is important, be aware that the translation in the other language may present a problem. "For example, if you intend to emphasize the word 'early' in 'Early will I rise and seek thee' (Psalm 63:1), it may interest you to know that the word simply doesn't occur in the Romanian Bible. Likewise, knowing that the Romanian version of Hebrews 4:16 admonishes us to 'hurry' to the throne of grace rather than to approach it 'boldly' may affect how you use that verse" (Veldt 1998, 62).

- Debrief with the interpreter after the first teaching sessions. Are you speaking too quickly? Is your voice audible? Are the concepts clear? Are learners following your train of thought? What can be done to address any difficulties? An interpreter may be reluctant to say anything negative about your teaching or style, so you will need to give him permission to be very frank with you, and thank him if he is. If possible, check with another bilingual person in the course to determine what adjustments might be necessary.

are unfamiliar or misunderstood by students. It also is prudent to consider whether examples and illustrations you use in your teaching may be culturally specific and thus unfamiliar to learners in another culture. For example, reference to the Fourth of July or to a television program such as *The Simpsons* may be meaningless to them. Many idioms, like "that's a hot potato" or "he put in his two cents," simply will not translate word for word. A story about Abraham Lincoln may illustrate your point perfectly, but your students may be clueless about who he is, when he lived, and why he would be important.

For further ideas on teaching students who speak a different language, see Jude Carroll's discussions of "Learning in English, Teaching in English" and "Practical Strategies for Developing Student's English Language Proficiency" (2015, 35–48; 67–78), and Pamela George's "Structuring Language Supports for Teaching" (1995, 173–91).

Reading and Writing Assignments

Most formal education, especially tertiary education, makes heavy use of reading and written assignments. Here too cultural expectations and standards vary widely. Reading and writing in a foreign language can be an enormous, time-consuming challenge.

Reading Assignments

Readings are a convenient way to cover large amounts of information efficiently. However, they present numerous challenges when teaching across cultures.

Availability and relevance. Appropriate, relevant literature is often unavailable in the language of instruction. If learners do not read English or a major language, the availability of high-quality literature drops off dramatically. What is available is often translated from another language and originated in a different cultural context, so examples or information may be foreign or irrelevant to the learners' context. Used or retired textbooks from America donated to schools in Ghana included "A" for apple and stories of foxes and bears, which are unfamiliar in Ghana (Goering 2006). The problem becomes even more serious when using texts written for ministry in suburban America being used to prepare for ministry in tropical villages in the Philippines, or when a textbook on sermon structure written for well-educated Western preachers is used to train preachers among oral learners in rural India.

Acquisition. Even if suitable literature is available, acquiring it presents a second challenge. International shipping can delay delivery of printed materials and texts. Then the package may be held up at a customs office, and a substantial customs duty may be imposed. Cross-cultural teachers, especially those on short-term assignments, frequently complain about materials arriving late or not at all. It is generally recommended that an instructor arriving from abroad bring the textbooks along in his luggage. A visiting teacher can consider sending a few copies of the textbook in advance to the school's library, where they can be placed on a reserve shelf and made available for students to share. Today many books are available as ebooks, which simplifies the purchase and delivery of texts. Articles and short documents can be scanned electronically and sent via email or shared in cloud-based storage. However, many students in under-resourced contexts do not have a tablet, Kindle, or even a laptop computer for reading ebooks. Audiobooks are increasingly available and may be especially suitable for oral learners.

Affordability. Books, especially academic literature, can be expensive. Thus, the instructor must carefully assess the affordability of texts. Is it realistic to expect that the learners will be able to purchase them? Are there alternatives, such as loaning the texts from a library, placing a few copies on reserve for students to share, or renting textbooks? Another solution is selecting short articles or chapters from books that can be distributed. Of course, students everywhere have discovered the ease of scanning or photocopying expensive texts at little or no cost and with no regard for copyrights. The joke in many places is that copyright means "the right to copy," or in other places, "when you copy, copy it right"!

Readability. Here the teacher asks: Is the level of writing suited to the students' comprehension level? Even the best textbook is useless if it employs vocabulary or argumentation incomprehensible to the readers. Thick books with small print and numerous footnotes can intimidate nonacademic learners. The text may assume background information that is entirely unfamiliar to them. The teacher cannot assume that learners with a high school diploma are able to understand what they are reading. This can be difficult to assess from a distance. Accordingly, first-time instructors will need to depend on the advice of experienced teachers in that cultural context (see George 1995, 175–80).

Student expectations. Perhaps an even greater cultural factor regarding reading assignments is students' expectations. Often the very idea of required reading is foreign. In countries as diverse as the Balkans, Thailand, and Japan, college students are expected to read about fifteen pages per week for a course, and by no means more than twenty (George 1995, 32–33). In many locations, the professor distills the most important points from textbooks in his lectures and there is little motivation for students to engage directly with the textbook (Slethaug 2007, 58). Professors who expect their students to have read the material and come to class ready to discuss it will in such cases be disappointed. In other contexts, one may encounter the opposite expectation: students assume that they must read required texts so thoroughly as to nearly memorize them. Jude Carroll writes, "A student once told me she shook with fear the first time she encountered a reading list because she assumed it would require the same kind of repetitive, whole text mastery that she was accustomed to achieving. How could we do that with twenty titles?" (2015, 23).

Time demands on students. In some universities students have twenty or even thirty-six hours of classes per week (George 1995, 12). This leaves little time for homework and reading. Students often work full-time jobs to support themselves and/or their families, which again leaves little time for assignments outside of class. Add to this the fact that in many, if not most, cases students are reading in a second language, which can double or triple the time needed to read a text.

In summary, this means that in most cases cross-cultural teachers need to include more content in class lectures that might otherwise be covered in readings. One cannot depend heavily on reading assignments to achieve course objectives. Handouts and short essential readings will be more important and more realistic than lengthy textbooks and long reading lists. Students who are not accustomed to reading long texts and processing written information can be aided by introducing them to shorter texts and coaching them on how to identify thesis statements and key points. If students are expected to discuss readings in class, it can be helpful to give them the discussion questions in advance so that they can prepare as they read. Assignments that ask students to apply principles from the readings to their personal lives and ministry will help them read with intentionality, process the information, and appreciate the practical relevance of the material.

Writing Assignments

Written assignments such as essays and research papers are common in formal education. Students writing in a foreign language will likely struggle with even the basics of expressing their ideas and using proper grammar and diction. But the challenge doesn't stop there. If students are expected to write a research paper using sources, the teacher must be clear about what "using sources" means. Carroll writes of master's level students who understood "using sources" to mean quoting verbatim from the textbooks (2015, 31). If the goal of a writing assignment is for students to critically evaluate ideas, they may not feel it is their place as students to make such judgments, or they may not have developed the necessary critical evaluation skills. Here are some questions that a teacher should ask if expecting students to write research papers:

- What kind of sources are students expected to use? Do students have access to the necessary resources, such as a library or internet databases?
- Do they know how to sort through possible sources and judge their quality or importance? Can they assess the value and reliability of internet sources?
- Do they know how to frame an argument and present supporting evidence?
- Have they developed critical and evaluative thinking skills that enable them to arrive at their own conclusions and form their own opinions?
- Do they know how the paper is to be structured?
- Are students expected to write the paper by hand or on a computer? Do they own or have access to a personal computer, and if so do they know how to use it?
- Do they know the school standards for plagiarism and academic honesty, and the consequences if the rules are violated?
- Are students allowed to collaborate on the writing assignment, and if so to what extent?

If students have little experience writing research papers, the teacher may want to break the assignment down into smaller parts, such as topic selection, how to find sources, how to evaluate sources and arguments, how to take notes, how to craft an outline, and so on. As students gain experience, the steps can be eliminated. Giving them writing samples will help them understand the expectations and provide a model of exemplary research and writing. Allowing them to rewrite poorly written papers is another way to help them improve writing skills.

It must be kept in mind that sometimes student living quarters—be it in a tiny apartment or in a dormitory—are cramped and may have no personal space or desk (see fig. 13.3 on page 287). Desk space also may be very limited in the library or study halls. This means that physical conditions alone create a challenge for students who need to find privacy and a desk and chair where they can write.

Programmed Learning

Programmed learning describes the use of learning materials that are highly structured so as to enable independent learning or self-study and give students immediate feedback. Study guides often break tasks into step-by-step learning units or exercises. Typically, a workbook, video, or computer-based media is used. Such programmed learning has been a major feature of Theological

Education by Extension (TEE) programs.[1] Questions for each learning unit are available in workbooks or online formats. Most are multiple choice or fill-in-the-blank questions that require minimal verbal skills. The answers often appear in the back of the book, so students can immediately check and correct their own answers. Many TEE materials are quite basic, employing repetition, questions based on simple observation of Bible texts, or giving definitions and then testing comprehension.

The advantage of such materials is that learners can experience immediate reinforcement by checking their answers. This can give them a sense of success and progress, which is particularly important to learners who lack confidence or have had little formal schooling. Students can learn at their own pace, though they are often part of a group that meets together to discuss each lesson. Because TEE study guides are standardized and easily reproducible, they can be widely distributed and used. There are, however, limitations. The question-answer approach can seem overly analytical and confusing to more holistic and oral learners. Instead of learning through the Bible story or passage as a whole, TEE questions typically require a more analytical approach, examining individual verses or words. There is little place for more open-ended questions about interpretation or application. The materials are rather rigid and not easily adapted to the local context or the educational level of the learners.

However, Aylett and Green write enthusiastically about the program's expansion of learners' analytic capabilities:

> Programmed instruction is often seen as indoctrinating and paternalistic, stifling critical thought. This is a serious point because many (not all) TEE courses do use programmed textbooks. However, programmed texts are not necessarily shackled to a rigid behaviourist philosophical foundation. Also when reflective questions are used alongside didactic ones in a well-designed TEE lesson, it leads to an appropriate combination of formative and critical education and hence to the possibility of transformative learning. . . . Programmed texts provide the secure bottom rungs of a ladder which takes them toward the higher cognitive levels of analysis, synthesis and evaluation. These higher cognitive skills may be honed gradually by moving away from strictly programmed texts as learners progress through the curriculum. (2015, 75–76)

Lecturing

Lecturing may be the most common form of instruction used in formal education. In the context of teaching across cultures, it too has potential difficulties.

1. For a good overview of the philosophy, history, and practice of TEE, see Aylett and Green 2015.

Student Note-Taking

In many cultures students are accustomed to writing in their notebooks only what the teacher writes on the blackboard. That is what is important and what must be mastered for examinations. Anything not written on the board is considered unimportant. Students may even be expected to record the lectures in their notebooks verbatim as if they were taking dictation. Many learners will not know how to take notes from lectures apart from simply copying from the board or transcribing verbal dictation. Such learners may be frustrated or confused by teachers who lecture rather freely, mixing in discussion or stories and not adhering to a lecture script.

Some years ago I lectured at a rural seminary in the Democratic Republic of the Congo where each semester, each student received one spiral-bound block of lined notepaper. Class notes for all the courses that semester would need to be condensed into that notebook. Very few of them could afford textbooks, so their class notes constituted their future library. In such situations it is no wonder that students want to write down every word that proceeds from the teacher's mouth. Field-dependent learners will be helped most if handouts are not a running script of the lecture but are structured in outline form or with clear section headings to organize the lecture content. A visiting lecturer who brings photocopied handouts or makes available electronic documents of her class lectures will be especially beloved. However, it may be best to bring your own copies of handouts. A Bible school in central Asia prepared photocopies of my lecture notes where I was teaching. However, I discovered in the course of teaching that one lesson had been copied four times, and other lessons were not copied at all.

Even in remote locations, most students own a cell phone with recording capabilities. Allowing students to make audio recordings of lectures can help them process lecture material. Oral learners and those learning in a foreign language will find it especially helpful. They can listen again to the lectures, correct their notes, and store the audio for future reference. Students who are not familiar or comfortable with technology may need assistance in learning how to make use of such tools. If students are taking notes with a laptop computer, they should be taught how to back up and transfer data in the event that their laptop is damaged, lost, or needs replacement.

Providing Structure

Earlier we saw that field-dependent learners can benefit from advance organizers such as outlines or diagrams. A handout or slide presentation with clear lecture outlines and key concepts or quotations is a good starting point. However, students may be unaccustomed to filling in the content corresponding to the main outline points in their personal lecture notes. They may not have learned how to distinguish important ideas from less important ones or how to formulate those ideas in their own words as they take notes. This comment from a Chinese student in an American MBA course could be echoed by learners from many cultures: "In China, we are accustomed to the instructors' ways of recapping points for us. Here, the instructors talk about a lot of things. They should let us know the most important things that we need to grasp" (Liu and Magjuka 2011, 175). Recapping the most salient points of a lecture at its end may be helpful. The teacher may also need to instruct students on note-taking skills and clarify expectations about how they are to record lecture material. A teacher in Papua New Guinea taught students how to take lecture notes by writing lecture notes on the blackboard as he lectured. He would explain why some points were written, but not others, thus giving students an example of identifying important content and of good note-taking. Gradually the students learned to take much improved lecture notes on their own (Strässler 2005a).

Contextually Relevant Illustrations and Examples

As we have repeatedly noted, both teaching methods and teaching content must be contextualized to the needs, questions, worldview, and local challenges that learners face. This applies not only to the curriculum and topics that are taught but also to the illustrative material used during instruction. Most good teaching includes relevant, practical examples, and this is especially important when teaching across cultures or teaching oral learners. Finding culturally relevant illustrative material can be a challenge if the teacher is not well acquainted with the context. Examples familiar in the world of the lecturer may be entirely unknown to the learners.

Imagine, for example, a teacher describing methods of youth ministry he knows from his experience in an urban American church to learners who work in rural churches where "youth ministry" includes anyone not yet married, regardless of age. Although the teacher may not have examples to draw on from the learners' cultural context, giving a variety of examples from other contexts or inviting learners to themselves contextualize a principle or give their own examples can alleviate this limitation. When teaching internationally, I often ask organizers to invite local persons to present case studies from their setting. This provides examples that are culturally relevant. However, for this to function well, presenters must be clearly instructed about the expectations for their presentation.

Body Language and Use of Humor

Two elements of intercultural communication that are easily overlooked in teaching are the teacher's body language and use of humor in the classroom. In Ethiopia, for example, speaking while facing the blackboard or failing to have eye contact with learners is considered rude. When learners are not native speakers of the instructional language, visual contact with the teacher can be important for understanding. American professors tend to be very casual when teaching, sitting on a desk or wandering around the classroom. This can be very distracting or appear undignified to learners. Here is a small sampling of behavior that can be considered especially rude or inappropriate:

- Placing one's foot on a table or chair.
- Crossing one's legs and pointing the toe at a person.
- Showing the bottom of one's foot.
- Using the left hand for gesturing, eating, or anything (except for one private thing). This can be a challenge for left-handed instructors.
- Blowing one's nose in the presence of others.

Cross-cultural teachers should familiarize themselves with local norms for nonverbal communication and etiquette.

Lecturers often use humor to lighten the atmosphere, sustain interest, or highlight a memorable point. Laughing together can create a sense of camaraderie, and humor can make teachers or professors can seem more approachable. Skillfully used, humor can diffuse tension or conflict. In America and England the use of humor in college teaching is considered to have numerous benefits (e.g., Lei, Cohen, and Russler 2010; Nesi 2012), and one older study found that college teachers use humor an average of 3.34 times in a fifty-minute class period (Bryant, Cominsky, and Zillmann 1979).

However, humor is a very cultural matter and can easily backfire.[2] One should always check first with a native speaker to be sure a joke or humorous expression will be understood and appropriate. Few things can make a speaker feel more foolish than attempting to be funny, only to find that the learners fail to see the humor and take it seriously. This can leave learners simply confused and the teacher embarrassed.

Some types of humor rarely make the jump smoothly from one cultural context to another. Puns seldom work in another language. Sarcasm and irony are especially tricky and often problematic. Some topics over which one might casually joke may be deeply offensive or even a taboo topic in another culture. A good rule of thumb is to avoid any humor relating to sexuality,

---

2. See, for example, Yue 2010 on how the use of humor has evolved in China.

gender difference, specific ethnic groups or nationalities, and religion. Fundamentally, one must discern how much humor, if any, is even appropriate for the setting. Will the use of humor cause the learners to not take anything that the teacher says seriously? Will it be interpreted as the teacher not taking her role or the learners seriously? This is a risk especially when a teacher employs silly antics or humorous behaviors. In some church traditions, any use of humor in teaching or preaching is considered irreverent or flippant.

Use of Visual Media

Modern technology offers many easy ways to employ visual instructional media such as diagrams, graphs, photos, videos, and cartoons. They can bring information to life and help learners conceptualize, and they are particularly valuable to oral learners and those more visually oriented. An and Carr cite numerous empirical studies that suggest "combining both verbal and visual/spatial processing would promote learning and achievement" (2017, 412; see also, e.g., Riding and Rayner 1998, 148–51; Angeli and Valanides 2004). However, people interpret images quite differently depending on their culture, their level of literacy, and their exposure to various conventions of visual communication. This is sometimes referred to as visual literacy. In selecting images to integrate into instruction, cross-cultural teachers must consider whether they are culturally appropriate and whether learners will understand them. When using electronic media, another factor to consider is the possibility of power outages and other technical difficulties common in much of the world. Before preparing instructional media, teachers need to inquire about technical possibilities and limitations.

Photographs and Drawings

One might assume that pictures and drawings would be the least problematic when teaching across cultures. But consider these examples of how that is not the case. Muslims may take offense at images involving drinking of alcoholic beverages, pigs, or women dressed immodestly. Animals can have various metaphoric meanings: for example, in Western culture owls are associated with wisdom, but some American Indian tribes associate them with evil or death, and in parts of Asia they represent stupidity. For Hindus monkeys are not a symbol of folly; they are sacred and not to be photographed. Gestures and body language may be misunderstood. For example, the extended tongue is a rude gesture in many cultures, but in Nepal it is a welcome greeting (for a good list of other examples, see McAnany 2009). Some years ago a photograph was used in American advertising of a middle-aged man in a business suit having breakfast at a penthouse window overlooking a city. American students interpreted the photo as an image of wealth and power, which was what the advertiser intended. But Chinese students focused on why such a person would be eating alone without his family (cited in Messaris 1995). The Chinese students' collectivist orientation directed their attention to an entirely different element of the photograph.

Depictions of objects may not be readily understood by persons unfamiliar with photographs and books. A literacy worker in Brazil found that illustrating the word *jaguar* for the Kayapo people would need to depict the animal as seen from the front, not the side, because that is how they see it when hunting (Lingenfelter and Lingenfelter 2003, 106–7). A health worker made an oversized mock-up of a mosquito as a visual aid for group instruction on the danger of malaria-bearing mosquitos. Later he found that villagers were not using mosquito nets because they claimed that they had never seen mosquitos as large as the one in the illustration (107–8). It is generally recommended that in oral cultures drawings should not include too much detail that distract from the central purpose or message of the drawing. Contrary to what one might expect, one study in Papua New Guinea found that among the nonliterate, simple black-and-white line drawings involving people were best understood, followed by faceless outlines, detailed black-and-white drawings, and watercolors. Least understood were black-and-white photographs. Although people preferred color pictures, they were not the best understood form (Cook 1981). On the other hand, another study found that field-dependent learners could recall illustrations better when color was added to them; this reduced the performance gap between them and field-independent learners, who generally outperformed them (Moore and Dwyer 1994).

Cartoons and comics are often used to teach not only children but also adults. Educators are increasingly recognizing that "comic books (or graphic novels) can teach literacy skills and critical thinking in ways that other formats can't" (Rapp 2011, 64). Combining text with pictures has been demonstrated to increase recall among college students (Brunyé et al. 2006). The global popularity of comics is staggering. In Japan, manga comic book sales in 2014 topped $2 billion[3] and comic sales in 2019 outnumbered book sales for the first time.[4] Sales of comics and graphic novels in the US and Canada in 2018 are estimated at over $1 billion.[5] Until recently, in the Philippines comics

3. "Sales Value of Manga Comic Books in Japan from 1985 to 2014," Statista, February 28, 2016, https://www.statista.com/statistics/688461/japan-manga-comics-sales-value.

4. "Sales of Online Manga Overtake Book Editions for 1st Time," *Jakarta Post*, February 27, 2018, https://www.thejakartapost.com/life/2018/02/26/sales-of-online-manga-overtake-book-editions-for-1st-time.html.

5. Milton Griepp, "Comics and Graphic Novel Sales Hit New High in 2018," ICv2, May 2, 2019, https://icv2.com/articles/markets/view/43106/comics-graphic-novel-sales-hit-new-high-2018.

were more popular than newspapers and other media, with top issues selling easily 400,000 copies in a week. Now internet and other media have hurt the comic industry.[6]

However, comics can face the same misunderstandings described above. Some learners may not understand common features of comics and cartoons such as a speed lines and speech or thought bubbles. Causal or temporal connections from one picture frame to the next may not be grasped. Teachers utilizing comics with learners who are unfamiliar with the medium may need to explain these features.

Film and Video

Video material such as Hollywood films or excerpts, illustrative material, and documentary reports are motivational, visual, and concrete. As noted above, they are especially helpful for oral learners. In the words of one Mongolian who viewed short films of Bible stories, "I have been reading the Bible, but I didn't understand it. When I saw Abraham in the movie I then understood what the Bible was saying and I then understood who God really is." Another said, "The film of the person's life and how he/she dealt with God is the trigger that allows me to understand what the written Bible is talking about" (Posey 2008). Increasingly, Christian films are being produced internationally and so have greater relevance for local cultures. Johannes Merz writes, "Film has become an integral part of West African Christianity, and in a wider sense of the urban public square" (2010, 120).

If a teacher intends to use video material available on the internet, such as a YouTube video, it should be downloaded to the computer so that the presentation is not dependent on a strong internet connection. One should not underestimate the challenges associated with using video material in a foreign classroom.

- *Unreliable or missing technology*—Lack of electricity, missing projectors or cables, incompatible cable connections, burned-out bulbs, poor image quality, lack of loudspeakers, inability to darken the room, outdated or missing software, and so on.
- *Language*—Many videos suitable for instructional purposes are only available in English or a major European language. Will the learners be able to understand them? In rare instances videos can be translated using subtitles by a competent translator with some video editing skills.

6. Mynardo Macaraig, "'Komiks' Industry Fights for Survival," *Planet Philippines*, October 17, 2010, http://planetphilippines.com/entertainment/komiks-industry-fights-for-survival.

SIDEBAR 11.2

Understanding and Misunderstanding the *Jesus Film*

A good example of some of the challenges and opportunities of using video and film is the *Jesus Film*, based on the Gospel of Luke. It is one of the most widely used evangelistic tools. It has been translated into over 1,700 languages and is reportedly instrumental in over 490 million persons coming to faith in Jesus Christ (www.jesusfilm.org). Numerous reports indicate that many people better understand who Jesus is and have a more positive attitude toward Jesus after viewing the film (e.g., Mansfield 1984). It is not unusual to hear viewers in non-Western contexts comment after seeing the film, "So Jesus wasn't a Westerner after all!" (Because most missionaries and Christians they know are Westerners, they assumed that Jesus was, too.) They may more readily relate to Jesus who lives in a world more like theirs: he wears sandals, walks on dusty roads, and cooks fish on open coals.

However, elements of the Jesus film can distract from the intended message.

People may misinterpret the images and behaviors through their culture and worldview.

- "The Sawi identified Judas as the hero of the gospel story. Some Mongolians believed Jesus to be a Buddhist monk" (Steffen 1993a).
- In remote Guinea (West Africa) viewers believed Jesus could perform miracles because he was a shaman. This was evident because he carried a satchel with magical fetishes, like other shamans in their society (Wiher 1997, 70).
- Although in the film Jesus lives in a nonindustrialized world, he is presented as a Western personality (fair skin and light hair color) with relatively little emotional expression. In the words of Johannes Merz, "Particularly during the time of his ministry, Jesus is depicted as exemplary and immaculate, merging the conventions of Hollywood with the evangelical pietistic tradition" (2010, 113).

- *Cultural relevance*—If appropriate reading material is difficult to find, such videos are even more difficult to find.
- *Misunderstanding of cultural meanings*—Body language, social interactions, cultural references, symbols, and so on may be unfamiliar to or misunderstood by viewers (see sidebar 11.2).

Some viewers may not understand that in dramatic films, scenes are enacted, not a filming of actual events. High-quality special effects can give the impression that scenes are the filming of actual miracles, angels, or spiritual powers (Merz 2010). A Nigerian woman was once asked why she was so confident that Jesus had risen from the dead; her reply was that she had seen it in a movie. Even Bible films that attempt to simply portray the biblical story are in fact interpretations, but often neither the producers nor the viewers are aware of this. Because the visual elements of a film are the more powerful communicative elements, they can overshadow the verbal messages (the biblical text). Because the visual is more culturally specific than the verbal, potential for culturally related misunderstandings is greater (Merz 2010).

Podcasts of short lectures or presentations have become a popular tool of instruction. A study of the use of video podcasts among Chinese students found that the best learning outcomes were obtained by using podcasts that included both the instructor and slide presentations versus podcasts including only slide presentations with narration. However, the social element increased the cognitive load. The study also found that mental fatigue began to set in at ten minutes, and by twenty-two minutes heavy mental fatigue was evident (Pi and Hong 2016). These findings contrast with findings of studies of American students, whose learning was not significantly improved by showing the face of the instructor. Pi and Hong attributed this to Chinese students being more relationally oriented, and Americans more task oriented: "Chinese students can be expected to be particularly sensitive to social cues and their cognitive outcomes are consequently more based on relationships than Western students. In contrast, American students may pay less attention to social cues but more attention to the content of the study" (142). All this highlights again the importance of taking culture into account when producing and selecting video material. Short ten-minute segments are most likely to hold attention in most cultures.

Maps, Diagrams, and Tables

Maps, diagrams, and tables present information in a comprehensive manner that visualizes relationships with an abstract depiction. From childhood, most Westerners have been exposed to these media and almost intuitively understand their meaning. This is by no means the case everywhere. For example, at least in the past, diagrams and graphs were seldom used in Chinese textbooks and were thus less familiar to Chinese students (Mitschian 1991, 347). Even giving verbal directions on how to get from one place to another can be a challenge (see sidebar 11.3).

Linda Achren (1991) described her experience teaching recent immigrants in Melbourne who had no more than six years of schooling in their home country. She discovered that they had difficulty reading city maps, a necessary skill to navigate job interviews and shopping. Although modern GPS guidance programs have made map reading less essential than previously, maps are still

SIDEBAR 11.3

Getting from Here to There

Birte Pappenhausen describes her experience teaching German as a foreign language at Khovd University in Mongolia. Her students came mostly from the least developed rural part of the country. One lesson was on "giving directions," including vocabulary such as "left/right, straight ahead, across from, etc." She thought students would be motivated by the opportunity to assist tourists who do not understand the local language and cannot read the signs in Cyrillic script. Such visitors are grateful when someone can help them find their way. She writes:

> The first assignment was to describe the way from the University building to a nearby neighborhood. However, despite giving several examples, they couldn't do it. I then drew a map of the center of Khovd with streets and buildings on the blackboard, but the map didn't seem to help. They confused right and left, used the wrong prepositions, and counted the number of streets randomly where one should turn or stop. To assist, I used chalk to trace the described route on the blackboard map so that students could see how their directions were interpreted. But this did not help either.
>
> I decided to simulate the situation of a taxi ride by setting up two chairs. I was the driver and the student sat next to me and was to give me directions how drive from the airport to a certain hotel. Alas, this exercise was also unsuccessful. I was simply unable to teach them how to give directions in German.

Mongolians have a remarkable sense of orientation and can find their way without recognizable streets through the prairie even in snowstorms. The challenge with this lesson was not the German language, but a different way of thinking. Mongolians are a largely nomadic people and do not have buildings or streets as orientation points, but rather navigate by the sun, rivers, property ownership and the like. Furthermore, they do not use definite lengths, e.g., *third street on the left*, or timeframes, e.g., *stop after ten minutes*, but rather *a little bit this way*, or *after a while*. Mongolians generally do not have city maps, and even in the capital city some streets do not have names. I would have had to teach them a whole new way of looking at a city in terms of maps, distances, and streets, and instead of east/west, right/left, etc.

My failed attempt at the taxi simulation made evident that the situation was simply too unrealistic. Firstly, taxi drivers don't need to have directions (they already know the way to hotels); and secondly, in rural areas all taxi drivers are men, but I was a woman. (Pappenhausen 2015)

I had a similar experience in Manila attempting to explain to a taxi driver the directions to my destination by drawing a map. He spoke English, so language wasn't the problem. He simply couldn't understand the map, and I didn't know the street names or landmarks. Eventually I had to find another taxi.

a major feature in many books and online sources. More fundamentally, the idea of an aerial view—not only with maps but also in floor plans and other diagrams—was unknown to these learners. It took about six months for them to acquire skills for understanding such diagrams. Achren taught the concept of aerial view through direct experience; she had students look down upon simple objects such as cups, chairs, and tables "as a bird sees them" and draw pictures of them as seen from that angle. The exercise was expanded to draw the classroom, then the floorplan of the building, and so on.

Basic graphs and charts may be difficult for even students with more years of formal education to understand. For instance, adult students in a German as a foreign language course were given the assignment to describe in words the meaning of simple bar graphs: 20 percent could not understand them whatsoever, another 20 percent gave up on the assignment before completing it, less than half could even partially clarify the diagrams, and only a quarter did so accurately. Students' comments included "I couldn't describe these graphs even in Polish" and "I didn't even know where to begin with interpreting the diagrams, they're just not clear" (Kiefer 2005). Here again, one cannot assume that such material can be used and understood by students without considerable explanation.

In conclusion, it should be added that various studies show that adding an image or picture to text is a good instructional strategy. Learners' recall increases across all learning styles. The combination of text, image, and sound increased recall even more (Riding and Rayner 1998, 149–50). Thus, use of multiple media is likely to increase learning, wherever one teaches and with almost any learners. One must simply give attention to use of images that are understandable and relevant to the learners and that do not miscommunicate.

Song, Drama, and Other Arts

Whereas most Western approaches to teaching are highly propositional and verbal, more participative, affective approaches to teaching are common in more traditional, nonindustrial, or semiliterate societies. Song, drama, and other art forms can be highly effective instructional modes for children and for adults. Not only can they communicate a particular content, such as a story or moral principle; but their aesthetic, participative, and more emotive nature involves the whole person, and can touch the heart as well as the mind. Brian Schrag describes how use of the arts "enriches the experience of a message. Tapping into existing arts allows new messages of truth to be marked as particularly important, uniquely memorable, and distinctly engaging. Artistic expressions are often the most powerful and enduring means of communication within a culture" (2007, 201).

Song

Many societies use song as a way to instruct and pass on traditional values and stories. Songs are memorable, easily passed on, and touch the emotions. One example of this is the *matjapat* form of song used in Javanese and Sundanese societies. "Performed by unaccompanied solo singer or interpreted to the accompaniment of elaborate ensemble, *tembang matjapat* comprises love songs, religious songs, moral-didactic songs, songs for and by children, lullabies, songs paying respect to parents and superiors, ceremonial songs of court and village, and songs of dramatic intent" (Kartomi 1973, v). Furthermore, "A large number of *matjapat* songs play an educative role. Moral and religious teachings, albeit sometimes with a feudal tinge, are taught through the song texts" (10–11). This form of song has been used by an Indonesian Christian to communicate the Gospel of Matthew to Javanese learners (Lingenfelter and Lingenfelter 2003, 103).

Songs have been a significant factor in the positive response to the gospel among the Dinka in Sudan. Several features contributed to their impact:

> First, the song outpouring emanates from a deeply seated wrestling with suffering and faith. . . .
>
> Second, the song outpouring articulates the Christian proclamation in idioms and nuances familiar to the Dinka heart and mind. Because of this, the rural Dinka, in particular, have very little struggle to comprehend or receive the message of the gospel that the songs convey. . . .
>
> Third, the song outpouring provides a basis of identification with a sense of ownership of the Christian proclamation. The Christian message, expressed in the songs and conveying local, familiar cultural idioms and meanings, is unlikely to be treated as foreign. . . .
>
> Finally, the song outpouring among the Bor Dinka contains a large and influential women's contribution, providing a unique gender balance. Contrary to the traditional Dinka culture, women lead the way in composing and popularizing the new Dinka songs. This is highly unusual in a male-dominated society. (Dau 2011, 197–200)

A study examining conversion narratives of how Ethiopians became Protestants found that for over a third of the individuals who were interviewed, Christian songs opened the way to receive the gospel message (E. Chang 2015, 163). In the words of one of the study participants, "The Pente[7] songs revealed the message of the Bible. The song of the Pentes itself is the Word of God; it is the preaching; it is a sermon by itself. Therefore, it is not hard to understand the Word of God presented in the Protestant songs" (164).

---

7. *Pente* is a term used in Ethiopia for all Protestants, not just Pentecostals.

Another said, "The song just walked into my heart. Unconsciously I was singing the song. And I was shocked to find myself singing the Protestant songs
while I was sitting in the Orthodox Church" (165–66). Because songs are
repeatedly listened to, the message of a song can be more easily understood
and memorized. Numerous similar examples could be recounted in various
cultural contexts (see sidebar 11.4).

While songs are not a replacement for use of texts or the oral communication of information, a study among the Yoruba in Nigeria found that among
oral learners, adding singing to other oral communication methods increased
learning significantly (Klem 1982, 173–74).

Drama

Most cultures are familiar with some type of drama. Drama involves some
form of actors imitating persons or events, usually involving a story. Having
learners observe dramatic performances and participate as actors in a drama
or skit are effective ways to engage them in simulated real-life scenarios.
Educational drama sometimes employs improvisation, with similarities to
role-playing (see below). African forms of drama may include music, people

---

SIDEBAR 11.4
Story in Song

Tom Steffen relates how the Antipolo/
Amduntug Ifugao people located in Central Luzon of the Philippines use song to
tell stories. This illustrates not only the
use of song as a popular mode of storytelling but also creativity, part-to-whole
thinking, participation, and repetition as
means of learning.

The Ifugao love to hear the sweep of
Scripture or selected large slices of it,
such as a whole book or letter, whether
storied or sung. One example of this
is the Bible story from creation to the
ascension. Using a traditional Salidu-
may tune, the lead singer (often female)
composed the story as she went along
(creativity within boundaries that pro-

motes mystery), with the first stanza
being a short summary of the direction of the story (whole-to-part); those
listening would sing the chorus (participation) after each of the 52 stanzas
(repetition). The formulaic end of the
song demonstrated a high respect for
the ability of each participant to discern
truth without outside pressure: "Ngenamung hu nemnem yu tep ag pepilit
Jesus, ngenamung kayun tuu" ("Your
minds are free to decide, Jesus does not
force, it's up to you"). This song offers
singer and searchers exposure to the
Source of Truth; they sing their way to
Truth. Similarly, followers of Jesus sing
their way to biblical authenticity. (Steffen 2010, 142–43)

dressing as animals, masquerades, and puppetry (Finnegan 2012, 485–501). Drama has been employed in a host of development projects, including education for sustainable development (e.g., McNaughton 2010), and perhaps most widely in HIV/AIDS education (e.g., Barnes 2013; see also fig. 11.2).

For example, Themba Interactive in South Africa "uses interactive theatre techniques from various drama and theatre forms such as forum theatre, dramatherapy, process drama, drama in education, psychodrama, and theatre for development" (Chipatiso 2013, 253). Playing a role allows participants to experience various emotions and inner conflicts, thus enhancing achievement of affective learning objectives and behavioral change. Follow-up discussion can lead to reflection and direct application of meanings to everyday life.

FIGURE 11.2

Skits have been used in AIDS education in East Africa using this simple drawing with Swahili text as a guide

Drawing courtesy of Annette Schumacher

SIDEBAR 11.5

Grain Banks, Loan Repayment, and Drama

Viggo Søgaard describes a development project that was implemented among the Garo people of Bangladesh and northeast India who were poor farmers. A grain bank cooperative was formed with some 352 villages participating. The cooperative had a revolving loan fund. Due to the low literacy rates among the people, audio cassettes were determined to be the most efficient way to communicate to them the procedures for obtaining and repaying loans. The information was presented not as a recording of the rules and expectations, but rather as an audio drama. Later, research was conducted to determine the effectiveness of the program. "There was a direct correlation between the number of people listening to the tapes and the rate of repayment. Where the cassettes had been used widely, the rate of return was high, and where only a few people had listened to the cassettes, the rate of return was low. . . . It was obvious to everybody concerned with the project that the communication system helped to make it work. Without the cassettes, the project would have failed and large sums of money would have been wasted" (Søgaard 1993, 167–68).

The example in sidebar 11.5 shows how drama can be particularly effective with oral or concrete learners. Even audio recordings with dramatic narrations of behaviors and procedures are much easier to understand and more memorable than discursive text, leading to application of the message. Sidebar 11.6 explains how song and drama together became a powerful means of encouraging mothers in Haiti to breastfeed their babies.

Cross-cultural teachers who intend to use drama in their teaching need to become informed of the various genres of drama and theater and of their meanings and appropriate usage. For example, in India there are classical Indian dance drama, traditional Indian theater, Indian folk theater, Indian puppet theater, contemporary Indian theater, and Indian street theater.[8] These forms often have religious meanings that may communicate unintended messages.

Puppets are yet another simple form of drama. Although today they are no longer a very popular feature of American entertainment, in other parts of the world they are still widely used and enjoyed.

For example, in Indonesia a form of shadow puppetry called *wayang* (puppets made of buffalo hide) entertain both children and adults for hours. An ancient poet once said of them, "There are people who weep, are sad and aroused watching the puppets, though they know they are merely carved pieces of leather manipulated and made to speak" (Brandon 1993, 3).

8. https://www.indianetzone.com/5/forms_indian_theatre.htm.

FIGURE 11.3

Use of puppets to teach about shamanism in Peru

Today *wayang* performers even appear on television, and their impact has not been lost. Starting in the sixteenth century this art form was used for Islamic instruction.[9] Christians have since adapted it for shadow puppet shows with the purpose of both evangelism and deepening understanding (Poplawska 2004).[10] In the words of one recent observer, "These puppets and their stories impacted people in ways that three-point sermons could not. The *wayang* theater reached the people's hearts. The stories they told were personal and memorable" (Sessoms 2016, 5).

Role-Playing and Simulation Games

A popular instructional method for developing certain skills is role-playing. While similar to drama, role-playing more often includes improvisation

9. Many believe that *wayang* was used in the sixteenth century to help convert Indonesians to Islam. "In any case, *wayang Sasak* is associated with earlier understandings and practices of Islam and it clearly functioned in introducing, teaching, and popularizing the religion" (Harnish 2003, 93).

10. Nineteenth-century Protestant missionary Coenraad Laurens Coolen used *wayang* in evangelism, but its use was rejected by other missionaries and it became controversial (Goß-weiler 1999).

FIGURE 11.4

Wayang puppet shows narrate Bible stories in Indonesia

around a real-life situation. It is similar to case study in that participants are often given a situation (case) that they must act out. Behaviors are modeled, practiced, and explored holistically. Role-playing has been particularly useful in developing interpersonal skills, counseling and coaching techniques, strategies for facing ethical dilemmas, and problem-solving abilities. Role-playing has been used for such diverse learning objectives as raising environmental awareness (Gordon and Thomas 2018) and in theological classrooms for value formation and faith integration (Howard 2018).

However, role-playing involves cultural dynamics that are not entirely unproblematic. Several misunderstandings or difficulties can arise. Participants may not understand that the circumstance being simulated is fictitious; for example, in a role play simulating a counseling session, participants may assume that the person playing the role of someone with a problem marriage actually has a problem marriage in real life. Also, because a role play is often observed by others and discussed afterwards, role players are exposed to potential criticism and they may feel terribly vulnerable. That could be especially difficult in a more shame-oriented society. Because role-playing often involves improvising behavior in response to a specific situation or question, participants may simply not know how to respond. Finally, participants may not understand the very concept of role-playing. While teaching coaching

SIDEBAR 11.6

The Power of Song and Drama in Public Health Education

Charles Madinger tells this story of the power of song and drama in communication and encouraging change in behavior.

A friend and former USAID senior AIDS advisor, Shelagh O'Rourke, started her life's work of serving the poor by empowering women in Haiti, but faced a monumental challenge created by American baby formula companies. Regardless of communication strategies, mothers resisted breastfeeding their babies but preferred baby formulas like that which was used by women in the United States. Consequently the babies suffered partly due to contaminated water, and partly due to diluting the expensive formulas. Then a co-worker composed a song about the benefits of nursing, and soon women started singing it while working or shopping in local markets. Another woman channeled the power of drama and crafted one that connected with mothers who dumped the formula and nursed their babies, and the community health picture took a giant step forward. (Madinger 2014)

skills for church planters in Nepal, our teaching team attempted to have the participants role-play coaching one another. Not only was the idea of coaching by asking questions and not giving answers somewhat foreign, but the hypothetical nature of the role-play was not understood. They ended up just discussing their challenges with one another. A better approach used in subsequent trainings was for instructors to demonstrate role-playing with another instructor. In this way, learners could observe the modeled behavior and then imitate it.

However, not all role-playing is improvised. A role-play can be rehearsed or scripted, similar to drama, in order to demonstrate the behavior for the class to observe. Alternatively, participants in a role-play can be given the scenario in advance and given time to think through their response. Such adaptations can remove some of the confusion and risk involved in having course participants spontaneously attempt to play a role.

Simulation games attempt to recreate the dynamics of a real-life situation through a controlled or analogical exercise. Often they are useful to illustrate problem-solving skills. When working with concrete learners, the facilitator needs to ensure that the simulation is neither too abstract nor too difficult. If it is too abstract, learners may have difficulty transferring the principles of simulation game to real life. If it is too difficult, participants may experience frustration or shame or simply not achieve the simulation's intended objective.

When using any of the media described in this chapter, it is wise to have persons from the intended audience review the material in advance to check for clarity and appropriateness. There are often nuances that even the most informed cultural sojourner simply will not catch. Observing teachers who are described by learners as gifted and effective is another way to learn how to best utilize teaching tools in the cultural context.

The Media Dimension

Part 2: Online Learning and Culture

Online learning and other electronic learning (e-learning) formats are the fastest growing forms of delivery in higher education and in many non-formal programs. Although experts often make a distinction between these formats, for our purposes the terms will be used more or less interchangeably to describe teaching and learning formats that primarily use the internet for learning exercises and teacher-learner interactions and do not require learners to be physically present in a classroom or with the instructor. Online learning, as used here, involves more than a learner merely reading online texts, viewing videos, or listening to audio recordings;[1] it includes interactive elements via internet between the participant and the course facilitator and usually with other learners also. Sometime courses are offered in a blended format that integrates some in-person classroom instruction with online instruction, but the focus here is on the distance learning element.

CHAPTER OVERVIEW

- The Hopes and Realities of International Online Education
- Advantages of Online Learning in Cross-Cultural Perspective
- Limitations of Online Learning in Cross-Cultural Perspective
- Addressing the Cultural Challenges of Online Learning
- Conclusion

The technological possibilities for online learning are advancing rapidly, and the number of learners becoming more comfortable with online learning is increasing dramatically. The COVID-19 pandemic of 2020 accelerated the use of remote learning and birthed new and creative methods that continue

---

1. Countless online courses, lectures, podcasts, and videos are available at no cost to anyone with internet access. Often the quality of the material is very good. Some courses require participants to register, and perhaps take quizzes. But these have little or no interactive element that engages the learner with others or directly with an instructor.

to evolve. Therefore, some information presented in this chapter reflects only a momentary snapshot of a rapidly evolving field. Indeed, some studies cited in this chapter are more than ten years old, which in the world of online learning is an eternity. Nevertheless, many of the insights are still valid. It must be remembered that in many places these technologies are still very new and unfamiliar. Learners in many parts of the world still face the challenges described here, and many of the underlying dynamics remain the same.

The Hopes and Realities of International Online Education

Online courses have become a standard, if not required, element of many educational programs. Remote leadership and professional development courses are commonplace in industry, education, the church, and community development. Informal and non-formal online programs are now a common feature of lifelong learning almost everywhere. The number of online degree programs via e-learning has grown particularly in Asia, Africa, and Latin America as a way to expand international academic programs in an accessible, economically feasible format.

Online education has been hailed as means of democratizing education, overcoming the elitism of higher education, and making it more universally accessible and affordable. Learning should be brought to the student, not the student to learning. Anonymity is welcomed as an advantage to learners who face prejudice and discrimination. But the visionary expectations of e-learning have yet to be fully realized. For example, so-called MOOCs (massive open online courses) are often accessible at little or no cost to anyone who wants to enroll. They may or may not count toward a degree. Some universities have started outsourcing online learning to MOOC providers. Initially they were expected to revolutionize higher education, but more sober assessments have settled in. Although the quality of MOOCs is often very high, dropout rates are too: 90 to 94 percent in recent years, and increasing (Reich and Ruipérez-Valiente 2019). MOOC courses in Korea experience similar dropout rates of over 90 percent (Lee and Chung 2019). In Colombia, for example, the 2019 retention rate in higher education was 87 percent for students in traditional classroom courses, but only 27 percent in virtual courses.[2] The promise of making high-quality MOOC courses accessible to students in low-income countries, who might benefit the most, has also not materialized; about 80 percent of enrollees are from the most affluent countries (Reich and Ruipérez-Valiente 2019).

2. Servicio Nacional de Aprendizaje (SENA), "Informe de Gestión 2019," 2019, http://www.sena.edu.co/es-co/transparencia/Lists/Informes%20de%20gesti%C3%B3n/info_gest_2019.pdf.

Idealistic expectations of online learning are further tempered by research indicating that "by most indications, students typically do worse in online courses than in on-campus courses, and the challenges of online learning are particularly acute for the most vulnerable populations of first-generation college students, students from low-income families, and underrepresented minorities" (Reich and Ruipérez-Valiente 2019, 131; see also Jaggars and Bailey 2010).[3] Merely placing a good classroom course online does not mean that it will lead to effective learning or to genuine accessibility for underserved populations. Extra efforts must be made to structure online learning in a manner suitable to its medium. Fortunately, there are abundant resources available. Great progress has been made to improve e-learning and better discern its possibilities and limitations. However, only recently have resources become available to help adapt e-learning for students from diverse cultures.

Programs developed in non-Western countries often differ from programs developed in the West. In China and South Korea, for example, they tend to be more teacher-centered and involve one-way communication (M. Wang 2007). Our discussion will deal mainly with online courses that feature a more interactive and learner-centered approach, created and/or managed in Western cultural contexts. The reach of such courses is international. However, this presents challenges for participants who are from under-resourced, less technologically advanced cultures. Concerns have also been raised that such international reach and influence presents a new form of colonialism.

Although there is a growing body of research on cultural factors influencing the effectiveness online learning, awareness of these factors has played a relatively minor role in the actual development of e-learning programs and course design. The culturally related challenges of online learning are further complicated by the fact that courses may include students from widely diverse cultural backgrounds who live in different parts of the world. Once created, online courses are by nature relatively uniform and inflexible in their structure compared to face-to-face classroom instruction. This heightens the challenges of providing user-friendly, culturally sensitive, relevant instruction online. The discussion here will not attempt to review or summarize the massive literature available on e-learning in general. Rather, we will consider some of the specific advantages and limitations of e-learning relating to cross-cultural instruction and suggest ways to overcome the cultural challenges.

3. However, there is an ongoing debate as to the difference in student performance between traditional classroom and online instruction. Researcher bias may be responsible for some of the contradictory findings (Bernard, Borokhovski, and Tamim 2014).

Advantages of Online Learning in Cross-Cultural Perspective

The advantages of online learning over in-person classroom instruction are well known, but the online format has added benefits for international and culturally diverse students.

Overcoming Time and Space Limitations of Classroom Instruction

Students anywhere with internet access, a personal computer, and basic computer skills can participate without having to obtain a visa, travel, and be physically present in a classroom. Learners who would never have the time or resources to study in more traditional educational programs can gain access to almost unlimited educational opportunities. Cell phones and tablets are increasingly being used to facilitate e-learning. Some online courses have synchronous real-time sessions, whereby participants come together online at predetermined times for virtual meetings such as chats, videoconferences, lectures, and discussion groups. But many courses are asynchronous: participants can log in at times convenient for them. Students can also complete learning exercises while offline. Often they can complete the entire course at their own pace. This is a great advantage for participants living in different time zones or who have personal schedules unsuitable for synchronous meetings. Course participants and online course creators and tutors can live almost anywhere there is adequate internet access.

Lower Cost, Higher Efficiency

The cost-effectiveness of online courses has made them a key to the financial viability of many institutions of higher learning. They open up new student markets and the possibility of increased enrollment, and the cost of instruction per student is generally lower than traditional classroom instruction. Once an online course has been created, it can frequently be repeated with only minor changes to the format and content as necessary. Although experts and professors may create the online course, often adjunct teachers (who cost less to employ than regular professors) serve as online course tutors who actually conduct the course and interact with students. Online programs save the expense of acquiring and maintaining traditional brick-and-mortar classrooms. Although creating a high-quality online course requires additional technical skill and time to prepare, which increases some initial production costs, those costs are often recovered after the course has been taught a few times. This also makes e-learning more accessible to lower income learners—not only in terms of tuition or registration fees but also in saved travel and housing expenses.

Advantages for Non-native Speakers of the Instructional Language

Students who are not native speakers of the instructional language may be more comfortable participating online and may make more thoughtful contributions. In traditional classroom instruction, such learners are often reluctant to speak up during class discussions due to introversion or lack of confidence in their language skills. Sometimes by the time they have formulated a sentence to contribute to a class discussion, the topic of discussion has moved on and their comment is no longer relevant. With an asynchronous online format, learners can take their time to formulate their thoughts carefully before posting their contributions to discussion forums and online interactions. For example, a study of Malaysian online students found that "as the online programme was time-independent it allowed learners to be reflective, critical and creative, and compose thoughtful rather than spontaneous responses" (Subramaniam 2008, 15).

Participants can also adjust the speed of information intake. This is especially helpful for learners who are not native speakers of the instructional language, who take notes slowly, or who have short attention spans. In traditional classrooms, if the learner doesn't understand something that the speaker says, they are usually reluctant to ask for clarification and don't have time to look up unfamiliar terms in a dictionary or otherwise clarify the meaning. Instruction simply moves on. In contrast, most online courses' videos and audio recordings can be paused or replayed, or the volume adjusted to increase comprehension.

Willingness to Express Opinions Online

Unfortunately, in most classrooms there are students who feel inferior, intimidated, or not respected by fellow students. Because of this, they are often reluctant to speak up in classroom discussions. Sadykova and Dautermann observe that "some researchers have found computer-mediated communication to increase participation of students whose gender, cultural background, low self-assessment of language fluency or low status in groups hinder equal contribution to discussion in face-to-face formats" (2009, 97). Studies have shown that in an online format such learners are more likely to participate and express their opinions more freely. For example, a study of students from Arab Gulf States taking online courses produced in the United States found that "although learners in this study were not anonymous to their peers because real names and, in most cases, an introduction about each person was posted, the lack of physical appearance gave an impression of anonymity. This made both male and female participants feel freer to speak their minds and more able to participate online. In addition, it reduced assumptions associated with race and gender biases" (Al-Harthi 2005, 7). This was especially the case for female students. Another study of Malaysian students found similarly that "students whose profile described them as shy or introverted and had difficulty participating in face-to-face classroom interaction found the online environment liberating as it allowed them the luxury of time to plan and contribute, without the competition from more vocal students" (Subramaniam 2008, 15). Robert Hogan writes of his experience with online learning at the University of South Pacific, Fiji, which serves students from twelve countries in Oceania: "Gender and ethnicity dominates every aspect of society and learning. . . . In the online environment, shyness disappears, and students judge one another on their quality of thought; not their culture, ethnicity, and gender" (2011).

We have seen in previous chapters that Chinese students are often characterized as reticent about expressing ideas contrary to their professor's or peers' and are concerned with saving face. However, research by Cong and Earl found that this was not necessarily the case with Chinese online learners, who "saw challenging lecturers' and peers' ideas as a positive and meaningful thing because different ideas could attract others' attention and enlighten others' thinking as well. . . . Posting different ideas to others in the online discussion was acknowledged as a positive way of learning, and was thought of as to be encouraged" (2011, 82).

Expansion of Cognitive Skills

Online learning requires certain analytical and even perceptual skills such as navigating the web-based platform and completing self-directed learning exercises. There is some evidence that participation in online learning develops these skills and may lead to students become more field-independent in their cognitive style. This was found to be the case, for example, in a study of 246 Hong Kong Chinese nursing students in an online distance-education program (Ching 1998). Field-independent learners tend to require less structure and guidance than field-dependent learners, provide their own structure to information, are less dependent upon personal feedback from the teacher, and do better with self-directed learning. The online learning format tends to reward such characteristics, thus shaping learners in a more field-independent direction. Although it is debatable whether greater field independence is necessarily a positive development (as discussed in chap. 6), field-independent learners do tend to be more successful in formal learning environments.

Limitations of Online Learning in Cross-Cultural Perspective

For all the advantages of online learning, formidable challenges arise when utilizing the format with learners from different cultures. The high dropout rate from online courses has already been noted. Reasons include technology failure, limited instructor feedback, lack of technical support, and a student's sense of isolation. These lead to frustration, lack of confidence, and sinking motivation (Lehman and Conceição 2014, 5–10). In addition to the other challenges of teaching across cultures already discussed, the following apply particularly to online learning that crosses cultures.

Inadequate Connectivity and Other Technical Deficits

Teachers living in industrialized countries where advanced technology is a given of modern-day life may underestimate the challenges of online learning in many parts of the world. Consider these technical factors that are conditions for participation in online learning:

- *A dependable power grid* providing a consistent source of electricity without unexpected power outages or damaging surges.
- *Reliable internet access* that is not intermittent; ideally, high-speed internet enabling videoconferencing and the downloading of large documents or data in a reasonable amount of time.
- *Adequate computer hardware* with processing and storage capabilities capable of running the necessary software. A webcam and microphone are necessary for videoconferencing. Dust, tropical climates, and extreme temperatures wreak havoc with computer hardware. Hardware malfunctions can lead to frustrating loss of data.
- *Up-to-date computer software* must typically be able to read documents, process information, stream video, process data, create presentations, and enable virtual meetings. Recent versions of multiple programs may be necessary to read current document formats.
- *Access to social media and online databases* is sometimes required for online research and for social interaction with other course participants. However, certain online platforms and data sources are blocked by governments with restrictive policies. For example, China blocks social media such as Facebook, Twitter, Instagram, Google platforms, and WhatsApp.

Some of these challenges are overcome when learners use cell phones for their internet access. But cell phones present their own limitations, such as difficulty reading texts in slide presentations and inadequate connection speed.

When taken together, the technical and infrastructure challenges to e-learning in low-resource contexts may be insurmountable, or frequent frustration can lead to high dropout rates. Add to this the inconvenience that many

SIDEBAR 12.1

Challenges of International Internet Access

Szu-Yu Chen, Dareen Basma, Jennie Ju, and Kok-Mun Ng describe internet access challenges that some of their international students in an online counseling program have faced:

> For example, a student from the Central African Republic is sometimes unable to log in to class meetings when she is unable to turn on generators in a remote village for fear that this could alert guerilla gangs and prompt additional warfare. A student in Peru who does her internship in rural areas is unable to submit her assignments on time because of a lack of internet access. Students in Beijing experience tight internet firewalls preventing them from accessing sites such as Google, Gmail, and YouTube; this problem intensifies during the week of the governmental National People's Congress annual meetings. (2020, 127)

e-learning participants have no internet access in their home or workplace and must go to an internet café, expensive coffee shop, or library to get online. Whereas in many industrialized nations the cost of high-speed internet is part of one's daily living expenses, in other countries participants may need to pay extra for broadband connections, hourly rates at an internet café, or data plans for their cell phone. This adds a not-so-hidden additional cost to the expense of the course. In a study of international distance-education students at the University of South Africa, "WhatsApp emerges as 'the' key social media tool that opens up opportunities for IDE students to transfer, translate and transform their educational journey when studying 'at a distance'" (Madge et al. 2019, 267). Videoconferencing apps are increasingly used for online instruction, with some 300 million daily participants on Zoom, and 100 million daily participants on Google Meet during the 2020 pandemic.[4] Technology is advancing rapidly, and it can be expected that user-friendly apps and software will have increasing capabilities at ever lower costs to enhance online learning.

Lack of Technical Skills Required to Navigate E-Learning

Inadequate technical skills were a source of anxiety among Arab Gulf State students (Al-Harthi 2005). Problems can range from poor keyboard

---

4. Shawn Knight, "Zoom Usage Soars to 300 Million Despite Security Concerns," *Techspot*, April 23, 2020, https://www.techspot.com/news/84964-zoom-usage-soars-300-million-despite-security-concerns.html; and Jay Peters, "Google's Meet Teleconferencing Service Now Adding about 3 Million Users per Day," *The Verge*, April 28, 2020, https://www.theverge.com/2020/4/28/21240434/google-meet-three-million-users-per-day-pichai-earnings.

skills and lack of coordination of using a computer mouse to the ability to navigate the internet, store data, create documents, type on a cell phone, or install software. The time it may take participants to post forum comments and write papers can be burdensome. They may not know how to create slide presentations, how to create a spreadsheet, and how to upload them to the learning platform. Course designers may need to consider using platforms with which learners are already familiar and free software or apps.

Student Expectations and Anxiety about E-Learning

Early studies found that anxiety was common among students who were new to distance learning, and particularly common among students from cultures that are more status oriented and shame oriented. This was the case, for example, with students from Arab Gulf States. "For example, one participant was very anxious and even 'scared' regarding her distance education at the beginning because she thought distance education meant total dependence on yourself with complete absence of help from the instructor" (Al-Harthi 2005). A rural South African teacher described her terrifying first experience in an online continuing education course this way: "When I wrote my first discussion posting I was so afraid. Would this get to the others? Will they laugh? What will Prof say? I am still very much mixed up. I feel I have not the same control as before. I type and I read and I am scared to click, because when I do that I feel I am falling down—like I slip and I slide on the wet ground" (Henning 2003, 308). Studies involving Chinese and South Korean students found concerns about online interaction and uncertainty about how to interact online (M. Wang 2007, 304–5; H. Wang 2006, 76). As learners everywhere become more familiar with online learning formats, often being exposed to it even in elementary school, these anxieties can be expected to disappear. However, that will still not be the case for many learners in underserved communities.

It is an illusion to think that computers, the internet, and e-learning are value-neutral tools. Alison A. Carr-Chellman may be overly pessimistic, but nevertheless she identifies a fundamental problem: "Making a single course that is available around the world for anyone interested in it is efficient, but culturally and contextually bankrupt" (2005b, 9). In much of online learning that does not include synchronous videoconferencing, the participant may have little or no face-to-face contact with others in the course, and thus learning takes place in isolation, whether in the privacy of one's home or workplace or in a public space such as an internet café. For more collectivistic learners, this can undercut motivation. An early study found this to be the experience of international students in online programs in the US (Anakwe and Christensen 1999).

As noted in earlier chapters, Western education values learner autonomy and a constructivist approach to knowledge. Most online learning is conceived on the basis of this pedagogical conviction. But as we also have seen in previous chapters, such values are not shared by all cultures. This can disadvantage non-Western learners involved in distance education. For example, "For Chinese learners, autonomous learning may be seen as an abdication of responsibility by the teacher. . . . The concept of students taking responsibility for managing their own learning should not be assumed given the wide diversity of students currently studying in online programs" (Catterick 2007, 126).

A study involving ninety-six participants from nineteen countries in an online professional development course found that expectations regarding learner participation led to discomfort for some learners. For example, "Although [the Chinese participants] expected to complete assignments and answer questions according to the instructor's directions, the Chinese participants had not anticipated bi-directional interaction with instructors in the course. One Chinese participant said that interacting with the instructional team felt uncomfortable because she did not expect instructors to converse freely with students" (Dennen and Bong 2018, 386). The Chinese participants tended to interact primarily with other Chinese, reflecting features of collectivism. Their discomfort with interacting individually with the course instructor may reflect high power distance and deference to the expertise and authority of the instructor. "Chinese students indicated the desire to learn *from* the instructor rather than *with* the instructor, and as nonexperts hesitated to offer contributions. This is particularly notable because the instructor repeatedly referred to herself as a 'co-learner' and suggested that any course member might share valuable content" (389).

These examples demonstrate that the online medium in itself, even apart from the content, is not value-neutral. Learners come with different social orientations and needs, different pedagogical convictions, and different expectations of the experience. To alleviate the problem of disadvantaging certain learners and to be effective in various cultural settings, e-learning will need to address these concerns.

Culturally Specific Instructional Content

Often courses are created using case studies, texts, and examples that are very culturally specific, typically from the context of the creator of the course. These can be irrelevant, difficult to understand, or hard to apply for international learners living in another context. The one-size-fits-all nature of online courses makes it difficult to tailor course content to multiple international contexts. Online course creators are often oblivious to the need to even try. In the words of an Asian student in an international online course, "[the courses need] more global thinking, because they focus on US examples. . . . Sometimes, you think that this case is difficult to apply to my country. They have to think about what is happening in other countries" (Liu et al. 2010, 184). Contextualization of content is no less important in online learning than in traditional classrooms, but if learners come from a diversity of cultural backgrounds, the challenge is compounded.

Lack of Visual Cues in Asynchronous E-Learning

In online courses that have no visual interaction, international course participants who struggle with learning in a foreign language do not have the advantage of reading body language and other visual cues as an aid to understanding. Their participation depends more on verbal cues that can be misunderstood.

> International students are also at risk of misinterpreting postings and assignments or of being misinterpreted by others thanks to misused vocabulary or grammar structures. There is also great potential for misreading communicative strategies such as turn taking, criticizing, apologizing, recasting, switching registers, and more. Idiomatic expressions, colloquialisms, regional or professional slang, references to local pop culture may also confuse second/foreign language speakers. (Sadykova and Dautermann 2009, 98)

One study of Asian learners participating in international online courses found "the delayed text-based communication of an asynchronous discussion is unable to convey the nuances of human interaction and, therefore, the students felt that it was difficult for them to figure out the intentions of the other students during group work due to their different working styles and cultures" (Liu et al. 2010, 183).

Similarly, the course instructor may not pick up on the needs of students from other cultural backgrounds. In a classroom setting, visual cues and extended in-person interaction help the instructor identify ways in which international students may be struggling to understand, to keep up with class discussions, or to feel a part of the learning community. Even with synchronous videoconferencing it is more difficult for the instructor or facilitator of an online course to identify such problems.

Culturally Influenced Web Design and Graphics

Web design is influenced by culture. A study by Faiola and Matei (2005) found that Chinese online learners performed significantly better on certain online tasks when the web layout was created by Chinese designers than when viewing layouts created by Americans. Conversely, American students performed best when the layout was created by American designers versus Chinese. The researchers concluded that the web layouts were influenced by the designers' culturally conditioned cognitive styles, which matched or mismatched the learners' cognitive styles. They explain how holistic and analytic cognitive styles are reflected in web design:

> For example, Chinese are more likely to find a strong association among objects that are functionally or contextually related. Specifically, the format of information in a Chinese-designed Web menu system may often create implicit relationships between its parts and the whole. Conversely, Americans are more likely to find a strong association among objects belonging to the same category. Specifically, sites designed by American designers may emphasize the division of different kinds of information into hierarchical categories that keep most information hidden within the hierarchy of information. (Faiola and MacDorman 2008, 365)

Furthermore, many images, cartoons, and graphics can be easily misunderstood by persons from different cultures, as we saw in chapter 11. For example, red text may indicate importance to Americans, but Chinese may understand it as a warning or correction. A Chinese student related this experience, "I received an e-mail from the instructor. The text was all in red. I almost passed out. I guessed I might have done or said something wrong or offensive to the teacher, otherwise, the teacher wouldn't [have] written to me this way" (Tu 2001, 52). It is well documented that computer desktop icons are not universally understood, such as the small "i" to click for information or the "?" to access a "help" feature. The magnifying glass icon that represents the search function was correctly interpreted by barely over a quarter of Moroccans and Sri Lankans (Knight, Gunawardena, and Aydin 2009, 25). Sadykova and Dautermann summarize research on cultural differences in web design preference:

> A number of studies suggest that cultural background may influence the way users respond to web content and design features. Wurtz found that websites developed for Japan, China and Korea made images more prominent thus providing an elaborate communication alternative to the text. In contrast, websites in Germany, Denmark, Finland used less animation and a more linear navigation. Evers reported that subjects from English-speaking countries derived most of their understanding of the website from text rather than graphics, while Japanese students were more influenced by the graphics. Cultural variability was also prominent in studies by Marcus and Gould and Faiola and Matei who showed that web content is processed faster when created by designers from the user's culture. (2009, 95)

Addressing the Cultural Challenges of Online Learning

Despite its challenges, e-learning remains for many students the most feasible means of acquiring further education and for strengthening personal and professional skills. This is especially so for learners in less-developed or underserved communities in many parts of the world. As noted above, although some of the studies cited in this chapter are dated, similar challenges remain with many learners less familiar with technology. Online instructors and web designers should be alert to these issues. Armed with an understanding of the structural limitations and potential instructional challenges, cross-cultural teachers can take intentional measures to maximize learning for cross-cultural learners. Here are some suggestions.

Help Learners Strengthen Their Technical Skills

Provide an orientation to online learning, and perhaps offer an introductory course or session on the basic technical skills needed. Remind participates that there is no shame in asking for assistance. Course instructors can make themselves available to meet individually with learners who struggle with technology. Assignments involving more advanced computer skills, such as preparing a slide presentation or a spreadsheet, should be given only if participants already have such skills or if technical assistance is offered as part of the course. Over time, most learners will gradually gain confidence, overcome anxiety, and become adequately proficient to benefit from e-learning.

Offer Materials and Assignments Less Dependent on Technology

Today most e-learning requires adequate internet access and speed to download materials and interact with the course instructor and peers. To alleviate slow download speeds or poor connectivity, course materials—especially large documents and videos—can be loaded on flash drives and sent to learners. Conversely, it may be difficult or impossible for some students to upload presentations they prepare, such as videos or large slide presentation files. Kirk St. Amant recommends that teachers allow students to submit class materials using cell phones or alternative media (2007, 19). He also recommends that webpages be designed to load quickly and be easy to navigate, to reduce the time students need to be online (20–21). Reducing the number of graphic images that must be downloaded will also reduce the time to load pages and data usage (23). Requiring students to log in no more than once a week will reduce their internet costs and, for students who lack internet access at home, cut down on trips to internet cafés (21).

Files, documents, and media should be provided in formats that do not require the newest versions of expensive software.[5] For example, PDF or RTF formats can be used for texts. Sadykova and Dautermann recommend briefing students thoroughly in advance about a course's technical requirements: "No matter what technologies are employed, each [international online distance] course needs to be equipped with a 'technology roadmap' that informs students of minimum hardware and software requirements *prior* to registration. This roadmap would also provide links to inexpensive downloadable programs and tutorials for those unfamiliar with the tools" (2009, 96). Such basic requirements cannot be taken for granted everywhere in the world. Course designers must also remember that, as noted above, social media and online resources may be blocked in politically restrictive countries.

Increase Cultural Sensitivity in Web Design

Web designers need to give attention to cultural factors involved in web layout and imagery. As one international study concludes, "Designers must incorporate research in the early stages of the design process that investigates the various sociocultural contexts and perspectives of users" (Knight, Gunawardena, and Aydin 2009, 33). Archee and Gurney advise care regarding "culture-specific color connotations, preferences in layout, animation, sounds, and other effects that are characteristic of today's generation of websites" (2011, 28). Web designers should become familiar with the norms and standards familiar to the intended learners. Indigenous color schemes, icons, and imagery can make webpages' appearance more comfortable and inviting for users. Photos or images of persons and places from the local culture can be used. A cultural insider should review all graphics and imagery to ensure that the material is inoffensive and user-friendly, and will be correctly understood. The International Standards Organization (www.iso.org) offers an internationally consistent set of icons that can be used in web design.

Additional design features can enhance the user friendliness and cultural appropriateness of online courses for a diversity of students. Learners who are more group oriented and struggle with motivation in online learning can be helped by embedding automatic assignment reminders in the online system. Course maps with a "you are here" feature can help students track their progress and gain sense of accomplishment (Alias 2011, 19).

Questions related to cognitive style and web design are considerably more complex. As Faiola and Matei recommend, "Web technology developers should increasingly take into account the complexity of the cognitive ap-

---

5. OpenOffice (www.openoffice.org) and LibreOffice (www.libreoffice.org) are examples of free alternatives available in many languages.

paratus that intersects with a cultural dimension, including the human-like responses that users often seek when engaging interactive systems" (2005, 390). Just how web designers accomplish this in practical terms is not yet entirely clear. One study explored different web features that appeal to holist learners and serialist (analytic) learners (Clewley, Chen, and Liu 2011). But more research is necessary to better understand cognition and web design.

Develop Instructors' Cultural Awareness

Course instructors and tutors can be given basic training in intercultural communication skills. Communication across cultures is always a complex undertaking fraught with potential misunderstanding. Because so much of online learning is in written form, without opportunities to visually perceive body language, the likelihood of miscommunication increases dramatically. Even something as basic as how students and instructors address each other can be problematic. For example, an online videoconference-based training for physicians in Ethiopia ran into confusion because American physicians followed the convention of addressing participants by title and family name (e.g., "Dr. Smith") and addressed the Ethiopian participants accordingly. But the Ethiopian convention is to address a person using their title and given name (e.g., "Dr. Abebe" for Dr. Abebe Kebede) (Negash 2011). There are many different traditions and conventions around the world for forms of address, and using the wrong one can lead not only to confusion but also to unintentionally offending others by use of forms of address that in their culture are considered disrespectful.

Another aspect of cultural sensitivity that online instructors must consider is time spent with online learners. Online learners who are unfamiliar with the medium and who may be reluctant to interact freely online may need extra time and assistance from the course instructor. Technical or instructional staff support has been found to be one of the most important factors contributing to learning effectiveness and anxiety reduction, especially with international students (e.g., Jung 2011; 2012).

Provide Resources to Bridge Language Gaps

Research has found that improving online learning formats alleviates some, but not all, challenges related to learning in a foreign language (Dillon, Wang, and Tearle 2007). For learners who are not native speakers of the instructional language, several steps can be taken to facilitate their learning. A glossary of key terms that may be unfamiliar, but frequently used in the course, can be posted on the course website. Links can be provided to free online dictionaries, aids for improving writing skills, or even for tutoring and proofreading services (see St. Amant 2007, 26–27). Course instructors and the students should be reminded that not all participants are native speakers of the instructional language and that they should be patient if responses are slow. Extra effort must be given to avoid colloquialisms or terms easily misunderstood. Finally, participants' contributions should be judged on the merits of the ideas, not largely on the basis of poor grammar or diction.

Create Course Content Appropriate for Diverse Learning Preferences

A wide variety of content-specific material and examples should be made available. Assignments can be made intentionally flexible, allowing learners to adapt assignments so as to be relevant to their local needs and interests. Everything already discussed in previous chapters regarding the importance of contextualization, needs of oral learners, different cognitive styles, use of images, and the nature of assignments applies just as much to online learning as it does to traditional in-person classroom teaching. All of this requires considerable extra effort from web designers and instructors in order to become aware of the context, preferences, and needs of the intended learners. It will not be adequate to merely translate course materials.

Reduce Anxiety with Clear Guidelines and Expectations

Clarity about expectations for appropriate online interaction can go a long way to alleviate the anxiety of participants who are less familiar with e-learning and the cultural social norms for online interactions. This would include conventions of online etiquette that may be unfamiliar to novices in online learning. For example, when using synchronous videoconferencing for instruction, these questions should be answered:

- What is acceptable dress and appearance? Are students allowed to participate with their webcam turned off? Is eating or multitasking allowed during instruction?
- What locations are unacceptable for synchronous learning? Can one be in public spaces, outdoors, or in a coffee shop where there may be distractions or privacy violations? Walking or driving in an automobile during instruction are generally prohibited.
- To what extent should students reduce visual or audio distractions, such as interruptions by children or background noises? Can they use virtual background images?
- How should they indicate that they want to ask a question or contribute to a discussion?

- What is the appropriate usage of messaging and chat functions?
- What level of privacy is expected? Can persons not enrolled in the course listen or participate? How should confidentiality be protected regarding personal information? This is especially important if course participants live or work in security-sensitive locations.
- Can instruction be recorded? If so, can recordings be shared with others?

Course participants should also be instructed on how to interact with others who represent different backgrounds and perspectives, the appropriate level of familiarity with the course instructor, and the like. For example, Haidong Wang recommends, "Instructors teaching Asian students could involve all students in online communication by building a casual, friendly, and safe atmosphere through sharing biographical information, stories, experiential learning, and reflections; journaling; using asynchronous and synchronous discussion; and encouraging collaboration on course assignments and problem solving" (2006, 78). Participants who are apprehensive can be encouraged to approach the online experience as an adventure and to experiment with new approaches to learning. They may need encouragement to express their opinions, even if contrary to opinions of their peers or instructor. The course instructor may need to find ways to help them gain confidence. The course facilitator can also reach out personally to students to create trust and more familiar atmosphere. For example, a study of Asian international students in the US found that when an instructor met online with small groups of students and encouraged them, after five or six weeks of participation in online learning "they became more trusting of the new environment and comfortable expressing themselves in front of peers and instructors; some students actually became very talkative. . . . They transitioned into the new culture and online learning format with positive perspectives and achieved academic success" (F. Tan 2018, 34).

Create Group Cohesion and Social Participation

A sense of group cohesion has been found to be one of the keys to student completion of and satisfaction with online learning. "Online distance education students need to feel connected to their peers, instructors, and the program. This sense of community and feeling connected helps increase student academic success and persistence" (Green et al. 2017, 6). In more collectivistic cultures, individuals undertake very few tasks in life alone; a partner or a group is associated with almost every activity. For such persons, sitting alone in front of a computer screen and completing assignments by reading and writing can sap their motivation. This is a common concern among students as they approach online learning, as these responses in a research study make clear:

> "I was afraid I wouldn't get the same interaction with others as I would sitting in a classroom" (self-identified as Mexican-American), "I felt that I would be missing on the intimate experience of being able to have discourse with my professors and peers in a face-to-face setting" (self-identified as White), and "I enjoy working alongside others and felt that the online course may not afford me the opportunity to do this" (self-identified as Indian). (Green et al. 2017, 9)

Extra effort must be made to create a sense of learning community for more collectivistic learners. This can be done in a variety of ways, such as structuring online course with frequent, high-quality communication among participants, including the instructor; assigning collaborative projects; building nonacademic social interactions into the course; offering virtual real-time (synchronous) group meetings or discussions; being responsive to learner needs; and allowing participants to introduce themselves, including their personal backgrounds and interests.

Minjuan Wang describes the ways that students present themselves in the virtual setting of online learning: "Social presence is about presenting oneself as a 'real person' in a virtual learning environment. Cognitive presence is about sharing information and resources, and constructing new knowledge. Emotive presence is about learners' expression about their feelings of self, the community, the learning atmosphere and the learning process" (2007, 295). Participants learn best when they are engaged in all three aspects. However, the focus of much Western learning is on the cognitive dimension. When the cross-cultural teacher intentionally creates elements that strengthen participants' social and emotive presence, learners from more collective and socially oriented cultures are likely to be more motivated to participate and improve their learning. This can be facilitated by having participants share biographical information, photos, and personal prayer requests, and, where possible, arranging in-person group meetings. Real-time videoconferencing with the whole class, interactive forums, and personalized interaction between course tutor and student have proven effective means to overcome the individualistic nature of e-learning (see F. Tan 2018). Teachers of online courses with large numbers of participants should consider breaking the class into smaller groups to allow for more personal interaction.

Assigning teamwork as part of an online course is another way to strengthen students' motivation, especially for more collectivistic learners. However, culturally diverse participants may need extra guidance. Minjuan Wang offers these tips:

> When guiding online teamwork, the instructor should not assume that teamwork will just "happen"' when they assign a few students to a team. Also, they should not assume that team members will learn to resolve conflicts without external help. The instructor should remain as an informal member to each team and should help build healthy, collaborative and functioning teams from the very beginning. There must be clearly set team goals, trust, social networks and an atmosphere for open exchange and communication for teams to be productive online. (2007, 308)

Because some learners from more collectivist cultures may be reluctant in online discussions to be critical of viewpoints held by peers or the instructor, assignments that will involve critical discussion should be scheduled for at least a few weeks into the class schedule, to allow time for a sense of community and trust to develop.

Gunawardena, Frechette, and Layne frame the concept of online education as creating "online wisdom communities." Their conviction is that everyone possesses wisdom in terms of practical knowledge and sound judgment. "The truly wise share their gift with others in their communities through storytelling, mentoring, and leadership. We view wisdom as a personal quality that can be cultivated to enhance a community; a wisdom community honors the gifts its members bring and promotes imparting those gifts to others" (2019, 7). To create online community, each individual must be valued and welcome to contribute to the common learning experience.

Integrate Asynchronous and Synchronous Features

We have seen that there are pros and cons to synchronous and asynchronous formats. The best solution may be to provide some of each in a given course. If synchronous meetings will take place, St. Amant (2007, 24) recommends providing clear course schedules so that students can plan accordingly and including a link to an international time and date calculator so that participants can determine the correct time to enter the meeting.

Learners' locations in different time zones should be considered not only for synchronous meetings or exercises but also for asynchronous assignments, as evidenced in one study of Asian online learners:

> The students mentioned that time zone differences had an impact on their timely participation in the asynchronous discussion forums, as this factor was not usually considered in the course design of most of the courses. In the program,

some instructors would post questions requesting the students' answers in a timely manner, and would request that the students not repeat points already made in previous posts. One student noted that "sometimes it would be very difficult to find a question to answer once I woke up in the morning finding that every single question had been answered." (Liu et al. 2010, 183)

Course instructions must specify the time zone used for determining meeting times and deadlines for submitting assignments. A twenty-four-hour clock should be used instead of a.m. and p.m. (e.g., not 1:00 p.m. but 13:00 hours). Date formats should be unmistakable, spelling out the month and year, since 12/11/21 might be interpreted in different countries as December 11, 2021; or 12 November, 2021; or as 2012 November 21st!

On the whole, given time zone differences, bandwidth issues, and language challenges, asynchronous assignments are the most practical. Minjuan Wang's study of American, Chinese, and South Korean online courses revealed that students from all cultures preferred asynchronous elements over synchronous ones.

> This is reflected in the 82% "somewhat helpful or very helpful" rating for asynchronous tools and the 65% rating for synchronous tools. The American group had similar mean ratings on the helpfulness of both types of tools. The Chinese and Korean groups, in particular, preferred delayed-time discussion over same-time discussion. The primary factors reducing the popularity of live-meeting tools included technical difficulties, low audio quality, necessity to be online at certain times, lack of opportunities to interact in live meetings and their language abilities. (M. Wang 2007, 302–3)

Technological advancements since Wang's study may have alleviated some of the difficulties; nevertheless, in poorly resourced regions challenges remain. Chih-Hsiung Tu notes another advantage of asynchronous online interactions for students concerned with *face*: "Chinese students are still very much concerned with face saving in the online environment despite the absence of a face-to-face contact and non-verbal cues. . . . [Computer mediated communication] provided Chinese students with opportunities to manipulate their images and facilitate face-saving. The nature of asynchronous communications afforded the students the time necessary to create the image they wished to project" (2001, 52–53).

Conclusion

E-learning is not the ultimate solution to every educational need. Nevertheless, online learning has become an important option for millions of learners, and progress is being made to resolve its limitations. Technological advances will no doubt continue to increase the accessibility, affordability, and effectiveness of remote instruction. Depending on the learning objectives, e-learning remains for many the most affordable and accessible access to higher education. It opens up possibilities to those who otherwise would not have the opportunity to participate in more traditional educational programs and lifelong learning opportunities. Greater awareness of the cultural challenges and greater intentionality in course design can go a long way toward maximizing the potential of e-learning for *all* participants.

Although the cultural challenges of online learning are many, most are not insurmountable. Most online learners will adapt to the format and benefit despite its limitations. As one study of Asian participants in international online courses happily found, "almost all of the students agreed that the cultural differences, which originated from ethnicity, existed, but did not negatively affect their communication or collaboration in learning. The participants seemed ready to accept the differences and looked for the positive aspects that cultural differences bring" (Liu et al. 2010, 185). Fortunately, more resources for developing culturally sensitive e-learning are becoming available (e.g., Carr-Chellman 2005a; Edmundson 2007; 2011a; Gunawardena, Frechette, and Layne 2019). Andrea Edmundson provides a concise and especially helpful overview of practical steps for adaptation in her chapter "The Cultural Adaptation of E-Learning: Using Appropriate Content, Instructional Design, and Media" (2011b).

The Environmental Dimension

Sweltering heat, power outages, inadequate classrooms, missing equipment. Frequent student absences. Conflicting messages from organizers or administrators, and abrupt schedule changes. These are the among the most common frustrations experienced by cross-cultural teachers. Some of them are anticipated; others are surprises. The ability to adapt, cope, and endure under less than ideal circumstances will have much to do with the effectiveness, longevity in service, and satisfaction of the cross-cultural teacher.

In this final chapter we come to the most obvious aspect of how culture influences teaching and learning: the environmental dimension.

CHAPTER OVERVIEW
- The Physical Environment
- The Societal Environment
- The Institutional Environment

FIGURE 13.1

Five dimensions of culture's influence on teaching and learning

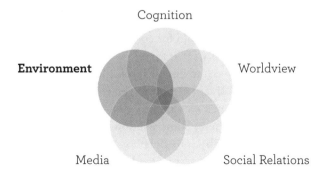

Cognition

Environment

Worldview

Media

Social Relations

A teacher has very little control over the physical, institutional, and societal aspects of the teaching environment—yet they have a profound impact on the teaching-learning experience. Unlike the previous chapters that dealt with various theories and empirical research related to teaching across cultures, this chapter will be based more upon the personal experiences of cross-cultural teachers, including my own.

The Physical Environment

Upon arriving at a teaching assignment, the cross-cultural teacher is immediately confronted with the physical environment of the location: classrooms, resources, climate, living arrangements, and more. One's initial experience may be exciting and perhaps quaint, but especially in under-resourced schools, churches, or institutions, difficult physical conditions can quickly become major obstacles to one's ability to effectively teach and one's personal sense of well-being.

Geography, Climate, and Health

To arrive at the location of an international teaching assignment may take many hours of travel, not only by commercial airlines but perhaps also long bus or car rides over rough roads. One arrives exhausted and with jet lag. Seasoned sojourners recommend arriving days or even weeks early to allow enough time to recover and adjust to the local climate, elevation, and so on before having to teach. However, it may take months or years to acclimate to some factors.

In poorly resourced areas in cold regions, schools, universities, and churches seldom have adequate heating for winter conditions; in warmer climates, they rarely have air-conditioning. I have taught in classrooms that were so cold that I had to wear a heavy winter jacket during instruction. Once, teaching in the tropical heat of the Philippines, I had the good fortune of having a classroom with air conditioning—or so I thought. I arrived early and was able to cool the room. But as soon as the students arrived, they quickly turned it off—for them, it made the room far too cold for comfort. Extreme temperatures, hot or cold, are not only uncomfortable for those unaccustomed to it, but can be physically and mentally exhausting. Extreme climate conditions can also lead to other challenges. When I taught in the Democratic Republic of the Congo, a thunderstorm struck so violently that class was interrupted—not an uncommon occurrence there. Some windows had no glass, and sheets of rain were blowing horizontally into the classrooms! Within a few minutes the storm passed, and instruction resumed. Other climate challenges such as drought or flooding may lead to more serious interruptions, which delay instruction for weeks or months as students return home and others are pre-occupied with basic survival.

Local climate, diet, and living conditions can create a host of health challenges for cross-cultural teachers. One's body must adjust to unfamiliar foods, which may entail digestive problems. In addition to the proper immunizations, one should leave home with a supply of medications, such as Imodium and Ciprofloxacin. One must drink plenty of filtered water and liquids and avoid going from a sweltering classroom to an air-conditioned room, because radical temperature changes can cause health problems. On two occasions when I was teaching in extreme heat, my body reacted by completely shutting down my vocal cords. I could hardly even whisper.

If one is residing for a long time in a foreign country, one will discover that it takes time for the body to develop resistance to local viruses and bacteria. The first couple of years one can experience an unusual frequency of illness. The extreme air pollution in many of the world's large cities can cause serious respiratory problems, too, especially for persons with asthma. It is generally wise to become informed of the health conditions of the location and how this might affect one's own health. This can be found at websites such as the US Center for Disease Control and Prevention[1] and the United Nations World Health Organization.[2] One should also investigate the availability of necessary prescription medicines in the country of service. While sometimes medications are available at a very low cost, the quality is not always reliable.

Times and Seasons

Many Westerners are unaware that the typical "summer vacation" from school originally was timed that way so that children could work in the fields on farms with their families. In many parts of the world that is still the case. Instruction must be scheduled around harvest seasons, rainy seasons, work schedules, holidays, elections, strikes, and other national or community events. This can be exasperatingly unpredictable. Romanowski and McCarthy describe the frustration of "showing up for class prepared with a carefully honed lesson, only to learn that your students are gone for four weeks picking potatoes somewhere in Ukraine" (2009, 146). A three-day workshop that I was conducting in Argentina had been planned many months in advance. We discovered shortly before our arrival that the date for a national holiday had been abruptly changed and the new holiday came in the midst of our work-shop. It was too late to change our dates, so we had to adapt the schedule at

1. wwwnc.cdc.gov/travel.
2. www.who.int/ith/en.

the last minute, losing one full day of the three-day workshop. That afforded us the unexpected delight of taking part in an Argentine barbeque, but we lost precious instructional time for the workshop. Pamela George's survey of American scholars who had served in international teaching assignments found that spontaneous or unscheduled holidays were a major cause of loss of class time. Add to this the reality that students often "extend" holidays by a few days, and up to a fourth of expected class time may be lost (1995, 114).

On one occasion while I was teaching in Nepal, a national general strike was called on the second day of a training seminar. All traffic in the capital city was blocked by barricades. We were informed by the seminar organizers that morning that the training would have to be canceled for the day. But twenty minutes later we received a second phone call with the news that the participants had managed to arrive at the training venue and the event should proceed. We were then transported on motorcycles that weaved through the barricades to bring us to the training location.

Because in so many countries the majority of pastors and Christian workers have secular day jobs, pastoral training and continuing education often take place on evenings or weekends. After a long workday or workweek, participants are motivated but tired. In such situations, particular attention needs to be given to use of instructional methods that actively engage learners. The opposite situation can be found in places like parts of Western Europe, where even at entry-level positions, the average employee receives four weeks of paid vacation per year. One- or two-week courses or retreats offered by schools, seminaries, retreat centers, and training institutes attract numerous participants who are happy to use their vacation time for personal enrichment, continuing education, or equipping for Christian ministry.

The cross-cultural teacher must be aware of the various traditions that may impact scheduling and instructional hours. In some cultures it is typical for instruction to take place in the early morning or evening to avoid the afternoon heat. In the afternoon students may take a siesta (afternoon nap) or work in the fields and do chores. It is not unusual at a seminar or workshop for participants to be found sleeping on chairs, tables, church pews, or on the floor during the noon break after lunch. Wise teachers will do the same and adopt the local life rhythms.

Classrooms and Buildings

The most immediate environment for most formal teaching is the classroom. It may be equipped with high-tech media and the latest amenities, or it may have four bare walls where a blackboard is the only "technology." Electricity may or may not be available. Romanowski and McCarthy (2009,

155) suggest in some places bringing a small gift for the maintenance person as a sign of appreciation and to elicit cooperation in the event of technical problems. I taught a short course at a ministry training program in Thailand where no classroom was available, so the course met in a church sanctuary and pews served as desks. Often there is a shortage of the most basic materials such as a blackboard, chalk, or writing paper. In some places, children have no classroom whatsoever and meet outdoors under a tree. In elementary schools, desks and chairs may be adult size, and several children may need to share a desk.

Some Bible schools have only small libraries containing mainly popular books donated by pastors in America, although the students can't read English. Books are sometimes locked up so that they do not "disappear," which limits the ability of students to do library research for assigned papers. However, this is not all bad. Since some pastors will have little access to a library after they

---

SIDEBAR 13.1

Teaching and Learning in Under-Resourced Schools

La Poudrière primary school in Brazzaville, the capital of the Republic of the Congo, unfortunately is typical of many under-resourced schools in Africa. In 2019, geometry teacher Saturnin Serge Ngoma taught a first-year class of seventy-six children crammed into one room. The school is described by journalist Laudes Martial Mbon as consisting of "two makeshift shacks that house six classrooms, surrounded by tall grass and vegetable gardens."

> On rainy days, the clay courtyard turns into sticky mud. The school is not enclosed. During the year, teachers give their classes with the doors open, under the gaze of passers-by who cross the courtyard to walk from one part of the neighbourhood to another.
>
> Everything is lacking in this school, which has no fences and no latrines. Before more tables were found at the start

of the school year, Ngoma's students were packed in, four to a desk. The others sat on the floor....

> The children also have to share the few textbooks available at the school, getting together in groups of three or four to do exercises, or during reading time.

Teacher Ngoma, who has a master's degree in sustainable economic development, is undaunted and committed to student success; he has no plans of leaving. With efforts like his and when children are eager to learn, progress can be made even under such circumstances. The report continues:

> In spite of these precarious conditions, sixty-two students from Ngoma's class successfully moved up to the next grade at the end of the school year. (Mbon 2019)

FIGURE 13.2

Overcrowded, poorly furnished schoolrooms, such as this one in Kenya with nearly fifty students, are common in many parts of the world

Joseph Sohm / Shutterstock.com

graduate, and may never own many books, it is best that they learn to prepare sermons and Bible studies by studying the Bible itself with the aid of a few basic tools such as a Bible dictionary or one-volume commentary on the whole Bible.

The situation of public schools in some under-resourced regions is truly dire (see sidebar 13.1). Large classes are common in many countries. UNESCO reported in 2016 that in a third of the African nations reporting data, the average class size in primary schools was more than fifty. In Malawi, the Central African Republic, and Tanzania, the average class size exceeded seventy (UNESCO 2016b).

In sub-Saharan Africa even basic sanitation needs are often unmet: in 2016 only half of primary schools had access to drinking water and only one out of three had toilets. Textbooks and other resources were extremely limited. The UNESCO report continued, "On average, 14 students share the same mathematics textbook in Cameroon, 5 in Chad and South Sudan, and 4 in Equatorial Guinea. There is on average 1 reading book for 2 students or more in sub-Saharan Africa and 1 mathematics textbook for about 3 students." Not surprisingly, the attrition rate of teachers in such contexts is quite high, with as much of a 14 percent loss per year in Ghana (UNESCO 2016b).

How one assesses the negative impact of large class sizes depends in part on one's understanding of teaching and learning. If good learning depends more on good teaching than on the circumstances under which a student learns, then large class sizes are considered less problematic. Cortazzi and Jin comment, "Thus while many Western policy makers see large classes as essentially a barrier to quality learning, their Chinese counterparts probably see the quality of the teachers, teachers' preparation and their performance in classroom interaction as keys to the quality learning of students" (2001, 116). Primary and middle school class sizes in China may range from thirty to seventy students or more (115).

Seating Arrangements

In classrooms where tables and chairs can be reconfigured, the teacher should consider carefully the possible unintended consequences of re-arranging the furniture. Seating arrangements send a message, but the message is not necessarily the same in every culture. In Western classrooms, seats arranged in auditorium-style rows indicate more one-way communication by a lecturer who stands in front of the class. Chairs arranged around separate tables is suitable for small group discussion or projects around the tables. Many Western teachers prefer to arrange seats in a semicircle or U-form to facilitate face-to-face discussion and eye contact among students and with the teacher. At least initially, though, arranging seating this way may actually hinder open discussion in some contexts. In the words of a student in Hong Kong, "when we sit in the traditional way [in rows facing the teacher], students can only see their lecturers (and the backs of their classmates), and they may feel freer to express their opinions. And in this sitting mode, students are more active and relaxed in expressing themselves" (Slethaug 2007, 68). Gordon Slethaug reports that "Hong Kong, mainland Chinese, Japanese and Korean students are often uncomfortable when having to sit in a large circle, finding that it discourages them from expressing themselves freely" (69). It's not just that such seating is unfamiliar; particularly in more shame-oriented cultures, students may feel exposed or somewhat intimidated by direct, uninhibited eye contact with the teacher and their peers. They may feel pressure to participate when they are unprepared or uncertain of their answers if called upon. Slethaug further points out that sitting in a circle with students directly next to the teacher may be considered too informal and uncomfortable (71). Experimenting with unfamiliar seating arrangements can be initially uncomfortable for students, and it may take some time for them to become accustomed to the change (George 1995, 57).

Noise and Distractions

The elementary school I attended was just a quarter mile from the north runway of Los Angeles International Airport, and the junior high school I attended was under the landing approach. Teachers frequently had to pause and wait for the roar of the jet engines to pass. Eventually those schools were closed and the entire neighborhoods were turned into parking lots. Western schools and educational settings today seek to create an uninterrupted environment for instruction, with minimal distraction.

This is not the case in many parts of Africa, Asia, and Latin America. I've taught seminars and workshops during which chickens or dogs would rummage through the classroom. Once when I was teaching in a large tent in Costa Rica, a large parrot would occasionally fly through the tent, barely clearing the heads of the students. On another occasion mothers brought their children, who would run about or cry loudly as I taught. A teacher unaccustomed to such conditions can find it difficult to maintain concentration. However, the learners are typically undaunted. Distractions are a regular part of their daily lives, and they filter them out easily.

What is not so easily tuned out is when an uproarious incident occurs just *outside* the classroom. Students may rush to the window or door to see what is happening, and it is usually no use trying to hold them back. It may take quite some time for them to refocus, so is often best to just take a break and allow the students to process the incident before trying to return to teaching.

When teaching a course in Southeast Asia I thought it was a bit odd that I was expected to use a microphone in a class with fewer than twenty students. I have a strong voice and the quality of the microphone was rather poor. However, when teaching students for whom English is not their native language, extra amplification helps them hear the instructor more clearly. This also helps overcome outdoor noise such as traffic, construction, or children playing.

Living Arrangements

In residential schools and universities it is common for single students to live in dormitories or some form of student housing. I've visited schools in India and the Philippines where there were as many as sixteen beds in one small room occupied by nearly as many students (see fig. 13.3). (One or two unoccupied beds could be used as extra storage space.) There were no desks, bookshelves, or other amenities. For students to have a desk for study or writing, they need to go to the library. But often the library doesn't have enough desk space for all students, so students may be found on benches, in unused classrooms, or wherever they can find a flat surface to write.

FIGURE 13.3

This dormitory room at a Bible school in India has eight beds and no desks

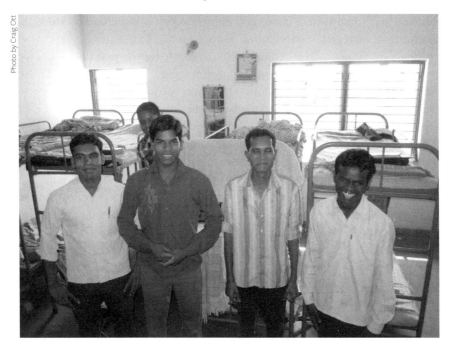

Photo by Craig Ott

Many Bible schools and seminaries require students to clean, cook, tend a vegetable garden, or perform other maintenance tasks for a certain number of hours per week to compensate for school expenses. In addition to the theological curriculum, some such schools also provide various forms of vocational training so that graduates can later earn a living with a secular occupation while they serve in or plant a new church. All of these factors consume time, so less is available for study.

In many non-Western Christian colleges and seminaries, students, faculty, and staff all live in campus housing. Often they eat meals together and live in close proximity. This learning community in which families are involved in daily life with one another is an optimal arrangement for modeling Christian character and spiritual formation. I have heard over and over that students remember informal interactions with teachers or professors as the most significant part of their education.

However, such arrangements also mean that one has little privacy by Western standards. Most Americans see family time as private time. Many cultures do not so strictly separate private and public life, or narrowly limit the role and responsibility of a teacher to the classroom (Chinchen 1997). Consequently, a teacher is engaged with students at one level or another all hours of the day and evenings. In one location, children who lived on the campus regularly peered in the windows of my room to observe how the strange foreigner lived. The teacher who too strictly protects her privacy may be viewed by students as uncaring, overly professional, and simply not a good teacher. Yet students' frequent spontaneous visits to one's home, or the feeling that one is always being watched, can become taxing for persons who value their privacy. Those who are not accustomed to constant interaction and interruptions can become emotionally drained and eventually burn out. Some cross-cultural teachers embrace this role and have little need for privacy. Others make themselves available but take frequent weekend excursions to get away from the campus for a few days. Yet others set boundaries and communicate them to their students. One teacher signaled to students that he was available for spontaneous visits by sitting on the porch of his house. If he was there, that meant that students were welcome to drop by. If he was not on the porch, that meant he did not want to be disturbed. I recall teaching for a week in the Democratic Republic of the Congo at a rural seminary where the students knew that American professors like their privacy. In the evening, if a student wanted to visit with me he would walk very slowly past the house where I was staying, hoping I would step out and invite him in. Cross-cultural teachers will need to honestly assess their personal privacy needs and discern what is reasonable for their individual or family situation. But they should be prepared for the stress they may experience living in a highly communal setting.

The Societal Environment

The broader societal context of a nation or region frames daily life and the educational experience in countless ways. Political or economic instability may create insecurity and stress for everyone. Natural disasters, civil unrest, ethnic conflict, and even war are unfortunately all too common disruptions in many parts of the world. For Christian teachers, the religious context is of particular interest, fraught with its own challenges.

Wealth, Poverty, and Opportunity

Teachers coming from wealthier countries will often be approached by students from regions characterized by poverty and lack of opportunity. They often come with a variety of requests including favors and material assistance. I've experienced that at the end of a week of teaching abroad it is not unusual to receive from students personal notes or requests for my email address, or to be approached in person with a variety of requests. Cross-cultural teachers may want to consider in advance how to respond graciously to such appeals. Resources such as David Maranz's *African Friends and Money Matters: Observations from Africa* (2001) can be invaluable in navigating such matters. Sometimes students hope that through a relationship with a foreign teacher they can acquire a scholarship or sponsorship to study abroad. One can grow weary of such requests, but understanding the context from which they come can help one keep a positive attitude and not become calloused.

In contexts where any education is better than no education, ambitious individuals may enroll in any available, affordable educational program—even if it is not of particular interest to them. They know it may provide a stepping-stone to another educational or vocational opportunity. Because Christian colleges and Bible schools typically offer education at a very low cost, they sometimes attract students who have little genuine interest in Christian ministry but see it as an opportunity to get ahead. It is a dangerous undertaking to judge the motivation of others, especially when working in a foreign culture. Therefore, the cross-cultural teacher needs to depend upon the judgment of local people in discerning such matters.

Politics

We live in a world in which much of life is politicized and polarized. A challenge that cross-cultural teachers sooner or later face is how to navigate sensitive political discussions. For example, the international sojourner will inevitably hear criticism of his home country by those of the host country. The temptation is to become defensive, or counter by pointing out weaknesses of the host country. This is rarely a wise response. Usually it is best to simply shrug and admit that one's homeland is not perfect. Sometimes such critique can open the door for a meaningful conversation about cultural differences and values, but wisdom is needed.

Teachers coming from societies where freedom of speech and conscience are considered basic human rights need to exercise discernment if working in a more restrictive society. What might seem to be an innocent debate about politics could be viewed by the host government as subversive. One may become incensed at observed injustices in the host culture. But one should weigh the cost: Is it is worth risking alienation or even deportation by speaking out, making negative comments about the government, or becoming embroiled in political debates? Such behavior can not only jeopardize the status of the expatriate teacher but also may have negative repercussions for the host institution and its leadership. Educational institutions are often under particular scrutiny and are not a context for free expression of opinion on sensitive matters. Xenophobic governments often keep a close eye on foreigner teachers. Cross-cultural teachers should become well informed of the local laws, political situation, and possible pitfalls that await naive foreigners.

Family

Teachers from more individualistic cultures can easily underestimate the importance of family obligations, including obligations to extended family, of persons in more collectivistic cultures. Family priorities can often conflict with educational goals. For example, in much of sub-Saharan Africa, students may abruptly miss a week of class in order to travel home for a family funeral, and this may happen multiple times in the course of a year. Money set aside for tuition or school fees may need to be sent home to assist in a crisis. This may interrupt study for a semester or longer. In many cultures older siblings are expected to provide for the education of younger siblings after they have completed their own education and have started their occupation.

Many non-Western Bible schools and seminaries offer a separate course of study for spouses, typically the wives. The wife may, however, be illiterate, and it is not unusual that the wife is not a Christian even though the husband is preparing for Christian ministry. Because often a pastor's wife is expected to be involved in ministry, Bible and counseling courses are included in their special curriculum. Sometimes instruction is also offered in vocational or practical skills such as sewing, cooking, and personal hygiene. Such cultural differences in gender roles and expectations sometimes offend Westerners' sensibilities. But in such matters the cultural outsider does well to follow the advice of James 1:19: "Everyone should be quick to listen, slow to speak and slow to become angry."

Social Unrest, Personal Safety, and Ethical Dilemmas

Teaching in locations where there is social unrest can entail risk for the expatriate teacher. Westerners, especially Americans, are often the target of popular protests. It is wise before traveling abroad to become informed of security alerts and risks in the host country. Such information, as well as general travel safety tips, can be found at the international travel webpage of the US Department of State[3] and similar agencies of other nations. Persons residing long-term are advised to register their presence with their consulate so they can receive security alerts and assistance if necessary. Agencies also exist that offer security services for organizations and individuals who work abroad, including consulting, training, crisis resolution services, and security

---

3. https://travel.state.gov/content/travel/en/international-travel.html.

updates. Personal crisis management training is available and especially rec-ommended for workers in high-risk locations.

Even serving in a stable, friendly foreign country has certain risks. Although one should not harbor a general distrust and suspicion toward the local people, as a cultural outsider it can take months or years until one is able to discern a scam or dangerous situation. Every major city has neighborhoods with high crime rates that require extra precautions to maintain personal safety. Naivete can result in avoidable misfortunes. Having trusted friends who are members of the host culture is the best starting point for developing such discernment and learning what safety measures are necessary and appropriate. Once one has gained some confidence in protecting personal safety, living in a foreign country and developing deep friendships with local people is a wonderful, life-enriching experience. But common sense and cultural awareness in secu-rity matters will help to keep the international sojourn a positive experience.

A dilemma frequently faced in many countries is the matter of bribery. A "gratuity" may be expected for anything from obtaining a visa in a government office, to obtaining a package from the customs office, to having the electricity turned on in one's residence. Such practices raise serious ethical questions. A culture of bribery ultimately perverts justice, granting services or favors to persons with the means to pay while others without means are discriminated against. The cross-cultural teacher may encounter such dilemmas personally or in the practices of the host educational institution as it seeks to obtain permits, accreditation, or services. However, one should be slow to judgment. A newcomer to a culture is seldom able to discern local distinctions between a bribe, extortion, a payment, and a gift, not all of which are necessarily un-ethical (J. Tan 2011). Here again, at least initially, one will need to trust the wisdom of local colleagues regarding the most appropriate way to ethically navigate such situations.[4] Works such as Bernard T. Adeney's *Strange Virtues: Ethics in a Multicultural World* (1995) are helpful for appreciating cultural differences in ethical issues.

Religion

Religion cannot be overlooked as a significant part of the teaching context. This is most obvious to Christian missionaries who work in locations where evangelism, proselytization, and other religious activities are strictly pro-hibited. However, even development workers and teachers in secular schools must know what activities are allowed and appropriate and be cognizant of how their behavior may be interpreted. In general, one should always speak

4. For various views on the ethics of missionaries and bribery, see the entire January 1999 issue of *Evangelical Missions Quarterly* (35, no. 1), and Koukl et al. 2014.

respectfully of other faiths and religious leaders even if one strongly disagrees with their beliefs or practices. But in Islamic countries, even a casual remark in private conversation that reflects negatively on the prophet Muhammad or the Qur'an can quickly land a person in serious trouble. If asked about one's faith, one is usually free to share one's personal story and the basic Christian message. But one must be aware of the risks of distributing literature and videos or more actively sharing one's faith.

Some cross-cultural workers teach in so-called underground churches, seminaries, or training institutes that are deemed illegal in the country in which they are located. Although government authorities sometimes turn a blind eye to such activities, the involvement of a foreigner may draw attention and place not only the teacher but also local people at risk. If a teacher has chosen to teach clandestinely in such a setting, he must be ready to face the consequences if discovered by government authorities. This activity may violate the terms of the teacher's visa. Deportation is the most likely outcome, but in some cases discovery could result in arrest and incarceration.

Jesus calls his followers to be willing to suffer for his name's sake (e.g., Matt. 5:11–12; 1 Pet. 3:13–17), and they must obey God and not people or governments (Acts 5:29). But they should also be wise and not unnecessarily provoke opposition (Matt. 10:16).

The Institutional Environment

The institutional context in which a cross-cultural teacher serves may be a formal school, university, or seminary; a local church; or a development organization. We speak here of the organizational framework within which teaching and learning take place. Romanowski and McCarthy describe some of the frustrations related to expectations and procedures when teaching abroad: "Things like not receiving the class roster until the end of the semester, only to realize that out of the sixty papers you've painstakingly graded, only twenty-five were actually signed up for the class. Or going to class to give your students their final exam and finding that another teacher has taken your classroom because he thought it was better for test taking—squatter's rights" (2009, 146). While teachers are usually patient with their students, they are often less flexible and more readily frustrated with challenges related to the institution. Unpredictable schedules, erratic class attendance, chaotic registration processes, bureaucratic red tape, different grading standards, and dealing with disciplinary matters are just a few of the institutionally related issues that may perplex and test the character of a cross-cultural teacher. Educational institutions, like most human organizations, develop their own subculture and traditions that reflect in part the larger cultural context and, in part, their own idiosyncrasies. The cross-cultural teacher may experience more culture shock within the parameters of the institution than they do living in the broader culture.

Expectations and Agreements

As the examples above illustrate, the institution's expectations and the cross-cultural teacher's expectations often do not match, even when they are negotiated in writing. On one occasion a teaching partner and I arrived for what we thought would be a private consultation with a committee of seven or eight regional leaders as a follow-up to a conference that I had led the previous year. Since this was billed as an informal discussion, we had not prepared much. However, when we arrived the organizers told us how excited they were that registration for the event now topped one hundred participants from all over the country! Needless to say, we had to scramble at the last minute to prepare to work with the larger group. In Nepal I taught a course in a small Bible school and brought along one of my former American seminary students, who was also to teach a course. On arrival he was informed that he was to teach an entirely different course from what he had prepared.

One might expect contractual agreements to be binding, but that is not always the case. Typically, teachers of English as a second language who travel to another country will have signed a contract that may stipulate the number of instructional hours per week, the provision of housing, financial remuneration, and other details. However, upon arrival they may be confronted with quite different conditions, such as increased instructional hours. The housing may be unheated (not unusual in China), or may be canceled after a few months, after which the teacher must fend for herself and find another place to live. In some cultures, contracts are considered to be only a momentary agreement. Westerners expect them to be strictly binding, but in many cultures the assumption is that circumstances always change, and thus conditions of a contract can be spontaneously and one-sidedly altered with little or no negotiation. Cross-cultural teachers should adjust their expectations accordingly. If a major conflict arises, one should discover culturally appropriate ways to negotiate the matter before too quickly taking legal measures or making harsh accusations. The reality is that in some countries there is little legal recourse and courts will seldom rule in favor of a foreigner, especially if the teacher is viewed as a wealthy Westerner.

Punctuality and Scheduling

Different expectations regarding punctuality are one of the best known, most frustrating differences between cultures. In one culture, arriving ten minutes after the arranged time is considered "late," whereas in another culture one is not "late" until thirty minutes after the appointed time. Furthermore, what is considered late when arriving for a business meeting may be different than for a family picnic. Some cultures are considered more "time oriented," and in those it is important to keep to tight schedules and arrive for an appointment or event within a few minutes of the arranged time. Time is viewed as a commodity that should not be wasted, and thus punctuality is more than a matter of efficiency: it expresses respect for the others who are present. On the other hand, some cultures are more "event oriented." People live more "in the moment." Relationships are more important than keeping schedules. If one encounters a friend on the way to an appointment, taking time for the friend is more important than arriving on time. Events begin when the most important people are present, not according to a clock on the wall. Everyone knows that eventualities may arise that may delay a meeting, so they are accustomed to conducting other activities to fill the time while waiting for someone to arrive. In fact, arriving right on time for a social event such as a dinner might be interpreted by the host as too businesslike and not indicating a real friendship (see discussions in Lingenfelter and Mayers 2016, 25–38; Moreau, Campbell, and Greener 2014, 142–53; Neuliep 2012, 156–62).

It may be hard to learn about local norms regarding punctuality and scheduling until one has arrived and begins teaching. Formal schools are usually good at keeping schedules, but my experience with non-formal teaching in many non-Western settings is that schedules are extremely flexible. Starting "on time" (by Western standards) is a rarity, and breaks are longer than anticipated. Participants will trickle in at the start of the day or after a break, and teaching does not begin until a majority is present. What was scheduled as a morning with four instructional hours may end up with only three. (It is interesting, however, to note that mealtimes are kept relatively punctual!) Cross-cultural teachers should prepare a flexible teaching plan in which content that is less essential can be omitted to adjust to the time actually available. One good strategy is to structure teaching content in small units that are complete in themselves. This makes it easier to accommodate last-minute changes.

One should not become frustrated and expect organizers to enforce a strict schedule that is out of sync with local norms. Social interactions during coffee breaks are often opportunities for participants to process information or ask questions that they were uncomfortable asking in class. Thus, long breaks can actually be important to the learning process (apart from merely increasing caffeine intake, which can also have pedagogical value!). Furthermore, one should not cut off class discussions too quickly just to stay on schedule. Conversely, a teacher from a culture where schedules are flexible who enters a culture that is more time oriented will need to adapt accordingly, too.

Otherwise students will become frustrated, fear that important content will not be covered, and feel that their time is being wasted.

In some cultures the daily schedule is so detailed that even time-oriented Westerners are amazed. Take for example this description of the daily routine at a Chinese university:

> The daily schedule for students is tightly regimented. At the latest the lights are turned off in the student residence at 11:00 pm (and the students' flashlights are turned on). At 6:00 in the morning the students are awakened by music and the first public announcements, which are loudly broadcast through speakers that are installed around the campus. During the instructional breaks, music is broadcast laced with commands to exercise, that are largely ignored. With this are broadcast also local, national, and international news reports. The mandatory afternoon nap is ended by an announcement over the loudspeakers, and at 10:00 pm a trumpet sounds bedtime. (Mitschian 1991, 213)

Although what is described above might no longer be the case in most Chinese universities, it is an accurate description of schedules elsewhere. A seminary I visited in India had a strict schedule down to the minute for the students: wake up, devotions, meals, class, chapel, chores, study time, and bedtime. A student I spoke with said that he had never experienced such a rigid lifestyle so totally antithetical to his home culture. Although it was difficult for him to adjust at first, he admitted that the discipline was good for him, and he is now a better person for it.

Boards, Stakeholders, and Accreditors

Virtually all formal educational institutions feature sponsors, stakeholders, and accreditors. These various groups have differing agendas, which may conflict. A theological seminary's board may be composed of local pastors and church leaders; the primary financial support may come from a mission organization or foreign partner; and accreditation may be through a government office or an international theological accrediting agency. The first group may desire the practical equipping of future pastors; the second may want to ensure that certain theological distinctives are maintained; and the third may be more focused on academic excellence. The cross-cultural teacher must take care not to become entangled in the various agendas and debates without first understanding the complexity of the local situation.

Different cultures also have different standards and qualifications for leadership roles. What are the most important qualifications for the president or principal of an institution? Should she be academically qualified, have administrative experience, or have high social status and close relationships with donors and other community leaders? Not a few cross-cultural teachers have found themselves working under the leadership of someone they regard as unqualified and incompetent—yet in that cultural setting, other qualities may be more important for the survival of the institution. Compensating creatively without undermining the leadership requires skill and diplomacy that a newcomer has rarely acquired. Patience and humility are virtues that every cross-cultural teacher needs.

Two other aspects of the institutional environment that are particularly disconcerting to many Western teachers are nepotism and preferential treatment of certain students. For example, a school may admit a student who does not meet the formal qualifications but comes from the same ethnic group as the principal. A school may be obligated to admit a quota of students from different regions, even if they are not qualified. In some Bible schools it would be simply unacceptable for the son of the local bishop to fail his exams. Such conditions can quickly cause a conflict between the teacher's ethical values and the institution's unspoken policies. The cross-cultural teacher may be tempted to react quickly and even make harsh accusations. The only change that such behavior is likely to effect is the termination of the teacher. In all these scenarios, an appreciation of the cultural dynamics and institutional history are necessary before attempting to introduce change, resolve conflicts, or address matters that are genuinely inappropriate. Cross-cultural teachers do well to familiarize themselves with the cultural dynamics around power, leadership, decision-making, and exercise of authority (see sidebar 13.2).

Expectations of Students

One of the first things that a cross-cultural teacher needs to clarify in formal teaching settings is what the institution expects of students. Are they required to do work outside of class? If so, what is normal? What are the standards for grading exams and assignments? Does the teacher have the freedom to fail students who are performing poorly, or is failure simply not allowed? Is attendance required? Some universities do not require students to attend classes. Consequently, if a student thinks that she can pass the exams by reading the books or copying other students' lecture notes, she may seldom attend lectures. Even where class attendance is expected, students may regularly miss class and the teacher may have little recourse for discipline. Students may be allowed to register for two classes that meet at the same time, and so may miss at least half the class sessions in each of them (George 1995, 116).

Sooner or later every teacher will encounter student behavior that requires some form of intervention or discipline. The question then arises: does the teacher have authority to directly deal with the matter? In serious cases, the administration is normally involved, but the teacher may be exasperated if no

SIDEBAR 13.2

Resources on Leadership and Culture

Abramson, Neil Remington, and Robert T. Moran. *Managing Cultural Differences: Global Leadership Strategies for the Twenty-First Century*. 10th ed. New York: Routledge & Kegan Paul, 2018.

Dimmock, Clive, and Allan Walker. *Educational Leadership: Culture and Diversity*. Thousand Oaks, CA: SAGE, 2005.

Lewis, Richard D. *When Cultures Collide: Leading across Cultures*. 3rd ed. Boston: Nicholas Brealey, 2005.

Lingenfelter, Sherwood G. *Leading Cross-Culturally: Covenant Relationships*. Grand Rapids: Baker Academic, 2008.

Plueddemann, James. *Leading across Cultures: Effective Ministry and Mission in the Global Church*. Downers Grove, IL: InterVarsity, 2009.

Thomas, David C., and Mark F. Peterson. *Cross-Cultural Management: Essential Concepts*. 4th ed. Thousand Oaks, CA: SAGE, 2018.

Trompenaars, Fons, and Charles Hampden-Turner. *Riding the Waves of Culture: Understanding Cultural Diversity in Business*. 3rd ed. London: Nicholas Brealey, 2012.

real corrective action is taken. Chapter 10 discussed cheating and plagiarism. As noted there, the cross-cultural teacher must understand and for the most part accept the institutional policy for dealing with plagiarism, cheating, and other behavioral problems.

Although institutions of higher education often consider themselves liberal and progressive, in reality they can be woefully bound to tradition. Change comes slowly. A cross-cultural teacher has the potential to bring fresh insights, an international perspective, and new ideas into an institution. However, the teacher should not be naive about this ability to be a change agent (see sidebar 1.1 on p. 9). One may encounter polite nods of agreement, only to experience no change in reality. Good ideas go ignored. Being a team player, appreciating the positive, giving and earning respect, exercising patience, discerning how decisions are made, and observing how change occurs are keys to making a positive contribution. There are no shortcuts: time, patience, demonstrating a genuine commitment to the institution, and evidence of sincere love for the people are the necessary prerequisites.

· · · · ·

This book has taken readers on a long and somewhat complex journey through the five dimensions of how culture influences teaching and learning: cognition, worldview, social relations, media, and the environment. One could easily conclude that the obstacles to effective teaching across cultures are insurmountable. This would be a mistake. While it is naive to assume that "good teaching is just good teaching . . . anywhere," there is a grain of truth in the statement. This is not because teachers can indiscriminately teach and relate to learners everywhere as they would at home. Rather, it's because, like Anna Leonowens, the schoolteacher in *The King and I*, good teachers everywhere become students of their students, getting to know them. What's more, good teachers everywhere personally *care* about their students. One can commit many cultural mistakes, but learners are usually forgiving when they know that the teacher really cares and is there to serve them. Still, there are no shortcuts to teaching effectiveness when entering another cultural world. It is hard work and at times frustrating. Christian teachers will learn to depend upon God's grace and enablement. They will commit themselves and their students to God in prayer, asking the Holy Spirit to be the ultimate teacher and life transformer. Diligence in understanding learners, perseverance in the midst of setbacks, and flexibility in the use of methods will pay rich dividends. Not only will learners be helped to reach their potential, but each teacher will be enriched through the experience of cultural diversity and the joy of having invested in the lives of others.

Works Cited

Aberbach, Moses. 1967. "The Relations between Master and Disciple in the Talmudic Age." In *Essays Presented to Chief Rabbi Israel Brodie on the Occasion of His Seventieth Birthday*, edited by H. J. Zimmels, J. Rabbinowitz, and I. Finestein, 1:1–24. London: Soncino.

Achren, Linda. 1991. "Do We Assume Too Much? Measuring the Cross-Cultural Appropriacy of Our Teaching Aids." *Prospect* 6 (2): 25–41.

Adeney, Bernard T. 1995. *Strange Virtues: Ethics in a Multicultural World*. Downers Grove, IL: InterVarsity.

AHSE (Association for the Study of Higher Education). 2012. "Understanding Intercultural Competence and Its Development." *ASHE Higher Education Report* 38 (2): 23–43.

Ajisuksmo, Carla R. P., and Jan D. Vermunt. 1999. "Learning Styles and Self-Regulation of Learning at University: An Indonesian Study." *Asia Pacific Journal of Education* 19 (2): 45–59.

Alexander, Jeffrey C., Bernhard Giesen, and Jason L. Mast, eds. 2006. *Social Performance: Symbolic Action, Cultural Pragmatics, and Ritual*. Cambridge: Cambridge University Press.

Alfieri, Louis, Timothy J. Nokes-Malach, and Christian D. Schunn. 2013.

"Learning through Case Comparisons: A Meta-Analytic Review." *Educational Psychologist* 48 (2): 87–113.

Al-Harthi, Aisha S. 2005. "Distance Higher Education Experiences of Arab Gulf Students in the United States: A Cultural Perspective." *International Review of Research in Open and Distance Learning* 6 (3): 1–14.

Alias, Nor Aziah. 2011. "Incorporating Cultural Components into the Design of an Affective Support Tool for the Malaysian Online Distance Learners." In *Cases on Globalized and Culturally Appropriate E-Learning: Challenges and Solutions*, edited by Andrea Edmundson, 1–26. Hershey, PA: Information Science Reference.

Alves, Rubem A. 1990. *The Poet, the Warrior, the Prophet*. Philadelphia: Trinity Press International.

Amaya, Ismael E. 1983. "A Latin American Critique of Western Theology." *Evangelical Review of Theology* 7 (1): 13–27.

Ambrose, Susan, Michael W. Bridges, Michelle DePietro, Marsha C. Lovett, and Marie K. Norman. 2010. *How Learning Works: Seven Research-Based Principles for Smart Teaching*. San Francisco: Jossey-Bass.

An, Donggun, and Martha Carr. 2017. "Learning Styles Theory Fails to Explain

Learning and Achievement: Recommendations for Alternative Approaches." *Personality and Individual Differences* 116 (October): 410–16.

Anakwe, Uzoamaka P., and Edward W. Christensen. 1999. "Distance Learning and Cultural Diversity: Potential Users' Perspective." *International Journal of Organizational Analysis* (1993–2002) 7 (3): 224–43.

Angeli, Charola, and Nicos Valanides. 2004. "Examining the Effects of Text-Only and Text-and-Visual Instructional Materials on the Achievement of Field-Dependent and Field-Independent Learners during Problem-Solving with Modeling Software." *Educational Technology Research and Development* 52 (4): 23–36.

Apfelthaler, Gerhard, Katrin Hansen, Stephan Keuchel, Christa Mueller, Martin Neubauer, Siow Heng Ong, and Nirundon Tapachai. 2007. "Cross-Cultural Differences in Learning and Education." In *Learning and Teaching across Cultures in Higher Education*, edited by David Palfreyman and Dawn Lorraine McBride, 15–35. New York: Palgrave Macmillan.

Archee, Ray, and Myra Gurney. 2011. "Integrating Culture with E-Learning Management System Design." In *Cases on Globalized and Culturally Appropriate E-Learning: Challenges and Solutions*, edited by Andrea Edmundson, 27–40. Hershey, PA: Information Science Reference.

Archibald, Jo-ann (Q'um Q'um Xiiem). 2008. *Indigenous Storywork: Educating the Heart, Mind, Body, and Spirit*. Vancouver: University of British Columbia Press.

Arensen, Brian. 1995. "How to Teach Using the Inductive Method." *Evangelical Missions Quarterly* 31 (3): 338–43.

Arnold, Clinton E. 1996. *The Colossian Syncretism: The Interface between Christianity and Folk Belief at Colossae*. Grand Rapids: Baker.

Asia Theological Association. 1982. "The Seoul Declaration: Toward an Evangelical Theology for the Third World." *Missiology* 10 (4): 490–94.

Atkinson, George. 1991. "Kolb's Learning Style Inventory: A Practitioner's Perspective." *Measurement and Evaluation in Counseling and Development* 23 (4): 149.

Au, T. K. 1983. "Chinese and English Counterfactuals: The Sapir-Whorf Hypothesis Revisited." *Cognition* 15 (1–3): 155–87.

Avoseh, Mejai B. M. 2012. "Proverbs as Theoretical Frameworks for Lifelong Learning in Indigenous African Education." *Adult Education Quarterly* 63 (3): 236–50.

Aylett, Graham, and Tim Green. 2015. "Theological Education by Extension (TEE) as a Tool for Twenty-First Century Mission." In *Reflecting on and Equipping for Christian Mission*, edited by Stephen Bevans, Teresa Chai, J. Nelson Jennings, Knud Jørgensen, and Dietrich Werner, 59–78. Oxford: Regnum.

Babaii, Esmat, and Hassan Nejadghanbar. 2017. "Plagiarism among Iranian Graduate Students of Language Studies: Perspectives and Causes." *Ethics & Behavior* 27 (3): 240–58.

Bagley, Christopher, and Kanka Mallick. 1998. "Field Independence, Cultural Context and Academic Achievement: A Commentary." *British Journal of Educational Psychology* 68 (4): 581–87.

Bain, Ken. 2004. *What the Best College Teachers Do*. Cambridge, MA: Harvard University Press.

Bandura, Albert. 1997. *Self-Efficacy: The Exercise of Control*. New York: W. H. Freeman.

Barnes, Hazel. 2013. *Applied Drama and Theatre as an Interdisciplinary Field in the Context of HIV/AIDS in Africa*. Amsterdam: Rodopi.

Barrett, Justin L. 2011. *Cognitive Science, Religion, and Theology: From Human Minds to Divine Minds*. West Conshohocken, PA: Templeton.

Barth, Fredrik, ed. 1998. *Ethnic Groups and Boundaries: The Social Organization of Culture Difference*. Prospect Heights, IL: Waveland.

Bartle, Neville. 2005. *Death, Witchcraft and the Spirit World in the Highlands of Papua New Guinea*. Goroka, Papua New Guinea: Melanesian Institute.

Bechlivanidis, Christos, David A. Lagnado, Jeffrey C. Zemla, and Steven Sloman. 2017. "Concreteness and Abstraction in Everyday Explanation." *Psychonomic Bulletin and Review* 24 (5): 1451–64.

Bedford, Olwen A. 2004. "The Individual Experience of Guilt and Shame in Chinese Culture." *Culture & Psychology* 10 (1): 29–52.

Bekaan, Michaela. 2009. Paper submitted for the course Interkulturelles Lehren und Lernen at the European School of Culture and Theology.

Bell, Joyce. 2007. "Reading Practices: Postgraduate Thai Student Perceptions." *Reading Matrix* 7 (1): 51–67.

Bennal, Amruta S., Raju H. Taklikar, and Manohar Y. Pattar. 2016. "Effectiveness of 'Case-Based Learning' in Physiology." *National Journal of Physiology, Pharmacy and Pharmacology* 6 (1): 65–67.

Bernard, Robert M., Eugene Borokhovski, and Rana M. Tamim. 2014. "Detecting Bias in Meta-Analyses of Distance Education Research: Big Pictures We Can Rely On." *Distance Education* 35 (3): 271–93.

Berry, John W. 1991. "Cultural Variations in Field Dependence-Independence." In *Field Dependence-Independence: Cognitive Styles across the Life Span*, edited by Seymour Wapner and Jack Demick, 289–308. Hillsdale, NJ: Lawrence Erlbaum Associates.

Berry, John W., Ype H. Poortinga, Marshall H. Segall, and Pierre R. Dasen. 1992. *Cross-Cultural Psychology: Research and Applications*. New York: Cambridge University Press.

Bhagat, Anumeha, Rashmi Vyas, and Tejinder Singh. 2015. "Students' Awareness of Learning Styles and Their Perceptions to a Mixed Method Approach for Learning." Supplement, *International Journal of Applied and Basic Medical Research* 5, no. S1: S58–S65.

Biggs, John B. 2001. "Teaching across Cultures." In *Student Motivation: The Culture and Context of Learning*, edited by Farideh Salili, Chi-yue Chiu, and Ying-yi Hong, 293–308. New York: Kluwer Academic.

Biggs, John B., and David A. Watkins. 1996. "The Chinese Learner in Retrospect." In *The Chinese Learner: Cultural, Psychological, and Contextual Influences*, edited by David A. Watkins and John B. Biggs, 269–85. Hong Kong: Comparative Education Research Centre.

Black, Stephanie L. 2018. "Scholarship in Our Own Words: Intercultural Rhetoric in Academic Writing and Reporting." In *Challenging Tradition*, edited by Perry Shaw and Havilah Dharamraj. Carlisle, UK: Langham Global. Kindle edition.

Boas, Franz. 1911. *The Mind of Primitive Man*. New York: Macmillan.

Bowen, Earle, and Dorothy Bowen. 1991. "What Does It Mean to Think, Learn, Teach?" In *Internationalizing Missionary Training: A Global Perspective*, edited by William David Taylor, 203–16. Grand Rapids: Baker.

Brandon, James R. 1993. *On Thrones of Gold: Three Javanese Shadow Plays*. Honolulu: University of Hawaii Press.

Brescia, Raymond M. 2018. "Dominance and Disintermediation: Subversive Stories and Counter-Narratives of Cooperation." *Southern California Interdisciplinary Law Journal* 27 (3): 429–81.

Brew, Christine R. 2002. "Kolb's Learning Style Instrument: Sensitive to Gender." *Educational and Psychological Measurement* 62 (2): 373.

Brewer, Paul, and Sunil Venaik. 2011. "Individualism-Collectivism in Hofstede and GLOBE." *Journal of International Business Studies* 42 (3): 436–45.

Brislin, Richard. 1993. *Understanding Culture's Influence on Behavior*. Orlando, FL: Harcourt, Brace.

Brock, Colin, and Nafsika Alexiadou. 2013. *Education around the World: A Comparative Introduction*. New York: Bloomsbury Academic.

Brouwers, Symen A., Fons J. R. van de Vijver, and Ramesh C. Mishra. 2017. "Cognitive Development through Schooling and Everyday Life." *International Journal of Behavioral Development* 41, no. 3 (May): 309–19.

Bruner, Jerome S. 1966. "On Cognitive Growth I" and "On Cognitive Growth II." In *Studies in Cognitive Growth*, edited by Jerome S. Bruner, Rose R. Oliver, and Patricia M. Greenfield, 1–29, 30–67. New York: Wiley & Sons.

———. 1996. *The Culture of Education*. Cambridge, MA: Harvard University Press.

Bruner, Jerome S., Rose R. Oliver, and Patricia M. Greenfield. 1966. *Studies in Cognitive Growth*. New York: Wiley & Sons.

Brunyé, Tad T., Holly A. Taylor, David N. Rapp, and Alexander B. Spiro. 2006. "Learning Procedures: The Role of Working Memory in Multimedia Learning Experiences." *Applied Cognitive Psychology* 20 (7): 917–40.

Bryant, Jennings, Paul Cominsky, and Dolf Zillman. 1979. "Teachers' Humor in the College Classroom." *Communication Education* 28 (2): 110–18.

Buck, Tina, Carol M. Baldwin, and Gary E. Schwartz. 2005. "Influence of Worldview on Health Care Choices among Persons with Chronic Pain." *Journal of Alternative and Complementary Medicine* 11 (3): 561–68.

Buconyori, Elie A. 1991. "Cognitive Styles and the Development of Reasoning in African Christian Students in Higher Education." PhD diss., Trinity Evangelical Divinity School, Deerfield, IL.

Burnett, Russell C., and Douglas L. Medin. 2008. "Reasoning across Cultures." In *Reasoning: Studies of Human Inference and Its Foundations*, edited by Jonathan E. Adler and Lance J. Rips, 934–55. New York: Cambridge University Press.

Burton, Pauline. 2010. "Creativity in Hong Kong Schools." *World Englishes* 29, no. 4 (December): 493–507.

Cai, Deborah A., and Edward L. Fink. 2002. "Conflict Style Differences between Individualists and Collectivists." *Communication Monographs* 69 (1): 67–87.

Carr-Chellman, Allison A., ed. 2005a. *Global Perspectives on E-Learning: Rhetoric and Reality*. Thousand Oaks, CA: SAGE.

———, 2005b. "Introduction." In *Global Perspectives on E-Learning: Rhetoric and Reality*, edited by Allison A. Carr-Chellman, 1–16. Thousand Oaks, CA: SAGE.

Carroll, Jude. 2015. *Tools for Teaching in an Educationally Mobile World*. New York: Routledge & Kegan Paul.

Catterick, David. 2007. "Do the Philosophical Foundations of Online Learning Disadvantage Non-Western Students?" In *Globalized E-Learning Cultural Challenges*, edited by Andrea Edmundson, 116–29. Hershey, PA: Information Science Publishing.

Chan, Carol K. K. 2009. "Classroom Innovation for the Chinese Learner: Transcending Dichotomies and Transforming Pedagogy." In *Revisiting the Chinese Learner: Changing Contexts, Changing Education*, edited by Carol K. K. Chan and Nirmal Rao, 169–210. Hong Kong: Comparative Research Centre, University of Hong Kong.

Chang, Eunhye. 2015. "Becoming a Pente: Factors Influencing the Conversion to Protestant Christianity among Urban Ethiopian Orthodox Young Adults."

PhD diss., Trinity International University, Deerfield, IL.

Chang, Peter S. C. 1984. "Steak, Potatoes, Peas and Chopsuey: Linear and Nonlinear Thinking." In *Missions and Theological Education in World Perspective*, edited by Harvie M. Conn and Samuel F. Rowen, 113–23. Farmington, MI: Associates of Urbanus.

Chen, Szu-Yu, Dareen Basma, Jennie Ju, and Kok-Mun Ng. 2020. "Opportunities and Challenges of Multicultural and International Online Education." *Professional Counselor* 10 (1): 120–32.

Chen, Wain-Chin. 2007. "Some Literature Review on the Comparison of the Chinese *Qi-Cheng-Zhuan-He* Writing Model and the Western Problem-Solution Schema." *Whampoa* 52:137–48.

Chen, Zhiwei, and Ying Liu. 2019. "The Different Style of Lifelong Learning in China and the USA Based on Influencing Motivations and Factors." *International Journal of Educational Research* 95 (May): 13–25.

Cheney, Lynne V. 1994. "The End of History." *Wall Street Journal*, October 20, 1994. http://online.wsj.com/media/EndofHistory.pdf.

———. 2015. "The End of History, Part II." *Wall Street Journal*, April 1, 2015. http://www.wsj.com/articles/lynne-cheney-the-end-of-history-part-ii-1427929675.

Cheng, Hongyu, Heidi L. Andrade, and Zheng Yan. 2011. "A Cross-Cultural Study of Learning Behaviours in the Classroom: From a Thinking Style Perspective." *Educational Psychology* 31 (7): 825–41.

Cheng, Xiaotang. 2000. "Asian Students' Reticence Revisited." *System* 28 (3): 435–46.

Chiang, Samuel E., and Grant Lovejoy, eds. 2014. *Beyond Literate Western Practices: Continuing Conversations in Orality and Theological Education*. Hong Kong: International Orality Network.

Chinchen, Delbert. 1997. "The Return of the Fourth 'R' to Education: Relationships." *Missiology* 25 (3): 321–35.

Ching, Luk Suet. 1998. "The Influence of a Distance-Learning Environment on Students' Field Dependence/Independence." *Journal of Experimental Education* 66 (2): 149–60.

Chipatiso, Remo. 2013. "Evaluation of Applied Drama and Theatre in HIV/AIDS Interventions." *Matatu: Journal for African Culture and Society* 43 (1): 251–67.

Chiu, Chi-Yue, Angela K.-Y. Leung, and Letty Kwan. 2007. "Language, Cognition, and Culture: Beyond the Whorfian Hypothesis." In *Handbook of Cultural Psychology*, edited by Shinobu Kitayama and Dov Cohen, 668–88. New York: Guilford.

Chomsky, Noam. 1965. *Aspects of the Theory of Syntax*. Cambridge, MA: MIT Press.

———. 1968. *Language and Mind*. New York: Harcourt Brace Jovanovich.

Christy, T. Craig. 2013. "Vygotsky, Cognitive Development and Language." *Historiographia Linguistica* 40 (1/2): 199–227.

Clewley, Natalie, Sherry Y. Chen, and Xiaohui Liu. 2011. "Mining Learning Preferences in Web-Based Instruction: Holists vs. Serialists." *Journal of Educational Technology and Society* 14 (4): 266–77.

Coffield, Frank, David Moseley, Elaine Hall, and Kathryn Ecclestone. 2004a. *Learning Styles and Pedagogy in Post-16 Learning: A Systematic and Critical Review*. London: Learning and Skills Research Centre.

———. 2004b. *Should We Be Using Learning Styles? What Research Has to Say to Practice*. London: Learning and Skills Research Centre.

Collins, Gary R., ed. 1991. *Case Studies in Christian Counseling*. Dallas: Word.

Cong, Yan, and Kerry Earl. 2011. "Chinese Postgraduate Students Learning Online in New Zealand." In *Cases on Globalized* and Culturally Appropriate E-Learning: Challenges and Solutions, edited by Andrea Edmundson, 73–89. Hershey, PA: Information Science Reference.

Cook, Bruce L. 1981. Understanding Pictures in Papua New Guinea. Elgin, IL: David C. Cook Foundation.

Cortazzi, Martin, and Lixian Jin. 2001. "Large Classes in China: 'Good' Teachers and Interaction." In Teaching the Chinese Learner: Psychological and Pedagogical Perspectives, edited by David Watkins and John B. Biggs, 115–34. Hong Kong: Comparative Education Research Centre.

Cothran, Donetta J., Pamela Hodges Kulinna, Dominique Banville, Eui Chang Choi, Chantal Amade-Escot, Ann MacPhail, Doune Macdonald, Jean-François Richard, Pedro Sarmento, and David Kirk. 2005. "A Cross-Cultural Investigation of the Use of Teaching Styles." Research Quarterly for Exercise and Sport 76 (2): 193–201.

Cozens, Simon. 2018. "Shame Cultures, Fear Cultures and Guilt Cultures: Reviewing the Evidence." International Bulletin of Mission Research 42, no. 4 (October): 326–36.

Cushner, Kenneth, and Jennifer Mahon. 2009. "Intercultural Competence in Teacher Education." In The SAGE Handbook of Intercultural Competence, edited by Darla K. Deardorf, 304–20. Thousand Oaks, CA: SAGE.

Darwish, Abdel Fattah E., and Günter L. Huber. 2003. "Individualism vs. Collectivism in Different Cultures: A Cross-Cultural Study." Intercultural Education 14 (1): 47–56.

Das, J. P., and U. N. Dash. 1989. "Schooling, Literacy and Cognitive Development." In Understanding Literacy and Cognition, edited by Che Kan Leong and Bikkar S. Randhawa, 217–44. New York: Plenum.

Dau, Isaiah. 2011. "How Can We Not Sing for the Lord?" In Global Mission: Reflections and Case Studies in Contextualization, edited by Rose Dowsett, 195–200. Pasadena, CA: William Carey.

Davis, Barbara Gross. 2009. Tools for Teaching. 2nd ed. San Francisco: Jossey-Bass.

Davis, J. Kent. 1991. "Educational Implications of Field Dependence-Independence." In Field Dependence-Independence: Cognitive Styles across the Life Span, edited by Seymour Wapner and Jack Demick, 149–75. Hillsdale, NJ: Lawrence Erlbaum Associates, 1991.

Day, Samuel B., Benjamin A. Motz, and Robert L. Goldstone. 2015. "The Cognitive Costs of Context: The Effects of Concreteness and Immersiveness in Instructional Examples." Frontiers in Psychology 6:1–13.

DeCapua, Andrea, and Helaine W. Marshall. 2010. "Students with Limited or Interrupted Formal Education in US Classrooms." Urban Review 42, no. 2 (June): 159–73.

De Ciantis, Steven M., and M. J. Kirton. 1996. "A Psychometric Reexamination of Kolb's Experiential Learning Cycle Construct." Educational and Psychological Measurement 56 (5): 809–20.

Demele, Isolde. 1988. "Interkulturelles Lernen zwischen traditioneller und Industriegesellschaft." Unterrichtswissenschaften 1:16–27.

Dennen, Vanessa P., and Jiyae Bong. 2018. "Cross-Cultural Dialogues in an Open Online Course: Navigating National and Organizational Cultural Differences." TechTrends 62 (4): 383–92.

Denny, J. Peter. 1986. "Cultural Ecology and Mathematics: Ojibway and Inuit Hunters." In Native American Mathematics, edited by Michael P. Closs, 129–80. Austin: University of Texas Press.

———. 1991. "Traditional Thought in Oral Culture and Literate Decontextualization." In Literacy and Orality, edited by David R. Olson and Nancy Torrance, 66–89. New York: Cambridge University Press.

Dillon, Patrick, Ruolan Wang, and Penni Tearle. 2007. "Cultural Disconnection in Virtual Education." *Pedagogy, Culture and Society* 15 (2): 153–74.

Dockery, David S., and Gregory Alan Thornbury, eds. 2002. *Shaping a Christian Worldview: The Foundations of Christian Higher Education*. Nashville: Broadman & Holman.

Drążkowski, Dariusz, Jakub Szwedo, Aleksandra Krajczewska, Anna Adamczuk, Krzysztof Piątkowski, Marcin Jadwiżyc, and Adam Rakowski. 2017. "Women Are Not Less Field Independent than Men—The Role of Stereotype Threat." *International Journal of Psychology* 52 (5): 415–19.

Eaves, Mina. 2011. "The Relevance of Learning Styles for International Pedagogy in Higher Education." *Teachers and Teaching* 17 (6): 677–91.

Edmundson, Andrea, ed. 2007. *Globalized E-Learning and Cultural Challenges*. Hershey, PA: Information Science Publishing.

———, ed. 2011a. *Cases on Globalized and Culturally Appropriate E-Learning: Challenges and Solutions*. Hershey, PA: Information Science Reference.

———, ed. 2011b. "The Cultural Adaptation of E-Learning: Using Appropriate Content, Instructional Design, and Media." In *Cases on Globalized and Culturally Appropriate E-Learning: Challenges and Solutions*, edited by Andrea Edmundson, 308–25. Hershey, PA: Information Science Reference.

Elliot, Julian G., and Janine Bempechat. 2002. "The Culture and Contexts of Achievement Motivation." In *Learning in Culture and Context: Approaching the Complexities of Achievement Motivation in Student Learning*, New Directions for Child and Adolescent Development 96, edited by Janine Bempechat and Julian G. Elliot, 7–26. San Francisco: Wiley & Sons.

Elman, Benjamin A. 2009. "Eight-Legged Essay: Bāgǔwén 八股文." In *Encyclopedia of China*, 695–98. Great Barrington, MA: Berkshire. https://www.princeton.edu/~elman/documents/Eight-Legged%20Essay.pdf.

Elmer, Duane. 1993. *Cross-Cultural Conflict: Building Relationships for Effective Ministry*. Downers Grove, IL: InterVarsity.

Engelbrecht, Petra, and Shirley G. Natzel. 1997. "Cultural Variations in Cognitive Style: Field Dependence vs. Field Independence." *School Psychology International* 18 (2): 155–64.

Enns, Marlene. 2005a. "'Now I Know in Part': Holistic and Analytic Reasoning and Their Contribution to Fuller Knowing in Theological Education." *Evangelical Review of Theology* 29 (3): 251–69.

———. 2005b. "Recovering the Wisdom Tradition for Intercultural Theological Education." *Journal of European Baptist Studies* 5 (3): 5–23.

Evans, Carol, John T. E. Richardson, and Michael Waring. 2013. "Field Independence: Reviewing the Evidence." *British Journal of Educational Psychology* 83 (2): 210–24.

Fabritius, Friederike, and Hans W. Hagemann. 2017. *The Leading Brain: Powerful Science-Based Strategies for Achieving Peak Performance*. New York: Penguin Random House.

Faiola, Anthony, and Karl F. MacDorman. 2008. "The Influence of Holistic and Analytic Cognitive Styles on Online Information Design." *Information, Communication & Society* 11 (3): 348–74.

Faiola, Anthony, and Sorin A. Matei. 2005. "Cultural Cognitive Style and Web Design: Beyond a Behavioral Inquiry into Computer-Mediated Communication." *Journal of Computer-Mediated Communication* 11 (1): 375–94.

Fajana, A. 1986. "Traditional Methods of Education in Africa: The Yoruba Example." In *The Arts and Civilization of*

Black and African Peoples, vol. 6, *Black Civilization and Pedagogy*, edited by Benjamin Olatunji Oloruntimehin, Joseph Ohiomogben Okpaku, and Alfred Esimatemi Opubor, 42–50. Lagos, Nigeria: Center for Black and African Arts and Civilization.

Fernández-Llamazares, Álvaro, and Mar Cabeza. 2017. "Rediscovering the Potential of Indigenous Storytelling for Conservation Practice." *Conservation Letters* 11, no. 3 (May): 1–12.

Ferrell, Barbara G. 1983. "A Factor Analytic Comparison of Four Learning-Styles Instruments." *Journal of Educational Psychology* 75 (1): 33–39.

Finnegan, Ruth H. 2012. *Oral Literature in Africa*. Cambridge: Open Book.

Fischer, Bettina, and Birgitta Kopp. 2007. "Evaluation of a Western Training Concept for Further Education in China." *Interculture Journal* 6 (4): 57–75. http://www.interculture-journal.com/index.php/icj/article/view/61/85.

Fite, Kathleen E., and John L. Garcia. 2006. "A Perspective on Ritual: Toward a Direction for Revitalizing Learning Communities." *Journal of Creativity in Mental Health* 2 (1): 75–84.

Fitzgerald, Kaitlin, Elaine Paravati, Melanie C. Green, Melissa M. Moore, and Jeffrey L. Qian. 2020. "Restorative Narratives for Health Promotion." *Health Communication* 35 (3): 356–63.

Flannery, Daniele D. 1993. "Global and Analytical Ways of Processing Information." *New Directions for Adult and Continuing Education* 59 (Fall): 15–24.

Fleer, Marilyn, and Avis Ridgway. 2007. "Mapping the Relations between Everyday Concepts and Scientific Concepts within Playful Learning Environments." *Learning and Socio-Cultural Theory: Exploring Modern Vygotskian Perspectives International Workshop 2007* 1 (1): 24–45. http://ro.uow.edu.au/llrg/vol1/iss1/2.

Forns-Santacana, Maria, Juan Antonio Amador-Campas, and Francesca Roig-López. 1993. "Differences in Field Dependence-Independence Cognitive Styles as a Function of Socioeconomic Status, Sex, and Cognitive Competence." *Psychology in the Schools* 30 (2): 176–86.

Foster, James D., and Glenn T. Moran. 1985. "Piaget and Parables: The Convergence of Secular and Scriptural Views of Learning." *Journal of Psychology and Theology* 13 (Summer): 97–103.

Fougère, Martin, and Agneta Moulettes. 2007. "The Construction of the Modern West and the Backward Rest: Studying the Discourse of Hofstede's Culture's Consequences." *Journal of Multicultural Discourses* 2, no. 1 (June): 1–19.

Frambach, Janneke M., Erik W. Driessen, Philip Beh, and Cees P. M. van der Vleuten. 2014. "Quiet or Questioning? Students' Discussion Behaviors in Student-Centered Education across Cultures." *Studies in Higher Education* 39 (6): 1001–21.

Frambach, Janneke M., Erik W. Driessen, Li-Chong Chan, and Cees P. M. van der Vleuten. 2012. "Rethinking the Globalisation of Problem-Based Learning: How Culture Challenges Self-Directed Learning." *Medical Education* 46, no. 8 (August): 738–47.

Freire, Paulo. 2005. *Education for Critical Consciousness*. New York: Continuum International.

Fung, Dennis, and Angie Su. 2016. "The Influence of Liberal Studies on Students' Participation in Socio-political Activities: The Case of the Umbrella Movement in Hong Kong." *Oxford Review of Education* 42, no. 1 (February): 89–107.

Garner, Iain. 2000. "Problems and Inconsistencies with Kolb's Learning Styles." *Educational Psychology* 20 (3): 341–48.

Gay, John, and Michael Cole. 1967. *The New Mathematics and an Old Culture: A Study of Learning among the Kpelle of Liberia*. New York: Holt, Rinehart & Winston.

Geertz, Clifford. 1973. "Religion as a Cultural System." In *The Interpretation of Cultures*, 87–125. New York: Basic Books.

Gentner, Dedre, Jeffrey Loewenstein, and Leigh Thompson. 2003. "Learning and Transfer: A General Role for Analogical Encoding." *Journal of Educational Psychology* 95 (2): 393–408.

George, Pamela Gale. 1995. *College Teaching Abroad*. Boston: Allyn & Bacon.

Georges, Jayson, and Mark D. Baker. 2016. *Ministering in Honor-Shame Cultures*. Downers Grove, IL: IVP Academic.

Gerstetter, Paul. 1999. "Traditionelles Lehren und Lernen bei den Guarani-Indianern und die Konsequenzen für den Aufbau einer Bibelschule." Research paper for the course Interkulturelles Lehren und Lernen at the European School for Culture and Theology, Korntal, Germany.

Gibbs, Raymond W., Jr. 1999. "Taking Metaphor out of Our Heads and Putting It into the Cultural World." In *Metaphor in Cognitive Linguistics*, edited by Raymond W. Gibbs and Gerald J. Steen, 145–66. Philadelphia: John Benjamins.

Giger, Martha. 1991. "Traditionelle Lern- und Lehrverhalten bei den Daba." BA thesis, Freie Hochschule für Mission, Korntal, Germany.

Glick, Peter, Susan T. Fiske, Dominic Abrams, Benoit Dardenne, Maria Christina Ferreira, Roberto Gonzalez, Christopher Hachfeld, et al. 2006. "Anti-American Sentiment and America's Perceived Intent to Dominate: An 11-Nation Study." *Basic and Applied Social Psychology* 28 (4): 363–73.

Goering, Laurie. 2006. "Ghana Schools Get Chicago Lift." *Chicago Tribune*, June 11, 2006. https://www.chicagotribune.com/news/ct-xpm-2006-06-11-0606110279-story.html.

Godó, Ágnes M. 2008. "Cross-Cultural Aspects of Academic Writing: A Study of Hungarian and North American College Students L1 Argumentative Essays." *International Journal of English Studies* 8 (2): 65–111.

Gordon, Sue, and Ian Thomas. 2018. "'The Learning Sticks': Reflections on a Case Study of Role-Playing for Sustainability." *Environmental Education Research* 24 (2): 172–90.

Goßweiler, Christian. 1999. "Syncretismus, Kontextualisierung, und Zusammenleben der Religionen auf Java (Indonesien)." In *Kein anderer Name: Die Einzigartigkeit Jesu und das Gespräch mit nichtchristlichen Religionen*, edited by Thomas Schirrmacher, 406–16. Nuremberg: Verlag für Theologie und Religionswissenschaft.

Green, Tim, Malia Hoffmann, Loretta Donovan, and Nawang Phuntsog. 2017. "Cultural Communication Characteristics and Student Connectedness in an Online Environment: Perceptions and Preferences of Online Graduate Students." In *International Journal of E-Learning and Distance Education* 32 (2): 1–27.

Greenfield, Patricia M. 1966. "On Culture and Conservation." In *Studies in Cognitive Growth*, edited by Jerome S. Bruner, Rose R. Oliver, and Patricia M. Greenfield, 225–56. New York: Wiley & Sons.

———. 1972. "Oral or Written Language: The Consequences for Cognitive Development in Africa, the United States and England." *Language and Speech* 15 (2): 169–78.

———. 2005. "Culture and Learning." In *A Companion to Psychological Anthropology*, edited by Conerly Casey and Robert B. Egerton, 72–89. Malden, MA: Blackwell.

Greenfield, Patricia M., and Carla P. Childs. 1977. "Weaving Color Terms and Pattern Representation: Cultural Influences and Cognitive Development among the Zinacantecos of Southern Mexico."

Inter-American Journal of Psychology 11:23–48.

Greenman, Jeffrey P., and Gene L. Green, eds. 2012. *Global Theology in Evangelical Perspective: Exploring the Contextual Nature of Theology and Mission.* Downers Grove, IL: InterVarsity.

Grimes, Joseph E., and Barbara Grimes. 1974. "Individualism and the Hiuchol Church." In *Readings in Missionary Anthropology,* edited by William A. Smalley, 199–203. Pasadena, CA: William Carey.

Gruenfeld, Leopold W., and Ann E. MacEachron. 1975. "A Cross-National Study of Cognitive Style among Managers and Technicians." *International Journal of Psychology* 10 (1): 27–55.

Gunawardena, Charlotte Nirmalani, Casey Frechette, and Ludmila Layne. 2019. *Culturally Inclusive Instructional Design: A Framework and Guide for Building Online Wisdom Communities.* New York: Routledge & Kegan Paul.

Günther, Susanne. 1990. "Sprichwörtliche Redensarten in interkulturellen Kommunikationssituationen zwischen Deutschen und ChinesInnen." In *Interkulturelle Kommunikation,* edited by Bernd Spillner, 53–61. Frankfurt am Main: Peter Lang.

Gutiérrez, Kris D., and Barbara Rogoff. 2003. "Cultural Ways of Learning: Individual Traits or Repertoires of Practice." *Educational Researcher* 32 (50): 19–25.

Habermas, Ronald T. 2008. *Introduction to Christian Education and Formation.* Grand Rapids: Zondervan.

Haidt, Jonathan. 2014. "Three Stories about Capitalism." WORLD.MINDS Annual Symposium. YouTube video, 23:52. https://www.youtube.com/watch?v=iOu_8yoqZoQ.

Hall, Edward T. 1983. *The Dance of Life: The Other Dimension of Time.* Garden City, NY: Anchor Press/Doubleday.

Hamill, James F. 1991. *Ethno-logic: The Anthropology of Human Reasoning.* Urbana: University of Illinois Press.

Harnish, David. 2003. "Worlds of *Wayang Sasak*: Music, Performance, and Negotiations of Religion and Modernity." *Asian Music* 34 (2): 91–120.

Harris, William V. 1989. *Ancient Literacy.* Cambridge, MA: Harvard University Press.

Harvey, John D. 1998. *Listening to the Text: Oral Patterning in Paul's Letters.* Grand Rapids: Baker.

Hattie, John. 2009. *Visible Learning.* London: Routledge & Kegan Paul.

Hauerwas, Stanley, and Gregory L. Jones, eds. 1997. *Why Narrative? Readings in Narrative Theology.* Grand Rapids: Eerdmans.

Henning, Elizabeth. 2003. "'I Click, Therefore I Am (Not)': Is Cognition 'Distributed' or Is It 'Contained' in Borderless E-Learning Programmes?" *International Journal of Training and Development* 7 (4): 303–17.

Henrich, Joseph, Steven J. Heine, and Ara Norenzayan. 2010. "The Weirdest People in the World?" *Behavioral and Brain Sciences* 33 (2/3): 61–135.

Henson, Robin K., and Dae-Yeop Hwang. 2002. "Variability and Prediction of Measurement Error in Kolb's Learning Style Inventory Scores: A Reliability Generalization Study." *Educational and Psychological Measurement* 62 (4): 712.

Hesselgrave, David J. 1991. *Communicating Christ Cross-Culturally.* 2nd ed. Grand Rapids: Zondervan.

Hezser, Catherine. 2001. *Jewish Literacy in Roman Palestine.* Tübingen: Mohr Siebeck.

Hiebert, Paul G. 1987. "Critical Contextualization." *International Bulletin of Missionary Research* 11 (3): 104–12.

———. 1994. *Anthropological Reflections on Missiological Issues.* Grand Rapids: Baker.

———. 2008. *Transforming Worldviews: An Anthropological Understanding of How*

People Change. Grand Rapids: Baker Academic.

Hiebert, Paul G., and Francis F. Hiebert. 1987. *Case Studies in Missions*. Grand Rapids: Baker.

Hiebert, Paul G., and Eloise Hiebert Meneses. 1995. *Incarnational Ministry: Planting Churches in Band, Tribal Peasant and Urban Societies*. Grand Rapids: Baker.

Ho, David Yau-Fai, Wai Fu, and S. M. Ng. 2004. "Guilt, Shame and Embarrassment: Revelations of Face and Self." *Culture & Psychology* 10 (1): 64–84.

Ho, Irene T. 2001. "Are Chinese Teachers Authoritarian?" In *Teaching the Chinese Learner: Psychological and Pedagogical Perspectives*, edited by David Watkins and John B. Biggs, 99–114. Hong Kong: Comparative Education Research Centre.

———. 2004. "A Comparison of Australian and Chinese Teachers' Attributions for Student Problem Behaviors." *Educational Psychology* 24 (3): 375–91.

Hobsbawm, Eric J., and Terence Ranger, eds. 1983. *The Invention of Tradition*. Cambridge: Cambridge University Press.

Hodge, Felicia Schanche, Anna Pasqua, Carol A. Marquez, and Betty Geishirt-Cantrell. 2002. "Utilizing Traditional Storytelling to Promote Wellness in American Indian Communities." *Journal of Transcultural Nursing* 13, no. 1 (January): 6–11.

Hodkinson, Chris S., and Arthur E. Poropat. 2014. "Chinese Students' Participation: The Effect of Cultural Factors." *Education & Training* 56, no. 5 (June): 430–46.

Hofstede, Geert. 1980. *Culture's Consequences: International Differences in Work-Related Values*. Beverly Hills, CA: SAGE.

Hofstede, Geert, Gert Jan Hofstede, and Michael Minkov. 2010. *Cultures and Organizations: Software of the Mind*. 3rd rev. ed. New York: McGraw-Hill.

Hogan, Robert. 2011. "Online Learning: The Comfortable Environment." In *Cases on Globalized and Culturally Appropriate E-Learning: Challenges and Solutions*, edited by Andrea Edmundson, 72. Hershey, PA: Information Science Reference.

Holmes, B. H. 1997. "Want Participation? Have Them 'Vote with Their Feet'!" *Journal of Management Education* 21 (1): 117–20.

Honeck, Richard P. 1997. *A Proverb in Mind: The Cognitive Science of Proverbial Wit and Wisdom*. Mahwah, NJ: Lawrence Erlbaum Associates.

House, Robert J., Paul J. Hanges, Mansour Javidan, Peter W. Dorfman, and Vipin Gupta, eds. 2004. *Culture, Leadership, and Organizations: The GLOBE Study of 62 Societies*. Thousand Oaks, CA: SAGE.

Howard, Melanie A. 2018. "A Game of Faith: Role-Playing Games as an Active Learning Strategy for Value Formation and Faith Integration in the Theological Classroom." *Teaching Theology and Religion* 21 (4): 274–87.

Hunter, James Davison. 2010. *To Change the World: The Irony, Tragedy and Possibility of Christianity in the Late Modern World*. New York: Oxford University Press.

Hvitfeldt, Christina. 1986. "Traditional Culture, Perceptual Style, and Learning." *Adult Education Quarterly* 36 (2): 65–77.

Hwang, Alvin, Anne Marie Francesco, and Eric Kessler. 2003. "The Relationship between Individualism-Collectivism, Face, and Feedback and Learning Processes in Hong Kong, Singapore, and the United States," *Journal of Cross-Cultural Psychology* 34, no. 1 (January): 72–91.

Hwang, Kwang-Kup. 1999. "Filial Piety and Loyalty: The Types of Social Identification in Confucianism." *Asian Journal of Social Psychology* 2 (1): 129–49.

Ingelhart, R., and W. E. Baker. 2000. "Modernization, Cultural Change, and the Persistence of Traditional Values." *American Sociological Review* 65 (1): 19–51.

Ingram, Jenni, and Victoria Elliott. 2016. "A Critical Analysis of the Role of Wait Time in Classroom Interactions and the Effects on Student and Teacher Interactional Behaviours." *Cambridge Journal of Education* 46, no. 1 (March): 37–53.

Issina, Gaukhar I., and Natalya P. Serebryakova. 2013. "Mythological Consciousness Transformation in Terms of the Modern Society." *European Researcher* 39, no. 1–2 (January): 164–68.

Jaggars, Shanna Smith, and Thomas Bailey. 2010. "Effectiveness of Fully Online Courses for College Students: Response to a Department of Education Meta-Analysis." Community College Research Center, Columbia University. ERIC Document Reproduction Service No. ED512274. Available at https://files.eric .ed.gov/fulltext/ED512274.pdf.

James, Waynne B., and William E. Blank. 1993. "Review and Critique of Available Learning-Style Instruments for Adults." *New Directions for Adult & Continuing Education* 59 (Fall): 47–57.

Jereb, Eva, Matjaž Perc, Barbara Lämmlein, Janja Jerebic, Marko Urh, Iztok Podbregar, and Polona Šprajc. 2018. "Factors Influencing Plagiarism in Higher Education: A Comparison of German and Slovene Students." *PLOS One* 13 (8): 1–16. https://doi.org/10.1371/journal .pone.0202252.

Jerrim, John. 2015. "Why Do East Asian Children Perform So Well in PISA? An Investigation of Western-Born Children of East Asian Descent." *Oxford Review of Education* 41 (3): 310–33.

Ji, Li-Jun, Kaiping Peng, and Richard E. Nisbett. 2000. "Culture, Control, and Perception of Relationships in the Environment." *Journal of Personality and Social Psychology* 78 (5): 943–55.

Jones, M. L. 2007. "Hofstede—Culturally Questionable?" Paper presented at the Oxford Business and Economics Conference, Oxford, UK, June 2007. https://ro .uow.edu.au/commpapers /370.

Joyce, Bruce R. 1984. "Dynamic Disequilibrium: The Intelligence of Growth." *Theory into Practice* 23 (1): 26–34.

Jung, Insung. 2011. "The Dimensions of E-Learning Quality: From the Learner's Perspective." *Educational Technology Research and Development* 59 (4): 445–64.

———. 2012. "Asian Learners' Perception of Quality in Distance Education and Gender Differences." *International Review of Research in Open and Distributed Learning* 13 (2): 1–25. https://doi.org/10.19173 /irrodl.v13i2.

Kamis, Mazalan, and Mazanah Muhammed. 2007. "Islam's Lifelong Learning Mandate." In *Non-Western Perspectives on Learning and Knowing*, edited by Sharan A. Merriam and Associates, 21–40. Malabar, FL: Krieger.

Kandarakis, Helen M. 1996. "Learning and Learning Strategies: Perceptions of Ethnic Minority Students." Paper presented at the Annual Meeting of American Psychological Association, Toronto, Ontario, August 1996. ERIC Document Reproduction Service No. ED409276. Available at https://files.eric.ed.gov/full text/ED409276.pdf.

Kaplan, Robert B. 1966. "Cultural Thought Patterns in Intercultural Education." *Language Learning* 16 (1): 1–20.

Kappe, F. R., L. Boekholt, C. den Rooyen, and H. Van der Flier. 2009. "A Predictive Validity Study of the Learning Style Questionnaire (LSQ) Using Multiple, Specific Learning Criteria." *Learning and Individual Differences* 19:464–67.

Karaslaan, Hatice, Annette Hohenberger, Hilmi Demir, Simon Hall, and Mike Oaksford. 2018. "Cross-Cultural Differences in Informal Argumentation: Norms, Inductive Biases and Evidentiality." *Journal of Cognition and Culture* 18 (3/4): 358–89.

Kartomi, Margaret J. 1973. *Matjapat Songs in Central Java and West Java*. Canberra: Australian National University Press.

Käser, Lothar. 2014. *Foreign Cultures: An Introduction to Ethnology for Development Aid Workers and Church Workers Abroad*. Nuremberg, Germany: VTR.

Kefela, Ghirmai. 2010. "Knowledge-Based Economy and Society Has Become a Vital Commodity to Countries." *International NGO Journal* 5 (7): 160–66.

Kember, David. 2000. "Misconceptions about the Learning Approaches, Motivation and Study Practices of Asian Students." *Higher Education* 40 (1): 99–121.

Kennedy, Peter. 2002. "Learning Cultures and Learning Styles: Myth-understandings about Adult (Hong Kong) Chinese Learners." *International Journal of Lifelong Education* 21 (5): 430–45.

Kenworthy, Scott A. 2020. "Research and Recommendations for Teaching Secondary School in Nigeria." Seminar paper submitted for the course Teaching across Cultures at Trinity Evangelical Divinity School, Deerfield, IL.

Khatib, Mahalaqua Nazli, Abhay Gaidhane, Mahjabeen Ahmed, Deepak Saxena, and Zahiruddin Quazi Syed. 2020. "Early Childhood Development Programs in Low Middle-Income Countries for Rearing Healthy Children: A Systematic Review." *Journal of Clinical and Diagnostic Research* 14 (1): 1–7.

Khoo, Hoon Eng. 2003. "Implementation of Problem-Based Learning in Asian Medical Schools and Students' Perceptions of Their Experience." *Medical Education* 37 (5): 401–9.

Kiefer, Karl-Hubert. 2005. "Die sensorische und verbale Verarbeitung grafischer Darstellungen oder wie Fremdsprachenlerner mit einem Angstgegner fertig werden." *Informationen Deutsch für Ausländer* 32, no. 4 (August): 336–58.

Kiewra, Kenneth A., and Bernard M. Frank. 1988. "Encoding and External-Storage Effects of Personal Lecture Notes, Skeletal Notes, and Detailed Notes for Field-Independent and Field-Dependent Learners." *Journal of Educational Research* 81 (3): 143–48.

Kiki, Gwayaweng. 2010. *Wokabaut-Karikulum: A Community Praxis for Theological Education Training in the Evangelical Lutheran Church of Papua New Guinea*. Köln, Germany: Lambert Academic.

Kiki, Gwayaweng, and Ed Parker. 2014. "Is There a Better Way to Teach Theology to Non-Western Persons? Research from Papua New Guinea That Could Benefit the Wider Pacific." *Australian eJournal of Theology* 21 (2): 108–24.

Kim, Eun-Young Julia. 2017. "Academic Writing in Korea: Its Dynamic Landscape and Implications for Intercultural Rhetoric." *TESL-EJ (Electronic Journal for English as a Second Language)* 21 (3): 1–15.

Kim, Min-Sun. 2007. "Our Culture, Their Culture and Beyond: Further Thoughts on Ethnocentrism in Hofstede's Discourse." *Journal of Multicultural Discourses* 2 (1): 26–31.

Kimmel, Michael. 2004. "Metaphor Variation in Cultural Context: Perspectives from Anthropology." *European Journal of English Studies* 8 (3): 275–94.

Kitayama, Shinobu, Hyekyung Park, A. Timur Sevincer, Mayumi Karasawa, and Ayse K. Uskul. 2009. "A Cultural Task Analysis of Implicit Independence: Comparing North America, Western Europe, and East Asia." *Journal of Personality and Social Psychology* 97 (2): 236–55.

Klem, Herbert V. 1982. *Oral Communication of the Scripture: Insights from African Oral Art*. Pasadena, CA: William Carey.

Kleppin, Karin. 1987. "Deutsche Lehrer - Chinesische Lerner: Zur Unterrichtssituation an den Hochschulen in China." *Informationen Deutsch als Fremdsprache* 14, no. 3 (June): 252–60.

Klotz, Monika. 2000. Case study in the course Interkulturelles Lehren und Lernen at the European School of Culture and Theology, Korntal, Germany.

Knight, Eliot, Charlotte N. Gunawardena, and Cengiz Hakan Aydin. 2009. "Cultural Interpretations of the Visual Meaning of Icons and Images Used in North American Web Design." *Educational Media Internati*onal 46 (1): 17–35.

Knowles, Malcolm. 1970. *The Modern Practice of Adult Education: From Pedagogy to Andragogy*. New York: Association Press.

Koehler, Paul F. 2010. *Telling God's Stories with Power: Biblical Storytelling in Oral Cultures*. Pasadena, CA: William Carey.

Kolb, David A. 1984. *Experiential Learning: Experience as the Source of Learning and Development*. Englewood Cliffs, NJ: Prentice Hall.

Konrath, Sara, Brad J. Bushman, and Tyler Grove. 2009. "Seeing My World in a Million Little Pieces: Narcissism, Self-Construal, and Cognitive–Perceptual Style." *Journal of Personality* 77 (4): 1197–228.

Koski, Jessica, Hongling Xie, and Ingrid R. Olson. 2015. "Understanding Social Hierarchies: The Neural and Psychological Foundations of Status Perception." *Social Neuroscience* 10 (5): 527–50. https://www.ncbi.nlm.nih.gov/pmc/articles/PMC5494206.

Koukl, Gregory, Samuel Kunhiyop, Sharon Mumper, and Marvin Wilson. 2014. "Under What Circumstances Should an Overseas Missionary Pay a Bribe?" *Christianity Today*, May 19, 2014, 26–27. Available at https://www.christianitytoday.com/ct/2014/may/circumstances-should-overseas-missionary-pay-bribe.html.

Kövecses, Zoltán. 2004. "Introduction: Cultural Variation in Metaphor." *European Journal of English Studies* 8 (3): 236–74.

Kozhevnikov, Maria. 2007. "Cognitive Styles in the Context of Modern Psychology: Toward an Integrated Framework of Cognitive Style." *Psychological Bulletin* 133 (3): 464–81.

Kozma, Tamás. 1992. "Ethnocentrism in Education: Can We Overcome it?" In *Ethnocentrism in Education*, edited by Klaus Schleicher and Tamás Kozma, 281–86. Frankfurt am Main: Peter Lang.

Krain, Matthew. 2010. "The Effects of Different Types of Case Learning on Student Engagement." *International Studies Perspectives* 11 (3): 291–308.

Kuhn, Thomas S. 1996. *The Structure of Scientific Revolutions*. 3rd ed. Chicago: University of Chicago Press.

Kühnen, Ulrich, Bettina Hannover, Ute Roeder, Ashiq Ali Shah, Benjamin Schubert, Arnold Upmeyer, and Saliza Zakaria. 2001. "Cross-Cultural Variations in Identifying Embedded Figures: Comparisons from the United States, Germany, Russia, and Malaysia." *Journal of Cross-Cultural Psychology* 32 (3): 365–71.

Lau, Te-Li. 2020. *Defending Shame: Its Formative Power in Paul's Letters*. Grand Rapids: Baker Academic.

Lawrence, Randee Lipson, and Dennis Swiftdeer Paige. 2016. "What Our Ancestors Knew: Teaching and Learning through Storytelling." In *Tectonic Boundaries: Negotiating Convergent Forces in Adult Education*, edited by Carmela R. Nanton, 63–72. New Directions for Adult and Continuing Education 149 (Spring). San Francisco: Jossey-Bass.

LCHC (Laboratory of Comparative Human Cognition). 1983. "Culture and Cognitive Development." In *Handbook of Child Psychology*, vol. 1, edited by R. Sternberg, 295–356. New York: Cambridge University Press.

LCWE (Lausanne Committee for World Evangelization). 2005. "Making Disciples of Oral Learners." Lausanne Occasional Paper (LOP) 54. https://www.lausanne.org/docs/2004forum/LOP54_IG25.pdf.

Lebra, Takie Sugiyama. 1983. "Shame and Guilt: A Psychocultural View of the Japanese Self." *Ethos* 11 (3): 192–209.

Lee, Moonjang. 1999. "Identifying an Asian Theology: A Methodological Quest." *Asia Journal of Theology* 13 (2): 256–75.

Lee, S., and J. Y. Chung. 2019. "Lessons Learned from Two Years of K-MOOC Experience." *Educational Media International* 56 (2): 134–48.

Lee, Wing On. 1996. "The Cultural Context for Chinese Learners: Conceptions of Learning in the Confucian Tradition." In *The Chinese Learner: Cultural, Psychological and Contextual Influences*, edited by David A. Watkins and John. B. Biggs, 25–42. Hong Kong: Comparative Education Research Centre.

LeFever, Marlene D. 2004. *Creative Teaching Methods: Be an Effective Christian Teacher*. Colorado Springs: David C. Cook.

Legrain, Philippe. 2006. "Globalization Benefits the World's Cultures." In *Globalization: Opposing Viewpoints*, edited by Louise I. Gerdes, 34–41. Detroit: Thomson Gale.

Lehman, Rosemary M., and Simone C. O. Conceição. 2014. *Motivating and Retaining Online Students: Research-Based Strategies That Work*. San Francisco: Jossey-Bass.

Lei, Simon A., Jillian L. Cohen, and Kristen M. Russler. 2010. "Humor on Learning in the College Classroom: Evaluating Benefits and Drawbacks from Instructors' Perspectives." *Journal of Instructional Psychology* 37 (4): 326–31.

Lewis. David. 1993. *The Unseen Face of Japan*. Gloucester, UK: Wide Margin Books.

Lewis, Helen. 1971. *Shame and Guilt in Neurosis*. New York: International Universities Press.

Li, Jin. 2002. "Learning Models in Different Cultures." In *Learning in Culture and Context: Approaching the Complexities of Achievement Motivation in Student Learning*, New Directions for Child and Adolescent Development 96, edited by Janine Bempechat and Julian G. Elliot, 45–63. San Francisco: Wiley & Sons.

Li, Jin, Lianqin Wang, and Kurt W. Fischer. 2004. "The Organisation of Chinese Shame Concepts?" *Cognition and Emotion* 18 (6): 767–97.

Li, Mingsheng. 2002. "Roles, Expectations and Pedagogical Awareness: A Case Study of Expatriate English Teachers in China." Wellington, New Zealand: The Open Polytechnic University of New Zealand. Paper presented at the Annual Meeting of the Australian-New Zealand Communication Association, Queensland, Australia, July 2002. ERIC Document Reproduction Service No. ED475522.

Lingenfelter, Judith. 2001. "Training Future Leaders in Our Classrooms." *Missiology* 29, no. 4 (October): 449–59.

Lingenfelter, Judith, and Sherwood G. Lingenfelter. 2003. *Teaching Cross-Culturally: An Incarnational Model for Learning and Teaching*. Grand Rapids: Baker Academic.

Lingenfelter, Sherwood G., and Marvin K. Mayers. 2016. *Ministering Cross-Culturally: A Model for Effective Personal Relationships*. 3rd ed. Grand Rapids: Baker Academic.

Littlemore, Jeannette. 2001. "The Use of Metaphor in University Lectures and the Problems That It Causes for Overseas Students." *Teaching in Higher Education* 6 (3): 333–51.

Liu, Airan, and Yu Xie. 2016. "Why Do Asian Americans Academically Outperform Whites?—The Cultural Explanation Revisited." *Social Science Research* 58 (July): 210–26.

Liu, Xiaojing, Shijuan Liu, Seung-hee Lee, and Richard J. Magjuka. 2010. "Cultural Differences in Online Learning: International Student Perceptions." *Journal of*

Educational Technology and Society 13 (3): 177–88.

Liu, Xiaojing, and Richard J. Magjuka. 2011. "Learning in Cross-Cultural Online MBA Courses: Perceptions of Chinese Students." In *Cases on Globalized and Culturally Appropriate E-Learning: Challenges and Solutions*, edited by Andrea Edmundson, 168–83. Hershey, PA: Information Science Reference.

Livermore, David. 2004. "AmeriCAN or AmeriCAN'T? A Critical Analysis of Western Training to the World." *Evangelical Missions Quarterly* 40 (4): 458–66.

———. 2018. "Why You Need to Stop Teaching Cultural Differences." David Livermore. https://davidlivermore.com/2018/12/13/why-you-need-to-stop-teaching-cultural-differences.

Lodahl, Michael. 2008. *The Story of God: A Narrative Theology*. 2nd ed. Kansas City, MO: Beacon Hill.

Longacre, Robert E. 1976. *An Anatomy of Speech Notions*. Lisse, Netherlands: Peter de Ridder.

Luria, Alexander R. 1971. "Towards the Problem of the Historical Nature of Psychological Processes." *International Journal of Psychology* 6 (4): 259–72.

Madden, Elizabeth Stallman. 2015. "Cultural Self-Awareness." In *Encyclopedia of Intercultural Competence*, edited by Janet M. Bennett, 177–78. Thousand Oaks, CA: SAGE.

Madge, Clare, Markus Roos Breines, Mwazvita Tapiwa Beatrice Dalu, Ashley Gunter, Jenna Mittelmeier, Paul Prinsloo, and Parvati Raghuram. 2019. "WhatsApp Use among African International Distance Education (IDE) Students: Transferring, Translating and Transforming Educational Experiences." *Learning, Media and Technology* 44 (3): 267–82.

Madinger, Charles. 2014. "Applied Orality: More than Methods." *Mission Frontiers* 36 (3): 6–8.

———. 2017. "Orality in Missions: Applications of the Orality Discussion." *Evangelical Missions Quarterly* 53 (1). https://missionexus.org/applications-of-the-orality-discussion.

Magnus, Jan. R., Victor M. Polterovich, Dmitri L. Danilov, and Alexi V. Savvateev. 2002. "Tolerance of Cheating: An Analysis across Countries." *Journal of Economic Education* 33 (2): 125–36.

Maldonado Torres, Sonia Enid. 2016. "Understanding the Relationship between Latino Students' Preferred Learning Styles and Their Language Spoken at Home." *Journal of Latinos and Education* 15 (3): 244–52.

Mann, Leon. 1980. "Cross-Cultural Studies of Small Groups." In *Handbook of Cross-Cultural Psychology*, edited by Harry C. Triandis and Richard W. Brislin, 155–209. Boston: Allyn & Bacon.

Mansfield, Kathy Lee. 1984. "Cognitive and Attitudinal Changes Following Viewing of the *Jesus Film* among the Gwembe Tonga of Zambia." MA thesis, Trinity Evangelical Divinity School, Deerfield, IL.

Marambe, Kosala N. 2007. "Patterns of Student Learning in Medical Education—a Sri Lankan Study in a Traditional Curriculum." Doctoral thesis, Maastricht University, The Netherlands.

Marambe, Kosala N., Jan D. Vermunt, and Henny P. A. Boshuizen. 2012. "A Cross-Cultural Comparison of Student Learning Patterns in Higher Education." *Higher Education* 64 (3): 299–316.

Maranz, David E. 2001. *African Friends and Money Matters: Observations from Africa*. Dallas: SIL International.

Markus, Hazel Rose, and Shinobu Kitayama. 1991. "Culture and the Self: Implications for Cognition, Emotion, and Motivation." *Psychological Review* 98 (2): 224–53.

Marquez, Robert C., and Joel Ellwanger. 2014. "Independent and Interdependent Self-Construals Do Not Predict Analytic or Holistic Reasoning." *Psychological Reports* 115 (1): 326–38.

Marton, Ference, Gloria Dall'Alba, and Lai Kun Tse. 1996. "Memorizing and Understanding: The Keys to the Paradox." In *The Chinese Learner: Cultural, Psychological and Contextual Influences*, edited by David A. Watkins and John. B. Biggs, 69–105. Hong Kong: Comparative Education Research Centre.

Massa, Laura J., and Richard E. Mayer. 2006. "Testing the ATI Hypothesis: Should Multimedia Instruction Accommodate Verbalizer-Visualizer Cognitive Style?" *Learning and Individual Differences* 16 (4): 321–35.

Masuda, Takahiko, and Richard E. Nisbett. 2006. "Culture and Change Blindness." *Cognitive Science* 30 (2): 381–99.

Masuzawa, Tomoko. 2005. *The Invention of World Religions: Or, How European Universalism Was Preserved in the Language of Pluralism*. Chicago: University of Chicago Press.

Mbiti, John S. 1969. *African Religions and Philosophy*. Nairobi: Heinemann.

Mbon, Laudes Martial. 2019. "Congo: A Class of Seventy-Six." *UNESCO Courier* (October–December), 14–15. https://unesdoc.unesco.org/ark:/48223/pf0000370991_eng?posInSet=4&queryId=990e498f-3dd2-4105-b313-45b2fe16163c.

McAnany, D. 2009. "Monkeys on the Screen? Multicultural Issues in Instructional Message Design." *Canadian Journal of Learning and Technology* 35, no. 1. https://www.cjlt.ca/index.php/cjlt/article/view/26402/19584.

McBride, Ron E., Ping Xiang, David Wittenburg, and Jianhua Shen. 2002. "An Analysis of Preservice Teachers' Dispositions toward Critical Thinking: A Cross-Cultural Perspective." *Asia-Pacific Journal of Teacher Education* 30 (2): 131–40.

McCabe, Donald, Tony Feghali, and Hanin Abdallah. 2008. "Academic Dishonesty in the Middle East: Individual and Contextual Factors." *Research in Higher Education* 49 (5): 451–67.

McIlwain, Trevor. 1987. *Building on Firm Foundations*. Vol. 1 of *Guidelines for Evangelism and Teaching Believers*. Sanford, FL: New Tribes Mission.

McNaughton, Marie Jeanne. 2010. "Educational Drama in Education for Sustainable Development: Ecopedagogy in Action." *Pedagogy, Culture and Society* 18 (3): 289–308.

McSweeney, Brendan. 2002. "Hofstede's 'Model of National Cultural Differences and Consequences': A Triumph of Faith—A Failure of Analysis." *Human Relations* 55, no. 1 (January): 89–118.

Medin, Douglas L, Sara J. Unsworth, and Lawrence Hirschfeld. 2007. "Culture, Categorization, and Reasoning." In *Handbook of Cultural Psychology*, edited by Shinobu Kitayama and Dov Cohen, 615–44. New York: Guilford.

Meng, Lingqi, Marco Muñoz, Kristin King Hess, and Shujie Liu. 2017. "Effective Teaching Factors and Student Reading Strategies as Predictors of Student Achievement in PISA 2009: The Case of China and the United States." *Educational Review* 69, no. 1 (January): 68–84.

Mercier, Hugo. 2011. "On the Universality of Argumentative Reasoning." *Journal of Cognition and Culture* 11 (1/2): 85–113.

Mercier, Hugo, Jiehai Zhang, Yuping Qu, Lu Peng, and Jean-Baptiste Van der Henst. 2015. "Do Easterners and Westerners Treat Contradiction Differently?" *Journal of Cognition and Culture* 15 (1/2): 45–63.

Merriam, Sharan B. 2007. "An Introduction to Non-Western Perspectives on Learning and Knowing." In *Non-Western Perspectives on Learning and Knowing*, edited by Sharan A. Merriam and Associates, 1–20. Malabar, FL: Krieger.

Merz, Johannes. 2010. "Translation and the Visual Predicament of the 'Jesus Film' in West Africa." *Missiology* 38, no. 2 (April): 111–26.

Messaris, Paul. 1995. "Visual Literacy and Visual Culture." In *Imagery and Visual Literacy: Selected Readings*, edited by Darrell G. Beauchamp, Roberts A. Braden, and Robert E. Griffin, 51–56. Loretto, PA: International Visual Literacy Association.

Messick, Samuel. 1994. "The Matter of Style: Manifestations of Personality in Cognition, Learning, and Teaching." *Educational Psychologist* 29 (3): 121–36.

———. 1996. "Bridging Cognition and Personality in Education: The Role of Style in Performance and Development." *European Journal of Personality* 10 (5): 353–76.

Metallidou, Panayiota, and Maria Platsidou. 2008. "Kolb's Learning Style Inventory-1985: Validity Issues and Relations with Metacognitive Knowledge about Problem-Solving Strategies." *Learning and Individual Differences* 18 (1): 114–19.

Mezirow, Jack. 1991. *Transformative Dimensions of Adult Learning*. San Francisco: Jossey-Bass.

Milco, Michael R. 1997. *Ethical Dilemmas in Church Leadership: Case Studies in Biblical Decision Making*. Grand Rapids: Kregel.

Miller, Alan. 1987. "Cognitive Styles: An Integrated Model." *Educational Psychology* 7 (4): 251–68.

Mishra, Ramesh C. 2001. "Cognition across Cultures." In *The Handbook of Culture and Psychology*, edited by David Matsumoto, 119–35. New York: Oxford University Press.

———. 2014. "Piagetian Studies of Cognitive Development in India." *Psychological Studies* 59 (3): 207–22.

Mitschian, Haymo. 1991. *Chinesische Lerngewohnheiten*. Frankfurt am Main: Verlag für Interkulturelle Kommunikation.

Miyamoto, M. 1985. "Parents' and Children's Beliefs and Children's Achievement and Development." In *Cross-Cultural and National Studies in Social Psychology*, edited by R. Diaz-Guerreri, 209–23. Amsterdam: Elsevier Science.

Moon, W. Jay. 2009. *African Proverbs Reveal Christianity in Culture*. American Society of Missiology Monograph Series 5. Eugene, OR: Pickwick.

———. 2017. *Intercultural Discipleship: Learning from Global Approaches to Spiritual Formation*. Grand Rapids: Baker Academic.

———. 2018. "Chicken Theology: Local Learning Approaches in West Africa." In *Challenging Tradition: Innovation in Advanced Theological Education*, edited by Perry Shaw and Havilah Dharamraj, 269–85. Carlisle, UK: Langham Global. Kindle edition.

Moore, David M., and Francis M. Dwyer. 1994. "Effect of Cognitive Style on Test Type (Visual or Verbal) and Color Coding." *Perceptual and Motor Skills* 79 (3): 677–80.

Moreau, A. Scott, Evvy Hay Campbell, and Susan Greener. 2014. *Effective Intercultural Communication: A Christian Perspective*. Grand Rapids: Baker Academic.

Nabi, Robin L., and Melanie C. Green. 2015. "The Role of a Narrative's Emotional Flow in Promoting Persuasive Outcomes." *Media Psychology* 18 (2): 137–62.

Nagashima, Nobuhiro. 1973. "A Reversed World, or Is It?" In *Modes of Thought: Essays on Thinking in Western and Non-Western Societies*, edited by Robin Horton and Ruth H. Finnegan, 92–111. London: Faber.

Nancekivell, Shaylene E., Priti Shah, and Susan A. Gelman. 2020. "Maybe They're Born with It, or Maybe It's Experience: Toward a Deeper Understanding of the Learning Style Myth." *Journal of Educational Psychology* 112 (2): 221–35.

Nandwa, Jane, and Austin Bukyena. 1983. *African Oral Literature for Schools*. Nairobi: Longman Kenya.

Nash, Gary B., Charlotte Crabtree, and Ross E. Dunn. 2000. *History on Trial: Culture Wars and the Teaching of the Past*. New York: Vintage.

Naugle, David K. 2002. *Worldview: The History of a Concept*. Grand Rapids: Eerdmans.

Nederveen Pieterse, Jan. 1995. "Globalization as Hybridization." In *Global Modernities*, edited by Mike Featherstone, Scott Lash, and Roland Robertson, 44–68. Thousand Oaks, CA: SAGE.

———. 2020. *Globalization and Culture: Global Mélange*. 4th ed. Lanham, MD: Rowman & Littlefield.

Neely, Alan. 1995. *Christian Mission: A Case Study Approach*. Maryknoll, NY: Orbis Books.

Negash, Solomon. 2011. "The Doctor Doesn't Know My Name." In *Cases on Globalized and Culturally Appropriate E-Learning: Challenges and Solutions*, edited by Andrea Edmundson, 92–93. Hershey, PA: Information Science Reference.

Nemati, Majid, and Shiva Kaivanpanah. 2013. "'He or She?' Examining Cultural Influences on Iranian Language Learners' Perceptions of Teacher Efficacy." In *Researching Cultures of Learning*, edited by Martin Cortazzi and Lixian Jin, 203–21. New York: Palgrave Macmillan.

Nesi, Hilary. 2012. "Laughter in University Lectures." *Journal of English for Academic Purposes* 11 (2): 79–89.

Neudecker, Reinhard. 1999. "Master-Disciple/Disciple-Master Relationship in Rabbinic Judaism and in the Gospels." *Gregorianum* 80 (2): 245–61.

Neuliep, James W. 2012. *Intercultural Communication: A Contextual Approach*. Thousand Oaks, CA: SAGE.

Ngaruiya, David Kimiri. 2008. "Death and Burial Practices: A Study of Contextualization of Rituals in Some Nairobi Multi-ethnic, Multi-racial Churches." PhD diss., Trinity International University, Deerfield, IL.

Nida, Eugene A. 1960. *Mission and Message: The Communication of the Christian Faith*. Pasadena, CA: William Carey.

Nielsen, Tine. 2012. "A Historical Review of the Styles Literature." In *Handbook of Intellectual Styles: Preferences in Cognition, Learning, and Thinking*, edited by Li-Fang Zhang, Robert J. Sternberg, and Stephen Rayner, 21–46. New York: Springer.

Nisbett, Richard E. 2003. *The Geography of Thought: How Asians and Westerners Think Differently . . . and Why*. New York: Free Press.

Nisbett, Richard E., Kaiping Peng, Incheol Choi, and Ara Norenzayan. 2001. "Culture and Systems of Thoughts: Holistic versus Analytic Cognition." *Psychological Review* 108 (2): 291–310.

Norenzayan, Ara, Incheol Choi, and Kaiping Peng. 2007. "Perception and Cognition." In *Handbook of Cultural Psychology*, edited by Shinobu Kitayama and Dov Cohen, 569–94. New York: Guilford.

Ntseane, Gabo. 2007. "African Indigenous Knowledge: The Case of Botswana." In *Non-Western Perspectives on Learning and Knowing*, edited by Sharan A. Merriam and Associates, 113–35. Malabar, FL: Krieger.

Odden, Harold, and Philippe Rochat. 2004. "Observational Learning and Enculturation." *Educational and Child Psychology* 21 (2): 39–50.

OECD (Organisation for Economic Co-operation and Development). 2013. *Skills Outlook 2013*. http://www.oecd.org/site/piaac/Skills%20volume%201%20(eng)--full%20v12--eBook%20(04%2011%202013).pdf.

Okombo, Okoth, and Jane Nandwa, eds. 1992. *Reflections on Theories and*

Methods in Oral Literature. Nairobi: Kenya Oral Literature Association.

Olson, David R., and Nancy Torrance. 1991. "Introduction." In *Literacy and Orality*, edited by David R. Olson and Nancy Torrance, 1–7. New York: Cambridge University Press.

Ong, Walter J. 1982. *Orality and Literacy: The Technologizing of the Word*. London: Methuen.

Orsak, Lana. 1990. "Learning Styles versus the Rip Van Winkle Syndrome." *Educational Leadership* 48 (2): 19.

Ott, Craig. 2014. "The Power of Biblical Metaphors for the Contextualized Communication of the Gospel." *Missiology* 42, no. 4 (October): 357–74.

———. 2015. "Globalization and Contextualization: Reframing the Task of Contextualization in the Twenty-First Century." *Missiology* 43, no. 1 (January): 43–58.

Ott, Craig, and Harold Netland, eds. 2006. *Globalizing Theology: Belief and Practice in an Era of World Christianity*. Grand Rapids: Baker Academic.

Oyserman, Daphna, and Spike W. S. Lee. 2008. "Does Culture Influence What and How We Think? Effects of Priming Individualism and Collectivism." *Psychological Bulletin* 134 (2): 311–42.

Padilla DeBorst, Ruth. 2016. "Response by Ruth Padilla DeBorst." In *The Mission of the Church: Five Views in Conversation*, edited by Craig Ott, 139–48. Grand Rapids: Baker Academic.

Paige, R. Michael, and Matthew L. Goode. 2009. "Intercultural Competence in International Education Administration." In *The SAGE Handbook of Intercultural Competence*, edited by Darla K. Deardorf, 333–49. Thousand Oaks, CA: SAGE.

Paine, David R., Peter J. Jankowski, and Steven J. Sandage. 2016. "Humility as a Predictor of Intercultural Competence." *Family Journal* 24 (1): 15–22.

Pappenhausen, Birta. 2015. Case study for the course Interkulturelles Lehren und Lernen at the European School of Culture and Theology, Korntal, Germany.

Paschyn, Christina. 2014. "Check Your Orientalism at the Door: Edward Said, Sanjay Seth, and the Adequacy of Western Pedagogy." *Journal of General Education* 63 (2/3): 222–31.

Pashler, Harold, Mark McDaniel, Doug Rohrer, and Robert Bjork. 2008. "Learning Styles: Concepts and Evidence." *Psychological Science in the Public Interest* 9 (3): 105–19.

Peng, Shenli, Ping Hu, and Zheng Guo. 2018. "Within-Culture Variation in Field Dependence/Independence: A Region-Level Investigation across China." *Social Behavior and Personality* 46, no. 2 (February): 293–300.

Peterson, E. R., S. G. Rayner, and S. J. Armstrong. 2009. "Herding Cats: In Search of Definitions of Cognitive Styles and Learning Styles." *ELSIN Newsletter* (Winter 2008–2009). http://elsinnetwork.com/images/newsletters/2008elsinnewsletter.pdf.

Pewewardy, Cornel. 2002. "Learning Styles of American Indian/Alaska Native Students: A Review of the Literature and Implications for Practice." *Journal of American Indian Education* 41 (3): 22–56.

Pi, Zhongling, and Jianzhong Hong. 2016. "Learning Process and Learning Outcomes of Video Podcasts Including the Instructor and PPT Slides: A Chinese Case." *Innovations in Education and Teaching International* 53 (2): 135–44.

Pithers, R. T. 2002. "Cognitive Learning Style: A Review of the Field Dependent-Field Independent Approach." *Journal of Vocational Education and Training* 54 (1): 117–32.

Plueddemann, James E. 1990. "The Effects of Schooling on Thinking in Northeastern Nigeria with Implications for

Christian Education." *Journal of Psychology and Theology* 18 (1): 75–82.

———. 2018. *Teaching across Cultures: Contextualizing Education for Global Mission.* Downers Grove, IL: IVP Academic.

Poplawska, Marzanna. 2004. "*Wayang Wahyu* as an Example of Christian Forms of Shadow Theatre." *Asian Theatre Journal* 21 (2): 194–202.

Portera, Agostino. 2014. "Intercultural Competence in Education, Counselling and Psychotherapy." *Intercultural Education* 25 (2): 157–74.

Posey, Steve. 2008. Case study for the course Teaching across Cultures at Trinity Evangelical Divinity School, Deerfield, IL.

Pratap, Prashant. 2015. "Patna HC Takes Govt to Task over Cheating during State Board Exams." *Hindustan Times*, March 21, 2015. https://www.hindustantimes.co /india/patna-hc-takes-govt-to-task-over -cheating-during-state-board-exams/story -UZlecSHMzo9MKN2Oc29V0H.html.

Price, Linda, and John T. E. Richardson. 2003. "Meeting the Challenge of Diversity: A Cautionary Tale about Learning Styles." In *Proceedings of the 10th International Symposium of Improving Student Learning, Improving Student Learning Theory and Practice—10 Years On*, edited by C. Rust, 285–95. Oxford: The Oxford Centre for Staff and Learning Development.

Priest, Robert J. 2010. "US Megachurches and New Patterns of Global Mission." *International Bulletin of Missionary Research* 34 (2): 97–102.

Prince, Michael, and Richard Felder. 2007. "The Many Faces of Inductive Teaching and Learning." *Journal of College Science Teaching* 36 (5): 14–20.

Rahman, Saeed. 2011. "Choices to Make: Is Cheating Okay?" *The Express Tribune*, July 17, 2011. http://blogs.tribune .com.pk/story/6926/choices-to-make-is -cheating-ever-okay.

Rao, Nirmala, Ben Richards, Jin Sun, Ann Weber, and Alanna Sincovich. 2019. "Early Childhood Education and Child Development in Four Countries in East Asia and the Pacific." *Early Childhood Research Quarterly* 47 (April): 169–81.

Rapp, David N. 2011. "Comic Books' Latest Plot Twist: Enhancing Literacy Instruction." *Phi Delta Kappan* 93 (4): 64–67.

Rawlins, Roblyn. 2012. "'Whether I'm an American or Not, I'm Not Here So You Can Hit on Me': Public Harassment in the Experience of US Women Studying Abroad." *Women's Studies* 41 (4): 476–97.

Reagan, Timothy. 2000. *Non-Western Educational Traditions.* Mahwah, NJ: Lawrence Erlbaum Associates.

Reich, Justin, and José A. Ruipérez-Valiente. 2019. "The MOOC Pivot." *Science* 363 (6423): 130–31.

Rez, Helmut, Monika Kraemer, and Reiko Kobayashi-Weinsieher. 2011. "Warum Karl und Kiezon sich nerven: Eine Reise zum systematischen Verständnis interkultureller Missverständnisse." In *Interkulturelle Kommunikation: Methoden, Modelle, Beispiele*, edited by Dagmar Kumbier and Friedemann Schulz von Thun, 28–72. Hamburg, Germany: Ro, Ro, Ro.

Richards, E. Randolph, and Richard James. 2020. *Misreading Scripture with Individualist Eyes: Patronage, Honor and Shame in the Biblical World.* Downers Grove, IL: IVP Academic.

Richards, E. Randolph, and Brandon J. O'Brien. 2012. *Misreading Scripture with Western Eyes: Removing Cultural Blinders to Better Understand the Bible.* Downers Grove, IL: IVP Books.

Richardson, J. A., and T. E. Turner. 2000. "Field Dependence Revisited I: Intelligence." *Educational Psychology* 20 (3): 255–70.

Ricoeur, Paul. 1977. *The Rule of Metaphor.* Toronto: University of Toronto.

Riding, Richard, and Indra Cheema. 1991. "Cognitive Styles—an Overview and

Integration." *Educational Psychology* 11 (3/4): 193–216.

Riding, Richard, and Stephen R. Rayner. 1998. *Cognitive Styles and Learning Strategies: Understanding Style Differences in Learning Behaviour.* London: David Fulton.

Riener, Cedar, and Daniel Willingham. 2010. "The Myth of Learning Styles." *Change* 42 (5): 32–35.

Riesner, Rainer. 1984. *Jesus als Lehrer.* 2nd ed. Tübingen: Mohr.

Roberts, Peter. 2000. *Education, Literacy, and Humanization: Exploring the Work of Paulo Freire.* Westport, CT: Bergin & Garvey.

Robertson, Roland. 1995. "Glocalization: Time-Space and Homogeneity-Heterogeneity." In *Global Modernities*, edited by Mike Featherstone, Scott Lash, and Roland Robertson, 25–44. Thousand Oaks, CA: SAGE.

Rogers, Carl R. 1969. *Freedom to Learn.* Columbus, OH: Charles E. Merrill.

Rogers, T. B. 1989. "The Use of Slogans, Colloquialisms, and Proverbs in the Treatment of Substance Addiction: A Psychological Application of Proverbs." *Proverbium, Yearbook of International Proverb Scholarship* 6:103–12.

Romanowski, Michael H., and Teri McCarthy. 2009. *Teaching in a Distant Classroom: Crossing Borders for Global Transformation.* Downers Grove, IL: InterVarsity.

Ronson, Jon. 2015. *So You've Been Publicly Shamed.* New York: Riverhead.

Rose, Andreas. 1999. Research paper for the course Interkulturelles Lehren und Lernen at the European School of Culture and Theology, Korntal, Germany.

Rynkiewich, Michael. 2011. *Soul, Self, and Society.* Eugene, OR: Cascade Books.

Saathoff, Helga. 2007. Case study for the course Interkulturelles Lehren und

Lernen at the European School of Culture and Theology, Korntal, Germany.

Sadykova, Gulnara, and Jennie Dautermann. 2009. "Crossing Cultures and Borders in International Online Distance Higher Education." *Journal of Asynchronous Learning Networks* 13 (2): 89–114.

Safrai, S., M. Stern, D. Flusser, and W. C. van Unnik. 1974–76. "Education and the Study of the Torah." In *The Jewish People in the First Century*, edited by S. Safrai and M. Stern, 2:945–70. Philadelphia: Fortress.

Salili, Farideh. 1996. "Accepting Personal Responsibility for Learning." In *The Chinese Learner: Cultural, Psychological and Contextual Influences*, edited by David A. Watkins and John. B. Biggs, 85–106. Hong Kong: Comparative Education Research Centre.

———. 2001. "Teacher-Student Interaction: Attributional Implications and Effectiveness of Teacher's Evaluative Feedback." In *Teaching the Chinese Learner: Psychological and Pedagogical Perspectives*, edited by David Watkins and John B. Biggs, 77–98. Hong Kong: Comparative Education Research Centre.

Salili, Farideh, Chi-yue Chiu, and Simon Lai. 2001. "The Influence of Culture and Context on Student's Motivational Orientation and Performance." In *Student Motivation: The Culture and Context of Learning*, edited by Farideh Salili, Chi-yue Chiu, and Ying-yi Hong, 221–47. New York: Kluwer Academic.

Salter, Phia, and Glenn Adams. 2013. "Toward a Critical Race Psychology." *Social and Personality Psychology Compass* 7 (11): 781–93.

Sampeley, J. Paul, and Peter Lampe, eds. 2010. *Paul and Rhetoric.* New York: T&T Clark.

San Martin, Alvaro, Joanna Schug, and William W. Maddux. 2019. "Relational Mobility and Cultural Differences in Analytic and Holistic Thinking." *Journal of Personality and Social Psychology* 116, no. 4 (April): 495–518.

Sato, T., H. Namiki, J. Ando, and G. Hatano. 2004. "Japanese Conception of and Research on Human Intelligence." In *International Handbook of Intelligence*, edited by Robert J. Sternberg, 302–24. New York: Cambridge University Press.

Schleicher, Klaus, and Tamás Kozma, eds. 1992. *Ethnocentrism in Education*. Frankfurt am Main: Peter Lang.

Schliemann, Analúcia D., and David W. Carraher. 2001. "Everyday Cognition: Where Culture, Psychology, and Education Come Together." In *The Handbook of Culture and Psychology*, edited by David Matsumoto, 137–50. New York: Oxford University Press.

Schrag, Brian. 2007. "Why Local Arts Are Central to Mission." *International Journal of Frontier Missiology* 24 (4): 199–202.

Schwartz, Shalom H. 1990. "Individualism-Collectivism: Critique and Proposed Refinements." *Journal of Cross-Cultural Psychology* 21, no. 2 (June): 139–57.

Scott, Catherine. 2010. "The Enduring Appeal of 'Learning Styles.'" *Australian Journal of Education* 54, no. 1 (April): 5–17.

Scribner, Sylvia. 1979. "Modes of Thinking and Ways of Speaking: Culture and Logic Reconsidered." In *New Directions in Discourse Processing*, edited by Roy O. Freedle, 223–43. Norwood, NJ: Ablex.

Scribner, Sylvia, and Michael Cole. 1981. *The Psychology of Literacy*. Cambridge, MA: Harvard University Press.

Segall, Marshall H., Pierre R. Dasen, John W. Berry, and Ype H. Poortinga. 1999. *Human Behavior in Global Perspective*. 2nd ed. Needham Heights, MA: Pearson Education.

Sessoms, Rick. 2016. *Leading with Story: Cultivating Christ-Centered Leaders in a Storycentric Generation*. With Tim Brannigan. Pasadena, CA: William Carey.

Seth, Sanjay. 2007. *Subject Lessons: The Western Education of Colonial India*. Durham, NC: Duke University Press.

Shaules, Joseph. 2015. *The Intercultural Mind: Connecting Culture, Cognition, and Global Living*. Boston: Intercultural Press.

Shaw, Mark. 1988. *The Cultural Factor in Translation and Other Communication Tasks*. Pasadena, CA: William Carey.

———. 1993. *Doing Theology with Huck and Jim: Parables for Understanding Doctrine*. Downers Grove, IL: InterVarsity.

Signorini, Paola, Rolf Wiesemes, and Roger Murphy. 2009. "Developing Alternative Frameworks for Exploring Intercultural Learning: A Critique of Hofstede's Cultural Difference Model." *Teaching in Higher Education* 14, no. 3 (June): 253–64.

Simpson, Steven T. 2008. "Western EFL Teachers and East-West Classroom-Culture Conflicts." *RELC Journal* 39 (3): 381–84.

Sire, James W. 2015. *Naming the Elephant: Worldview as a Concept*. Downers Grove, IL: InterVarsity.

Sirriyeh, Elizabeth. 2015. *Dreams and Visions in the World of Islam: A History of Muslim Dreaming and Foreknowing*. London and New York: I. B. Tauris.

Slethaug, Gordon E. 2007. *Teaching Abroad: Intercultural Education and the Cross-Cultural Classroom*. Hong Kong: Hong Kong University Press.

Smith, Richard H., J. Matthew Webster, Heidi L. Eyre, and W. Gerrod Parrott. 2002. "The Role of Public Exposure in Moral and Nonmoral Shame and Guilt." *Journal of Personality and Social Psychology* 83 (1): 138–59.

Søgaard, Viggo. 1993. *Media in Church and Mission*. Pasadena, CA: William Carey.

Solórzano, Daniel G., and Tara J. Yosso. 2002. "Critical Race Methodology:

Counter-Storytelling as an Analytical Framework for Education Research." *Qualitative Inquiry* 8 (1): 23–44.

Squire, Gary. 2007. "What I Learned about Teaching at the Great Wall of China." *Phi Delta Kappan* 88 (7): 530–34.

St. Amant, Kirk. 2007. "Online Education in an Age of Globalization: Foundational Perspectives and Practices for Technical Communication Instructors and Trainers." *Technical Communication Quarterly* 16 (1): 13–30.

Stahl, William A. 2007. "Religious Opposition to Globalization." In *Religion, Globalization, and Culture*, edited by Peter Berger and L. Beaman, 335–53. Boston: Brill.

Steffen, Tom. 1993a. "Don't Show the Jesus Film . . ." *Evangelical Missions Quarterly* 29, no. 3 (July): 272–75.

———. 1993b. *Passing the Baton: Church Planting That Empowers*. La Habra: Center for Organizational and Ministry Development.

———. 2005. *Reconnecting God's Story to Ministry: Cross-Cultural Storytelling at Home and Abroad*. Rev. ed. Downers Grove, IL: InterVarsity.

———. 2010. "Pedagogical Conversions: From Propositions to Story and Symbol." *Missiology* 38 (2): 141–59.

———. 2018. *Worldview-Based Storying: The Integration of Symbol, Story, and Ritual in the Orality Movement*. Richmond, VA: Orality Resources International, Center for Oral Scriptures.

Steffen, Tom, and William Bjoraker. 2020. *The Return of Oral Hermeneutics: As Good Today as It Was for the Hebrew Bible and First-Century Christianity*. Eugene, OR: Wipf & Stock.

Steinbring, Richard. 2010. Research paper for the course Interkulturelles Lernen und Lehren at the European School of Culture and Theology, Korntal, Germany.

Sternberg, Robert J. 2007. "Intelligence and Culture." In *Handbook of Cultural Psychology*, edited by Shinobu Kitayama and Dov Cohen, 547–68. New York: Guilford.

Sternberg, Robert J., and Elena L. Grigorenko. 2001. "A Capsule History of Theory and Research on Styles." In *Perspectives on Thinking, Learning, and Cognitive Styles*, edited by Robert J. Sternberg and Li-Fang Zhang, 1–21. Mahwah, NJ : Lawrence Erlbaum Associates.

Stevenson, Harold W., and James W. Stigler. 1992. *The Learning Gap: Why Our Schools Are Failing and What We Can Learn from Japanese and Chinese Education*. New York: Simon & Schuster.

Stigler, James W., Patrick Gonzales, Takako Kawanaka, Steffen Knoll, and Ana Serrano. 1999. *The TIMSS Videotape Classroom Study*. Washington, DC: US Department of Education National Center for Education Statistics.

Stigler, James W., and James Hiebert. 1999. *The Teaching Gap: Best Ideas from the World's Teachers for Improving Education in the Classroom*. New York: Free Press.

Storti, Craig. 2017. *Cross-Cultural Dialogues: 74 Brief Encounters with Cultural Difference*. 2nd ed. Boston: Intercultural Press.

Strack, Herman L., and Paul Billerbeck. 1965–69. *Kommentar zum neuen Testament und Midrasch*. Vol. 1. Munich: Beck.

Strässler, Beat. 2005a. "Eine Klausur Zeigt, wie effektiv ein Lehrer gearbeitet hat." Research paper for the course Interkulturelles Lehren und Lernen at the European School for Culture and Theology, Korntal, Germany.

———. 2005b. Case study for the course Interkulturelles Lehren und Lernen at the European School for Culture and Theology, Korntal, Germany.

Subramaniam, Ganakumaran. 2008. "Confronting Asian Concerns in Engaging Learners to Online Education." *International Education Studies* 1 (4): 1–18.

Svinicki, Marilla D., and Wilbert J. Mc-Keachie. 2014. *McKeachie's Teaching Tips: Strategies, Research and Theory for College and University Teachers*. 14th ed. Belmont, CA: Wadsworth.

Swetland, Kenneth L. 2005. *Facing Messy Stuff in the Church: Case Studies for Pastors and Congregations*. Grand Rapids: Kregel.

Talhelm, T., X. Zhang, S. Oishi, C. Shimin, D. Duan, X. Lan, and S. Kitayama. 2014. "Large-Scale Psychological Differences within China Explained by Rice versus Wheat Agriculture." *Science* 344 (6184): 603–8.

Tam, Cecilia S. Y., Shane N. Phillipson, and Sivanes Phillipson. 2016. "'Creativity' Reform in Hong Kong: Validation of the Creative Inventions Test." *Talent Development and Excellence* 8, no. 2 (July): 3–19.

Tam, Kai Yung (Brian), Mary Anne Heng, and Gladys H. Jiang. 2009. "What Undergraduate Students in China Say about Their Professors' Teaching." *Teaching in Higher Education* 14, no. 2 (April): 147–59.

Tan, Charlene. 2015. "Education Policy Borrowing and Cultural Scripts for Teaching in China." *Comparative Education* 51, no. 2 (May): 196–211.

———. 2017. "Confucianism and Education." In *Oxford Research Encyclopedia of Education*, edited by George W. Noblit, 1–18. New York: Oxford University Press.

Tan, Fujuan. 2018. "Facilitating International Chinese Students' Transformation in an Online Course." *Adult Learning* 29 (1): 32–34.

Tan, Jason Richard. 2011. "Missionary Ethics and the Practice of Bribery." *Evangelical Missions Quarterly* 47 (3): 278–82.

Thaker, Swathi Nath. 2007. "Hinduism and Learning." In *Non-Western Perspectives on Learning and Knowing*, edited by Sharan A. Merriam and Associates, 57–73. Malabar, FL: Krieger.

Thigpen, L. Lynn. 2016. "Connected Learning: A Grounded Theory Study of How Cambodian Adults with Limited Formal Education Learn." PhD diss., Biola University, La Mirada, CA.

Tinajero, Carolina, Alba Castelo, Adelina Guisande, and Fernanda Páramo. 2011. "Adaptive Teaching and Field Dependence-Independence: Instructional Implications." *Revista Latinoamericana de Psicología* 43 (3): 497–510.

Tippett, Alan R. 1967. *Solomon Islands Christianity: A Study of Growth and Obstruction*. London: Lutterworth.

Tobin, Kenneth. 1987. "The Role of Wait Time in Higher Cognitive Level Learning." *Review of Educational Research* 57, no. 1 (Spring): 69–95.

Triandis, Harry C. 1995. *Individualism and Collectivism*. Boulder, CO: Westview.

———. 2001. "Individualism and Collectivism: Past, Present, and Future." In *The Handbook of Culture and Psychology*, edited by David Matsumoto, 35–50. New York: Oxford University Press.

Tu, Chih-Hsiung. 2001. "How Chinese Perceive Social Presence: An Examination of Interaction in Online Learning Environment." *Educational Media International* 38 (1): 45–60.

UNESCO (United Nations Educational, Scientific, and Cultural Organization). 2016a. "Education for People and Planet: Creating Sustainable Futures for All." Global Education Monitoring Report. https://unesdoc.unesco.org/ark:/48223/pf0000245752.

———. 2016b. "School Resources and Learning Environment in Africa." http://uis.unesco.org/sites/default/files/school-resources-and-learning-environment-in-africa-2016-en/school-resources-and-learning-environment-in-africa-2016-en.pdf.

———. 2017. "Literacy Rates Continue to Rise from One Generation to the Next." Fact Sheet 45. http://uis.unesco.org/sites

/default/files/documents/fs45-literacy
-rates-continue-rise-generation-to-next
-en-2017_0.pdf.

Unseth, Peter. 2013. "Using Local Proverbs in Ministry." *Evangelical Missions Quarterly* 49 (1):16–23.

Uygur, Nermi. 1988. "Türkisch-Deutsch— Eine transkulturelle Betrachtung." In *Interkulturelle Pädagogik im Internationaler Vergleich*, edited by Michele Borrelli and Gerd Hoff, 189–98. Bultmannsweiler: Pädagogischer Verlag Burgbücherei Schneider.

Vágvölgyi, Réka, Andra Coldea, Thomas Dresler, Josef Schrader, and Hans-Christoph Nuerk. 2016. "A Review about Functional Illiteracy: Definition, Cognitive, Linguistic, and Numerical Aspects." *Frontiers in Psychology* 7, article 1617. https://doi.org/10.3389/fpsyg.2016 .01617.

Veldt, Luke. 1998. "Translating: How to Avoid Pitfalls." *Evangelical Missions Quarterly* 34 (1): 60–62.

Venaik, Sunil, and Paul Brewer. 2008. "Contradictions in National Culture: Hofstede vs GLOBE." Paper presented at the Academy of International Business annual conference, June–July 2008, Milan, Italy. https://www.academia.edu/880772 /Contradictions_in_national_culture _Hofstede_vs_GLOBE

———. 2010. "Avoiding Uncertainty in Hofstede and GLOBE." *Journal of International Business Studies* 41 (8): 1294–315.

Venkateswaran, Ramya T., and Abhoy K. Ojha. 2019. "Abandon Hofstede-Based Research? Not Yet! A Perspective from the Philosophy of the Social Sciences." *Asia Pacific Business Review* 25, no. 3 (July): 413–34.

Viale, Riccardo. 2006. "Introduction: Local or Universal Principles of Reasoning." In *Biological and Cultural Bases of Human Inference*, edited by Riccardo Viale, Daniel Andler, and Lawrence A. Hirschfeld,

1–31. Mahwah, NJ: Lawrence Erlbaum Associates.

Viale, Riccardo, and Dan Osherson. 2006. "Cognitive Development, Culture, and Inductive Reasoning." In *Biological and Cultural Bases of Human Inference*, edited by Riccardo Viale, Daniel Andler, and Lawrence A. Hirschfeld, 33–48. Mahwah, NJ: Lawrence Erlbaum Associates.

Vygotsky, L. S. 1978. *Mind in Society: The Development of Higher Psychological Processes*. Cambridge, MA: Harvard University Press.

Wagner, Daniel A. 1978. "Memories of Morocco: The Influence of Age, Schooling, and Environment on Memory." *Cognitive Psychology* 10 (1): 1–28.

Wagner, John A., III. 1995. "Studies of Individualism-Collectivism: Effects on Cooperation in Groups." *Academy of Management Journal* 38 (1): 152–73.

Walker, Deron. 2011. "How to Teach Contrastive (Intercultural) Rhetoric: Some Ideas for Pedagogical Application." *New Horizons in Education* 59 (3): 71–81.

Wallace, Margaret, and Susan C. Hellmundt. 2003. "Strategies for Collaboration and Internationalisation in the Classroom." *Nurse Education in Practice* 3 (2): 89–94.

Wallbott, Herald G., and Klaus R. Scherer. 1995. "Cultural Determinants in Experiencing Shame and Guilt." In *Self-Conscious Emotions: The Psychology of Shame, Guilt, Embarrassment, and Pride*, edited by June Price Tangney and Kurt W. Fischer, 465–87. New York: Guilford.

Wan, Lisa. 2020. "Research and Recommendations for Teaching Chinese Missionary Trainees." Research paper for the course Teaching across Cultures at Trinity Evangelical Divinity School, Deerfield, IL.

Wang, Haidong. 2006. "Teaching Asian Students Online: What Matters and Why?" *PAACE Journal of Lifelong Learning* 15:69–84.

Wang, Minjuan. 2007. "Designing Online Courses That Effectively Engage Learners from Diverse Cultural Backgrounds." *British Journal of Educational Technology* 38 (2): 294–311.

Weigl, Robert C. 2009. "Intercultural Competence through Self-Study: A Strategy for Adult Learners." *International Journal of Intercultural Relations* 33 (4): 346–60.

Wells, David. 1993. *No Place for Truth: Or Whatever Happened to Evangelical Theology?* Grand Rapids: Eerdmans.

Wendland, Ernst R. 1998. "The Case for a 'Case Study' Approach to Theological Education in Africa." *Africa Journal of Evangelical Theology* 17 (1): 41–57.

Wenthe, Dean O. 2006. "The Social Configuration of the Rabbi-Disciple Relationship: Evidence and Implications for First Century Palestine." In *Studies in the Hebrew Bible, Qumran, and the Septuagint: Presented to Eugene Ulrich*, edited by James C. VanderKam, Peter W. Flint, and Emanuel Tov, 143–74. Vetus Testamentum, Supplements, vol. 101. Leiden: Brill.

Wertsch, James V., and Peeter Tulviste. 1992. "Lev Semyonovich Vygotsky and Contemporary Developmental Psychology." *Developmental Psychology* 28 (4): 548–57.

Whiteman, Darrell L. 1997. "Contextualization: The Theory, the Gap, the Challenge." *International Bulletin of Missionary Research* 21 (1): 2–7.

Whorf, Benjamin Lee. 1956. *Language, Thought, and Reality*. New York: Wiley & Sons.

Wiher, Hannes. 1997. "Der Jesus-Film: Sein Gebrauch in der animistischen und islamischen Bevölkerung Westafrikas unter Berücksichtigung von Erfahrungen in der Waldregion Guinea." *Evangelikale Missiologie* 13 (3): 66–74.

———. 2003. *Shame and Guilt: A Key to Cross-Cultural Christian Ministry*. Bonn: Verlag für Kultur und Wissenschaft.

Wildcat, Daniel R. 2001. "The Schizophrenic Nature of Metaphysics." In *Power and Place: Indian Education in America*, edited by Vine Deloria Jr. and Daniel R. Wildcat, 47–55. Golden, CO: Fulcrum.

Willhauck, Susan. 2009. "Crossing Pedagogical Borders in the Yucatan Peninsula." *Teaching Theology and Religion* 12 (3): 222–32.

Wingo, Ted. 2010. Research paper for the course Church in Cultural Context at Trinity Evangelical Divinity School, Deerfield, IL.

Wisse, Maarten. 2005. "Narrative Theology and the Use of the Bible in Systematic Theology." *Ars Disputandi* 5 (1): 237–48.

Witherington, Ben, III. 1998. *The Acts of the Apostles: A Socio-rhetorical Commentary*. Grand Rapids: Eerdmans.

Witkin, H. A., and D. R. Goodenough. 1981. *Cognitive Styles: Essence and Origins, Field Dependence and Field Independence*. New York: International Universities Press.

Witkin, H. A., C. A. Moore, D. R. Goodenough, and P. W. Cox. 1977. "Field-Dependent and Field-Independent Cognitive Styles and Their Educational Implications." *Review of Educational Research* 47 (1): 1–64.

Wong, Joseph Kee-Kuok. 2004. "Are the Learning Styles of Asian International Students Culturally or Contextually Based?" *International Education Journal* 4 (4): 154–66.

Wong, Mary. 2000. "The Influence of Gender and Culture on the Pedagogy of Five Western English Teachers in China." PhD diss., University of Southern California, Los Angeles, California.

Wong, Ying, and Jeanne Tsai. 2007. "Cultural Models of Shame and Guilt." In *The Self-Conscious Emotions: Theory and Research*, edited by Jessica L. Tracy, Richard W. Robins, and June Price Tangney, 209–23. New York: Guilford.

Wright, Brian J. 2015. "Ancient Literacy in New Testament Research: Incorporating a Few More Lines of Enquiry." *Trinity Journal*, n.s., 36 (2): 161–89.

Wu, Su-Yueh, and Donald L. Rubin. 2000. "Evaluating the Impact of Collectivism and Individualism on Argumentative Writing by Chinese and North American College Students." *Research on Teaching English* 35, no. 2 (November): 148–78.

Wu, Xiaoxin. 2009. "The Dynamics of Chinese Face Mechanisms and Classroom Behavior: A Case Study." *Evaluation and Research in Education* 22, no. 2–4 (June–November): 87–105.

Wuthnow, Robert. 2009. *Boundless Faith: The Global Outreach of American Churches*. Berkeley: University of California Press.

Yang, Lin, and David Cahill. 2008. "The Rhetorical Organization of Chinese and American Students' Expository Essays: A Contrastive Rhetoric Study." *International Journal of English Studies* 8 (2): 113–32.

Yang, Yuchen, and Zhong Zang. 2010. "Problem-Solution in English vs. *Qi-cheng-zhuan-he* in Chinese: Are They Compatible Discourse Patterns?" *Chinese Journal of Applied Linguistics* 33 (5): 65–79.

Yeung, Philip. 2016. "Blame Hong Kong's Failed Education Reform for Independence Activism in Schools." *South China Morning Post*, September 5, 2016. https://www.scmp.com/comment /insight-opinion/article/2014894/blame -hong-kongs-failed-education-reform -independence.

Young, Serenity. 2003. "Dreams." In *South Asian Folklore: An Encyclopedia*, edited by Margaret A. Mills, Peter J. Claus, and Sarah Diamond, 166–69. New York: Routledge & Kegan Paul.

Yousef, D. A. 2019. "Exploring the Reliability and Validity of the Learning Styles Questionnaire (LSQ) in an Arab Setting." *Quality Assurance in Education: An International Perspective* 27 (4): 446–64.

Yu, A. B., and K. S. Yang. 1987. "Social-Oriented and Individual-Oriented Achievement Motivation: A Conceptual and Empirical Analysis." *Bulletin of the Institute of Ethnology, Academia Sinica* 64:51–98. In Chinese.

Yue, Xiao Dong. 2010. "Exploration of Chinese Humor: Historical Review, Empirical Findings, and Critical Reflections." *Humor: International Journal of Humor Research* 23 (3): 403–20.

Yung, Hwa. 1997. *Mangoes or Bananas? The Quest for an Authentic Asian Christian Theology*. Oxford: Regnum.

———. 2010. "A 21st Century Reformation: Recover the Supernatural." *Christianity Today*, September 2, 2010, 32–33. http:// www.christianitytoday.com/ct/2010 /september/yung.html.

Zahniser, A. H. Matthias. 1997. *Symbol and Ceremony: Making Disciples across Cultures*. Monrovia, CA: MARC.

Zhang, Li-Fang, and Robert J. Sternberg. 2001. "Thinking Styles across Cultures: Their Relationships with Student Learning." In *Perspectives on Thinking, Learning, and Cognitive Styles*, edited by Robert J. Sternberg and Li-Fang Zhang, 197–226. Mahwah, NJ: Lawrence Erlbaum Associates.

———. 2012. "Culture and Intellectual Styles." In *Handbook of Intellectual Styles: Preferences in Cognition, Learning, and Thinking*, edited by Li-Fang Zhang, Robert J. Sternberg, and Stephen Rayner, 131–52. New York: Springer.

Zhang, Li-Fang, Robert J. Sternberg, and Stephen Rayner. 2012. "Intellectual Styles: Challenges, Milestones, and Agenda." In *Handbook of Intellectual Styles: Preferences in Cognition, Learning, and Thinking*, edited by Li-Fang Zhang, Robert J. Sternberg, and Stephen Rayner, 1–20. New York: Springer.

Zhou, Ning, Shui-Fong Lam, and Kam Chi Chan. 2012. "The Chinese Classroom Paradox: A Cross-Cultural Comparison of Teacher Controlling Behaviors." *Journal of Educational Psychology* 104 (4): 1162–74.

Zlatev, Jordan, and Johan Blomberg. 2015. "Language May Indeed Influence Thought." *Frontiers in Psychology* 6 (October): 1–10.

Zurlo, Gina A., Todd M. Johnson, and Peter F. Crossing. 2020. "World Christianity and Mission 2020: Ongoing Shift to the Global South." *International Bulletin of Mission Research* 44, no. 1 (January): 8–19.

Index

academic
  achievement, 51, 62, 119, 120, 127, 148, 153, 156, 188, 213, 215, 219, 242, 273
  integrity, 209, 223–27. *See also* cheating; plagiarism
accreditation, 15, 59, 291, 295
acculturation, 42
achievement. *See* academic: achievement
Achren, Linda, 246, 248
adaptation of teaching, 17, 19–23
Adeney, Bernard T., 291
affective learning, 57, 103, 105, 169, 248, 251. *See also* character
Africa, 14, 95, 114, 132, 142, 161, 177, 188, 224, 250, 286, 289
  cognition, 119, 121
  power distance, 189
  proverbs, 100–102
  schools, 283, 284
  writing style, 85
  See also East Africa; North Africa; South Africa; sub-Saharan Africa; West Africa
African American, 121
AIDS education, 251, 255
Al-Ghazzali, 13
Alves, Rubem A., 94
Amaya, Ismael, 133
ambiguity
  of narrative, 131
  of research, 51, 127, 206
  tolerance of, 45, 79, 133
Ambrose, Susan, 91, 139

America, 3, 7, 9, 36, 92, 100, 166, 201, 234, 252, 271, 287, 290
  communication, 86
  field articulation, 121–22
  individualism, 36, 214–17, 222
  reasoning, 82, 84, 86–87, 98, 113–15, 149, 223
  stereotypes of, 8
  students, 18, 220, 225, 243, 246, 258, 276
  teachers, 6, 22, 57, 177, 183–88, 192, 219, 223, 240, 241, 282, 288
  worldview, 141, 143, 152–55
Antipolo/Amduntug Ifugao, 250
apprenticeship, 231
Arab Gulf States, 187, 261, 264, 265
Arensen, Brian, 147
Argentina, 212, 281
argumentation, 17, 78, 82, 84–87, 91, 101, 131, 235. *See also* rhetoric
Aristotle, 82, 97. *See also* Greek philosophy/ logic
Ashanti, 103
Asia, learning and, 38, 55, 65, 83, 95, 101, 132, 152–54, 183, 186, 196, 213, 239, 242, 286
  active vs. passive learners, 35, 61, 187, 189
  e-learning, 267, 273, 275, 277
  "face," 209, 211
  field dependent/independent, 121
  outperform Western students, 154, 188
  reasoning, 79–82, 113–14, 149–50
  theology in, 18, 132–33
  writing style, 85–87, 144
  See also East Asia; South Asia; Southeast Asia; *individual countries*

assessment of learning, 2, 15–16, 39, 59, 113, 146, 154, 156, 227

attitude of teachers, 1, 33, 41–43, 45, 57, 95, 98, 153, 161–62, 192, 289

attrition rate of teachers, 284

Australia, 57, 61, 186

Austria, 38, 155–56, 189

Avoseh, Mejai B. M., 102

Bain, Ken, 192

Balkans, 235

Bangladesh, 252

Barrett, Justin L., 139

Bartle, Neville, 167–68

Bedford, Olwen, 208–10

behavior, 11, 28, 35, 40, 44–46, 202, 205–6, 207, 255
    and collectivism/individualism, 202, 205–7, 215–17, 219, 225, 226–27
    of learners, 31–32, 93, 115, 109, 115, 149, 188, 219, 221, 140, 143, 149, 251, 255, 296–97
    and shame/guilt, 207–11, 213
    of teachers, 6, 55, 57, 59, 180, 241–42, 289, 291, 296
    and worldview, 152–53, 161, 165, 167, 172–73, 245

Bekaan, Michaela, 112

Benedict, Ruth, 207

Berry, John W., 67, 70, 75, 119, 123

Bible, 19–20, 90, 99, 104–5, 110, 113, 134, 147, 218, 233, 238, 249, 284
    authority of, 17, 164, 187, 198
    storying, 77, 93, 96–97, 168, 238, 244, 246, 250, 254
    and worldview, 139, 145, 152, 161–64, 168–69, 171

Bible school, 147, 220, 239, 283, 287, 289, 290, 293, 296. See also seminary

Bjoraker, William, 90, 133

Boas, Franz, 72

body adjustment test, 116

body language, 183, 210, 241–42, 245, 267, 271

Bolivia, 157

Boniface, St., 172

Botswana, 14, 145

Brazil, 99, 108, 145, 151, 156, 218, 243. See also Guarani

bribery, 190, 291. See also gift giving

Bruner, Jerome, 75, 93, 123, 137

Buddhism, 19, 96, 145, 150, 183

Bulisa, 105

Canada, 6, 57, 243

Carr-Chellman, Alison A., 265, 277

Carroll, Jude, 2, 21–22, 39, 45, 130, 179, 234, 236

categorization and cognition, 65, 70, 83–84, 112, 124, 149

Central African Republic, 264, 284

ceremony, 174–75, 183, 212– 213

Chad, 284

challenges, 1–2

character
    formation, 15, 287. See also affective learning
    of teachers, 8, 147, 180, 292

Chayahuita, 168–69

cheating, 201, 223–27, 297. See also academic: integrity

Chen, Wain-Chin, 87

China, 5–7, 25, 42, 57, 70, 123, 154, 163, 177, 179, 183–84, 206, 214–15, 219, 223, 241, 243, 246, 263, 265–68, 276, 285, 293, 295
    collectivism, 36, 205, 217, 243, 246, 266
    field articulation, 122–23, 262
    passive/active learning, 36, 60, 115, 154, 184, 186–89, 219, 240, 259, 266
    reasoning, 68, 81–82, 84–85, 141
    shame/honor, face, 202, 208–10, 212, 220–21, 262, 285
    writing style, 70–72, 86–87

Chinchen, Delbert, 179, 184, 190, 192, 288

Chomsky, Noam, 70

Christy, T. Craig, 70

Chuis, 99

classroom environment, 3, 10, 22, 51, 53, 56, 59, 178, 182–84, 188–89, 215, 217, 219, 241, 280–83, 285–86

class size, 195, 284–85

climate, 11, 263, 280–81

Cole, Michael, 75, 122, 124

Columbia, 258

comics, comic books, 168–69, 243–44

community development. See development

conflict, 4 –5, 14, 32, 38, 42–45, 138, 145, 155, 158, 176, 188, 196, 211, 225, 226, 241, 275, 293, 295, 296
    resolution strategies, 43, 204

Confucius, Confucianism, 57, 86, 150, 154, 163, 184, 209

constructivism, 13, 55, 57, 135, 195

contextualization of teaching content, 18–21, 59, 89, 105, 240, 267

contracts, 2, 81, 293

credentials, 146. *See also* diploma;
    qualifications
credibility of the teacher, 8, 146–48, 185, 231
Cree, 71
critical contextualization, 20
Cuicatec, 72, 99
culture shock, 11, 42, 293
curriculum, 9, 15, 19, 92, 119, 134, 154, 177,
    194, 195, 238, 240, 287, 290

Dalib, 230
David, J. Kent, 119, 127
Demele, Isolde, 193–95
Democratic Republic of the Congo, 239, 280,
    288
Denny, J. Peter, 69, 71–72, 74, 76, 78, 82
development, 3–4, 16, 131, 144, 152, 156, 258,
    291
diagrams, use of, 129, 233, 239, 242, 246–48
Dinka, 249
diploma, 15, 17, 146, 212, 235
disciple, disciple making, 62–63, 96–97, 131–
    32, 160–61, 175
discipline of learners, 183–84, 191, 223, 226,
    296
discrimination, 32, 161, 181, 258, 291
discussion, in class, 5, 38, 77, 95, 104, 106–8,
    132, 142, 163, 189, 195, 196, 216, 218–21,
    226, 232, 236, 238, 239, 251, 254, 285, 289,
    294
  online discussion, 261–62, 267, 274–75
  reluctance to discuss in class, 10, 35, 115,
    187–89, 194, 218–21, 261, 275
disequilibration, 63, 163, 169–72
drama, use of, 14, 75, 93, 95, 97, 107, 165, 169,
    250–53, 255
dreams, 19–20, 76, 94, 145, 167, 186
dress, 184–85, 242, 272
Dyer, Gwynne, 32

East Africa, 71, 251
East Asia, 79, 81–82, 85–86, 113, 121, 149
Eaves, Mina, 50, 55–57, 61
Edmundson, Andrea, 277
educational traditions, 14, 22, 53, 61, 64, 292,
    297
embedded figures test, 116–17
enculturation, 15, 30–31, 54, 230. *See also*
    acculturation

England, 57, 241
English. *See* teaching English as a second
    language
Enns, Marlene, 134–35
Equatorial Guinea, 284
essentialization, essentialism, 32–33, 48, 54
ethics, 104, 106, 233n6, 291. *See also* academic:
    integrity; bribery; morals; plagiarism
Ethiopia, 211, 230, 241, 249, 271
ethnic minority, 7, 53, 173
Europe, 8, 12–13, 32, 38, 53, 65, 82, 121–22,
    149, 163, 189, 225, 244, 282
evaluation. *See* assessment of learning; grades
everyday cognition, 125–27
exams, 11, 59, 201, 212. *See also* testing of
    learning
experiential learning, 50, 171, 273

face, face-saving, loss of face, 9, 188, 198,
    209–12, 219–22, 226, 276
fatalism, 155
Finnegan, Ruth H., 92–93, 101, 103n4, 104,
    144, 251
formal education, 3–4, 11, 14–16, 33, 55, 61,
    89, 95, 146, 148, 193–94, 230, 234, 236, 238,
    248, 294–96
  and cognition, 66, 75, 77, 79, 84, 112, 124–25,
    262
  theological, 108, 131
formal logic, 68, 78–79, 81–82, 149
France, 28–29, 32
Freedom Writers, 173–74
Freire, Paulo, 156
friendship, 2, 42, 45, 63, 71, 129, 158, 178, 181,
    210, 217, 273, 291, 294

Garo, 252
Geertz, Clifford, 28
gender, 1, 8, 30, 44n5, 119, 181, 182, 184, 242,
    249, 261–62, 290
George, Pamela Gale, 22, 183, 219, 225, 232,
    234–36, 282, 285, 296
Germany/German, 8, 25, 38, 57, 72, 77–78,
    102, 112, 121, 147, 155–57, 163, 172, 189,
    202, 216, 217, 224–25, 247, 248, 268
Gerstetter, Paul, 145, 151, 219
Ghana, 105, 224, 234, 284
Gibbs, Raymond W. Jr., 98
gift giving, 179, 190–92, 211, 283, 291. *See also*
    bribery

globalization, 2, 5, 12, 20, 21, 27, 31, 32–34, 110, 160, 205
GLOBE Project, 37–38, 203
Godó, Ágnes M., 87
grades, 16, 58–59, 86, 154, 190, 216–18, 220n5, 223, 226, 292, 29. *See also* assessment of learning
Greece, 38
Greek philosophy/logic, 68, 91. *See also* Aristotle; Plato
Greenfield, Patricia M., 73–75, 115, 119,123
Gruwell, Erin, 173
Guarani, 145, 151, 218, 219
guilt, 154, 203, 207–9, 212, 227. *See also* shame

Haidt, Jonathan, 165
Haiti, 252, 255
Hall, Edward, 157
Hamill, James F., 81
Hesselgrave, David J., 72, 150, 211
Hiebert, Paul G., 20, 21, 33, 106, 139, 140, 152, 159, 161n2, 162n3, 167, 170, 174, 214
Hinduism, 142, 145, 242
Hmong, 75–76, 98, 112, 215
Hofstede, Geert, 30, 36–38, 177, 185, 189, 202–7
Hofstede's dimensions of culture, 36–38, 185, 189, 202–7
Hogan, Robert, 262
Holy Spirit, 159, 164, 171, 298
homework, 1, 225, 227, 236
homework cartels, 225
homogenization, 32–33
Honeck, Richard P., 100–102
Hong Kong, 121, 154, 185–86, 196–97, 205, 212, 220n5, 221, 262, 285
Huichol, 93
humor, use of, 241–42
Hungary, 87, 98
Hvitfeldt, Christina, 76, 112, 215
hybridization, 29, 33

illiteracy. *See* literacy
imitation, 13–14, 126, 193–94. *See also* observation, learning by
India (South Asia), 8, 39, 81–82, 124, 126, 145, 159, 177, 182, 184, 185, 188, 197, 226, 252, 274, 286, 295
Indian (American). *See* Native American
Indonesia, 115, 214, 249, 252–54
informal learning, 15–16, 33, 89, 177, 230, 258

instructional strategies, 22, 51–55, 58, 60, 130, 234, 248, 294
integrity. *See* academic: integrity
intellectual traditions, 12, 68, 81–82, 84, 97, 134–35
intelligence, 120–22, 152–54
International Standards Organization, 270
intuition, intuitive, 11, 13, 41, 48, 68, 81, 103, 134, 139, 150, 222, 246
Inuit, 76
Islam, 13, 145–46, 193, 253, 292
Israel, 114

Japan, 19, 57, 79, 114, 11, 150, 185, 197, 201–2, 209, 214, 235, 243, 268, 285
Jesus, 6, 96, 99, 104–5, 157, 161, 168, 171, 218, 246, 250
    teaching of, 62–64, 90–91, 170–71, 180, 292
Jesus Film, 245
Joyce, Bruce, 61–62
Jungle, The (Sinclair), 166

Kaplan, Robert B., 84–85
Käser, Lothar, 30
Kayapo, 23
Kazakhstan, 19, 216, 225
Keillor, Garrison, 92
Kenya, 19, 92, 105, 114, 121–22, 142, 161, 175, 284
kiasu, 206
King and I, The, 1, 298
Knowles, Malcolm, 13, 103
Koehler, Paul F., 96
Kolb, David A., 50
Kolb's Learning Style Inventory, 50
Korea, 57, 81, 87, 149, 179, 184, 186, 190, 205, 258, 259, 265, 268, 276, 285
Kpelle, 124
Kuhn, Thomas, 170

Latin America, 8, 77, 132, 133, 189, 258, 286
learning strategies, 48, 52–56, 61–62, 67, 89, 110, 115, 128, 197
lecture, 5, 39, 61, 98–99, 114, 118, 129–30, 183, 189, 196, 229, 232–33, 235–36, 238–42, 246, 260, 262, 296
Lee, Moonjang, 131, 133
Lee, Wing On, 154
Lewis, C. S., 132, 168
Li, Mingsheng, 7, 60

Liberia, 124, 179, 190–91, 212
library, 148, 235, 237, 239, 264, 283, 286
Lingenfelter, Judith, and Sherwood Lingenfel-
    ter, 108, 181, 191, 224, 243, 249
literacy, 14, 66–67, 69n1, 70–71, 73–76, 81–83,
    90n1, 112, 156, 193–94, 215, 224, 242–43,
    248, 252. *See also* oral literature
Littlemore, Jeanette, 98
Livermore, David, 6, 44
Longacre, Robert, 70
Luria, Alexander, 79–80, 83

Madinger, Charles, 75, 95, 255
Malawi, 179, 190–91, 284
Malaysia, Malay, 121, 152, 182, 261–62
maps, map reading, 246–48
Maranz, David E., 289
match/mismatch
    of cognitive styles, 89, 110, 127–28, 130, 268
    of expectations, 7, 177, 293
    of learning and teaching styles, 7, 49–55,
        58–62
Maxakali, 99
Maya, 125
Mbiti, John, 71
Mbon, Laudes Martial, 283
McCarthy, Teri, 184, 188, 281–83, 292
McIlwain, Trevor, 96–97, 198–99
Mead, Margaret, 207
Melanesia, 151
Mercier, Hugo, 80
Merriam, Sharan B., 12, 15, 144
Meru, 105
Merz, Johannes, 244–46
metaphor, 69, 71–72, 85, 97–99, 101, 103–4,
    167, 168, 222, 242
Mexico, 75–76, 93, 99, 218
Mezirow, Jack, 170
minority. *See* ethnic minority
Mishra, Ramesh, 122–26
missionary, 3–4, 8, 17, 75, 95–96, 152, 162,
    167–68, 172, 198, 211, 245, 253n10, 291. *See
    also* short-term missions
Mongolia, 19, 244, 245, 247
Montreal, 7
MOOC (massive open online courses), 258
Moon, W. Jay, 105, 108, 175
morals
    development, 104, 193–94
    example of teacher, 8, 178, 184

and proverbs, 99–100, 104
reasoning, 63, 141, 164–65
and shame, 208–9
and songs, 248–49
and stories, 72, 91, 93
    See also ethics; academic: integrity
Morocco, 114, 122–25, 185, 268
motivation
    and competition, 221
    and field articulation, 131
    and individualism/collectivism, 212–15, 226
    and leadership style, 186
    of learners, 16, 57, 59, 93, 129, 188, 206, 235,
        244, 247, 282
    and learning style, 48, 52
    and online learning, 263, 265, 270, 274
    and problem-based learning, 196–97
    and shame/guilt, 202, 207–9, 212
    of teachers, 42
    and worldview, 149, 152–56, 173, 176
Mozambique, 157
My Fair Lady, 28

Nagashima, Nobuhiro, 79
narrative, 72, 75, 91, 93–97, 108–9, 114, 156,
    165–69, 174, 249
    theology, 90–91, 96–97, 131–32
    See also storytelling
Native American/American Indian, 54, 72–73,
    151, 242
Naugle, David K., 140n1, 140n2, 162n3, 164
Navaho, 72
Netherlands, 115, 196
Ngaruiya, David Kimri, 175
Nida, Eugene A., 72, 99
Nigeria, 8,38, 101, 114, 121, 144, 186, 213, 245,
    250
Nisbett, Richard E., 90, 94, 97, 133, 164, 167,
    175, 24, 250
non-formal learning, 4, 15–16, 61, 89, 212,
    257–58, 294
North Africa, 9, 97
notetaking, 61, 129, 147,232, 233, 237, 239–40,
    261
Ntseane, Gabo, 14, 145
numeracy, 74–76

Obelix distortion, 35–36
observation, learning by, 14, 120, 126, 149, 173,
    193–94, 230–31, 255. *See also* imitation

Occam's razor, 149
Ojibway, 76
Ong, Walter J., 14, 72, 74
oral literature, 92
Oz moment, 41

Pakistan, 197
Palawano, 96, 198
Pappenhausen, Birte, 247
Papua New Guinea, 75, 108, 134, 151, 167, 201, 220, 240, 243
parables, teaching with, 63, 69, 90–91, 132, 170–71
parents, 19–20, 48, 122, 127, 145, 153–54, 167, 183, 190–91, 193, 210, 213–14, 216, 249
passive learners, 11, 35–36, 38–39, 61, 187–89, 219
patron-client relationship, 190–92, 224
perception
    and cognition, 66–67, 70, 115, 118, 122
    of social relations, 185, 215
    of teachers, 6, 8
    of teaching effectiveness, 6
    of Western theology, 132–33
    and worldview, 138, 151
Peretti, Frank E., 168
Peru, 168–69, 253, 264
Pewewardy, Cornel, 54
Philippines, 38, 96,164, 197, 198, 243, 250, 280, 286
philosophy, 12–13, 18, 68, 71, 97, 131–32, 150n6, 167–68, 173
    of education, 14–15, 238
photographs, 113, 115n1, 213, 233, 242–43, 270, 274
Piaget, Jean, 122–24, 170, 172
plagiarism, 2, 17, 223–24, 227, 237, 297
planning, 155, 158, 262, 281. See also teaching plan
Plato, 101
    Platonic idealism, 68
Plueddemann, James E., 84, 188, 297
politeness, 6, 9, 196, 297
political environment, 16, 24, 39, 155, 270, 288–90
politics, 40n4, 165, 190, 202
poor, 112, ,161, 190, 252, 255, 276, 280, 284
Portera, Augostino, 42
Portugal, 57
poverty, 16, 138, 145, 288–89
power distance, 156, 185–89, 194, 203, 266

PowerPoint. See slide presentations
prayer, 63, 91, 152, 171–72, 176, 274, 298
preferential treatment, 190, 217–18, 296
prejudice, 7–9, 12, 22, 32, 41, 43–45, 53, 68, 167, 258
preparation
    of learner, 126, 212, 217, 226, 230, 236, 269, 281, 285
    of teacher, 4–5, 10, 18, 20–22, 38–39, 187, 189, 232–34, 239, 242, 260, 285, 293–94
problem-based learning, 195–97
programmed learning, 119, 237–38
proverbs, use of, 14, 69, 86, 90, 99–105, 108, 144, 211, 222
psychology, psychologist, 40, 70, 79, 84, 115, 122, 133–34, 137, 165, 167, 202
psychometric testing, 50, 51, 67, 116–25
punctuality, 158, 293–95

qualifications
    of students, 17, 226
    of teachers, 15, 146–47, 295–96
    See also credentials; diploma
question asking
    by learners, 14, 187–88, 219–21, 294
    by teachers, 13, 135
    See also discussion, in class
Qur'an, 13, 193, 292

rabbi, 62–64, 180
racism, 32, 41, 161, 167. See also discrimination
reading
    ability, 2, 10, 119. See also literacy
    assignments, 51, 76, 129, 229, 234–36, 245
reflective/non-reflective beliefs, 139–40, 163, 165, 171
rhetoric, 81, 84–87, 90–91, 93. See also argumentation
rhetorical questions, 86, 218
ritual
    cultural, 14, 28, 31, 161, 172, 172, 174, 184, 205
    religious, 150, 168, 172, 174, 175
    teaching using, 108, 174–75, 193
rod-and-frame test, 116
Romania, 233
Romanowski, Michael H., 184, 188, 281–82, 292
Russia, Russian, 70, 121, 216
Rwanda, 201
Rynkiewich, Michael, 28, 32

Saathoff, Helga, 216
safety, 44, 290–91
Sapir, Edward, 70
Sapir-Whorf hypothesis, 70
schedule, 2, 5, 59, 260, 275, 279, 281–82, 292–95
Schrag, Brian, 248
Schulz, Terry, 168–69
science, scientific method, 13, 15, 37, 81, 89, 68, 94, 100, 118–19, 126, 132, 141, 143–45, 149, 151, 154, 166, 188. *See also* social science
Scott, Catherine, 49, 52, 153
seating arrangements, 59, 285
self-directed learning, 12, 197, 262
self-efficacy, 61, 154–56, 167
seminary, 2, 4, 18, 97, 188, 239, 288, 292–93, 295
Senegal, 123
Seth, Sanjay, 13
sex/sexuality, 8, 241. *See also* gender
Shaules, Joseph, 41
Shaw, Mark, 132
Shintoism, 150
short-term assignment/teachers, 5, 60, 73, 89, 130, 147, 185, 231, 235
short-term missions, 3–4, 17
Simpson, Steven T., 5
Singapore, 38, 155–56, 189, 197, 206, 207n5, 221
Sire, James W., 140, 161
Slethaug, Gordon E., 223, 235, 285
slide presentations, 30, 232–33, 239, 246, 263, 265, 269
Slovakia, 224
social science, 25, 28, 37, 40, 106, 202
Socrates, 142
Søgaard, Viggo, 252
song, use of, 93, 97, 108, 148–50, 252, 255
South Africa, 121, 251, 264–65
South Asia, 73
Southeast Asia, 18, 286
South Sudan, 147, 284. *See also* Sudan
Spain, 114
spiritual formation, 2, 16, 61–62, 135, 162, 168, 171–72, 218, 287
Sri Lanka, 55, 115, 185, 214, 268
stakeholders, 62, 295–96
St. Amant, Kirk, 269, 272, 275
standards
   educational, 15, 16–17, 146, 258, 187, 195
   grading and testing, 59, 292, 296

See also academic: integrity; accreditation; ethics; testing of learning
Steffen, Tom, 90, 94, 97, 133, 164, 167, 175, 245, 250
storytelling, 14, 30, 92–97, 134, 165, 167, 169, 275, 250. *See also* Bible: storying; narrative
Strässler, Beat, 108, 220, 240
strategies, 4, 14, 20, 28, 30, 31, 45, 59. *See also* learning strategies; instructional strategies; conflict: resolution strategies
student-directed learning, 195–97
sub-Saharan Africa, 73, 155, 194, 284, 290
Sudan, 148, 249
Switzerland, 38, 114, 122, 201
symbols, 20, 28, 31, 75, 105, 108, 125, 167–68, 172, 174–75, 183, 211–12, 245

Taiwan, 19, 186, 208, 209n3, 221–22
Tan, Charlene, 141, 184
Tanzania, 147, 284
Tarahumara, 75, 76
teaching English as a second language (ESL, TOEFL), 2–3, 5–7, 75–76, 84 112, 225, 293
teaching plan, 5, 9, 168, 216, 275, 294. *See also* planning
technology, 32–33, 92, 119, 205, 224
   classroom, 239, 282, 242, 244
   and online learning, 257, 258, 259, 263–64, 269–70, 276–77
   and worldview, 143, 160, 163
TEE. *See* theological education by extension
Terkel, Studs, 92
testing of learning, 16, 59, 61, 154, 197, 224–25, 238. *See also* exams; psychometric testing
textbooks, 5, 10, 18–19, 86, 129, 193, 195, 231, 233–39, 246, 283–84
Thailand, 38, 155, 183, 189, 255, 235, 283
Thaker, Swathi Nath, 142
theological education by extension (TEE), 237–38
theology
   teaching, 17–21, 89, 91, 97, 106, 131–34
   Western, 18, 20, 68, 131–33, 152
   See also narrative: theology
time
   measuring, 157
   monochronic/polychronic, 157–58
   orientation, 294–95
   understanding of, 156–58
   See also punctuality; schedule

Tippett, Alan R., 172
torah, 135
Totonacs, 99
tradition
  and change, 20, 32, 63, 91
  See also educational traditions; intellectual
    traditions
traditional classroom instruction, 258–61, 267,
    272, 277, 285
traditional culture, 9, 15, 28–29, 32–33, 43, 60,
    62, 91, 175, 187, 214, 226, 249, 271, 282
traditional knowledge, 12, 13–22, 72, 101,
    142–47, 150–51
traditional learning, 193–97, 230–31, 248, 249
Triandis, Harry C., 202, 205
Tu, Chih-Hsiung, 268, 276
Tylor, E. B., 68

Ukraine, 281
UNESCO, 73, 194, 284
United States, 3n3, 8, 13, 57, 166, 177, 217,
    220n5, 225, 255, 261. *See also* America
unprepared. *See* preparation
Unseth, Peter, 105
Uygur, Nermi, 72, 78
Uzbekistan, 79–80, 83

Viale, Ricarrado, 67
Vonolszewski, Susan, 95
Vygotsky, Lev, 54, 70, 126

Walker, Daron, 85
Wang, Haidong, 265, 273
Wang, Minjuan, 259, 265, 274–76

wayang, 252–54
WEIRD people, 40
Wells, David, 134
West Africa, 163, 244–45
Western theology, 18, 20, 68, 131–33, 152. *See
    also* theology
Whiteman, Darrell, 19, 21
Whorf, Benjamin, 70
Wildcat, Daniel R., 150
Willhauck, Susan, 218
Wingo, Ted, 76
wisdom
  biblical, 19, 90, 164, 172
  communities, 275
  as a gift, 191–92
  goal of learning, 11, 14, 147, 162, 193, 222
  and proverbs, 99–105
  traditional, 13, 144–45
  and worldview, 8, 142–45, 147, 162, 163
Wisse, Maarten, 131
witchcraft, 161, 167
Witkin, H. A., 115–18, 120, 127
Wizard of Oz, The, 41
Wolof, 123
World Oral Literature Project, 92
World Values Survey, 203
writing style. *See* Asia, learning and; China

Yale (people), 75–76
Yoruba, 102, 250
Young, William Paul, 168
Yung, Hwa, 133, 152

Zahniser, Matthias, 175